FAITH & PHILOSOPHY
OF
HINDUISM

INDIAN RELIGIONS SERIES: 1

FAITH & PHILOSOPHY OF HINDUISM

Rajeev Verma

Faith & Philosophy of Hinduism

Rs. 180

ISBN: 978-81-7835-854-3

Published in 2010 in India by
Kalpaz Publications
C-30, Satyawati Nagar,
Delhi-110052
E-mail: kalpaz@hotmail.com
Phone: 9212729499

Printed at : Salasar Imaging System, Delhi

Contents

Preface

This volume will appeal to anyone interested in acquiring an authentic grasp of Hinduism as it lives and functions in today's world. The wide spectrum of Hinduism practice is represented here in great detail. The reader will discover the central tenets of Hinduism, Vedas, Karma, Nirvana, and others in terms of their contemporary relevance and active participation in the formation of society and culture. Likewise, commonly practiced rituals are portrayed in terms of their role in living Hinduism.

Hinduism, as a philosophy, a way of life and of course as a faith, has served like a lighthouse for the whole world. It has, as a force, influenced all civilizations. Be it education, social fabric or science, Hinduism has left its impact in all the spheres. In fact, Hinduism is basically a scientific and progressive religion.

This volume, unique in its presentation, is perhaps first of its kind, to take all the great events, developments, and personalities in Hinduism, in its fold. All the significant aspects have been covered in this volume. The painstaking research and thorough study over a period of time, has resulted in an authentic, comprehensive, exhaustive, exclusive, and interesting work, which is bound to fill a big vacuum in Hinduism studies.

A productive bibliography, along with references is provided to prove the authenticity of the work and in order to guide the scholars and readers for further studies. Hopefully, this volume would be able to satisfy the urge of all those who desire to know about real Hinduism and also to create a new awareness, regarding this religion, as a radical discipline, based on reason and opposed to fundamentalism and dogmatism.

1

Hinduism: An Introduction

Hinduism, a religious custom of Indian origin, comprising the beliefs and practices of Hindus is one of the oldest religious customs in the world. Hinduism is often equated with a giant banyan tree in whose shade thousands of faiths bloom. The word Hindu is derived from the river Sindhù, or Indus. Hindu was principally a geographical term that referred to India or to a region of India (near the Sindhu) as long ago as the sixth century BC. The word Hinduism is an English word of more recent origin. Hinduism got into the English language in the early nineteenth century to depict the beliefs and practices of those residents of India who had not converted to Islam or Christianity and did not exercise Judaism or Zoroastrianism. In the case of most religious faiths, beliefs and practices come first, and those who subscribe to them are recognized as followers. In the case of the Hindu custom, however, the acknowledgment of Hindus came first, and their beliefs and practices makes the contents of the religion.

The followers of Hinduism themselves are in favour of using the Sanskrit term Santana dharma for their religious custom. Santana dharma is often interpreted into English as "endless custom" or "endless religion" but the translation of dharma as "custom" or "religion" gives an exceedingly limited, even false, sense of the word. Dharma has a number of meanings in Sanskrit, the sacred language of Hindu scripture, including "moral order," "duty," and "right action." The Hindu custom encourages Hindus to seek spiritual and moral truth wheresoever it might be found, while acknowledging that no religious doctrine can contain such truth in its fullness and that each individual must recognize this truth through his or her own systematic effort. Our experience, our information, and our talks with others; particularly with educated individuals, provide various means of trying out our understanding of religious and moral truth. And Hindu scriptures, based on the insights of Hindu sages and visionaries, serves primarily as a guidebook. But at last truth comes to us through direct consciousness of the divine or the ultimate reality. In other religions this ultimate realism is known as God. Hindus refer to it by a number of names, but the most common name is Brahma. In a number of faiths truth is presented or disclosed from a divine source and comes in the world through a single agent.

These truths are then entered in sacred scriptures that serve as a reservoir of knowledge of inspired wisdom: the Bible, the New Testament, and the Quran. In the Hindu custom, by contrast, there is no exclusive divine revelation or orthodoxy (founded doctrine) by which people may achieve knowledge of the divine or lead a life backed by religious law. The Hindu custom recognizes that there are a number of ways by which people may seek and go through religious understanding and way. It also claims that every individual has the potential to achieve nirvana.

The Hindu people today are found out primarily in India and neighbouring Nepal, and in Bali. large Hindu communities are present in Sri Lanka and Bangladesh, Mauritius, Fiji, the West Indies, East Africa, and South Africa. Scattered Hindu communities are found in most parts of the Western world. Hindus today number nearly 900 million, including about 20 million who live in foreign countries, making them the third largest religious community in the world, after Christians and Muslims. Since ancient times, Hindu thought has surpassed geographical limits and determined religious and philosophical ideas throughout the world. The most influenced religions by Hinduism were Persian, ancient Greek, and ancient Roman.

Custom of Dharma

For Hindus Dharma is an all-significant concept. In addition to custom and moral order, it also signifies the path of knowledge and correct action. Because of Hinduism's stress on living in accordance with dharma, anyone who is endeavouring for spiritual knowledge and seeking the right course of honourable action is, in the broadest sense, a follower of Santana dharma. Buddhism, Jainism, and Sikhism share with Hinduism the concept of dharma along with other key concepts, and the four religions may be said to belong to the Dharma custom. At one level Hinduism can refer to the notions or exercises of followers of any of the dharmic customs. The word Hinduism retains this sense in some usages in the Indian Constitution of 1950. In the field of religious fields, however, Hinduism is used in a narrower sense to differentiate it from the other religions of Indian origin. A Hindu is thus distinguished by a double exclusion. A Hindu is someone who does not subscribe to a religious belief of non-Indian origin, and who does not lay claim to belong solely to any other religious belief of Indian origin.

A rather artificial distinction between Hinduism and other dharmic customs, is produced by this effort which stems from an attempt to limit a system that sees itself as universal to an identity that is strictly religious. In a number of ways, labelling the other dharmic customs as non-Hindu has a basis that derives more from politics than from philosophy. Indeed, deeper differences of belief and practices lie within the broad family labelled as Hinduism than distinguish Hinduism from other dharmic systems. Indian historian Irfan Habib makes this point when he quotes an early Persian source that Hindus are those who have been debating with each other within a common framework for centuries. If they recognize another as somebody whom they can either support or oppose intelligibly, then both are Hindus. Despite the fact that Jains reject a number of Hindu beliefs, Jains and Hindus can still argue and thus Jains are Hindus. As the Hindus and Muslims do not share any basic terms such discussion does not go on amongst them.

The objective of the Hindu custom is comprehensiveness so far as religious beliefs and practices are referred to. First, it wishes to make the wealth of Hinduism available to the Hindu and to any true searcher of truth and knowledge. But it does not limit Hindus to their custom. Instead, it encourages them to explore all avenues that would lead to a realization of the divine, and it provides a scheme with a number of paths for such realization. Second, in the manner of science, Hinduism is constantly experimenting with and assimilating new ideas. Also like science, it is far less concerned with the origin or history of ideas than with their truth as demonstrated through direct experience. The most effective feature of Hinduism which differentiates it from the those religions who believe particularly historical events, people, or revealings is receptiveness to new ideas, teachers, and practices, and its hope for universality rather than exclusivity.

The religious custom of Hinduism originated in the Indian landmass. In present-day usage Hinduism is also sometimes denoted to as Sanatana Dharma, a Sanskrit word meaning "eternal law". Hinduism, a number of whose beginnings can be traced to the ancient Vedic civilization, is the world's oldest extant religion. A accumulation of various beliefs and customs, Hinduism has no single founder. It is also the world's third largest religion after Christianity and Islam, with more or less a billion adherents, of whom about 905 million live in India and Nepal. Other countries with large Hindu populations include Bangladesh, Sri Lanka, Indonesia, Malaysia, Singapore, Mauritius, Fiji, Suriname, Guyana and Trinidad and Tobago. Hinduism comprises a vast body of scriptures. Divided as revealed and remembered and developed over millennia, these scriptures expound on theology, philosophy and mythology, providing spiritual insights and guidance on the practice of dharma (religious living). In the orthodox view, among such texts, the Vedas and the Upanishads are the foremost in authority, significance and antiquity. Other major Holy Scriptures include the Tantras, the sectarist Agamas, the Puranas and the epics Mahabharata and Ramayana. Sometimes Bhagavad Gita, a treatise extracted from the Mahabharata is called a sum-up of the religious teachings of the Vedas.

The term Hindu is mainly a Persian term which is derived from Sindhu, Sanskrit for the Indus River. The Rig Veda mentions the land of the Indo-Aryans as Sapta Sindhu. Hinduism is an extremely diverse religion. Although some tenets of the faith are accepted by most Hindus, scholars have found it hard to identify any doctrines with universal acceptance among all denominations. Prominent themes in Hindu beliefs include Dharma (ethics/duties), Samsara (The continuing cycle of birth, life, death and rebirth), Karma (action and subsequent reaction), Moksha (liberation from samsara), and the various yogas (paths or practices). The term Hinduism is of recent origin, having been applied mostly by Westerners to denote the majority religion of India. Only groups that had clear non-Hindu identities, such as Jains, Buddhists, Parsis, Muslims, Jews, and Christians, were not included in the generic Hindu category. The use of a foreign designation derives from the fact that there is no corresponding word indigenous to South Asia. There, people generally define themselves as per the local caste and community and, among these; there is no single scripture, deity, or religious teacher common to all that can be designated as the core of Hinduism. Yet, the very vagueness of the term makes it useful. This is because the word Hinduism comes from Hindu, a name used by medieval Muslims to refer to the people living around the Sindu (Indus) River. This then became an umbrella term for all the people residing in the Indian subcontinent. Most of the regional Customs that developed in India as the indigenous faith is included by Hinduism.

Other Indian religions that says themselves as non-Hindu, like Buddhism and Jainism, had to demark themselves in clear limits to discern themselves from the Hindus. But Hinduism itself has never acquired such clear boundaries and religious practices across the subcontinent show great regional variation. The amorphous quality of the term Hinduism makes it a convenient designation for the very varied customs of approximately 80 percent of the people in India and their kindred communities around the world. It is significant, however, to remember that the word is a modern invention and that to project "Hindu" religion back through time is to use an artificial category in order to distinguish the roots of modern Hinduism from other Indian religions. Hinduism has one of the most ethnically diverse bodies of adherents in the world. For some, it is hard to classify Hinduism as a religion because the framework, symbols, leaders and books of reference that make up a typical religion are not uniquely identified in the case of Hinduism. Most ordinarily it can be seen as a "way of life" which gives rise to a number of cultured forms of religions. Hinduism, its religious doctrines, traditions and observations are very typical and inextricable linked to the Indian culture and statistics.

Outstanding tribes and communities of indigenous origin are also intimately linked to the earliest synthesis and formation of Hindu civilization. People of East Asian roots living in the states of north eastern India and Nepal were also a part of the earliest Hindu civilization. Immigration and settlement of peoples from Central Asia and peoples of Indo-Greek heritage have brought their own influence on Hindu society. The deities of the Indus Valley Civilization bear resemblances to Hindu Gods such as Shiva. The Indus Valley Civilization is often taken to represent the historical continuum of Hinduism. The root of Hinduism in southern India, and amongst tribal and indigenous communities is just as ancient and fundamentally contributive to the foundations of the religious and philosophical system. Ancient Hindu kingdoms arose and spread the religion and customs across South East Asia, particularly Thailand, Burma, Malaysia, Indonesia, Cambodia and what is now central Vietnam. A form of Hinduism particularly various from Indian roots and customs is practiced in Bali, Indonesia, where Hindus form 90% of the population. Indian migrants have taken Hinduism and Hindu culture to South Africa, Fiji, Mauritius and other countries in and around the Indian Ocean, and in the nations of the West Indies and the Caribbean. The variations of Hindu practices have been borrowed by a number of recent Movements.

In What Sense Hinduism is a Religion

It is worth here to start with an account of the major religions of the world with Hinduism, because the instance of Hinduism shows how misleading our habit of cataloguing the religions of the world can be. It has been argued that what is called Hinduism is not one religion but several, related to each other as Judaism, Christianity and Islam are, though in a more complex way whose history is harder to trace. For various historical facts, a number of various customs have come to be regarded (at least by non-Hindus) as sects within one religion called Hinduism. For other historical facts, Jains and Sikhs have been counted as followers of religions distinct from Hinduism, though they can as factably be called Hindu as Lingayats. The word Hinduism is an extreme case of a term which disguises the multiplicity of an indefinite number of religious customs, and seem s to include some customs which might have been barred, and exclude some that might have been included. However, it is not a unique case.

Diversity and Unity

Nowadays Hinduism has become a world custom. In South Asia, it is the dominant religion of India and Nepal, it is a minority custom in Sri Lanka, and it has small memberships in Pakistan and Bangladesh. In Southeast Asia, there are a few Hindu enclaves, most notably on the Indonesian island of Bali, that are remnants of large populations who arrived in the medieval period. There are also new growing Hindu populations in urban centres like Singapore and Kuala Lumpur. Outside of Asia, well-founded Hindu communities exist in eastern and southern Africa, in the Persian Gulf states, on the island of Fiji, on the northeast coast of South America, in the Caribbean, in North America, and in Europe. In spite of this globalization, Hinduism is still irrevocably linked to the culture of South Asia and any understanding of the Hindu custom must begin with the land of India. The body of religious beliefs and practices covered by the arching over term of Hinduism is one of the most richly diverse religions in history. This is a natural condition for a custom that developed organically, over thousands of years, out of the interactions of the various peoples who have settled in South Asia. The wealth of human diversity is evident in the languages of the subcontinent. There are four distinct language families, Indo-European, Dravidian, Tibeto-Burman, and Austro-Asiatic. From these come the 17 official languages recognized in India, each with its countless dialects, and the minor, unofficial languages spoken in modern South Asia. Indo-European languages descended from Sanskrit are spoken in northern India and Nepal, and include languages like Hindi, Marathi, Bengali, and Nepali. Four Dravidian languages, Tamil, Telegu, Malayalam, and Kannada, are spoken in the four states of south India. The other two language families have much smaller numbers of speakers. Tibeto-Burman languages are used in the Himalayan and north-eastern areas such as the Kathmandu valley. The tribal peoples who are found in central, eastern, and north-eastern India still speak Austro-Asiatic languages.

A number of these languages are associated with specific regions. This regionalism, which is one of the hallmarks of Hinduism, is a by-product of South Asian geography. The subcontinent has geographically defined regions that have developed their own distinctive cultures. The northern boundary is formed by the Himalayan mountain range. These mountains have not prevented immigration, especially from the northwest. Peoples entering from that direction settled in the river valleys of the north, where they interacted with the previous inhabitants.

As these migrants step by step worked their way across to the eastern regions their cultures were continually changed. So, for example , the descendants of an Indo-European tribe that had come into India from the northwest would have a considerably altered culture by the time they reached the eastern coast. Thus, the northwest and the northeast developed distinct cultures, even when the influences that came together in each region had similar origins. Within the subcontinent, the distinctive geographical cultures have also been shaped by the necessity of adapting to their climates. In the northern plains, populations have clustered around the rivers that provide resources for agriculture. One such region lies on the rivers of the Punjab in the northwest, and a second exists along the Ganges and Yamuna Rivers in the northern plains.

Concept of Dharma

Similarly as there is no indigenous word to designate the religion of India, so too there is no one word equivalent to the Western concept of "religion." Perhaps the word that comes closest is dharma. Dharma means law, duty, justice, virtuousness. Like Western "morality" it refers to both religious and social obligations of behaviour. As such, the term brings out the emphasis on praxis, or correct behaviour that is central to the Hindu worldview. Hinduism is a religion that focuses on behaviour more than belief. There is great diversity in beliefs, there are diverse deities, philosophies, and paths, but all of these necessitate adherence to particular rules of behaviour. To understand what makes dharmic behaviour, one must understand the Hindu worldview. The ground to this worldview is the belief that the sacred is immanent in the world. The natural world, social order, and family life all have correlations to divine order. Because of this, all actions, whether ostensibly secular or obviously religious, have religious implications. This means that one's place within the world order affects one's dharma. The things that may not seem religious in

Western customs, such as places, objects, people, and moments in time, the immanence of the sacred also gives religious significance to them.

Characteristics of Hinduism

Any one at the first attempt to define Hinduism by recognizing in it the totality of religious forms which originated and developed on Indian soil. It would then be necessary to exclude Buddhism, which in ancient days spread across a large part of Hindustan and still remains very much alive in some areas of the continental borderlands. It would also be necessary to exclude Jainism, which has today about one and a half million followers although in the past it was, relatively at least, more widespread. Other religious groups would also have to be barred: six million Christians, Jews and Zoroastrians, and some twenty-five million fetishists and animists, who one might say participate in varying degrees in certain elementary forms of Hinduism. In relation to the mass of the Indian population, which at present numbers approximately four hundred million, these groups are practically negligible both statistically and culturally. This is not the case, however, with Islam. Since the eleventh century Islam has steadily drawn millions of persons from the Hindu community; and even today, in spite of the creation of Pakistan as a Muslim state within the subcontinent, Islam has some thirty-five million followers in the Indian Union. It is not regarded a heresy as for Sikhism, or the religion of the Sikhs, it may be regarded a religious movement at the uttermost limits of Hinduism.

To bound Hinduism within the boundary of India, however, would be to bypass the missionary character of this religion in the past. In the so-called Hinduization of southeast Asia, Indian religious influences combined with indigenous elements and in the course of time were assimilated by Buddhism, Islam or some form of national religion. In this way Hinduism has had a unplumbed influence, especially in Cambodia, ancient Champa and Bali. One should also recall that there are Hindus in Ceylon (among the Dravidian population), in Nepal, in Pakistan (an inestimable number) and in Indian settlements scattered all over the world. Can one rather define Hinduism by its elements?

In real, this will have to be done; but in attempting to find such a unifying definition we run the risk of generalizing to such an extent that we fail to grasp the infinite diversity of forms which constitute Hinduism. The primitive origin of Hinduism was in part of Indo-European origin; the framework at least was such, while the content was largely indigenous or was modified on the spot. The Aryan tribes which invaded India during the second millennium before our era brought with them a body of religious belief which was already well organized and which survived in classical Hinduism — at the cost of A number of modifications. This "Aryan" religion (that is, Indo-European on Indian soil) had already been sifted out during the so-called Indo-Iranian intermediary period. It was at the end of this period that a separation occurred between the original religion of Iran (pre-Zoroastrian) and what was to become the Vedic religion in north-western India. To this ancient foundation was added a succession of influences which made Hinduism a religion quite various from that of the Aryan invaders. Most of these new developments took place during historical time. The primary stages were the seem ance of great philosophical speculations and the fixation of the Smti (at the beginning of the Christian era), the first fragmentation into sects (first and second centuries A.D.), the seem ance of bhakti (600-800 A.D.), and Tantrism (since 800 A.D.). However all these movements existed, as early as the Vedic period.

Uniqueness of Hindu Religion

Among all the great Religions of the world Hinduism is unique as it had no single founder or Messiah nor a single book as a source but grew gradually over a period of several thousand years. The Hindu society is the product of A number of races and A number of cultures with several forms of practice. It evolved out of the varying faiths in various groups of the community as it was absorbing and assimilating all the diversified social movements and cultural practices of India. Consequently, it does not have a single Holy book as a source to guide all, like a Bible or Koran or Dhammapadam. Most of their beliefs and practices are based on the teachings of the Vedas, Agamas, Upanishads and several books written, based on these texts. Large portions of these texts are lost. Hindus believe that their religion is without beginning, even preceding the creation of human race and the creation of the universe. They believe that creation of the universe and their life are without beginning or end and is a continuous process, a cycle of creation and dissolution.

The Vedas are the very breath of this process with which Lord Brahma, the creator, creates the universe and all its lives. The name "Hindu" is said to have been derived from the name given by the Western and Persian scholars to the people settled on the River Sindhu. Some believe the name has a much older origin in the scriptures. Scholars often referred to this as the Brahmanical faith. Hindus called it "Vaideeha Dharma" or "Sanathana Dharma". Philosophers often do not want to refer to it as a mere religion, as that will narrow it down to a blind faith of prayers to God. It permits free thinking, questioning and facting. It allows both philosophy and rituals. As it accepts various forms of worship it accepts even atheists and agnostics.

Hindu Religion and the Eternal Truth

There are literally thousands of books, spiritual literature and scriptures to guide both the beginners and the scholars. There are several pathways given to the followers. It is not based on any single book or the words of any single teacher or prophet. It does not follow any blind doctrine. Everyone is allowed to study, question, and doubt, analyse, fact and then accept the teachings after their own spiritual experience. The first sets of books are known as "Sruthis" or "Vedas." They are "of Superhuman or Divine origin". They are unchangeable, highest spiritual knowledge of the Eternal Truth ever known. They are older than creation itself. In the beginning of each era (Kalpa), the Supreme God, Brahmam, creates Himself as Brahma, and gives Him the knowledge of Vedas as His own breath. The Universe and all its beings are created by Brahma out of the sound of Pranava Manthra "OM" and the knowledge of Vedas. Vedas are the primary authority and the very soul of Hinduism. They were revealed to the Rishis, the sages or seers, who received them as an intuition by direct revelations from God. Sage Veda Vyasa codified and organized the four Vedas, Rig, Yajur, Saama and Atharva.

His disciples Paila, Vaisampaya, Jobjectiveini and Sumanta taught them to their disciples and the latter in turn to their pupils. This way, the knowledge of Vedas was passed on through generations by memorizing and reciting the verses for thousands of years. The Rig Veda consists of 1028 Sookthas collected as 21 sections or Sakhas with hymns in praise of the Divine. Yajur Veda, with 109 sakhas, mainly consists of Hymns used in religious rituals and rites. Saama Veda has 1000 sections, and it is made of Verses from Rig Veda set to music. Atharva Veda has 50 sakhas with 598 hymns, gives a number of rites and rituals to guide man in his daily activities and materialistic life, to ward off evil and destroy enemies.

Religion with Various Gods and Goddess

It is the common belief of the Hindu people that three Gods rule the world. Brahma: the creator; Vishnu: the preserver and Shiva: the destroyer. These three Lords have consorts and they are goddesses too. Consort of Brahma is Sarasvati; goddess of learning. Vishnu's consort is Lakshmi; goddess of wealth and prosperity. Shiva's companion is Parvati who is worshipped as Kali or Durga. Besides these there are many other Gods and Goddesses. To cite a few, there is Ganesh, son of Shiva and Parvati; Hanuman, Surya Lord of sun; Ganga, Goddess of river Ganges; Samundra, sea; Indra, king of the Gods; Prithvi, Goddess of earth; Shakti, Goddess of strength. Heroes of eposes like the Mahabharata and the Ramayana are immortalised and are still alive in the daily existence of the common people.

The champion of the Ramayana; Lord Rama, exemplifies qualities such as pureness, bravery and valour and is held up as an example of virility. His wife Sita is the prototypal Indian wife who is carried off by Ravana, the king of Lanka, while Rama and Sita are on exile. Sita's eventual rescue by Rama, his brother Lakshmana, and Rama's faithful monkey-general Hanuman are all woven into this engrossing tale. Stories from this epic have been passed down orally from one generation to the next. Religious fairs, festivals and rituals have kept these legends alive, and there is never an occasion that does not offer an opportunity to retell the old stories. The stirring verses of the Mahabharata tell the story of the dynastic struggle between the Pandavas and the Kauravas, who were close cousins. Lord Krishna plays a very significant role in this Great Epic. He is a friend, philosopher and guide to Arjuna, one of the Pandavas, and he helps Arjuna overcome his hesitation to kill his close relatives in the battlefield. The judicious doctrine of Krishna and his commandments have been embodied in the Bhagwad Gita.

REFERENCES

F. Edgerton: *The Bhagavad-Gita*, Cambridge, Mass, Harvard University Press, 1944.

G. Buhler: *The Laws of Manu*, Oxford, Clarendon Press, 1886.

G. Buhler: *The Sacred Books of the East*, Oxford, Clarendon Press, 1897.

H. Oldenberg: *The Grhya-Sutras*, Oxford, Clarendon Press, 1886.

J. Eggeling: *The Uatapatha-BrahmaGa*, Oxford, Clarendon Press, 1900.

J. Jolly: *The Institutes of Vishnu*, Oxford, Clarendon Press, 1900.

J. Jolly: *The Minor Law-Books*, Oxford, Clarendon Press, 1889.

J. Muir: *Original Sanskrit Texts*, London: Trubner & Co., 1872.

M. Bloomfield: *Hymns of the Atharva-Veda*, Oxford, Clarendon Press, 1897.

M. Monier-Williams: *Indian Wisdom*, London, Allen, 1876.

M. Winternitz: *A History of Indian Literature*, Calcutta, University, 1927.

Nicol Macnicol: *Hindu Scriptures*, London, J. M. Dent, 1938.

Ph. J. Vogel: *Indian Serpent-Lore*, London, A. Probsthain, 1926.

R. E. Hume: *The Thirteen Principal Upanishads*, London, Oxford University Press, 1931.

S. Radhakrishnan, *The Principal Upanicads*, London, George Allen & Unwin, 1953.

S. Radhakrishnan: *The Bhagavad-gita*, London, George Allen & Unwin, 1948.

2

History

The meaning of the name of India has changed after independence it got in 1947. When British rule ended on 15 August 1947, India was partitioned into two countries: India, with a Hindu majority, and Pakistan, with a Muslim majority. While India inherited the name India, Pakistan inherited the river Indus. Pakistan consisted of two territories, one centred on the Indus basin, and the other in eastern Bengal, with about a thousand miles of Indian Territory between them. In 1971, the eastern portion separated to become Bangladesh.

When the name India refers to ancient India, or British India, it includes what are now India, Pakistan and Bangladesh. These countries are all included in the term South Asia, which also includes Afghanistan, Bhutan, Nepal, Skim and Sri Lanka. Another term covering approximately the same area is the Indian subcontinent. South Asia is separated from the rest of Asia by mountains. Leaving aside Afghanistan, which is the threshold between South Asia and Central Asia, it measures about two thousand miles from west to east and from north to south, and is divided into two roughly equal parts. The northern part is bounded by mountains but flat in the interior, and watered by three great rivers: the Indus, the Ganges and the Brahmaputra. This part is known as the Indo-Gangetic plain. The southern part of the subcontinent is a peninsula, mountainous in the interior and bounded by sea to the west and east. An significant part is played by the rivers in the history of northern India, and a number of its historic cities are inland, on rivers. Peninsular India, separated from the north by the Vindhya and other mountain ranges, is open to sea routes linking it to Arabia, Africa and Southeast Asia; a number of its historic cities and Hindu pilgrimage are on the coast of these holy rivers.

The external natural boundaries - mountains and sea - have given South Asia a cultural unity, while internal boundaries - mountains, forests and deserts - have helped to maintain the cultural distinctiveness of its regions. It has never been a political unity, though the ambition of ancient India kings was to rule an empire from the Himalayas to the eastern and western seas. Some powers have ruled most of this area, but not all of it: the Maurya dynasty in the third century BC., whose greatest emperor, Ashoka, is remembered as a patron of Buddhism; the Guptas in the fourth to sixth centuries AD.; the Mughals in the seventeenth century; the British in the nineteenth and twentieth centuries; and the present state of India. Within this area live people of diverse cultures but having some traits in common: loose, unsewn clothes, though sewn garments are also known; a concern to avoid pollution, and a respect for water, the sun and cattle as means of purification; a view of society as divided into hereditary groups, each with its own way of life and rules of purity; a belief that after death people are reborn in other bodies, as per the their previous deeds; a way of worshipping by placing offerings of food in front of images or other objects representing gods. These people are Hindus. A Hindu anthropologist has written: 'while it is not possible to define a Hindu, it is not very hard to identify a person as a Hindu'. However, not all Hindus fit the above description: both in South Asia and elsewhere, there are Hindus who wear suits, seek hygiene rather than ritual purity, and do not worship gods. If it is harder still to define a lapsed Hindu then it is impossible to define a Hindu.

Roughly we can divide the history of South Asia into the following periods. The dates, except 1947, are arbitrary approximations which do not refer to any specific events, and the dating of the first two periods is contested.

Harappan period	3000 BC. to 1500 BC.
Vedic period	1500 BC. to 500 BC.
Period of north Indian empires	500 BC. to 600 AD.
Period of regional kingdoms	600 AD. to 1200 AD.
Period of Muslim rule	1200 AD. to 1800 AD.
Period of British rule	1800 AD. to1947 AD.
Post-independence period	1947 AD. onwards

ORIGIN

Uniqueness of Hinduism among all other religions of the world is due to the fact that it has no founder or date of origin. While most major religions derive from new ideas taught by a charismatic leader, Hinduism is simply the religion of the people of India, which has gradually developed over four thousand years. The origins and authors of its sacred texts are largely unknown. Although today's Hinduism differs significantly from earlier forms of Indian religion, Hinduism's roots date back as far as 2000 BC, making it one of the oldest surviving religions. Because of its great age, the early history of Hinduism is unclear. The most ancient writings have yet to be deciphered, so for the earliest periods the researchers and scholars must rely on guesses based on archaeological excavations and the study of contemporary texts which are saved upto this time.

In the recent past, the history of India's religion has also become a matter of political controversy. The history of any nation (or individual) is a significant part of its self-identity, and this is especially true of India, which so recently gained independence after centuries of colonial rule. The controversy over India's history centres on the origin of the Aryan culture, as we will discuss in more detail in this chapter.

Archaeologists' in 1921 uncovered evidence of an ancient civilization along the Indus River, which today runs through northwest India into Pakistan. The so-called Indus Valley civilization (also known as the "Harappan civilization" for one of its chief cities) is thought to have originated as early as 7000 BC and to have reached is height between 2300 to 2000 BC, at which point it encompassed over 750,000 square miles and traded with Mesopotamia. Some writings of this period have been discovered, but unfortunately in such small amounts that they have yet to be deciphered. Knowledge of this great civilization's religion must hence be based on physical evidence alone. Baths have been found that may indicate ritual bathing, a component of modern Hinduism. Some altar-like structures may be evidence of animal sacrifice, and terracotta figures may represent deities. An significant seal features a horned figure surrounded by animals, which some conjecture is a prototype of Shiva, but it could be a bull similarly found on the seals of Mesopotamia.

The decline of this culture began around 1800 BC, due possibly to flooding or drought. Until recently, it was unquestionably held that it was at this time that the Aryans invaded or migrated into both India and Iran. As per the this hypothesis, both the Sanskrit language and the Vedic religion that is foundational to Hinduism are attributable to the Aryans ("noble ones") and their descendents. The original inhabitants of the Indus Valley are thought to have had a Dravidian language and culture, which became subordinate to that of the invading peoples. This hypothesis is supported by similarities between Zoroastrianism, the ancient religion of Iran, and the Vedic religion of ancient India. In addition, no trace of horses or chariots has been found in the remains of the Indus Valley culture, although they were central to Aryan military and ritual life. Starting from the 1980s, this hypothesis was challenged by some as a myth propagated by colonial scholars who sought to reinforce the idea that anything valuable in India must have come from elsewhere. In its place, a hypothesis is offered in which there was no invasion and Aryan culture developed out of the Indus Valley civilization. This view is sometimes called the "cultural transformation hypothesis."

EARLY HISTORY

The Harappan Period

Since 1920s the Harappan or Indus Valley civilization has been known to the archaeologists. Its chief sites are Mohenjodaro, in the Indus valley, and Harappa, 350 miles to the north-east. Sites have now been identified over an area about 700 miles from north to south and from east to west, with outlying sites at even greater distances. The sites are the remains of brick-built cities, showing a remarkable uniformity in the size of bricks and the width and geometrical layout of streets. The most remarkable artefacts are steatite seals, depicting human figures, plants and animals, and inscribed with characters. There have been a number of attempts to decipher the script and identify the language, but none has convinced all scholars. The antecedents of this civilization can be traced back to the seventh millennium BC., and its mature period is about 2300 to 2000 BC. It declined between 1800 and 1700 BC., probably as a result of climatic and geological change.

There is little evidence and much speculation as for the religion of the Harappan civilization. The large baths in the cities may have been for ritual bathing, like the pools known as tanks adjoining Hindu temples. The numerous exaggeratedly female clay figurines may be connected with the mother goddesses worshipped by Hindus in village shrines. A figure on one of the seals seem ed to Sir John Marshall, the pioneer of Harappan archaeology, to show features of the god Shiva; he tentatively identified it as 'Proto-Shiva'. Further examination makes this identification less likely. A number of writers on Indian religion have stated that the Hindu belief in rebirth was inherited from the Harappan civilization, but this is only conjecture. But it rests on a mistaken view that the doctrine of rebirth seem s suddenly in the Upanishads without any precedent in the earlier parts of the Veda. But although after all the efforts made by other religions of the world Hinduism still keeps it uniqueness and glory.

The Vedic Period

A great number of evidences have been gathered in due course of time from the Harappan civilization which provides us with a mass of material remains, much of them datable by radiocarbon and other techniques, but no literature. The Vedic period, on the other hand, is known from a mass of literature which carries no dates, and is hard to match with any archaeological record. This literature was not written down for some centuries, but was memorized and handed down orally with great exactness. The word Veda means 'knowledge' and the Veda is a collection of the knowledge which was preserved by a class of people called Brahmins, who needed it for the rituals they performed.

The most sacred text of Veda is a very large and varied collection of texts, composed over a long period, perhaps even a thousand years. The oldest part, known as the hymns of the Rig-Veda, may itself span some centuries. These hymns are poems addressed to various gods, and less commonly goddesses, spoken by a priest as part of the ritual. Modern scholars usually date them to the second millennium BC. However, there is no direct way of dating the Veda; as per the Hindu custom it is eternal. Vedic rituals became very elaborate, requiring a staff of priests with various specializes. Some of these rituals are described in texts called Brahmanas, which discuss their meaning and motive. These texts are part of the Veda, as are the Upanishads, which also discuss the meaning and motive of rituals, but often reach the conclusion that nothing of lasting value can be achieved by them. The Upanishads, which reject ritual, have proved the most influential part of the Veda. Among their key ideas is the contrast between the a number of things of this world of impermanence, and the One which is the origin and goal of all existence.

Rituals, which are performed for goals such as long life, wealth or security after death, are concerned with the a number of; infinitely more valuable than knowledge of rituals is knowledge of the ultimate truth, or Brahman, to be found in the cave of the heart. From the geographical names they contain, the hymns of the Rig-Veda seem to have been composed in the northern Punjab. In the later parts of the Veda the geographical horizon is extended eastwards along the Ganges and southwards towards the peninsula. Much of the territory known to the hymns is the same as that of the Harappan civilization, but city life is unknown, and the chief form of wealth is cattle. As per the Vedas the people of that time which were living on the land of India were called Arya, and those who were alien or living on the land various from the India were regarded as non-Arya regarding them as enemies to be conquered.

The Vedas are written in an early form of Sanskrit, the classical language of Hinduism. Languages of the same family are now spoken over most of northern and central South Asia, admitting Hindi, Bengali, Gujarati and Marathi. Together they are called the Indo-Aryan languages, after the name Arya by which the Vedic people referred to themselves. These languages are closely related to the Iranian languages. The ancient Iranians, incidentally, in the same manner called themselves and their language Arya; they also referred to Aryana Vaeja, 'the Arya country', and this is the origin of the name Iran. The Indo-Aryan languages are also concerned, though less closely, to most of the languages of Europe, making the Indo-European language family.

However, all the other branches of the Indo-European family were spoken outside South Asia, and since the river-names in the hymns of the Rig-Veda indicate that the hymns were composed in the Punjab, it seems that the Indo-Aryan branch came into South Asia from the north-west and subsequently spread over most of the subcontinent. This inference from the linguistic and literary evidence, which was well founded by the middle of the nineteenth century, is a very factable one.

This relative ness between temporal power and spiritual power, the king and the Brahmin, recurs in a number of forms in its whole history of Hinduism. Its development in the Vedic period depended on an accumulation of wealth in the hands of the king, which Marxist historians especially have attributed to material developments such as the iron-tipped plough, which enabled the land to produce a surplus which could be appropriated by the king. The king could then support a host of retainers who did not work the land: jewellers, artists, soldiers and others, including Brahmins, who were valued not only as ritualists but as advisers in worldly business as well as spiritual matters. Power and wealth were concentrated in cities. Wealth was no longer counted in cattle but in money. Some of these trends can be seen in a story in an early Upanishad. Janaka, king of Videha in the lower Ganges basin, one of the more recently Aryanized areas, invites the brahmins of the Kuru and Panchala countries further west, where Aryan culture has been long founded, to perform a great sacrifice. When they are assembled, he offers a thousand cows to the best Brahmin among them. Cows are a customal reward for Brahmins;

but these cows have ten gold coins tied to their horns, marking a transition from barter to a money economy.

The prize is immediately claimed by the great ritual theorist Yajnavalkya, and he upholds his claim by answering the questions of the Brahmins who challenge him. He out-talks them all; the questions use ritual terms and concepts, but are not so much on the ritual itself as on cosmology, the nature of a person, what becomes of a person after death, and the nature of ultimate reality.

The Period of the North Indian Empires

In Hindu history the concentration of power and wealth in cities, and the symbiosis of the king with the Brahmin who provided religious legitimation for his power and worldly advice on how to augment it, led to the ideal of the chakravarti, literally the 'wheel-turner': the emperor who conquers all neighbouring kings and makes the whole world revolve round the hub of his capital. No ruler in Indian history ever achieved this objective in its complete extent, but several came close to it, basing their power in the northern plains and extending it into the peninsula. In 4th BC., the short-lived Nanda dynasty, with its capital at Pataliputra (modern Patna), conquered the Ganges basin and parts of the peninsula; it was overthrown by Chandragupta Maurya. Chandragupta's grandson Ashoka, who reigned from 268 to 232 BC., ruled northern India and parts of the peninsula. Ashoka patronized Buddhism, and the Buddhist community may have helped to consolidate his power. The extent of the Maurya Empire decreased after Ashoka, and in 185 BC. the throne was seized by Pushyamitra Shunga, a Brahmin; the Shunga dynasty lasted till about 73 BC. The most successful north Indian empire, again based on Pataliputra, was that of the Guptas, from the middle of the fourth century to the middle of the sixth. This was a period of prosperity, when the arts flourished, and Indian culture spread to parts of Southeast Asia.

The natural barriers, especially in the south, and by the resistance of rival powers made hard the expansion of kingdoms. These included invaders from the north-west, the usual route for invasion from outside India. In second century kings of Greek descent or at least with Greek names and Hellenistic culture, from Bactria (now northern Afghanistan), occupied territories in India and may even have conquered Patliputra. In the last century Shakas, of Central Asian origin, conquered Bactria and north-western and western India. They were invaded in turn by Parthians, from northern Iran, but some Shaka rulers retained power in parts of western India. Another group of invaders from Central Asia, the Kushans, founded an empire which extended over most of northern India and across the mountains into Central Asia, around the second century AD. In the fifth century the Huns, also from Central Asia, invaded the north-west, and during the first half of the sixth century they reigned over a large part of western India, gradually they spread in other parts of India as well.

Basically all this literature was written in the earlier form of Sanskrit, which, after being standardized by Panini's grammar, hardly varied from one part of India to another, and remained largely unchanged while the various vernacular languages - those spoken by ordinary people - changed through the centuries. The authorities on Sanskrit language and literature, known as pandits, were generally Brahmins. Sanskrit was the language of diplomacy, since each king could be expected to have pandits at his court that could understand and reply to letters in Sanskrit, whether or not the king himself could. At the beginning of this period a variety of doctrines flourished, some of them based on the Veda and others openly opposed to it. The best-known teacher is known by his family name Gautama, but much better known by his title Buddha, meaning 'aware', which indicates that he has reached perfect knowledge of the nature of phenomena and of personality.

Gautama the Buddha came from the aristocracy of a small state on the northern fringe of the Ganges basin, near the present borders of Nepal. Estimates of his dates vary, but he probably lived in the fifth century BC., when the Ganges basin was being transformed by urbanization, the concentration of wealth in the city, and the alliance between king and Brahmin. Some modern interpreters see his teachings as a reaction to these changes. The Buddhist practice of maintaining monks (and a smaller number of nuns) through voluntary donations, to follow a discipline of meditation and study, allowed them to develop a well-structured body of ideas which was independent of brahminical thought, and eventually prompted the Brahmins to construct counter-arguments.

While Buddhism was a powerful religious and intellectual force in South Asia in the first millennium AD., it did not survive there long in the second millennium, except in Nepal and Sri Lanka. However, it founded itself in Central, East and Southeast Asia, and in the nineteenth and twentieth centuries was hailed by Indian intellectuals as one of ancient India's gifts to the world. Another teacher of about the same time was Mahavira, known by the title Jina, 'conqueror', because like the Buddha he had overcome the limitations of human existence. His followers are called Jains (meaning 'belonging to the Jina'), and whereas they did not carry his teachings outside South Asia, they survive there today, especially among the commercial class of Gujarat in western India. The teachings of non-violence by the Jains also influenced Mohandas Gandhi, who belonged to this class.

Jains and Buddhists reject the authority of the Veda. However, they agree with the Vedic schools that after death a person is reborn in a human, animal or other form as per the their previous deeds. Another school who originated at about the same time were the materialists or Lokayatas, founded by Charvaka, who denied any sort of existence after death. Their writings do not survive, but something is known of them from hostile accounts by Buddhist and brahminical writers. Twentieth-century Indian materialists have taken an interest in these ancient predecessors. Urbanization and the rise of kingship may help to explain the emergence of holy places in the geography of South Asia. The Vedic ritual was performed on ground ritually marked out and consecrated for the occasion; there is no indication of temples in the Veda. But permanent holy places may have been known in the Harappan civilization, and they are a feature of Hindu life today, whether in the form of a stone in the open air or a great temple. A number of the pilgrimage centres are also centres of commerce, such as Varanasi on the Ganges; they may have started as simple shrines which grew as the trade routes brought worshippers to them. As per the Arthashastra, a treatise on statecraft written around 300 BC., temples owned property including land, gold and cattle, and were a source of revenue for the king.

The deities mentioned in the Veda were various which were worshipped in temples. Indra, the god most frequently worshipped in the Vedic hymns, remained as king of heaven but had little to do with this world, though his name is often used as an element in the names of kings. Vishnu, who rose to prominence as lord of the sacrifice in the later Vedic period, became widely worshipped as supreme God. This position is also claimed for Rudra or Shiva, who in the Veda is a god of the wild, isolated from other gods. Goddesses, who are little mentioned in the Vedic hymns except as the wives of gods, were common in this period, as in India today. It is thus possible to describe certain deities and rituals as 'Hindu' as opposed to 'Vedic'. These differences, together with the significance of images and temples, mark the Hinduism of the past two millennia as substantially various from the religion of the Veda.

Especially in the nineteenth and early twentieth centuries, some modern scholars marked these differences by separating 'Hinduism' from what they called 'Vedism' or 'Brahmanism'. But such labelling gives a misleading impression of distinct systems succeeding each other, and raises the unanswerable and unprofitable question of when Vedism or Brahmanism ended and Hinduism began. It is more helpful to think of a great number of various religious practices which come into prominence at various times, and are recorded in various kinds of sources. The Veda, for example , is concerned mainly with a particular group of rituals performed by Brahmins for their patrons, in an expanding but limited geographical area, and cannot be taken as evidence that other kinds of ritual, such as worship of images in temples, did not take place outside, or even within, that area. Thus goddess worship, rather than an innovation, is probably a feature of Hindu life that went unrecorded for centuries, apart from archaeological evidence, but first seem s in texts in the last five centuries BC. Vedic ritual, on the other hand, continues to be practised in attenuated forms. Some elements of it occur regularly as part of Hindu marriage and death rituals, and large-scale Vedic sacrifices are occasionally performed.

The Buddhist monasteries and Temples, depended largely on the patronage of kings; similarly the Brahmin pandits. Particular kings favoured Buddhist, Hindu or Jain institutions, but not exclusively; South Asian states were not like European states after the Reformation, each supporting one form of religion and more or less forcibly suppressing others. Thus Ashoka favoured Buddhism, but also patronized Hindu temples, as did the Kushans, while the Guptas favoured Hinduism but also patronized Buddhist monasteries. In this way every ruler favoured one or the other religion.

MEDIEVAL HISTORY

The Period of Regional Kingdoms

The Gupta Dynasty ruled on a vast land of India, no later Hindu empire covered as much of South Asia as that of the; instead, the subcontinent was shared between a number of powers based in various regions. The regional distribution of power helps to account for the growth of regional cultures and literatures, and also for regional varieties of Hinduism. Dynasties rose and fell, but four regions remained significant: the land around the upper Ganges and its tributary the Yamuna, known as the Doab (from Persian doab 'two waters', like Punjab 'five waters'); Bengal, around the Ganges delta; the plateau to the west of the centre of the peninsula, known as the Deccan (from Sanskrit dakshina 'south'); and the far south, where the Tamil language was spoken, approximately

Tamil Nadu and Kerala. Literature in Tamil goes back at least to the first century AD. The language is unrelated in its origins to the Indo-Aryan languages such as Sanskrit, and Tamil culture is in A number of ways separate from that of north India.

However, the early literature mentions Brahmins, and early Tamil kings were influenced by northern ideals of kingship, performing Vedic rituals and claiming to rule as far as the Himalayas. Gods of the Tamils came to be identified with gods known in the north: the mountain god Murugan was identified with Shiva's son Skanda. There were three ancient Tamil dynasties: Chera, Chola and Pandya. These declined around the fifth century AD., and in the sixth century another dynasty, the Pallavas, emerged as the supreme power in the south. The Pallavas built temples on a larger scale than hitherto, setting the pattern for the distinctive South Indian style of temple building. While the typical north Indian temple consists of a hall with a small shrine at the east end, with a peak surmounting the shrine and an entrance at the west end, the great South Indian temples surround these with subsidiary shrines, courtyards, outbuildings and gateways. A feature which seem s first in the Pallava temples is the gopuram (literally 'cow-castle'), a tower built over a gateway, covered with statuary. The gopurams were multiplied, each overtopping the peak of the shrine as the South Indian style developed.

The power of Pallavas declined in the ninth century, to be succeeded by a resurgence of the Cholas of Tanjore (Thanjavur) which continued until the thirteenth century when the Cholas were eclipsed by the Pandyas of Madurai. The Cholas built some of the largest and finest South Indian temples, each with several courtyards, with high gopurams facing north, south, east and west. It was under the Cholas, too, that the art of casting sculpture in bronze was brought to perfection. The bronze images of the dancing Shiva, associated with the great temple of Shiva at Chidambaram, south of Madras, became in the twentieth century one of the best-known visual symbols of Hinduism. Further north, in the Deccan, the Shatavahana dynasty ruled from the end of the last century BC. to the beginning of the third century AD., its northward expansion checked by the Shakas and Kushans.

In the Doab, a new empire arose under Harsha, who ruled from 606 to 647 at Kanauj on the Ganges. He was a notable patron and author of Sanskrit literature, and had Buddhist monks as well as Brahmins at his court. Kashmir was the major power in north India for part of the eighth century, until a new empire was formed in Kanauj by the Gurjara-Pratiharas, who claimed descent from Lakshmana, brother of the hero

Rama. They belonged to the group of tribes called Rajput (from Sanskrit rajaputra 'king's son'), a title used by several ruling families in the western part of northern India. Their claim to the title rests on their success as fighters and rulers rather than their ancestry.

In this period the Gurjara-Pratiharas were confronted by the Rashtrakutas in the Deccan, and in Bengal by the Palas, who flourished from the mid-eighth to the mid-twelfth century. The Palas favoured Buddhism; and by their support of the long-founded Buddhist university of Nalanda, and their own foundation Vikramashila, they facilitated the development of Buddhist learning and art in Tibet and in Southeast Asia. They were overtaken by the Sens, who were Hindus; Ballal Sen, in the twelfth century, is credited with having founded a system of precedence among the Brahmins of Bengal. The chief rivals of Rashtrakutas were the Chalukyas, the Pallavas and the Cholas in the peninsula.

In this period conquered kings were often restored or retained on their thrones as vassals of the conqueror. This reduced the centralized bureaucracy of the earlier empires, but it also meant that the vassal could in turn seize power from the paramount king. The ebb and flow of empires helped to distribute ideas, styles of art and architecture, and so on through the subcontinent. At the same time, through the system of vassalage, and because certain regions remained prosperous and powerful while dynasties changed, each region developed a distinctive culture. While the use of Sanskrit throughout South Asia for ritual, diplomatic and literary motives continued or even increased, regional languages were also written. This had been the case for centuries with Tamil, with its rich literary heritage. The instability of power influenced the pattern of kingship. Conquest and marriage alliances were the usual devices for acquiring power, but they were not sufficient to secure it; power once gained had to be legitimated.

Gopala, the founder of the Pala dynasty in Bengal in the eighth century, is said to have been chosen by the leading members of the people: a form of legitimation suited to the dynasty's Buddhist ideology. A more typically Hindu way of legitimating kingship is through the support of Brahmins, and the Vedic ritual which only they are entitled to perform. A number of kings claimed in their inscriptions to have undergone the Vedic royal consecration, and even to have performed the horse sacrifice which makes a king into a chakravarti. They also claimed close connection, or even identity, with particular gods. For example , the Pandyas claimed descent from Shiva and his wife Parvati. To provide for their ritual necessitatements, and to show their piety, kings invited Brahmins to live in their realms, giving them grants of land so that they could live on the revenue which otherwise would have gone to the king. Remoter regions have customal accounts of Brahmins being brought there from the old centre of sanctity in the Punjab and Doab.

In Bengal, for example , the semi-legendary king Adishura is said to have brought Brahmins from Kanauj, while the Brahmin priests of the temple of the dancing Shiva at Chidambaram in Tamil Nadu are said to have come from the north. The Pandya and the Chola kings both laid claim the support of the Vedic sage Agastya, the legendary bringer of brahminical culture to the peninsula. Though Manu says that Aryas should live in the Indo-Gangetic plain, the boundaries of the Aryan country are elastic. In the ninth century, a commentator on Manu reconciled the text with current practice by explaining that any territory could become suitable for Vedic ritual if a righteous king conquered the barbarians and founded the system of four social classes there. Aryavarta remains the holiest territory, and the Ganges is the holiest of rivers, but this does not mean that other places are unholy.

We can see more instances showing that dharma is a matter of better and less good, not of absolute good and bad. Moreover, a holy river in the peninsula, for example , can be identified with the Ganges. Another instance of changing values concerns Vedic ritual and temple ritual. Temple ritual and the worship of images are disparaged in the dharma texts, yet in this period they were more commonly practised than Vedic ritual. This was justified by saying that Vedic ritual was appropriate for an earlier age, but temple worship is right in the present fallen age of the world (the Kali age, pp. 39, 47). The terminology and symbolism of Vedic ritual were transferred to the temple; a text of the sixth century says building a temple earns the same merit as Vedic sacrifices (Brihat-Samhita 55.2). Each large temple had its staff of Brahmins, to perform rituals and to manage the temple and its lands. Temples could act as banks, financing agricultural projects. The great temples are highly visible displays of the recognition and ritual support which kings received from Brahmins, and their munificence towards them. Less visible, but no less present to the minds of local people, are the myths about the temple's origins recorded in the local purana (sthala-purana).

Wars and conquest, the business of the king, was closely linked to sanctification, the business of the Brahmin. A good instance is the exploit of Rajendra Chola when he defeated Mahipala of Bengal in 1023. To commemorate his victory he built a new capital to the north of Tanjore, naming it Gangai-konda-chola-puram, 'Ganges-conquering Chola city'. As per the his inscription, he compelled the princes of Bengal to carry water from the Ganges to fill a tank in the new city. Thus he at the same time added the purifying and sanctifying power of the Ganges into his own country, and humiliated the Palas by making them his water-carriers.

The form of devotion known as Bhakti took shape in this period. In Sanskrit this word can refer to devotion of various kinds, such as a warrior's to his king, or a lover's to his or her beloved, or a worshipper's to a god or goddess; it is in this last sense that the word is used in English. It is already used in this sense in the Bhagavad-Gita, one of whose central themes is devotion to God, who seem s in the poem as the warrior prince Krishna. However, what is often called 'the bhakti movement' began later, around the seventh century in the far south; its founders are poets who used the Tamil language, and are revered as saints by Tamil Hindus today. They used the poetic devices of the Tamil literary custom to express intensely emotional devotion to Shiva or Vishnu. The longing of a girl for her absent lover, a common theme of Tamil poetry, was used to represent the devotee's longing for God. This theme was particularly set aside to the worship of Krishna, who is said to have arisen in a community of cowherds, inspiring ecstatic love in the women of that region.

Unlike Sanskrit Tamil, is a vernacular language, spoken in a particular region of South Asia, and it is during this period that the regional vernaculars came into written use, fostered by the regional bases of political power. The bhakti movement broke the Brahmin monopoly of communication with the great gods; a number of bhakti poets were non-Brahmins or even people of very low caste. It also broke the monopoly of men, since some of its saints were women. The practice of composing devotional poetry in vernacular languages spread northwards from Tamil Nadu. In the twelfth century, short poems to Shiva were composed in the Kannada language; they are still recited by the Virashaiva or Lingayat sect, in the south-west of the Deccan.

In general sects are not necessarily exclusive; the same person or family may follow the teachings and go to the temples of more than one sect. It has been said that Hinduism is polycentric; that is, it does not have one source of authority but a number of authorities. This polycentrism is seen in the way various sects hand on related but various customs, and in the number of local, regional and global places of pilgrimage. One of the most facts for it is the development of regional powers, each encouraging a distinctive culture, but united by a network of communication that included merchants, pilgrims and pandits. In this way Hinduism was distinct from other religions.

The Period of Muslim Rule

It can not be said in entirety that any single event founded Muslim power in South Asia, and no part became completely Islamized. Sind (now southern Pakistan) was conquered by Arabs in 711. Their power was checked by the Chalukyas, Rashtrakutas and Gurjara-Pratiharas, and the Muslim princes took their place among the competing dynasties. From 1000 to 1025, Mahmud of Ghazni (south of Kabul, in Afghanistan) repeatedly raided India, sacking Kanauj and other cities, and looting temples. Mahmud, whose empire extended into Central Asia, was the patron of Al-Biruni, but did not share his enquiring attitude to Hindu culture. Ghazni was sacked in 1151, and Ghur, further west, became the ruling power in Afghanistan. In 1175 Muhammad of Ghur conquered the Punjab, and afterwards most of northern India, but was checked in the east by another Muslim dynasty, the Khaljis, who had displaced the Sens in Bengal. Muhammad was murdered in 1206, and his viceroy in Delhi, Qutb-ud-din Aibak, became an independent ruler. Qutb-ud-din's successor Iltutmish, of Turkish origin, was created Sultan of Delhi by the Caliph of Baghdad, and the Delhi Sultanate became the major power in the north. Delhi, which stood approximately on the site of Hastinapura, remembered in the Mahabharata as the capital of the Bharata kings, had been one of several Rajput strongholds.

It now became the capital of a Muslim empire, and remained so until the eighteenth century. Around 1300, Sultan Ala-ud-din extended the empire into the Deccan, subduing Rajput and other Hindu rulers. In the far south he conquered the Pandyas of Madurai, and the Hoysalas of Dvarasamudra (also called Halebid), former vassals of the Cholas who had become an independent power. However, Muslim expansion was resisted on the east coast by the kings of Orissa, who built the great twelfth-century temple of Jagannath (Vishnu as 'lord of the world') at Puri and the thirteenth-century temple of the sun at Konarak.

In the fourteenth century the Delhi sultanate collapsed, after an attempt to replace vassalage with rule by centrally appointed Muslim governors. The governors of Madurai in the south and Bengal in the east declared themselves independent sultans, and the Bahmani sultanate was founded in Gulbarga (Karnataka), which in turn split into four around the end of the fifteenth century. A new Hindu kingdom in Vijayanagar (further south in Karnataka) dominated the south until the sixteenth century. Two remarkable Brahmins flourished under the early Vijayanagar kings: Vidyaranya and his younger brother Sayana. Vidyaranya wrote several works supporting the theology of Shankara, and is also credited with reconverting the founders of the dynasty who had been converted to Islam. Sayana wrote the standard Sanskrit commentary on the Rig-Veda. Both the Hoysalas and the Vijayanagar kings built magnificent and elaborately carved temples, which helped to consolidate their power by attracting the loyalty of Brahmins and others. The last and greatest of the Muslim dynasties was that of the Mughals from Samarkand in Uzbekistan, descendants of Timur, who himself had pillaged Delhi in 1398.

The Delhi sultanate was re-founded by the Lodi dynasty from Afghanistan, but was conquered in the sixteenth century by a Mughal ruler, Babur, who took the Persian title of Padishah. The Mughal Empire extended over north India and for a time over most of the peninsula, and influenced Indian culture even more profoundly than the preceding Muslim dynasties. It was confronted in the Deccan by the Muslim sultanates of Bijapur and Golkonda, and by the last Hindu empire, founded by the Maratha chieftain Shivaji, who was consecrated with Vedic royal rituals in 1674. The Maratha Empire enjoyed the support of school of Vishnu-worshipping saints who composed poems in the Marathi language. One of these, Ramdas, was Shivaji's personal guru, and hailed him as the protector of gods, cows and Brahmins. This period overlaps with the preceding, since the interplay of regional powers continued, with the difference that some were Hindu and some were Muslim. The practice of retaining conquered kings as vassals also continued.

Foreign powers from the north-west were nothing new; indeed, Hindus referred to the Muslim invaders by the same name, Yavana, which they had used for the Greeks. (Yavana is derived from the ancient Greek form of Ionian, which refers to the Greeks of the coast of Asia Minor; similar names are used in other Asian languages for the Greeks in general.) This new use of the name Yavana implies that, like the Greeks, the Muslims were respected for their custom of learning and material culture, which distinguished them from mere barbarians (mleccha).

A large number of people from the various religion were converted to Islam, so that in the twentieth century over a fifth of the South Asian population was Muslim. However, a number of these Muslims retained elements of Hindu culture. Within Islam, the Sufi custom was particularly congenial to Hindu religious ideas, since it sought knowledge through discipline and meditation under the guidance of a master. A new form of bhakti emerged, which rejected not only rituals and the authority of Brahmins, but the mythological attributes and images through which deities were known to earlier bhakti poets. Kabir, in the fifteenth century, composed poems in Hindi, ridiculing both Muslim and Hindu religious practices and asserting that God is neither in the mosque nor in the temple but in the heart. Nanak (1469-1539) proclaimed a similar message in the Punjab. His followers were known as Sikhs, this being the Punjabi form of the Sanskrit word shishya 'pupil'. Guru Nanak is known as the founder of the Sikh community.

MODERN HISTORY

The Period of British Rule

When the Mughal Empire was in decline in the eighteenth century, Britain and France competed for power in India. Each of these countries operated through a trading company, which became a military and political power by forming alliances with Indian rulers and raising its own Indian army. By 1760 the British had emerged as sole European power in India.

The East India Company, founded in 1600, had bases in three seaports: Calcutta (now Kolkata), Bombay (Mumbai) and Madras (Chennai). These were known as 'Presidency towns' because in the eighteenth century their governors were called 'presidents'. Each became the centre of an expanding territory called a 'presidency'. The largest of these territories was Bengal, which the Company administered as the agent of the Mughal emperor. By the middle of the nineteenth century, British India had acquired the shape which it retained, with some changes, until 1947. About two-thirds of the subcontinent was under direct British rule. About one-third was under Indian rulers, some Hindu and some Muslim, who were bound by treaties requiring them to accept the advice of British officials. The Maratha Empire, last of the regional powers and last Hindu empire, had been defeated in 1818 and divided between Bombay Presidency and a number of indirectly ruled states.

This company was headed by a Court of Directors in London, but the three governors could not always wait for instructions from the directors, and made their own policy. From 1773 the Company became increasingly under the control of Parliament, until in 1858 the Company was abolished and the government of India was placed directly under the Crown. The Regulating Act of 1773 provided for a Governor-General based in Calcutta, which thus became the capital of British India until 1911, when the capital was transferred to Delhi. The Company had a policy of not interfering with Indian society and religion, though this was modified in the course of the nineteenth century. Even before then, the British presence in India made religious and social change inevitable. The increasing use of English, and of printing in English and in Indian languages, together with gradually increasing uniformity in education, changed attitudes to authority.

Instead of a teacher handing on a custom of learning to a single pupil or a small group, writers addressed a more or less critical public, using arguments which were intelligible and acceptable to that public. A number of these writers kept abreast with ideas from the West, and some wrote for an international readership. There was lively debate between Christians (Indian as well as Western), Hindus and secularists; public debate with Christianity was also conducted in Sanskrit (Young 1981). Opponents of Hinduism cited social problems, especially caste and the condition of women, as evidence against it; a number of Hindus argued that these were false Hinduism, and advocated social reform in the name of true Hinduism. However, these reforms were suppressed by the Britishers in one or other form.

In that period the policy of governing the people as per the their own laws accidentally changed those laws, by requiring Hindu law to be codified and standardized, and persons to be categorized as Hindus, Muslims and others so that the appropriate law could be applied to them. It also brought matters of dharma, which had hitherto been the concern of specialists, into the public arena, and made caste identity more public and rigid. Much of the education, in English and the vernacular languages, was in the hands of missionaries, despite the Company's early hostility towards them.

Among the modern reformers Rammohun Roy, a Brahmin of Calcutta, was the first Indian of modern times to be at home in Indian and Western intellectual customs. Rammohun held that there was one God, revealed in the design of the universe; all religious customs taught this, and none possessed a unique revelation. True worship consisted in the contemplation of God without the aid of images or mythology, and in benevolent behaviour towards others. The various religious customs were in agreement on these essentials of religion, differing only on inessentials. Rammohun accused both Hindus and Christians of insisting on inessentials and obscuring the universal truths which they had received. The society which he founded, the Brahmo Samaj, though small in numbers, became an effective movement for modernization in Bengal, and inspired similar societies elsewhere, committed to monotheism and social reform. Its most influential member after Rammohun was Keshub Chunder Sen (1838-84), an enthusiastic preacher, who introduced the idea that Hindus inherited a custom of spirituality which had made India the source of all the great religious movements of the world. Keshub turned the quest for revelation from the external world to the human heart, and met the claims of Christianity with a counter-claim for Hinduism, without in realclaiming a unique revelation. Swami Vivekanand further developed these ideas.

The new ideas were not only confined to the centres of British influence. In the Kathiawar peninsula in Gujarat a Brahmin ascetic called Sahajanand (1781-1830), better known as Swaminarayan, founded a sect which is still strong in Gujarat and in Gujarati communities elsewhere. The name Narayan is one of the names of Vishnu, and reflects a belief that Swaminarayan was a expression of God. This sect was encouraged by British officials as a force for peace in a turbulent region. Later, another Brahmin ascetic of Kathiawar who knew no English, Dayananda Sarasvati (1825-83), interpreted the Veda and Manu in a way that showed the influence of Victorian thought, upholding monotheism, condemning idolatry and caste, especially the hereditary authority of Brahmins, and advocating scientific enquiry and commercial and military enterprise. Dayananda founded a sect, the Arya Samaj, which became a force for modernity in the Punjab. He also intended to spread Aryan culture, as he saw it, outside India, but did not put this into effect. Some notions of Hinduism were spread in the West by the Theosophical Society, founded in New York in 1875 by the Russian Helena Blavatsky (1831-91) and the American Henry Olcott (1832-1907) to investigate ancient wisdom. An attempt to join forces with the Arya Samaj failed, but in 1882 the society founded its headquarters at Adyar, near Madras, where its library remains a centre for research on Sanskrit texts.

Ideas such as karma, rebirth and the subtle body became widely known in the USA and Britain, in versions adapted to Blavatsky's ideas of spiritual evolution. For a time Theosophy provided some Hindus, whose English education had turned them away from Hinduism, with a route into their heritage, and encouraged them to study Sanskrit texts, especially the Bhagavad-Gita. The first effective Hindu missionary to the West was Swami Vivekananda (1863-1902), who made a dramatic seem ance at the World's Parliament of Religions at Chicago in 1893. His message was a modern form of Advaita Vedanta, which he claimed was the most rational and scientific religion.

Sri Aurobindo Ghose was another prominent religious nationalist, who was educated in England but on his return in 1893 threw himself into Indian culture and politics. He became a national figure over the partition of Bengal in 1905. The province of Bengal had become over-large by the addition of Bihar to the west and Orissa to the south, and the

Governor-General, Lord Curzon, solved this problem by creating a new province, East Bengal (approximately where Bangladesh is today). To Aurobindo and others, the partition was an assault on the land of Bengal, which he identified with the violent but nourishing mother goddess, Kali, whose worship is particularly popular in Bengal. Violent struggle in her defence was a sacred duty which Aurobindo equated with a Vedic sacrifice. Such appeals aroused Hindus but antagonized Muslims, who welcomed the partition because the new province had a Muslim majority. Aurobindo retired suddenly in 1910 to the French colony of Pondicherry though acquitted on a charge of seditious journalism, where he developed a new form of Vedanta.

Although Bengal was reunited in 1912, but the partition issue left a permanent scar. In turning the Congress into an independence movement, Tilak, Aurobindo and others had turned it into a Hindu movement which virtually barred Muslims. After the First World War, Mohandas Gandhi (1869-1948) attempted to bring together an independence movement that was founded on religion but transcended religious divisions - taking advantage of Muslim indignation at the dismemberment of the Turkish Empire after the war. Gandhi proclaimed that 'Truth is God', so that no one, not even an atheist, could be alienated by a struggle in the name of God.

Truth, however, he understood in his own way: as shown in his autobiography, The Story of my Experiments with Truth, he regarded it as something never to be completely known, but to be constantly sought after through vows of abstinence, and through a non-violent approach to political and interpersonal conflict which recognizes the truth in the opponent's position while refusing to abandon the truth as one sees it. Though Gandhi found support in a number of non-Indian sources, such as Ruskin and Tolstoy, his ideas about truth are rooted in Hindu custom. Rammohun, Keshub, Vivekananda and Radhakrishnan were also affined with his belief that true religion transcends the boundaries between religious customs.

However, Gandhi believed that God could be known by any name, his favourite name of God was Rama, the name he uttered as he died. Rama, the hero of the Ramayana, is worshipped by a number of Hindus as God. He is also the ideal king, who reigned in perfect peace, order and prosperity during the second age of the world. Gandhi's objective in the independence movement was not simply to end British rule, but to re-establish the reign of Rama (Rama-rajya). This would mean not only peace and prosperity, but an economy based on minimal consumption in self-sufficient villages, where all castes would be respected because all work was equally valued, under the authority of God, Truth, or Rama.

During the Bengal partition agitation one of the features of Hinduism that emerged as nationalist symbols was the Bhagavad-Gita: revolutionaries swore oaths on it, and recited it defiantly under the gallows. Later, Tilak, Aurobindo and Gandhi each wrote a commentary on it: Tilak in Marathi and Gandhi in Gujarati, both in prison, and Aurobindo in English in Pondicherry. Unlike the Sanskrit commentaries, each of which used the text as authority for the theology of a particular sect, the primary concern of these modern commentaries is action in the world. They all emphasize the ideal of action without desire for personal reward, a feature of the Bhagavad-Gita which had been highlighted earlier by the Bengali Bankim Chandra Chatterji (1838-94). While Aurobindo's shows the deepest understanding of the Gita, Gandhi's, brief and published as cheaply as possible, proved the most popular; it was translated into a number of languages and became a handbook of the independence movement. The Gita's popularity as a devotional text and as authority for the exposition of ideas increased rapidly.

V. D. Savarkar (1883-1966), a Marathi Brahmin and veteran of the Bengal partition agitation, wrote a book in 1924 called Hindutva: Who is a Hindu? When Hindu political ideologies were developed which made little or no attempt to accommodate non-Hindu communities. Savarkar explains that Hindutva, literally 'Hindu-ness' (a Persian name with a Sanskrit suffix), is more comprehensive than Hinduism; it is a matter of race, geography and culture. Savarkar, who also translated the Italian nationalist Mazzini into Marathi, presents a nationalism of blood and soil on the European Romantic model. For him, anyone who accepts this Hindutva is a member of the Hindu nation; but those who have loyalties outside the sacred land cannot be true Hindus. So long as Muslims look to Mecca, they exclude themselves from full membership of the nation, just as Jews exclude themselves by their Zionism from full membership of European nations; the analogy, more ominous now than when he wrote, is Savarkar's own views on the Hinduism.

REFERENCES

A. Avalon: *The Great Liberation*, Madras, Ganesh & Co., 1927.

A. Danielou: *Le polythéisme hindou*, Paris, Correa, 1960.

A. L. Basham: *The Wonder That Was India*, London, Sidgwick and Jackson, 1954.

E. B. Cowelleau and A. E. Gough: *The Sarva-darœana-sacgraha*, London, Kegan Paul, Trench, Trubner & Co., 1904.

F. E. Keay: *Kabir and His Followers*, Calcutta, Association Press, 1931.

F. E. Pargiter: *The Markandya Purana*, Calcutta, Asiatic Society, 1904.

F. Kingsbury and G. E. Phillips: *Hymns of the Tamil œaivite Saints*, Calcutta, Association Press, 1921.

Gordon Matthews: *Shiva*, New York, Oxford University Press, 1948.

H. H. Wilson: *Select Specimens of the Theatre of the Hindus*, London, Trubner & Co., 1835.

H. H. Wilson: *The Vishnu Puraana*, London, Trubner, 1864.

J. A. B. Van Buitenen: *Ramanuja on the Bhgavad-gita*, The Hague, H. L. Smits, 1953.

J. Brough: *Selections from Classical Sanskrit Literature*, London, Luzac & Co., 1952.

J. Muir: *Metrical Translations from Sanskrit Writers*, London, Trubner & Co., 1871.

J. S. M. Hooper: *Hymns of the Alvars*, Calcutta, Association Press, 1929.

Nicol Macnicol: *Psalms of Maraha Saints*, Calcutta, Association Press.

R. C. Temple: *The Word of Lalla the Prophetess*, Cambridge, Mass, Cambridge University Press, 1924.

W. Norman Brown: *The Saundaryalahari*, Cambridge, Mass, Harvard University Press, 1958.

3

Philosophy

Among all the surviving customs Hinduism is the longest surviving philosophical custom in India. We can recognize several historical stages. The earliest, from around 700 BC, was the proto-philosophical period, when karma and liberation theories arose, and the proto-scientific ontological lists in the Upanishads were compiled. Next came the classical period, spanning the first millennium ad, in which there was constant philosophical exchange between various Hindu, Buddhist and Jaina schools. During this period, some schools, such as Sankhya, Yoga and Vaisesika, fell into oblivion and others, such as Kashmir Saivism, emerged. At last, after the classical period only two or three schools remained active. The political and economic disturbances caused by repeated Muslim invasions hampered intellectual growth. The schools that survived were the Logic school (Nyaya), especially New Logic (Navya-Nyaya), the grammarians and, above all, the Vedanta schools. The chief concerns of the Hindu philosophers were metaphysics, epistemological issues, philosophy of language, and moral philosophy.

Various schools can be distinguished by their various approaches to reality, but all regarded the Vedas (the sacred scriptures) authoritative, and all believed that there is a permanent individual self (atman). They shared with their opponents (Buddhists and Jainas) a belief in the need for liberation. They used similar epistemic tools and methods of argument. In direct contrast to their opponents, who were atheists, Hindu philosophers could be either theists or atheists. In realwe can observe an increased tendency towards theistic ideas near the end of the classical period, with the result that the strictly atheistic teachings, which were more philosophically rigorous and sound, fell into disuse. Atma or soul was regarded as a part of larger reality in Hindu metaphysics.

These views of the world differed due to the fact that they had to be proved and properly founded. Similarly, logical and epistemological tools were developed and fashioned as per the needs and beliefs of individual philosophers. Most agreed on two or three sources of knowledge: perception and inference, with verbal testimony as a possible third. In this quest for philosophical rigour, there was a need for precision of language, and there were significant philosophical developments among the grammarians and the philosophers who explained the Vedas (the Mimamsakas). A culmination of these linguistic efforts can be seen in the philosopher of language Bharthari. One of his greatest accomplishments was the full articulation of the theory that a sentence as a whole is understood in a sudden act of comprehension.

It is customary to name six Hindu schools, of the more than a dozen that existed, thus lumping several into a single school. This is particularly the case with Vedanta. The six are listed in three pairs: Sankhya–Yoga; Vedanta–Mimamsa; Nyaya–Vaisheshika. This does not take account of the grammarians or Kashmir Saivism. In their quest for freedom from rebirth, all the Hindu schools operated within the same framework. Their ultimate goal was liberation. However they never doubted its real possibility that how much they were truly engaged in the quest for liberation apart from their philosophical preoccupations is not always clear.

Following the establishment of Vedic culture in the history of the Indian subcontinent, the development of philosophical and religious thought over a period of two millennia gave rise to what came to be called the six schools of aastika, or orthodox, Indian philosophy or Hindu philosophy. These schools have come to be synonymous with the greater religion of Hinduism, which was a development of the early Vedic Religion. Hindu Philosophy gives a clear understanding to the questions of cycle of life and death, the nature of Soul, the Universe and its creator and facts for joy and sufferings, happiness and sorrow, health and disease and the ultimate understanding of man's relationship with God. It also explains his duties during this birth as well as about his past and his future.

It investigates and inquires the Truth and tempts us to think and fact in our search for a solution. Even though the Agamas and Vedas seem to be professing various doctrines, they both are written on the same philosophy but for various population group. The Agamas give us the Theological aspect of our practice with prayers to God in various expressions. The Vedas give us all the rituals and also the philosophy of our religious practice. All of them are based on the principle that the Soul is a part of the Divine spirit and is covered by the sheaths of "Upadhis" as an effect of ones Karma. It goes through endless rebirth as per the ones Karma to purify itself. Every one should follow his Dharma and perform their duties or Karma without attachment, as an offering to God to receive eternal salvation and liberation as Moksha.

BASIC PHILOSOPHY

It is commonly said that philosophy is the rational aspect of the faith, in any culture or Religion. It is an integral part of Hindu religious beliefs and culture in India. It is a rational inquiry into the nature of truth or reality, giving clear solutions to A number of problems of life and human behaviour. It shows the ways to get rid of the pain and sufferings, to get happiness and peace of mind and to attain liberation and eternal bliss. Theology is regarded significant in most world religions. Philosophy is often agnostic and it is not part of the religious study. Hindus consider philosophy as an integral part of their religious experience. In Hindu culture, theology is well mixed in all aspects of life through its mythology, art, music and dance and they all carry a moral.

Hindu Philosophy is not merely a speculation or guess work of a solution for human problems and doubts, but an organized doctrine based on the mystical experience of the Sages and Seers. The teachings of Hindu philosophy are given to us in the Upanishads which are the wealth of our knowledge. The ethics and tenets are obtained from them through the Six Dharsanas and various later schools of philosophers. The glory of Hindu philosophy is seen in the teachings of Hindu dharma, the theory of karma and rebirth, the six dharsanas, and the four yogas or spiritual disciplines. They not only create the questions in our mind to think but also give us the answers to the problems. Dharma means "that which holds" the people of this world and the whole creation. It is the eternal Divine law of God. That which brings well being to man and supports the world with prosperity is dharma. It is the absolute Truth and laws of righteous living. The four Vedas are the authority of Dharma. The truth about dharma can not be realised through any other knowledge and one's own facting through any analysis alone can not be that authority. So it is appropriate to say here that Vedas are the real authority of the Dharma.

DIVINE LAWS

Law of Integrity

As per the law of integrity the whole universe is imbued with divine presence. "All this is for the habitation of the Lord," thus begins the Isa Upanishad. All religions acknowledge that the God is omnipresent and is the ruler as well as dweller of the whole cosmos. Since God is present in each and every aspect of His creation, it logically follows that the whole creation is divine and sacred and that each and every object in it and each and every aspect of it, including ourselves, the good and the bad, the high and the low, deserve our unconditional love, respect and attention. It also becomes clear that we cannot deal with the world as per the our needs and desire or fear and expectations, but with a sense of equanimity as if we are playing hide and seek with God Himself in his gigantic world. We realize that self-realization is possible only by staying within and accepting the objective world as the twisted truth that need to be explored and resolved by consciously searching for God in its myriad objects not by going away or escaping.

The Buddha taught this to His followers when he advised them to cultivate friendliness towards the whole world. If we look at the world objectively from this point of view, we realize why the world is in conflicts and why human relationships fail so frequently. Why the world is mostly polluted, dirty and disease ridden. We realize the price we are in realpaying for not honouring the divine connection we have with the world we live in. If the world or conditions are unkind or are not favouring us, we need not have to look far for facts but into ourselves. The world is against us, because we are against each other, in competition with each other, suspicious of each other and cannot visualize and work for a united world. If we want the world to be with us, we need to reconnect ourselves with the world and live in harmony with it, with a sense of gratitude and reverence and with an awareness that you cannot really be happy if a part of your body is sick or disjointed and you use your body purely for your selfish desires without any concern for its wellbeing. So its better that we trust in the existence of God.

By just going to a Church or temple truth can not be brought as it is solace, but we can bring it in the love we spread and receive. If we are selfish and disconnected, however hard we may try, we cannot experience oneness with God. The love that we block in our hearts also blocks our consciousness to the love that comes from others. A person who experiences this ordeal has but an emptiness within from which he is rarely free. But if he can manage to shake off his pettiness, he will have the opportunity to experience the sacred presence of God in the world around Him. He will grow in the light of that awareness and learn to see the world as an aspect of God. He will find the world in harmony with his own aspirations and personal goals and live with the confidence that when the need arises, he would get the necessitated help or counsel from the stranger.

Law of Integral Equilibrium

Biologically human beings cannot tolerate extreme physical or mental conditions. Beyond a point, we cannot withstand the joys and sorrows or the comforts or discomforts of life. Excessive self denial is as harmful as excessive self indulgence. Overeating is as harmful to our wellbeing as obsessive dieting. Too much alcohol would burn the system. A little once in awhile would perhaps relax the muscles and serve the heart. Extreme inaction or extreme exertions are equally harmful to our professional and personal lives. This is true in case of other things concerning our lives. For example in our relationships if we do not know where to stop, we may cause innumerable problems to ourselves and to others. If we do not know when to care and when to ignore our children or when to discipline them and when to pamper them, perhaps we may fail to bring them up as responsible adults. A certain degree of privacy and separation are necessitated for the relationships to survive even among the closest relationships.

This is the foremost if we can learn anything from our experiences. Life on earth is conditioned by this principle of moderation. Our bodies and minds have evolved on the principle of balance and control. We are safe if we remain within bounds and avoid the extremes. If we know our limitations and stay with in our control we are at peace with ourselves.

Law of Wealth

On the principle of abundance the universe exists. It is by giving that you receive. This is the law of abundance, which stipulates that we cannot enjoy the riches of the universe unless we are willing to share them with others. Health and happiness need not always go together. Not all who accumulate wealth enjoy their lives. It is because they guard their acquisitions jealously unwilling to share them with others. Abundance does not mean mere accumulation of material wealth. Happiness, peace of mind and harmony in life are also part of this universal abundance. Abundance comes into a person's life only when he facilitates its free flow from him and through him. You can block the flow and you may accumulate wealth. But there is no guarantee that the wealth you amassed would bring you peace and harmony. You would enjoy the love and acceptance of others it can not be guaranteed.

Only the selfish accumulation of wealth only generates negative consequences of abundance- its overwhelming capacity to inflict pain and suffering. Remember, whatever that comes to you today will leave you some day. For every thing is here is so transient and fleeting. At the end of life all that is sought is lost and all that is given is gained. This is the basis of divine life and the secret of life.

Law of Personal Realism

The law of personal realism says that you are the creator of your life and your reality. Your thoughts become your actions and your actions create the circumstances in your life. You are responsible for everything that happens to you in your life. This is the simple law of as you sow so you reap. It can also be called the law of motion and emotion. Every thought that we send out into the universe comes back to us with accumulated energy of its own kind. When negative thoughts go out of our minds, they will come back to us with redoubled negative energy and give us lot of pain and unhappiness. Positive thoughts on the other hand bring in positive energy and energize us, establishing in the process peace and harmony in our consciousness.

Our actions too yield the same results. Our positive actions bring in positive rewards and our negative actions bring negative rewards. The energy that we unleash either in the form of a thought or action always comes back to us with increased force. Thus through our actions and thoughts we are constantly creating our own realities. Whatever we give comes back to us. We should hence be very careful about our thoughts and actions as they have a lasting influence on the pattern of our lives. People blame others for what happens to them. Little do they know that if any one is to be blamed it is the person himself who made it happen to himself. Wisdom is when something happens to you, instead of looking around for excuses and placing the blame on others, look into yourself and ask yourself why you made it happen? Why you invited those circumstances into your life either intentionally or unintentionally?

May be it is because you wanted to learn something out of that experience or you wanted to strengthen some aspect of your personality or resolve some long troubling relationship. When you start accepting responsibility for the events of your life, you begin to learn more about yourself, your inner thoughts, your fears and aspirations. Out of this awareness you also start expanding your consciousness, become aware of your thought processes, and through this awareness you ultimately learn to change the conditions of your life. And in its end it gives you the happiness and satisfaction.

Law of Compatibility

As per the law of compatibility the ancient Aryans believed in 'rta' meaning the universal order or harmony. 'Rta' is an ancient word to which we can trace at least few significant words that are known to us today. One is the Sanskrit world 'ritu', which means season. The others are the Latin word 'rhythmus', the French word 'rhythme', the Greek word 'rhuthmos' and the English word 'rhythm' , all meaning, beat, pulse, metre, pattern, order, flowing, and harmony. Let us understand why the concept of harmony and rhythm was regarded so significant by our ancient generations and why they elevated it to the level of highest divinity. They regarded Truth, harmony and order to be the Ultimate Reality lying beyond all realities, the hidden secret behind all manifest creation, or the Absolute Truth above all relative truths so they did so.

What is truth? Or how can Truth be defined? Truth does not necessarily mean only verbal truths. Truth is the fundamental reality where there are no conflicts and confusion, no divisions and separation, but only unity and harmony. Truth is where there is movement without obstruction and where there is order without confusion. Where there is conflict, separation and feeling of alienation, there is no truth. Where there is division and alignment of divisions into opposing parts there is no truth. There is no truth in ones life and ones being unless there is total harmony in ones whole being, which include ones activities, thoughts and environment. Truth resolves all conflicts, divisions and differences and establishes permanent peace, order and harmony in ones life. When you consider the world outside is various and separate from you there is always a conflict.

Again there is conflict when you consider others are various and separate from you. There is conflict when you consider that some one is good, or some one is bad; that some thing is this or some thing is that. There is conflict as long as you pass petty judgements about yourself or about the world around you. Unless you learn to resolve these differences, by expanding your consciousness, and learn to appreciate them in their own light, you cannot have real harmony and peace in your life.

The ordinary mind cannot understand this truth because it is still steeped in ignorance. But at the highest level of consciousness, all conflicts and confusion resolve themselves into one beautiful, harmonious whole. You may call it divine. You may call it God, This or That. The fact is, it is One, it is whole, and it is harmony and order, without any divisions and without any conflicts. At that level even in the seemingly chaotic conditions of life one can perceive harmony and certain order. That which we understand as good or that we understand as bad, become but the facets of the same Truth. He who realizes this fundamental reality of our existence no more suffers from inner confusion and conflicts. He suffers no more from the relative conflicts of his life or relationships. He stops judging things from the limited values of his mind and consciousness. He learns to forgive people. He learns to tolerate opposition. He learns to accept the conditions of his life without complaint. The people and their weaknesses without reservations are accepted by him.

There is nothing higher or lower, nothing sacred or evil for him. Nothing motivates him to take sides or judge the diversity of creation. He lives in harmony with himself and with others, with the world within himself and with the world external to him. He suffers not from fear or insecurity, or from worries and anxieties about himself or his life. If you want to live in peace, stop categorizing and grouping things and people, and it includes you also. Stop judging things from the relative state of your mind, against the partial truths you know and believe in. Understand that harmony comes when you live in peace with the world around you, and when you accept it whole heatedly and unconditionally without measuring it against your limited knowledge. It only happens when you become an embodiment of 'Rta', the rhythm of life and creation.

Law of Rationale and Feelings

One should learn to use appropriately the three forces of your personality namely emotion, fact and faith, to achieve peace and harmony in your life and move closer to God. Emotion, fact and belief are equally significant in human life. They serve various motives. But they are complimentary, which means that you need them all equally to conduct yourself in this world. Without the one the other two do not take you far be it your ordinary life or spiritual.

All these three help us to conduct ourselves in this world, but in their own various ways. It is hard to say which is more useful than the other two. He who has mastery over these three forces, is a master of himself and is qualified to reach God than any one else. Emotion, fact and faith in realemanate from the body, the mind and the inner spirit, or alternatively, the animal, human and divine components of the human personality. They are the Great Trinity, namely Lord Siva, Vishnu and Brahma, the divinities that exist at the microcosmic level also, where as the whole human personality can be contrasted withthe Cosmic Man (Purusha) or Supreme Being of the macrocosm. Without these three components, creation and our existence is not complete.

In a common paralance emotions connect us to the world; fact helps us to solve the problems of our existence, while belief helps us to transcend ourselves to reach the world beyond. Emotions bring people together through the power of love or the joy of being together. But do not help us maintain them for long. Fact helps us to understand the world around us intelligently, but does not take us far in building relationships that are based upon unconditional love, especially when the relationship are no more yielding the expected results. Fact merely can't explain properly the mysteries of our existence or the need for us to become spiritual. Its vision and its field of activity are limited to the tangible and to the sensory world.

In real sense it helps us to fact beyond facts to pursue the path of spirituality so that we may realize Truth in a various way where faith comes to our aid. It enables us to overcome our selfishness and petty mindedness so that we learn to love others unconditionally and sacrifice our selfish interests for the common welfare of all. When hardships surround us and we have exhausted our rationale means to deal with them, or when we are overwhelmed with the negative emotions of fear and hostility, faith provides us with some meaningful clues and the necessitated answers to sustain ourselves. When emotions and fact let us down, faith is the comforting and soothing companion. If you have faith in yourself and in God, you can withstand greater hardships and maintain your inner balance. Trust is an aspect of faith only.

Trust can bring diverse individuals and groups together so that they can work together and live in harmony, though this does not happen all the time as we do not have enough faith in each other. It is trust which is responsible for our social, political or economic institutions. But when people lose faith in them, they either use fact to change them or succumb to their emotions to destroy them. Emotions on their own destabilize our lives. Fact on its own leads us to unlimited ambition and selfishness and in the process endangers the very safety and survival of our existence. On its own faith binds us to blind dogmatism and superstition.

Emotions may be harmful if used inappropriately or not regulated properly. The body can suffer from enormous damage because of negative emotions. But take emotions completely out of our systems and what you find will be automatons, devoid of any love for life or concern for themselves or others. If you take emotions completely of our consciousness, the institutions of family and society would collapse under the heavy burden of fact and conditional relationships alone. So we should know when and where to use these three instruments appropriately for the greater benefit of all instead of wasting these powers.

We should cultivate in ourselves the positive emotions of love, compassion, courage and inner joy, discarding wherever possible their corresponding negative emotions. Whether it is in your physical life, material life or spiritual life, learn to use three forces of your personality for your peace and inner happiness. Bring out the best of your emotions in your relationships. Use the best of your facting in times of hardships and when you stand alone in the contemplation of God, let the light of your faith shine through your heart.

Law of Misery

Just because of our inner imperfections suffering comes to us. To the extent we learn from our suffering and learn from it, our suffering is mitigated. Suffering is not a negative but a positive and dynamic force. Its objective is to open our eyes and correct our ways. It comes into our lives, not because we are destined to suffer, but because it has a message to deliver. When you pursue a wrong path, objective for a wrong goal, make some wrong choices or give expression to some inner imperfection, you suffer and in that suffering lays a warning that you need to change. Your suffering goes to the extent you become aware of it and respond positively to it and to the extent you correct yourselves or your actions.

The hidden motive of suffering hence is not to really subject to you physical or mental anguish, but to improve you in some aspect of your life. Those who refuse to listen to its message continue to suffer, perhaps more intensely, till good sense prevails and the necessitated change comes in them. The fact why every one suffers to some degree in the world is because every one is imperfect in some way and is in need of some improvement. It is because of the suffering that life evolves on earth.

Hence, when suffering comes into the life of an individual, he must look into himself deeply and find out the root cause. He must find out what its true message is, what it wants in him to change or improve. Once he identifies the cause, he must take necessary steps to change himself. He should strive sincerely to remove the cause. Suffering becomes not a dark affliction, but a beacon of light guiding us in the right direction towards the future in this way.

PRIMARY BELIEFS

Mainly the Hindu philosophy is divided into six orthodox (Sanskrit stika) schools of thought, or darshanas, discussed below.

Samkhya

In Hinduism Samkhya is the oldest of the orthodox philosophical systems. Samkhya postulates that everything in reality stems from purusha

(Self or soul) and prakriti (Matter, creative agency, energy). There are a number of souls and they possess consciousness, but they are devoid of all qualities. Prakriti/Matter consists of three dispositions: steadiness (sattva), activity (rajas), and dullness (tamas), known as the three gunas, or qualities. Because of the intertwined relationship between the soul and these dispositions, an imbalance in disposition causes the world to evolve. Liberation occurs with the realization that the soul and the dispositions are different.

Samkhya is a dualistic philosophy, but there are differences between Samkhya and other forms of dualism. Dualism is between the mind and the body in the West, whereas in Samkhya it is between the self and matter. The concept of the self is roughly equivalent to the Western concept of the mind. Originally Samkhya was not theistic, but in confluence with Yoga it developed a theistic variant.

Yoga

Yoga is the name of one of the six orthodox philosophical schools in Indian philosophy. The Yoga philosophical system is closely allied with the Samkhya school. The Yoga school as expounded by Patanjali accepts the Samkhya psychology and metaphysics, but is more theistic than the Samkhya, as evidenced by the addition of a divine entity to the Samkhya's twenty-five elements of reality. The parallels between Yoga and Samkhya were so close that Max Müller says that "the two philosophies were in popular parlance distinguished from each other as Samkhya with and Samkhya without a Lord." Heinrich Zimmer wrote about the intimate relationship between Samkhya and Yoga:

"These two are regarded in India as twins, the two aspects of a single discipline. Sekhya provides a basic theoretical exposition of human nature, enumerating and defining its elements, analyzing their manner of co-operation in a state of bondage (bandha), and describing their state of disentanglement or separation in release (moksha), while Yoga treats specifically of the dynamics of the process for the disentanglement, out outlines practical techniques for the gaining of release, or 'isolation-integration' (kaivalya)."

The foundational text of the Yoga school is the Yoga Sutras of Patanjali, who is regarded as the founder of the formal Yoga philosophy. The Sutras of the Yoga philosophy are ascribed to Patanjali, who, may have been, as Max Müller explains, "the author or representative of the Yoga-philosophy without being necessarily the author of the Sutras."

Nyaya

Basically the Nyaya school is based on the Nyaya Sutras. They were written by Aksapada Gautama, probably in the second century BC. The most significant contribution made by this school is its methodology. This methodology is based on a system of logic that has subsequently been adopted by the majority of the Indian schools.

This is comparable to the relationship between Western science and philosophy, which was derived largely from Aristotelian logic. Nevertheless, Nyaya was seen by its followers as more than logical in its own right.

They believed that obtaining valid knowledge was the only way to gain release from suffering, and they took great pains to identify valid sources of knowledge and distinguish these from mere false opinions. As per the Nyaya, there are exactly four sources of knowledge: perception, inference, comparison, and testimony. Knowledge obtained through each of these is either valid or invalid. Nyaya developed several criteria of validity. In this sense, Nyaya is probably the closest Indian equivalent to analytic philosophy. The later Naiyanikas gave logical proofs for the existence and uniqueness of Ishvara in response to Buddhism, which, at that time, was basically non-theistic.

Vaisheshika

The school of Vaisheshika was founded by Kanada and postulates an atomic pluralism. All objects in the physical universe are reducible to certain types of atoms, and Brahman is regarded as the fundamental force that causes consciousness in these atoms. Although the Vaisheshika school developed independently from the Nyaya, the two eventually merged because of their closely related metaphysical theories. In its classical form, however, the Vaisheshika school differed from the Nyaya in one crucial respect: where Nyaya accepted four sources of valid knowledge, the Vaisheshika accepted only two—perception and inference. But both Vesheshika and Nyaya schools were not entirely identical.

Purva Mimamsa

Chief objective of the Purva Mimamsa school was to establish the authority of the Vedas. Consequently, this school's most worthful contribution to Hinduism was its conceptualisation of the rules of Vedic interpretation. Its adherents believe that one must have unquestionable faith in the Vedas and perform the yajñas, or fire-sacrifices, regularly. They believe in the power of the mantras and yajñas to sustain all the activity of the universe. In keeping with this belief, they place great emphasis on dharma, which consists of the functioning of Vedic rites.

The Mimamsa assumed the logical and philosophical teachings of the other schools, but felt they did not sufficiently emphasise attention to right action. They believed that the other schools of thought that objectiveed for release (moksha) did not allow for complete freedom from desire and selfishness, because the very striving for liberation stemmed from a simple desire to be free. As per the Mimamsa thought, only by acting in accordance with the prescriptions of the Vedas may one attain salvation. The Mimamsa school later changed its views and commenced to teach the doctrines of Brahman and freedom. Its adherents then advocated the release or escape of the soul from its constraints through enlightened activity. Although Mimamsa does not receive much scholarly attention, its influence can be felt in the life of the practising Hindu, because all Hindu ritual, ceremony, and law is influenced by this school.

Vedanta

The Vedanta, or later Mimamsa school, focuses on the philosophical teachings of the Upanishads rather than the ritualistic injunctions of the Brahmanas. While the customal Vedic rituals continued to be exercised as meditative and propitiatory rites, a more knowledge-centred understanding began to emerge. These were mystical aspects of Vedic religion that focused on meditation, self-discipline, and spiritual connectivity, more than conventional ritualism.

The more recondite Vedanta is the essence of the Vedas, as encapsulated in the Upanishads. Vedantic thought drew on Vedic cosmology, hymns and philosophy. The Brihadaranyaka Upanishad seem ed as far back as 3,500 years ago. While thirteen or so Upanishads are accepted as principal, over a hundred exist. The most significant share of Vedantic thought is the idea that self-consciousness is continuous with and indistinguishable from consciousness of Brahman. The aphorisms of the Vedanta sutras are presented in a cryptic, poetic style, which allows for a variety of interpretations. Consequently, the Vedanta broke into six sub-schools, each interpreting the texts in its own way and producing its own series of sub-commentaries. Four of them are as follows.

ETHICS

With other philosophical trends and schools Hindu schools of philosophy developed in close, lively dialogue. As early as 400–300 BC, both Panini and the author of Manusmriti (a third century BC book of laws) identified two major intellectual trends, one involving belief in the sacred texts known as the Vedas, and one involving their rejection. Those who regarded the Vedas as their authority later developed into what we know as the Hindu schools. With a few exceptions, most of the religious and philosophical movements objectiveed at liberation, complete freedom from life and rebirth. From about the eighth century BC, belief in rebirth was found among most philosophical and religious leaders.

At first, the mechanism of rebirth was thought to be prompted by bad actions. It was also believed that by good actions a person became good and by evil actions a person became evil. Since with time this must have come to be perceived as rather simplistic, the idea of rebirth became more complicated. A person was reborn just by acts, regardless of whether those acts were good or evil. Liberation from rebirth could be attained by an absence of desire; desire of any sort, whether a craving for food, say, or for a new thing, entangled a person in the worldly repetition mechanism.

Various thinkers and teachers were specifically concerned with effective ways of achieving liberation. This meant establishing the basic presuppositions of the theory, such as what it is that truly exists, how this could be proved, and how liberation was to be viewed, and, moreover, how to promulgate such beliefs. There were constant discussions, an ongoing search for better ways of arguing with opponents. The formal necessitatements for building an argument were much disputed; each school believed that only its tools for debate were necessary, and that any others were useless.

An axiom held by most followers of the Vedic custom was that there is a self (atman) which travels from life to life. The 'life' in question need not be human; it can also be that of an animal. In the early philosophical sources, the Upanishads, there is little room for any sort of agency beyond individuals with selves. It is only later that we find the idea of God or gods actively creating the universe and directing individual persons towards liberation or towards realizing some sort of aspiration towards the divine. Both these objectives were combined in many instances.

The concept of atman was crucial in a number of debates, because there were a number of people who either had a various understanding of it or who claimed to need no such concept. Argument helped towards a more precise articulation of the term, although a number of Hindu thinkers held that knowledge of atman is only a partial understanding of reality; the individual self is only a part of the larger scenario of the universe. The universe was thought to be an all-encompassing spiritual entity, of which atman is a minute fragment. Experiencing this spiritually, through meditative practices, frees a person from the ordinary way of things: such a person is not reborn, and does not repeat the anguish, pain, disease, old age and death of ordinary mortals, but is instead forever free. This can be accomplished through one's own efforts, although often the guidance of a teacher, a guru, is necessitated. These efforts may necessitate to be extended over various lifetimes in order to work off all the accumulated karmic impressions. Karmic impressions, which may result from physical activities, speech or mental acts, are what in realbind people to the rotating process of rebirth.

Step by step, notions of divine intervention in the process of liberation found their way into numerous teachings. It was a compounding of one's own efforts plus divine grace which would grant final deliverance, which was now not only freedom from repeated cycles of lives, but also either an identification with the divine, or companionship with a god as a lover or eternal servant. Some Advaita philosophers postulated a single ultimate principle, whereas others argued for the existence of an ultimate cause of the universe, namely God. As it is to this day the worship of a multitude of gods was still widely practised.

Panini observed the need for a capacity for mutual connection between the meanings of words, and the Mimamsakas similarly developed a set of conditions for meaningful and correct sentences. They named the capacity for mutual connection between the meanings of words 'mutual expectancy'. For example , 'he rides an elephant' fulfils the condition of mutual syntactic expectancy, but a string of words such as 'elephant, house, riding' does not. But as per the this condition, the sentence 'he rides a house' is also a sentence. So another condition, 'semantic compatibility', was added. In a sentence like 'he rides a house', the semantic compatibility is absent. The Mimamsakas also necessitated that the condition of 'contiguity' be fulfilled: words must not be spoken at long intervals or be separated by other words. Another condition was 'the intention of the speaker', about which there were varying opinions. All chief branches of the Mimamsa school developed its own theory regarding the semantic relationship between words and sentences.

The adherents of Prabhakara believed that the meaning of a sentence arises directly from its collection of words. Conversely, words convey meaning only in the context of a sentence. Each word in a sentence conveys both its isolated meaning and the syntactic meaning. On the other hand, Kumarila Bhatta and his followers believed that the meaning of a sentence arises circuitously. Each word gives its individual meaning, and this uses up its significative power; hence the syntactic relation must be obtained by means of a secondary significative power. This view was also shared by the Advaita Vedantins, who, in order to be able to express truths about the Absolute, could not always use words with their primary meaning, but had instead to use the secondary meaning.

MORAL ISSUES

The two significant principles govern Indian moral philosophy: karma and dharma. The theory of karma was articulated early in Upanisadic times (which are usually placed from 700 BC onwards, but were possibly earlier). It concerns the causal relation between acts and their results, although neither was always understood in a uniform way. In general, the workings of karma were not interpreted as a fatalistic mechanism. With the exception of a few schools, most Indian thinkers came to conceive of karma in terms of a kind of naturalistic law of causation.

The best-known philosopher of the Upanishads, Yajñavalkya, was the first one to teach karma, which soon became discernible in almost all intellectual developments, as well as being a governing principle in everyday ethics. The precept of dharma is closely associated with karma. Dharma literally means 'to uphold what is correct', what we may call today 'morality'. The precise translation of the term depends on the context. For exampleFor example , we can understand dharma as 'justice' in cases where something that was illegally taken away is to be recovered. Thus, in the epic Mahabharata, it is justice for the Pandavas to regain their kingdom, which was illegally taken from them by their cousins, the Kauravas. There is also dharma as 'individual duty', as per the a person's social and economic status in society. This is in contrast with a certain extent with the Kantian idea of duty (responsibility for responsibility's sake). Then as a guide in moral and social issues there is general dharma which applies to society as a whole.

A significant idea in Hindu moral philosophy is that of the stages of life. It is depicted in the literature known as the Dharmauastras. This supports the determination of social station by birth, and dictates for each individual (at least, each male of the two highest classes, namely priests and royalty) the various stages to progress through in life. The prescribed chronological sequence is as follows: first, the socially responsible person should study and refrain from sexual relations; next, he should get married, bring up offspring and collect material possessions;

third, he should become a religious seeker, leaving behind the amenities of home, family and riches (although his wife may still supply some common comfort); ultimately, he should leave the company of his wife and roam alone as an ascetic until end. Two value systems, one socially engaged, the other with an ascetic tendency, seem to be combined here. Closely related are the four objectives of human life (purushartha): material wellbeing, pleasure and enjoyment, morality and social responsibility, and, the ultimate goal, liberation from repeated birth. Here, too, two value schemes are merged: the first three aims guide the socially engaged, whereas the last is the target of an individual in the end of life.

METAPHYSICS

Still Vedanta lives and is the most prestigious school of modern times, having great intellect and political figures among its adherents. 'Vedanta' describes several schools and legion of thinkers, and means 'the appendage to the Vedas', referring in this way to the body of texts known as the Upanishads. The Upanishads have been a source of encouragement and dogma since their beginnings around 700 BC. Embedded in them are ideas that came to dominate Indian thought, namely karma, rebirth, and liberation from the ever-revolving cycle of rebirth. The means of liberation is to know the identity of the ourself (atman) with a larger cosmic entity (Brahman). Individual thinkers each had several interpretation of these tenets, but all basically agreed on the means of liberation. Curiously, the development of Vedanta did not take place until more than a millennium after the earlier Upanishads. The most respected thinker of whom we know today was Sankara.

Like other Vedantins, Sankara built on an earlier custom. The work to which they all responded was Badarayana's Brahmasutra (or Vedantasutra) of around AD fifty. It stimulated A number of interpretive commentaries, which gave occasion for new schools to arise. The most prominent interpretation of the Brahmasutra is known as Advaita Vedanta. It focuses on Brahman, which is understood as identical with atman. Out of ignorance, the material world is superimposed on the ultimately empty Brahman; this superimposition is sometimes described as an illusory projection (maya). The first spectacular name in this custom is Gau apada, who taught Uankara's teacher.

Sankara was prolific in his philosophical output. He commented on all the major Upanishads and the Bhagavad Gita ([Upanishad, or Secret Teaching] Recited by the Lord Krishna), and a number of other works are ascribed to him. His Advaitism can be characterized as a strict nondualism: there is nothing other than Brahman, either real or unreal, and the goal is to know this through a trance-like experience which grants liberation from rebirth. Were it not for this experience of truth, which is the vision of identity between atman and Brahman, we would always superimpose this colourful world on transparent Brahman. This superimposition is an act of mistaking an unreal object for a real one, just as we superimpose silver on a piece of a glittering shell or a snake on a rope. If we could lift the superimposed object away from the real one, underneath we would find something altogether of varied form.

The significance of a personal God is diminished by this doctrine as it is austere. It failed to stimulate the imagination of A number of people, and with time there was a strong reaction to such an abstract portrayal of reality. The form of Vedanta that flourished subsequently tended to have a more theistic cast. The earliest work of theistic Vedanta was Bhaskara's interpretation of the Brahmasutra, whereby the individual self is both various and not various from God (Brahman). This doctrine was called 'the teaching of difference with no difference' (Bhedabhedavada). The Brahmasutra was often seen in the light of theology devoted to the god Vishnu.

The eleventh-century philosopher Ramanuja, commenting on the Brahmasutra in his Sribhasya, claims that everything is Brahman, yet acknowledges the reality of individual selves and the material world. This teaching is called 'qualified monism' (Viœicmadvaitavada) because Brahman is described as Knowledge and as being merciful, all-powerful and all-pervading. Everything that exists is contained in Brahman, understood as a personal God who should be approached with constant devotion. Other interpreters of the Brahmasutra postulated devotion to God; to a number of them, he was some form of Vishnu, which indicates that they too had a problem with absolute monism. Hence they introduced a modified monism: Nimbarka, for example , combined both dualism and nondualism.

The extreme position of disavowing monism was taken in the thirteenth century by Madhva (not to be confused with Madhava), who claimed that there is an absolute difference between Brahman and individual selves (Dvaitavada). Another extreme position was expressed by Vallabhacharya in his teaching of pure nondualism (Uudhadvaitavada). Still other thinkers with other interpretations, such as Chaitanya (1486–1534) of the Bengal Vaisnavism, did not leave a corpus of literature behind them.

With respect to epistemology and some ontological issues Sankhya and Vedanta are similar. Sankhya was an old dualistic school reaching back to the ontologies of Upanisadic times. It postulated an irreducible duality of consciousness and material stuff. Originally, the material stuff existed in an unvariousiated form, until it was disturbed by an intangible prodding of consciousness. Once disturbed, it produced twenty-three parts of the universe, with the human individual's parts in preponderance. Altogether, with consciousness and the unvariousiated material stuff, there are twenty-five things that exist. The goal of Sankhya was to experience the basic duality in a trance-like state, to discriminate between 'spirit' and 'matter'. Perhaps this dualism reflected vacillation between idealistic/metaphysical tendencies and naturalistic/materialistic tendencies.

Vaisheshika was another old school, which in some respects was close to Sankhya. Like Sankhya, it strove to list all the things that exist in reality, to name everything there is. Such a proto-scientific enumeration of categories marks the antiquity of these systems. The number of ontological categories as per the classical Vaisesika of Prauastapada is six. Other philosophers enumerated as A number of as ten, others only seven. Among these categories, such as substance, quality and activity, we find a category of relation, inherence. Inherence is a relation between things that do not exist in isolation. It holds between qualities and substances, and between particulars and universals; a quality inheres in its substratum, a substance, so that, with a red apple, the red colour is a quality of the substance apple. This red colour cannot exist on its own, but always has to inhere in something, whether an apple or a hibiscus flower.

The Vaisheshika are known as the Indian atomists. Motion inheres in the atoms, which, in their varying compositions as whole objects, are the substratum of motion. The Vaisheshika school is frequently lumped together with the Nyaya ('Logic') school. The fact for this might be that later Nyaya philosophers took it upon themselves to comment upon and revise the old atomistic school. The word nyaya is often used for a maxim or an instance in an argument, which is perhaps why it was adopted for the Logic school; earlier, however, it was used to refer to the system of Mimamsa.

The Nyaya school also had a list of basic categories. Their sixteen categories are quite obviously the parts of a rigorous argument: for example , instruments of knowledge, objects of knowledge, doubt, motive, instance, and so on. Thus the list consists of epistemological or proto-epistemological tools. The chief preoccupation among the Naiyayikas was to build proper arguments. They used a five-member syllogism based on the constant relation between logical fact and thing-to-be proved (sadhya). This relation came later to be known as concomitance or pervasion (vyapti).

The Naiyayikas also tried to safeguard against possible mishaps in argument by distinguishing three kinds of fallacy in facting. The early Mimamsakas were completely engaged in interpreting the scriptures, which conveyed injunctions for ritual actions such as sacrifices and ceremonies. These actions should be performed because the Vedas say so – the Vedas are authoritative. Other pursuits, such as acquiring knowledge of oneself or engaging in philosophical debates about God, serve no motive. Furthermore, any philosophical pursuit may give rise to doubts, and the doubts may extend to the authority of the Vedas. It was centuries before Mimamsa was freed from such dogmatism, by the philosophers Kumarila and Prabhakara (both seventh century).

REFERENCES

Aurobindo Ghose: *Speeches*, Calcutta, Arya Publishing House, 1948.

Aurobindo Ghose: *The Life Divine*, Calcutta, Arya Publishing House, 1947.

E. J. Thompson and A. Marshman Spencer: *Bengali Religious Lyrics*, Calcutta, Association Press, 1923.

Gandhi: *An Autobiography*, Mahadev Desai, Ahmedabad, Navajivan, 1927.

H. Jacobs: *Western Psychotherapy and Hindu-Sadhana*, London, G. Allen & Unwin, 1961.

Melville T. Kennedy: *The Chaitanya Movement*, Calcutta, Association Press, 1925.

R. Tagore: *One Hundred Poems of Kabir*, Madras, G. A. Natesan.

Raja Rammohun Roy: *The English Works of Raja Rammohun Roy*, Allahabad, The Panini Office, 1906.

Ramakrishna: *The Gospel of Ramakrishna,* New York, The Vedanta Society, 1907.

Ramanama: *The Infallible Remedy*, Karachi, 1947.

Sarvapalli Radhakrishnan: *An Idealist View of Life*, London, George Allen & Unwin, 1929.

4

Concept of God

As per the Hinduism God is not just as the Supreme All powerful One but also a personal God Whom the individual can worship out of love and not out of fear. Devotion or bhakti as often referred to is a very key concept in Hinduism, even for the philosophically inclined ones. While the shashtras describe the Glory of God, one finds abundance of sources that praise the God in love. For Hindus God, as is, is beyond any attributes of form or shapes, i.e., God does not have any specific form or name. In this state God is referred to as nirguna Brahman (attribute less god). However God takes forms as perceived by humans and this perceived form is called saguna brahman (god with good attributes). These forms could range from calm to fierce to yogic.

Each form has its significance. For example when one is depressed and sees the form of God Strong and Powerful, the seeker feels the moral boost that God would definitely be the support for the right thing. Similarly when in an auspicious ceremony would like the God to be the calm provider of boons. In a spiritually elevated state, the choice would be the yogic form of God. The forms provide a basis for the Hindu worshipper to easily pursue the otherwise incomprehensible Supreme. So Hinduism supports both form as well as formless worship of the God. It is ultimately the same God whether one worships in saguna or nirguna way.

DEFINING GOD

To the Hindu philosophy the concept of a divine god is not fundamental. What is the meaning of this word God? Customally God is regarded as a being or an entity. Since Hinduism is not an organized religion, not one founded by a code book, we can only go by what are the customal practices and beliefs of the people. These beliefs of the common

Hindu present a picture of a god not very various from the gods of other religions. But if we go by the fundamental philosophical treatises, the Vedas, the chief Upanishads and Bhagavad Gita, then a very distinct picture comes out.

The Riga-Veda is full of panegyric hymns venerating the numerous deities for their superhuman powers. Some scholars call it the prevalent polytheism. In realnone of these characters were in the category of a god. They were historical figures, like warlords who fought for the Aryans, and divine attributes got associated with them in time and legend. They lacked the status of absolute divinity. None of them was a supremo. The sages of the Vedic age also came up with the concept of Brahma, a concept that should not be confused with god.

However, since Brahma does not decide how the individual should act? Does anyone control? Or are we all absolutely free? Is all this uncontrolled and chaotic? We can not psychologically accept that it is all chaotic and haphazard. Scientifically also we do find some order in the scheme of things, some principles making things act in the way they do. Existences are not free to do anything they want. Krishna tells Arjuna that his resolve not to fight in the battle is vain and an offshoot of his ego. He tells Arjuna, 'You think you are going to take decisions. But no. Your own nature will compel you to fight.' Elsewhere also, Krishna says that even the sinner is a victim of his own nature; he is not a sinner in the real sense, as he is not the doer. Man is thus bound by his own nature in the context of his actions, but there is no extra-terrestrial control over him. This does put serious limitations on the individual's freedom but that is also true. It however relieves the individual from the dictates of stranger divine hand.

An abstract metaphysical force prevailing everywhere, in each entity, which causes the constituent factors to act in the way they do and hence is the cause of all actions is the Nature. It is not that nature is something outside the material entity. Rather nature is an innate and inseparable part of the material entity. It is that abstract factor which makes the material factor be or act whatever it is or does. And since it is an abstract quantity it can neither be fully understood nor completely controlled. Nature controls everything, but it is a sort of non-predetermined control. What will be the outcome of the action is nowhere predetermined because all action that is taking place is a continuous process of interplay of the nature of various existences in an extremely dynamic and fluid situation. The process can be predicted to some an extent by empirical methods and by logic (the laws of science) but not always and not to the absolute exactness, both because of the sheer complexity of the total interaction and due to the unknown factors of nature.

One of the factors of action is Providence, and this factor is unknown. No one can know this. It is mysterious like the uncertainty principle. We can understand a phenomenon on the basis of its principles but only to the extent of its singularity. There comes a point when the principle ceases to be applicable. That is its singularity stage. It is because of the principle itself is based on the phenomenon. Providence is not the divine but simply the unknown, the mysterious, the incalculable.

Hence, we do not find the concept of a divine god either logical, or empirically sustainable, nor supported by ancient Indian philosophy. That is why we hold that the Hindu philosophy was based on scientific perceptions, on rational and logical thought and there was no room in it for supernatural and divine concept of god. They believed in the concept of Brahma as the underlying universal cause of all existences. But the sages also realised that it was hard for the common man to understand and accept such concept which is abstract in nature. At the same time it was necessary not to break the simple belief in the divine of those people who were not capable of understanding a complex concept of Brahma. And so in the third chapter Krishna advises that the knowledgeable person should not confuse the simple minded one by his knowledge. Let the common man carry on with his simple faiths, or he will feel totally lost.

The man's answer to the mysteries of the existence was the concept of God. It was a reassurance in a system which was full of unknown, and full of inevitability of death. Belief in divinity satisfied a very basic need of human curiosity and bewilderment and of course, of fear. We must remember that the process of human survival was a very ruthless one. There was no democracy, no human rights and no concept of social justice to save the unfit. God was a part of man's quest for survival. Indeed god was the most sublime creation of the collective human mind. Indeed god was the most sublime creation of the collective human mind. The concept of god as a superior being capable of doing a rescue act was indeed a fascinating idea.

DIMENSIONS OF GOD

Generally Hinduism is associated with a multiplicity of Gods, and does not advocate the worship of one particular deity. The gods and goddesses of Hinduism amount to thousands or even millions, all representing the A number of aspects of only one supreme Absolute called "Brahman". Therefore, to believe that the multiplicity of deities in Hinduism makes it polytheistic is erroneous. The Rig Veda says: "Ekam sath, Vipraah bahudhaa vadanti" (The Truth is one). However, to equate "Brahman" with "God" is imprecise. It is neither the "old man in the sky" concept, nor the idea of something capable of being vengeful or fearful. The doctrine of Spiritual Competence (Adhikaara) and that of the Chosen Deity (Ishta Devata) in Hinduism recommend that the spiritual practices prescribed to a person should correspond to his or her spiritual competence and that a person should have the freedom to choose (or invent) a form of Brahman that satisfies his spiritual cravings and to make it the object of his belief and prayer.

Hence, Hindus have a number of gods and goddesses. Deities are represented by a complexity of images and idols symbolizing divine powers. A number of these idols are housed within ornate temples of unparalleled beauty and grandeur. Hindus also worship spirits, trees, animals and even planets. The most fundamental of Hindu deities, is the Trinity of Brahma, Vishnu and Shiva - creator, preserver and destroyer respectively. Other popular deities comprise Ganesha, Krishna, Hanuman and a number of Goddesses.

Theology

The ideas of God and the gods are expressed in a number of forms, including allusions and riddles in the Vedas, complex devotional poetry, simple chants, and elaborate theological arguments. When Yajnavalkya said there was one god, he identified him as Brahman, which is not a personal name like Vishnu or Shiva. Other passages in the Upanishads identify Brahman with the universe, and with the self (atman) hidden in each person's heart. What Brahman means is the central question of the custom of theology known as Vedanta (literally the 'end of the Veda' - that is, its ultimate motive), whose key text is the Vedanta-sutra. The Vedanta-sutra is so brief that it makes little sense without a commentary, and various commentators find very various meanings in it. The objective of Vedanta, as of all Hindu systems, is to show the way to salvation.

The most powerful commentator was Shankara, from Kerala in the far south-west, around the seventh century. Using the contrast between the one and the a number of which is found in the Upanishads, Shankara built a radical theology in which all multiplicity and individuality belong to the world of impermanence, and the true nature of Brahman is inexpressible. His theology is called Advaita (non-dualist) Vedanta, because it insists that Brahman is 'one only without a second' (Chandogya Upanishad 6.2.1). Shankara insists that salvation cannot be achieved by anything we do, which would only mean more karma, but only by knowledge.

He sees a fundamental opposition between knowledge and action; the highest knowledge is knowledge of Brahman, which is identical with the self. Ramanuja, a Tamil Brahmin of the eleventh century, provided Vaishnava bhakti with a closely argued theology, a form of Vedanta which replaces Shankara's idea of an inexpressible ultimate with loving descriptions of the god Vishnu. Ramanuja holds that God, the world and our own selves are one, but only in the sense in which one's self and one's body are one: neither can exist without the other. True knowledge involves the acknowledgment that we, like everything in the world, are part of God's body, and hence has no other motive than to serve him. Ramanuja's Vedanta is called Vishishtadvaita, 'non-dualism with differentiations', because it discerns eternal distinctions between God, the world and our selves. Other schools of Vedanta followed, supporting particular Vaishnava or Shaiva sects. The school developed by Bengali Vaishnavism, and propagated by ISKCON, argues that the relationship between God, the world and ourselves is beyond the reach of thought. But the influence of these Vedanta theologies is mainly confined to their own sects and regions, while Advaita is known throughout the region concerned.

The views of true Hinduism of Radhakrishnan suited the Westward-looking elite of mid-twentieth-century India, with their secularist politics. Today, it is harder to overlook those Hindus for whom images and sacred places are essential. Customal practices are promoted by militant Hinduism, and are facilitated and transformed by technology. Temples display neon signs, mantras are recited on audiotape, and videos take the place of oral storytelling at women's fasts. The power of modern communications was demonstrated in 1995, when images of Ganesha and other deities were widely reported to have consumed offerings of milk. The news spread immediately, and the miracle was replicated in temples more or less all over the world.

Migration in its entirety has affected the sacred geography of Hinduism in two ways. It has elaborated the catchment areas of customal holy places, so that people come from all over the world to Varanasi, for example , to bathe or to immerse the ashes of their dead. But Hindus have also founded holy places in the countries where they have settled. Besides temples, whose location normally depends on the property market and the planning system, there are private houses and public places where miracles have occurred or which holy people have visited. Just as rivers in South Asia are identified with the Ganges, rivers elsewhere can be regarded holy so that the ashes of the dead can be placed in them. And in this way Hinduism and its culture is surviving no matter where it is flourishing.

DEITIES

In contrast with the popular belief in the West, Hindu deities are not "individual gods", indicating a polytheistic faith. They are, rather, various representations of particular aspects of the one god, the source, known as Brahman. The "human" or physical representation of Brahman's aspects or attributes in the form of deities is a vehicle for the devotee to focus his or her attention, devotion or meditation on that particular aspect or attribute in a form more easily visualized and held in the mind.

A number of deities of Hinduism, which may be seen as reflecting various aspects of Brahman, are represented by images. Use is made of such features as posture, dress, multiple arms and symbolic objects to represent each deity. It should be noted, however, that there may be a range of various ways of representing a particular deity, particularly when the deity is seen to represent several various qualities. In some cases, symbols are used to show that a deity belongs to a particular 'family', e.g. there is a range of deities associated with Vishnu. In addition some symbols belong to the common heritage of Hinduism or more specifically of India.

The images found in temples will tend to be much more majestic than those found in Hindu homes. Images may be made from metal, stone, wood or plastic. The image only becomes a "murti", an embodiment of Brahman, through a special act of consecration when it is installed in the temple or home. It then becomes a focal point for worship. Some images are consecrated on a 'permanent' basis and will continue to be used on the temple or home shrine unless they become damaged. Broken or damaged images are discarded as they no longer fulfil their need of representing the deity. Sometimes an image will only be consecrated for a specific period of time, e.g. a festival, after which it will be destroyed, perhaps as part of the resolving ritual of the festival.

In Hindu mythology each deity is associated with a 'vehicle', a bird or animal on which it travels. The vehicles are used in Indian religious art to reflect and at times to extend the powers or qualities of the deity with which it is associated. These are often better expressed by an animal than by a human being. The vehicle also represents the close relationship between all living things. There is a range of views within Hinduism about images of the deities. Most accept that within the context of worship they mediate the presence of Brahman/the particular deity and help the worshipper to visualize the deity. To those outsiders who find it hard to empathize with the brightly colored plastic images which feature in a number of Hindu homes, some Hindu writers point to the very 'concrete' mental images of God held by a number of devotees in other customs, e.g. God as 'an old man in the sky'. Perhaps the very fact that there are a number of images makes the point that each can tell only a very small part of the complete story.

Seemingly, Hinduism seem s to have a vast pantheon of Hindu Gods and Goddesses. However, in fact, at the heart of this religion, is simply the Hindu Trinity that comprises Lord Brahma, Lord Vishnu, and Lord Shiva . These are the three aspects of the Supreme Being (Brahman). Respectively they represent creation, preservation and destruction for the process of recreation.

Lord Brahma, the Creator

As per the Hindu mythology it is said that Lord Brahma grew in a lotus out of the navel of Vishnu. In order to create the world, he made a goddess out of himself. This was Saraswati, the Goddess of Knowledge. Brahma has four heads, from which, it is believed, the four Vedas sprung. His children are Daksi, Dharma, Kama, Anger, Greed, Delusion (Maya), Lust, Joy, Death, Bharata and Angaja. Goddess Saraswati, the consort of Brahma, is the Goddess of Knowledge, music and the creative arts. She is dressed in white and holds a mala and a palm-leaf scroll (symbol of knowledge). She plays veena while riding on a swan or peacock.

Lord Vishnu, the Preserver

Among the Hindu gods and goddesses, Lord Vishnu embodies goodness and mercy. He is represented seated on the serpent Shesha. Vishnu never sleeps and is the Hindu deity of Shanti, peace. He has four weapons or attributes: the conch, disc, club and lotus. In the cosmos, good and evil forces are balanced. When this balance is disrupted, Vishnu takes a human form to set it right. There are nine avatars or incarnations of Vishnu. These are Matsya (fish), Kurma (turtle), Varaha (boar), Narasingha (lion), Vamana (dwarf), Parasurama, Ram, Krishna, Buddha. Kalki is the future incarnation which is to come at the end of Kaliyuga (present age).

Goddess Lakshmi is the associate of Vishnu. When the gods were exiled, Lakshmi took refuge in the ocean of milk. She was reborn when the ocean was churned. As soon as she seem ed, the gods fell in love with her. Shiva, claimed her, but her hand was given to Vishnu. Of the Hindu gods and goddesses, Lakshmi is the Goddess of light, beauty, good fortune and wealth. Lakshmi was reborn as Vishnu's consort in every incarnation of his, as Sita, Radha and Rukmini.

Ten Reincarnations of Vishnu: Among all the avataras of the most famous are Rama, whose life is depicted in the Ramayana, and Krishna, whose life is depicted in the Mahabharata and the Srimad Bhagavatam. The Bhagavad Gita, which comprises the spiritual teachings of Krishna, is one of the most widely-read scriptures in Hinduism.

1. Matsya, the fish, came out in the Satya Yuga. Represents beginning of life.
2. Kurma, the tortoise, came out in the Satya Yuga. Represents a human embryo just growing tiny legs, with a huge belly.
3. Varaha, the boar, came out in the Satya Yuga. Represents a human embryo which is almost ready. Its features are visible.
4. Narasimha, the Man-Lion, came out in the Satya Yuga. Represents a newborn baby, hairy and cranky, bawling and full of blood.
5. Vamana, the Dwarf, came out in the Treta Yuga. Represents a young child.
6. Parashurama, Rama with the axe, came out in the Treta Yuga. Represents both an angry young man and a grumpy old man simultaneously.
7. Rama, Sri Ramachandra, the prince and king of Ayodhya, came out in the Treta Yuga. Represents a married man with children in a very ideological society
8. Krishna came out in the Dwapara Yuga. Represents a person in more practical society, where there is one good or bad. Good or bad depends on society you live in.
9. Gautama Buddha is regarded an avatar that returned pure dharma to the world.
10. Kalki (Eternity), who is believed to come out at the end of Kali Yuga, the time period in which we presently exist, which will end soon.

Lord Shiva, the Destroyer

One of the principal deities of Hinduism is Shiva. Within Shaivism he is viewed as the Supreme deity, whereas in other branches of Hinduism such as the Smarta custom he is worshipped as one of the six expressions of the Divine. Followers of Hinduism who focus their worship upon Shiva are called Shaivites or Shaivas (Sanskrit Saiva). His role as the primary deity of Shaivism is reflected in his epithets Mahadeva (great god), Maheshvara (great lord) and Parameshvara (Supreme Lord). Shaivism, along with Vaisnava customs that focus on Vishnu, and Sakta customs that focus on the goddess (Devi) are three of the most influential denominations in Hinduism. Shiva is one of the six primary forms of the Divine in Smartism, a denomination of Hinduism that puts particular emphasis on six deities, the other five being Vishnu, Shakti, Ganesha, Kartikeya and Surya. Another way of thinking about the divinities in Hinduism identifies Brahma, Vishnu, and Shiva as each representing one of the three primary aspects of the divine in Hinduism, known conjointly as the Trimurti. In the Trimurti system, Brahma is the creator, Vishnu is the maintainer or preserver, and Shiva is the destroyer or transformer.

Shiva is commonly worshipped as the Shiva linga. In images, he is mostly represented as immersed in deep meditation or dancing the Tandava upon the demon of ignorance in his expression of Nataraja, the lord of the dance.

Goddesses in Hinduism

The Supreme Being comprises both masculine and feminine traits as per the Hindu religion. The female part is as significant as the male part. One has to consider the feminine aspect of the divine, in order to know the ultimate truth. It is believed that all goddesses of the Hindu pantheon are special forms of the divine mother- Shakti. To recognize the feminine aspect, it is necessary to restore wholeness, completeness and universality. There are a number of goddesses and local deities in the Hindu mythology. Here we will discuss some of the popular Hindu goddesses also called "devi".

Durga: The Goddess Durga represents the power of the Supreme Being that preserves moral order and righteousness in the creation. The Sanskrit word Durga means a fort or a place that is protected and thus hard to reach. Durga, also called Divine Mother, protects mankind from evil and misery by destroying evil forces such as selfishness, jealousy, prejudice, hatred, anger, and ego. The worship of Goddess Durga is very popular among Hindus. She is also called by A number of other names, such as Parvati, Ambika, and Kali In the form of Parvati, She is known as the divine spouse of Lord Shiva and is the mother of her two sons, Ganesha and Kartikeya, and daughter Jyoti. In India there are a number of temples dedicated to Durga's worship.

Durga is described as a warrior aspect of Devi Parvati with 10 arms that rides a lion or a tiger, carries weapons and assumes mudras, or symbolic hand gestures. This form of the Goddess is the embodiment of feminine and creative energy (Shakti). Each god also gave her their own most powerful weapons, Rudra's trident, Vishnu's discus, Indra's thunderbolt, Brahma's kamandal, Kuber's gada, etc.

Kali: Kali, also known as Kalika, is a Hindu goddess related with death and destruction. Despite her negative connotations, she is not in realthe goddess of death, but rather of Time and Change. Although sometimes presented as black and violent, her earliest incarnation as a figure of annihilation still has some influence. Kali is represented as the consort of god Shiva, on whose body she is often seen standing. Kali is pictured mostly in two forms: the popular four-armed form and the ten-armed Mahakali form. In both of her forms, she is described as being black in color but is most often showed as blue in popular Indian art. Her eyes are described as red with intoxication and in absolute rage, her hair is shown dishevelled, small fangs sometimes protrude out of her mouth and her tongue is lolling. She is often shown naked or just wearing a skirt made of human arms and a garland of human heads.

Saraswati: In Hindu mythology Sarasvati is the Hindu goddess of knowledge, music and the creative arts. The Sanskrit word sara means "essence" and swa means "self." Thus Saraswati means "the essence of the self." Saraswati is represented in Hindu mythology as the divine consort of Lord Brahma, the Creator of the universe. Since knowledge is necessary for creation, Saraswati symbolizes the creative power of Brahma. Students, teachers, scholars, and scientists worship Goddess Saraswati as she is regarded as the goddess of knowledge and education.

The Goddess Saraswati is often portrayed as a beautiful, white-skinned woman dressed in pure white often seated on a white Nelumbo nucifera lotus (although her actual vahana is believed to be a swan), which symbolizes that she is founded in the experience of the Absolute Truth. She is in general shown to have four arms, which represent the four aspects of human personality in learning: mind, intellect, alertness, and ego. Alternatively, these four arms also represent the 4 vedas, the primary sacred books for Hindus. The vedas, in turn, make up the 3 forms of literature:

Poetry — the Rigveda comprises hymns, representing poetry

Prose — Yajurveda comprises prose

Music — Samaveda represents music.

The four hands also depict this thusly — prose is represented by the book in one hand, poetry by the garland of crystal, music by the veena. The pot of sacred water represents purity in all of these three, or their power to purify the thought of Human being.

Lakshmi: In Hindu mythology Lakshmi is regarded as the Goddess of wealth and prosperity, both material and spiritual. The word ''Lakshmi'' is derived from the Sanskrit word Laksme, meaning "goal." Lakshmi, therefore, represents the goal of life, which includes worldly as well as spiritual prosperity. In Hindu mythology, Goddess Lakshmi, also called Shri, is the divine spouse of Lord Vishnu and provides Him with wealth for the maintenance and preservation of the creation. She is the consort of Vishnu and married Rama (in her incarnation as Sita) and Krishna (as Rukmini and Radha).

In Her images and pictures, Lakshmi is portrayed in a female form with four arms and four hands. She wears red clothes with a golden lining and is standing on a lotus. She has golden coins and lotuses in her hands. Two elephants (some pictures show four) are demonstrated next to the Goddess.

Parvati: Sometimes Parvati, spelled Parvathi or Parvathy, is a Hindu goddess and nominally the second consort of Shiva, the Hindu god of destruction and rejuvenation. She is the Kali in her unmarried state, who is known by the names of Maya, Sati and so on. She is described as beautiful and magnificent in her disposition.

Parvati when showed alongside Shiva comes along with two arms, but when alone, she is shown having four arms, and astride a tiger or lion. Sometimes, Parvati is regarded as the supreme Divine Mother and all other goddesses are referred to as her incarnations or expressions.

Parvati symbolises a number of noble virtues esteemed by Hindu custom. Just as Shiva is at once the presiding deity of destruction and regeneration, the couple jointly symbolise at once both the power of renunciation and asceticism and the blessings of marital felicity.

The Vedic Gods

Hinduism as the religion of the Hindus is one of the oldest religions in the world. It began prior to the emergence of the first known civilizations in the Orient and probably before the first scripts, which seem ed around 3000 BC. in Egypt and in Mesopotamia. The Aryans came in India and destroyed the cities of Harappa and Mohenjodaro. After setting on the plains they gradually spread out and pushed the original inhabitants to further south. However, they allowed them to venerate their own Gods and rituals.

As per the scholars the ancient Indian society honoured first the sun and the moon the latter often being regarded as a feminine deity who was both the companion of the sun and the Great Mother of life and the universe. This very ancient cult of a feminine deity had its origin in Indus valley civilization, which was stamped out by the Aryans who turned to patriarchal worship more suited to their aggressive and wild nature. However slow evolution towards Hinduism and intermarriage the Aryans return to ancient rituals and cult of the mother goddess. This was accompanied by worship of Shiva-the phallic God who was represented by 8 million yonis. There were no less than 3000 Gods venerated in Vedic times. The principal divinity was Indra - the God of War and Thunder whose power was capable of destroying the wall of cities of burning them down in order to conquer and pillage them. He was the King of Gods.

Brahma was the creator or protector who was also given the name of Narayana Prajapati or Pursha. He was the father of all creatures. Agni was the God of fire. He was the guardian of the world and giver of eternal life. Surya the Sun God was also deeply venerated. The other secondary Gods were Arjuna or the God of the dawn and the charioteer of the sun. He was the son of Vinata and the wise Kasyapa. The Kubera was the God of wealth. Vayu or the God of wind. Wind is the friend of fire—perfumed and caressing, it wonders around the abode of the gods, stimulating the senses. It is the messenger of the gods, the breath of the world, and the bringer of life to all beings of the earth.

PHILOSOPHY OF GOD

As per the Hinduism, God is like yarn, which, when woven into cloth, creates the Maya that is the universe. It is analogous to the idea that Energy becomes the fabric of Matter. The energy does not disappear, nor does it really change form, but it is there the whole time. There are two characteristics of God: 1) Purusha, which is man and the drama of the world, or the cloth. It consists of the soul (Jiva) plus inert matter (Jada). It is what is seen, the Maya, the female aspect called Shakti. 2)

Prakriti, the invisible, or the yarn. It is the unmanifest nature of God. It is the Seer, the male aspect called Siva.

Conjugation of these two characteristics, the union of the male and female aspects, Siva Sakhti, union of Prakrithi and Purusha creates the movable and immovable world. It is also called the Jiva-Brahma union, mukthi, or moksha. Hindu literature expounds the philosophy that all is really One (Adhvaitha) through its symbolic mythological epics, the Mahabharatha (the great battle epic, which includes the Bhagavad Gita), the Ramayana (story of Rama, an incarnation of Vishnu), and the Bhagavatham (story of Krishna, a later incarnation of Vishnu).

As per the great Hindu epic Mahabharata, the thousand Kauravas are the evil qualities (which exist in great numbers); the Pandavas are the five good qualities of Sathya (truth), Dharma (duty), Santhi (peace), Prema (love), and Ahimsa (detachment). The dispute is for kingship of the heart. Dritarashtra is Ajnani, the unwise personality, while Pandu is Sujnani, the wise. The millions of soldiers and charioteers represent the innumerable feelings, thoughts and impressions of the mind and body. The regiments are the ten Indriyas, the chariots, the five senses. Lord Krishna is the witness, the Atma, Sarathi (Charioteer) of the Chariot of the Jiva (Soul). The capital city Hastinapura is Asthinapura, or City of Bones, which is the Body itself, with its nine gates. Both the Kauravas and Pandavas grew up and played together in the capital, watched and opposed each other, resulting in war. They warred until Krishna, as the Atma (all pervasive Soul) discloses how to overcome so that only good remains, teaching us that one must investigate one's own soul to reach well.

MESSENGERS OF GOD

God is Omnipotent, Omniscient, and Omnipresent as per the Hinduism. God can do anything. God is all-powerful and can do anything. There are a number of instances in Hindu mythology when God has broken his own rules and defied his laws. In Mahabharata the saving of Draupadi is one such instance. God knows everything about this world. For him there is no mystery. He knows the past births of everything and knows about what that animal or person will do in this life and the coming lives. There is nothing left unidentified to God because he creates the world himself. God is present everywhere at the same time. As per the Hinduism God creates the whole cosmos/world in himself and there is nothing that is present without him. God is present in everything at all the times.

Similarly, as a single force in space can be mathematically conceived as having various spatial components, the Supreme Being or God, the personal form of the Ultimate Reality, is conceived by Hindus as having various aspects. A Hindu deity (god or goddess; note small g) represents a particular aspect of the Supreme Being. For example , Saraswati represents the learning and knowledge aspect of the Supreme Being. Thus, if a Hindu wants to pray for acquiring knowledge and understanding, he prays to Saraswati. Just as sunlight cannot have a distinguish and independent existence from the sun itself, a Hindu deity does not have a separate and independent existence from the Supreme Being. Thus, Hindu worship of deities is monotheistic polytheism and not simple polytheism.

The Hindu people declare that there is only one Supreme Being and He is the God of all religions. There is no "other God." Hindus view cosmic activity of the Supreme Being as comprised of three tasks: creation, preservation, and dissolution and recreation. Hindus associate these three cosmic tasks with the three deities, Brahma, Vishnu and Shiva. Lord Brahma brings forth the creation and represents the creative principle of the Supreme Being. Lord Vishnu maintains the universe and makes up the eternal principle of preservation. Lord Shiva represents the principle of dissolution and recreation. These three deities together form the Hindu Trinity.

One must clearly understand that Brahma, Vishnu and Shiva are not three independent deities. They represent the same power (the Supreme Being), but in three various aspects.

Just as a man may be called a doctor, father or husband based upon the tasks he performs, the Supreme Being is called Brahma, Vishnu or Shiva when conceived as performing the three various cosmic tasks of creation, preservation, and dissolution/recreation. Hindu religion is often labelled as a religion of 330 million gods. This misunderstanding arises when people fail to grasp the symbolism of the Hindu pantheon. As per the Hindu scriptures, living beings are not apart from God, since He lives in each and every one of them in the form of atman. Thus each living being is a unique expression of God. In ancient times it was believed that there were 330 million living beings. This gave rise to the idea of 330 million deities or gods. Actually, this vast number of gods could not have been possibly worshipped, since 330 million names could not have been designed for them. The number 330 million was simply used to give a symbolic expression to the fundamental Hindu doctrine that God lives in the hearts of all the creatures.

NIRVANA

In Hinduism, Nirvana is the Union with the Supreme Brahman (God) through moksha, the release from the cycle of birth and death as well as pain, sorrow, and suffering within the human condition of life. Nirvana is the immediate experience of ego-less with the blissful Brahman. The Bhagavad-Gita has one of the clearest expositions of nirvana, calling it Brahma-nirvana, that is, union with Brahman, or extinction (of the ego) in Him. The obtaining of the Gita's is by the practice of yoga (joy, peace, vision all turning inward), through which one can "come to Brahman and know nirvana."

However, it is hard to assign a dogmatic orthodoxy to Hinduism. A number of variations have developed from Hinduism over the years, and a number of non-Hindu cults and religious movements gained their inspiration from Hinduism. Even in India today, the most orthodox divisions of Hinduism have changed significantly over the last three thousand years to a greater extent.

Other way of salvation is the way of knowledge, or jnana yoga. The basic premise of the way of knowledge is that the cause of our bondage to the cycle of rebirths in this world is ignorance. As per the prevalent view among those committed to this way, our ignorance consists of the mistaken belief that we are individual selves, and not one with the ultimate divine reality – Brahman. It is this same ignorance that gives rise to our bad actions, which result in bad karma. Salvation is achieved through attaining a state of consciousness in which we realize our identity with Brahman. This is achieved through deep meditation, often as a part of the discipline of yoga.

And another significant way of salvation is the way of devotion, or bhakti yoga. This is the way most favoured by the common people of India. It satisfies the longing for a more emotional and personal approach to religion. It involves the self-surrender to one of the a number of personal gods and goddesses of Hinduism. Such devotion is expressed through acts of worship, temple rituals, and pilgrimages. Some Hindus conceive of ultimate salvation as absorption into the one divine reality, with all loss of individual existence. Others conceive of it as heavenly existence in adoration of the personal God. In Hindu custom, nirvana (more commonly called moksha) is the reuniting with Brahman, the universal God or universal soul. In customal Hinduism, a soul reaches this state after living a number of lives in which it climbs up through the caste system or varna.

Human being accumulate good karma by performing the duties of the caste they were born in. If a person is born in a lower caste, his only hope is to behave properly in that caste so he will move up to a higher caste in the next life. When a soul has reached the upper castes, it may escape the cycle of reincarnation by eliminating bad karma. This includes setting the scales right through good deeds (possibly over several lifetimes) and also removing oneself from all earthly distractions. When a soul finally escapes the karmic cycle, it becomes one with Brahman when the last bodily incarnation dies. This is a higher plane of existence that transcends the suffering of earthly life. Basically, the soul rejoins the intangible energy that created the universe. This is the way and teachings of Hinduism in which it is quite distinct and true rather than any other religion.

REFERENCES

A. Embree: *The Hindu Tradition and, with S. Hay*, Sources of Indian Tradition, 1988.

Allchin F. R.: *Neolithic Cattle-Keepers of South India*: A study of the Deccan ashmounds, Cambridge, 1963.

Basham A. L.: *A Cultural History of India*, Oxford, 1975.

Bowes Pratima: *The Hindu Religious Tradition*, A philosophical approach, London, 1978.

Brown W. N.: *Man in the Universe*, Some continuities in Indian thought, Berkeley, 1966.

Daniélou Alain: *Hindu Polytheism*, London, 1964.

Fairservis W. A.: *The Roots of Ancient India*: The archaeology of early Indian civilization, London, 1975.

Gonda Jan: *Vedic Literature,* Wiesbaden, 1975.

Hauer J. W.: *Der Vratya*; Untersuchungen uber die nichtbrahmanische Religion altindiens, Stuttgart, 1927.

K. H. Potter: *Presuppositions of India's Philosophies* (1963) and Guide to Indian Philosophy, 1988.

Macdonell A. A.: *Vedic Mythology*, Strassburg, 1897.

Rodhe Sten: *Deliver us from Evil: studies on the Vedic ideas of salvation*, Lund, 1946.

5

Main Figures

Hinduism poses a particular challenge for several facts when exploring chief figures. Firstly, it is impossible to trace the exact beginning. It has no single founder, but comprises a number of leaders who reformed and revived existing customs, either breaking them into innumerable sub-groups or consolidating them. The rather vague boundary between man and the immortal makes the subject even more complex. Almost universally, God is regarded the ultimate Father of religion, and a number of the sampradayas consider their founder an avatar. Custom holds that in ancient times there were seven great rishis (poet-sages) born from the mind of Brahma. They are often associated with the seven stars of the Big Dipper constellation. Hindu families claim to trace their dynasty (gotra) to one of them. They are Bhrigu, Gautama, Bharadvaja, Vishvamitra, Vashishta, Atri, and Angira. Though lists given by various sources vary, the names of these and other rishis seem repeatedly in the stories of the Puranas, Epics, and other texts. Despite their inconceivable age, living from the time of creation, some are still believed to be alive and continuously looking after their devotees.

MAIN FIGURES IN EARLY PERIOD

A number of Munis (Sages) and Rishis (Seers) of ancient India have, through the ages, compiled the scriptures that are today the binding force within Hinduism. Unfortunately, most of the lives of these great men are clouded by the mists of time and very little is known of them and their times. There are a few legends and myths that are based on the lives of a few of these great men but I have chosen not to include them here. Instead, I have only included the lives of those great religious figures that have definite historical records. In this section on Sages we have only included the name of one sage - Ved Vyasa who , though legendary, must be mentioned because of his paramount significance in the Hindu mythology and the ancient stories.

Ved Vyasa

The Great sage Ved Vyasa is a legendary figure in Hinduism. He is the great sage who has written down the Vedas as they were revealed to him by the Gods. Thus, he is the initiator of the sruti literature on which all of Hinduism is based. In fact, Hindu scholars hold, that which is derived from the Vedas - The Vaidika - is what constitutes True Hinduism. Whatever else that has some other source is Avaidika and not Hinduism. Vyasa is popularly known as Ved Vyasa as he has written down the Vedas. He is also credited with composition of the Mahabharata. Some scholars even go to the length of asserting that it is he who has written down the Puranas and a number of other ancient texts. The chief legend says that Vyasa Dev is born at the beginning of every Yuga to write down what is revealed by the Gods for the religion of the people of that Yuga.

Maharshi Aitreya Mahidasa

Hindus believe that his mother was a maid named Itara. This Rishi is credited with the compilation of the Aitreya Brahmana and sections 1-3 of the Aitreya Aranyaka (the latter comprises the Aitreya Upanishad- one of the 10 canonical Upanishads for Hindus) belonging to the Rigveda.

Rishika Lopamudra

As per the Hindu mythology Rishika Lopamudra was a Kshatriya princess from Vidarbha, who married Maharshi Agastya. She is the Seer of some verses of the Rigveda. Various edifying duologues between her and Sage Agastya are recorded in the Puranas.

Maharshi Vishwamitra

As per the hindu mythology he was originally a Kshatriya named Vishwaratha. He is credited with revealing the Gayatri Mantra, the Hindu prayer par-excellence. He was brought up to Brahminhood because of his spiritual luster.

Maharshi Valmiki

As per the Hindu Mythology he basically was descendant from Sages but had become a chandaala (an outcaste) named Ratnakara, because he took to murder and highway robbery. He was reformed by Prajapati Brahma and was inspired by the divine Sage Narada to compose the Hindu epic par excellence- the Ramayana.

MAIN FIGURES IN MEDIEVAL PERIOD

In the medieval period of Hinduism Shankaracharya is the first of the five great acharyas who reformed Hinduism by delivering the essence of the sacred texts to the common people. It should be noted that "Acharya" means "Great Teacher". Before Shankaracharya the Vedic texts, the srutis, were orally studied and transmitted by and within a particular class of people, especially the Brahmins. They were written in a very esoteric language which was quite beyond the scope of the common people. The true catholicity of Hinduism was interpreted and revealed by Shankaracharya (788-820 A.D.), Ramanujacharya (11th century A.D.), Nimbarkacharya (11th century A.D.), Madhvacharya (13th century A.D.) and Vallabhacharya (1479-1531 A.D.) and it is to their credit that Hinduism is still such a respected religion in the world with numerous adherents. Being studied the world over today present-day Hindu thought and philosophy, owes much to these five great men.

It is widely believed that all these five great saints are believed to be Avatars sent down to earth to perform a definite mission – to deliver Humankind from the clutches of evil, a task they all performed impeccably well. They all preached various forms of the same basic philosophy and it is discouraged to treat one as being greater than the other. That they propounded various schools of philosophy is not thought to be a disadvantage within Hinduism. Instead they established various paths to the same goal – the Godhead. People from various levels of spiritual development can find succor and be benefited. Thus, their diversity serves diverse peoples. They all gave rise to various schools of Vaishnavism.

Shankaracharya

It is said that Shankaracharya was born of poor but pious Nambudiri Brahmin parents. From an early age he was inclined towards the ways of God. His father died when he was a very young boy. He was an only child and, when he decided to renounce the worldly life in favour of a holy one, his mother resisted piteously. He somehow persuaded her to allow him the life of an ascetic though she managed to extract a promise from him to visit her death-bed and see to her funeral. A pious Hindu cannot die and go to heaven unless his or her son performs the funeral rites. At that very early age Shankaracharya set out to find a teacher and found an ideal one in Govinda Bhagavadpada, a disciple of another great guru Gaudapadacharya who had advocated monism or Advaita.

The philosophy taught him by his guru befitted Shankaracharya perfectly. He was a very intelligent man. At that time Hinduism had degenerated into a mess of dogmas and rituals which all seemed meaningless to the common people but were perpetrated by the Brahmins, the priestly class, in whose interest it was to control the reigns of society by dictating the will of the Gods. There was such diversity of complex and expensive rituals that it seemed beyond the means of common people to achieve the grace of the Gods. In this bleak scenario more tolerant religions like Buddhism and Jainism, which themselves were reformist reactions against the evils of Hinduism, and which advocated simple personal devotion as a means of gaining salvation had gained much popularity to the detriment of Hinduism. Sankaracharya understood the common people's problems in adhering to Hinduism in its composite state and set out to reform the religion onto a very much personal level.

It can be concluded that this great sage's short biography that, in the end, he did not fail to keep his promise to his own mother. When it was time for her to die he was there by her side and, when she subsequently died, he, though an ascetic who had given up all contact with the outside world, arranged for her funeral.

Ramanujacharya

Ramanuja was born in the village of Perumbudur, in the state of Tamil Nadu in the year 1017 A.D. His father was Keshava Somaji and his mother was Kantimathi, a very pious and virtuous lady. Ramanuja's Tamil name was Ilaya Perumal. At a very early age he lost his father. He persuaded his mother to let him set out of their village so that he could travel to one of the religious centers nearby and study under a Guru. He subsequently set out for Kanchipuram and started studying Advaita philosophy. His guru's interpretation of the Vedas was not quite to his liking and, after a rather colorful round of argument and insults, he left his guru for a better one in Kanchipurna, a Sudra who was much revered in the Vishishtadvaita community of Tamil Nadu.

The philosophy of Vishishtadvaita is Qualified Non-dualism. Ramanuja quickly found the philosophy to his liking and soon adopted it for his own. As per the interpretations of works left by him his Brahman is Sa-Visesha Brahman or Brahman with attributes. As per the Ramanuja's preachings Lord Narayana is Bhagwan or Supreme Being. The individual soul is Chit and all matter is Achit. The attributes are real and permanent but subject to the control of the Brahman. The attributes are called Prakaras or modes. Lord Narayana is the Ruler and Lord of the universe. All living things - Jivas are His servants and must worship Him and surrender to His will completely. The attributes are also called Shaktis and they are the manifest part of the Lord. He called his path of worship Bhakti. His followers are a particular sect among the chief sect of the Vaishnavites.

After thoroughly immersing himself in formulating his philosophy of God and the Causes of Creation set out of Kanchipuram to visit all the Vaishnavite Shrines in South India Ramanuja, he went about spreading his words and was widely accepted and revered wherever he went. Ultimately he reached Srirangam and settled there permanently. He lived a long and colorful life of 120 years full of holiness and religious zeal. He had several maths built and temples to his Lord established there. He formulated rules of worship and religious etiquette. He strove for the rest of his life to rid society of the evils that had crept into it subsequent to the degradation of Hinduism. He converted thousands of common people to his faith, alongwith a number of the outcastes of the time whom he lovingly welcomed to his community. He demolished barriers of caste and creed and welcomed all wholeheartedly. His religious precepts were easy to follow and keep. He advocated personal worship or Bhakti through which anyone could attain God. This was the main attractions of the branch of Hinduism he founded and thousands of people hungry for pointers to the right direction flocked to his maths to be converted. In this prominent quiet and singularly orderly manner he set about reforming Hinduism into a much more acceptable set of tenets that have stood the ups and downs of the a number of years that have passed from that time.

Alongwith the above qualities Ramanuja was an excellent controversialist and wrote commentaries on a number of ancient texts. His commentary on Badarayana's Brahma Sutras is known as Sri Bhashya. The Vishishtadvaita system was a very old one even at that time and Ramanuja followed the way of Bodhyana in this. Bodhyana had expounded this unique philosophy in his book Vritti written in 400 B.C. Ramanuja followed Bodhyana in his commentary on the Brahma Sutras. Ramanuja also wrote three other books - Vedanta Sara (Essence of the Vedanta), Vedanta Sangraha (Resume of the Vedanta) and Vedanta Deepa (Light of the Vedanta). Ramanujacharya's particular sect of Vaishnavites is called Sri Sampradaya and it still has an immense following today, particularly in South India, the birth place of this great sage.

Madhvacharya

As per the Hindu texts and scriptures Madhvacharya was born in around 1199 A.D. at a small village called Velali near Udipi in South Kanara district in South India. He was of Tula Brahmin birth born to Madhya Geha and Vedavati, a virtuous woman. His father named him

Vasudeva. Madhvacharya had an fantabulous physique and he could wrestle, run, jump and swim. People used to call him Bhima after the second Pandava brother in the Mahabharata. Madhva took up the study of the Vedas and the Vedangas early in his life and soon became well-versed in them. In his 25th year he took up Sanyash (Monkhood) and renounced the world. Achutaprakashacharya, a great guru at that time in Udipi, initiated him and thereafter he began to be known as Purna Prajna.

Madhva's command over the scriptures, especially of the components of the Vedanta, impressed Achutaprakashacharya so much that he soon made him head of his Math. Madhva now received the name Ananda Tirtha. He set out on a tour of Southern and Northern India. He preached to all and made a number of converts to his faith. He visited Badrinath, the Northern Dham, and, thereafter, returned to Udipi. Reinforced by both his studies and his travel experience he started to write his commentaries on the Bhagavad Gita and the Vedanta. He built several temples in Udipi to his Lord and acquired innumerable disciples. Upto this day Udipi is the center of the Madhva Sect and most orthodox Madhvas strive to visit Udipi at least once in a lifetime.

Advaita Philosophy was preached by Madhva. His sect is known as Sad Vaishnavism to distinguish it from the Sri Vaishnavism of Ramanujacharya. Madhva held that Vishnu or Narayana was the Supreme Being. This is the same as the doctrines of Ramanuja but Madhva's philosophy has certain distinctions. Madhva laid much stress on Smarana - remembering the Lord at all times. He said – "Form a strong habit of remembering God. Then only will it be easy for you to remember Him at the moment of death." He performed a number of miracles before he died. He is still remembered for the gentle faith he preached to all. His emphasis on personal devotion, as of the other great teachers, drew in a number of of people to Hinduism while it made it easy for those who were already Hindus to understand their religion better.

Nimbarkacharya

At Vaiduryapattam on the banks of the River Godavari, in the state of Andhra Pradesh in Southern India, there was born a boy-child to a great ascetic Aruna Muni and his pious wife Jayanti Devi in the 11th century A.D. The learned Brahmins around named him Niyamanandacharya. He also became famous as Aruna Rishi and Haripriyacharya. He was sent to Rishikul to study the Vedas, Vedangas, Darshanas and other holy books. He mastered the scriptures in a short time. He was in his teens then and people were astonished at his knowledge and came to see and listen to him from miles around.

Niyamananda was visited by Brahma himself in the guise of a sanyasin and, pleased with his hospitality, given him the name Nimbarka - "Nim" – from the "Neem" tree, and "Arka" from the "Sun" or "Surya", is said by the Hindus. After that incident his disciples and others started calling him Nimbarkacharya. Sri Nimbarkacharya is believed to be an avatar of Vishnu's Chakra Sudarshan or discus. Sri Nimbarkacharya was an exponent of the Dvaitadvaita School of Philosophy. His followers worship Lord Krishna and His cowgirl lover Radha. For them the Bhagavad Gita is the most significant scripture. Sri Nimbarkacharya held that Jiva, living being, and the material world are both separate from yet identical to the Supreme Being, Brahman. The sect he founded thrives prosperously at Mathura and Brindavan, principal centers of Radha-Krishna worship.

Chaitanya Mahaprabhu

It is said about the Chaitanya Mahaprabhu that he was a monk and social reformer of the 16th century Bengal, (present-day West Bengal and Bangladesh) and Orissa in India. Sri Krishna Chaitanya was a notable proponent for the Vaishnava school of Bhakti yoga (meaning loving devotion to Krishna/God) based on the philosophy of the Bhagavata Purana and Bhagavad Gita. Mainly he worshipped the forms of Radha and Krishna and popularised the chanting of the Hare Krishna maha mantra. His line of followers, known as Gaudiya Vaishnavas, revere him as an avatar of Krishna in the mood of Radharani who was prophesised to seem in the later verses of the Bhagavata Purana.

Sometimes he was also referred to by the names Gaura (Sanskrit for golden one) due to his light skin complexion, and Nimai due to his being born underneath a Neem tree. There are a number of biographies available from the time giving details of Chaitanya's life, the most prominent ones being the Chaitanya Charitamrita of Krishnadasa Kaviraja Goswami and the earlier Chaitanya Bhagavata of Vrindavana Dasa Thakura (both originally written in the Bengali language but now widely available in English and other languages) and the Chaitanya Mangala, written by Lochana Dasa Thakura.

Sai Baba of Shirdi

The scholars keep various views about the Sai Baba of Shirdi he is also known as Shirdi Sai Baba, was an Indian guru, yogi and fakir who is regarded by his Hindu and Muslim followers as a saint. Some of his Hindu devotees believe that he was an incarnation of Shiva or Dattatreya, and he was regarded as a satguru and an incarnation of Kabir. The name

'Sai Baba' is a combination of Persian and Indian origin; Sai is the Persian term for "holy one" or "saint", usually attributed to Islamic ascetics, whereas Baba is a word meaning "father" used in Indian languages.

The appellative thus refers to Sai Baba as being a "holy father" or "saintly father". His parentage, birth details, and life before the age of sixteen are obscure, which has led to a number of speculations and theories attempting to explain Sai Baba's origins. In his life and teachings he tried to reconcile Hinduism and Islam: Sai Baba lived in a mosque, was buried in a Hindu temple, practised Hindu and Muslim rituals, and taught using words and figures that drew from both customs. One of his epigrams which is widely known among both Hindus and Muslims says of God: "Allah Malik" ("God is Master").

Sai Baba in general and particular taught a moral code of love, forgiveness, helping others, charity, contentment, inner peace, devotion to God and guru. His philosophy was Advaita Vedanta and his teachings consisted of elements both of this school as well as of bhakti and Islam. Sai Baba remains a popular saint and is worshipped mostly in Maharashtra, southern Gujarat, Andhra Pradesh and Karnataka. Debate on his Hindu or Muslim origins continues to take place. He is also revered by several notable Hindu and Sufi religious leaders.

Sant Gyaneshwar

As per the Hindu custom and the religious texts Sant Gyaneshwar was a 13th century marathi saint, poet, philosopher and a yogi of Nath custom. His works Bhavartha deepika teeka, popularly known as Gyaneshwari, and Amrutanubhav are regarded to be the milestones in Marathi literature. The Vaishnav Sampraday or the Vitthal Sampraday of Pandharpur, Maharashtra, India considers "Gyaneshwar as its spiritual leader and Gyaneshwari as its Dharmagrantha (holy book). In Alandi, Maharashtra he entered into Sanjeevan Samadhi at the age of 21.

Tukaram

As per the Hindu Mythology Tukaram was a prominent Marathi Sant and religious poet in the Hindu custom in India. He was born and lived most of his life in Dehu, a town close to Pune city in Maharashtra, India. He was born to a couple with the family name Moray - the descendent of the Mourya Clan. Through a custom in India in bygone days, Tukaram's family name is rarely used in identifying him. Rather, in accord with another custom in India of assigning the epithet sant to persons regarded as thoroughly saintly, Tukaram is commonly known in Maharashtra as Sant Tukaram. It is also said that he was spiritual guru of Shivaji.

It is also believed that Tukaram was a devotee of Lord Vittala —an incarnation of Lord Krishna, who in turn, regarded to be an incarnation of Lord Vishnu. Tukaram is regarded as the climactic point of the so-called Bhagawat Hindu custom, which is thought to have begun in Maharashtra with Namdev. Gyasneshwar, Namdev, Janabai, Eknath, and Tukaram are revered especially in the warakari sect in Maharashtra. He has recived guru-mantra comprising names of Krishna, Rama and Hari. This was at the hands or by the media of a dream, of one Babaji Chaitanya — a possible indication that Tukaram had some connexion with prominent saint Chaitanya, and Gaudiya Vaishnavas believe that he was initiated and was a disciple of Chaitanya. Whatever information about the lives of the above saints of Maharashtra comes mostly from the works Bhakti-Wijay and Bhakti-Leelamrut of Mahipati. Mahipati was born 65 years after the death of Tukaram, (Tukaram having died 50 years, 300 years, and 353 years after the deaths of Ekanath, Namdev, and Dnyaneshwar, respectively.) Thus, Mahipati doubtlessly based his life sketches of all above "sants" primarily on rumours.

Public relgious preachings of Tukaram used to be mixed, by custom, with poetry, which included some of his own compositions. His discourses focussed on day-to-day behavior of human beings, and he emphasized that the true expression of religion was in a person's love for his fellow human beings rather than in ritualistic observance of religious orthodoxy, including mechanical study of the Vedas. His teachings covered a wide array of issues, including the significance of the ecosystem. Tukaram worked for his society's enlightenment in the warakari custom, which emphasizes community service and musical group worship.

Tukaram like Namdev, Janabai, and Eknath wrote in Marathi a large number of devotional poems identified in Marathi as abhang. A collection of 4,500 abhang known as the Gatha is attributed to Tukaram. Mantra Geeta, a Marathi translation in abhang form of the Sanskrit Bhagavad Geeta, is also attributed to him. It is an interpretation of Geeta from the perspective of Bhakti (devotion).

Vallabha Acharya

As per the Hindu Mythology Sri Vallabhacharya was a devotional philosopher, who founded the Pushti sect in India, following the philosophy of Shuddha advaita (Pure Non-dualism). He is regarded as an Acharya and Guru within the Vaishnava customs as promulgated and prescribed by the Vedanta philosophy. He is often associated with Vishnuswami, the founder of Rudra Sampradaya. Within Indian Philosophy he is known as the writer of sixteen 'stotras' (tracts) and produced several commentaries on the Bhagavata Purana, which discovers the a number of lilas (pastimes) of the avatar, Krishna. Vallabha Acharya occupies a unique place in Indian culture as a scholar, a philosopher and devotional (bhakti) preacher. He is widely regarded as the last of the four great Vaishnava Acharyas who founded the various Vaishnava schools of thought based on Vedantic philosophy, the other three (preceding him) being Ramanujacharya, Madhvacharya and Nimbarkacharya. He is especially known as a lover and a propagator of Bhagavata Dharma.

He was born in Champaranya near Raipur in the Indian state of Chhattisgarh. His education commenced at the age of seven with the study of four Vedas. He gained mastery over the books expounding the six systems of Indian philosophy. He also learnt philosophical systems of Adi Sankara, Ramanuja, Madhva, Nimbarka along with the Buddhist and Jain schools. He was able to recite hundred mantras, not only from beginning to end but also in reverse order. At Vyankateshwar and Lakshmana Balaji, he made a strong effect on the public as an incarnation of knowledge. He was now applauded as Bala Saraswati.

It is believed that when Vallabhacharya entered Gokul, he thought about the significant question of fixing people to the right path of devotion. He meditated on Krishna who seem ed to him in a vision in the form of Shrinathji, deity discovered by Madhavendra Puri and disclosed the 'Brahma Sambandha', a mantra of self dedication or consecration of self to Krishna. Vallabha Acharya related this experience to his worthiest and most beloved disciple. He became the first Vaishnava initiated by Vallabhacharya. He wanted to preach his message of devotion to God and God's grace called Pushti - Marga. He contracted three pilgrimages of India. He performed the initiation ceremony of religious rite by conferring on them 'NamaNivedana' mantra or 'Brahma Sambandha' mantra. Thousands turned to be his disciples, but 84 devoted servants are most famous and their life has been documented in Pushti Marg literature as the 'Story of 84 Vaishnavas'.

Bhagwan Swaminarayan

Bhagwan Swaminarayan or Sahajanand Swami is the main figure in a modern form of Hinduism known as the Swaminarayan Faith and is the founder of the Swaminarayan Sampraday in which followers offer devotion to Bhagwan Swaminarayan as the final expression of god. In this particular custom, Sahajanand Swami is respectfully addressed as Bhagwan Swaminarayan by his followers. Sahajanand Swami was born in Chhapaiya, Uttar Pradesh. He settled in the West Indian state of Gujarat, where he then preached his doctrine until his death in 1830. Sahajanand Swami is also known as Lord Swaminarayan, Ghanshyam Pande, Ghanshyam Maharaj, Shreeji Maharaj, HariKrishna Maharaj and Shri Hari.

As per the legend, it was events that took place at Badarikashram (Abode of NarNarayan) that led to the incarnation of Swaminarayan. It is believed that Narayan took birth as Swaminarayan due to a curse of Rishi Durvasa. With the advent of kaliyug, Adharm (immoral situation) had spread in Bharat Khand (India) and that Asur's (Evil people) had also tremendously increased. Hence he had accepted the curse, which was due to his own will, to take avatar on earth to demolish evil and establish Ekantik-dharm (Religion based on morality, knowledge, non-attachment and devotion). While there is indirect reference to Narayan taking birth in the form of Swaminarayan in the Geeta and Shreemad Bhagwad, there is a direct address to this in the Brahma Purana and Vishwaksena Samhita.

MAIN FIGURES IN MODERN PERIOD

Swami Prabhupada

Abhay Charanaravinda Bhaktivedanta Swami Prabhupada was the founder of the International Society for Krishna Consciousness, a movement to propagate Gaudiya Vaishnavism of Hinduism, not only in India, but also throughout the whole world, a devotional yoga custom that is popularly known as the "Hare Krishna". Born as Abhay Charan De, in Calcutta, he was educated at the prestigious local Scottish Churches College. Before adopting the life of a pious renunciate, vanaprastha, in 1950, he was married with children and owned a small pharmaceutical business. He later took a vow of renunciation, sannyasa, in 1959 and started writing commentaries on Vaishnava scriptures.

In his later years, as a travelling Vaishnava sadhu, he became an influential communicator of Gaudiya Vaishnava theology to India and mostly to the West through his leadership of the International Society for Krishna Consciousness (ISKCON), founded in 1966. As the founder of ISKCON, he has "emerged as a major figure of the Western counterculture, starting thousands of young Americans." Despite attacks from the anticult groups, he received a favourable welcome from a number of religious scholars, such as J. Stillson Judah, Harvey Cox, Larry Shinn and Thomas

Hopkins, who praised Prabhupada's translations and defended the group against distorted media images and misinterpretations. In respect to his achievements, religious leaders from other Gaudiya Vaishnava movements have also assigned him the credit.

He has been reported as a charismatic leader, in the sense used by the sociologist Max Weber, as he was successful in acquiring followers in the United States, Europe, India and elsewhere. After his death in 1977 his ISKCON, an authentic form of Hindu Krishnaism based on Bhagavata Purana, continues to grow, and is respected in India, but there have been a number of squabbles about leadership among the followers. Prabhupada is sometimes criticised by Neo-Vedantic relativistic philosophers, mainly due to uncompromising and 'unkind remarks' against non-Vaishnava systems, especially 'the mayavadis'. This may be taken in the perspective of universal underlying hostility of Neo-Vedantists towards fundamental truth of bhakti, devotion, and orthodox Vedanta system presented by Prabhupada being in conflict with heterodox views of mayavadis. As such his Hare Krishna movement is accepted by the academics as "the most genuinely Hindu of all the a number of Indian movements in the West". In 1922, when Prabhupada first met his spiritual master, Bhaktisiddhanta Sarasvati Thakura, Bhaktisiddhanta requested that Prabhupada spread the message of Chaitanya Mahaprabhu in the English language. Later in 1932 Prabhupada became a formally initiated disciple of Bhaktisiddhanta and in 1944 started the publication of Back to Godhead, an English language fortnightly, for which he acted as publisher, editor, copy editor and distributor.

The Gaudiya Vaishnava Society in 1947 recognised Prabhupada's scholarship with the title Bhaktivedanta, (bhakti-vedanta) meaning "one who has realised that devotional service to the Supreme Lord is the end of all knowledge" (with word Bhakti, indicating devotion and Vedanta indicating conclusive knowledge). His later well known name is Prabhupada. It is a Sanskrit title (prabhupada), literally meaning "he who has taken the position of the Lord" where prabhu denotes "Lord", and pada means "position" that is also explained to mean "at whose feet masters sit". This name was used as a respectful form of address by his disciples from late 1967 early 1968 onwards. Previous to this, as with his early disciples, followers used to call him "Swamiji".

From 1950 onwards, Prabhupada lived at the medieval temple in the holy town of Vrindavan, where he began his commentary and translation work of the Sanskrit work Bhagavata Purana. Of all notable Vrindavana's temples, the Radha-Damodara mandir had at the time the largest collection of various copies of the original writings of the Six Gosvamis and their followers - more than two thousand distinguished manuscripts, a number of them three hundred, some even four hundred years old. His guru in the sampradaya, custom, of Chaitanya Mahaprabhu, Bhaktisiddhanta Sarasvati had always encouraged Prabhupada, "If you ever get money, print books", referring to the necessitatement of literary presentation of the Vaishnava culture. Keshavaji Gaudiya Matha was the place where Prabhupada used to live, he had written and studied in the library of this building, here he edited the Gaudiya Patrika magazine and this is the place where he donated the murti of Lord Chaitanya who stands on the altar beside the Deities of Radha Krishna.

During his visit in September 1959 he entered the doors of this matha dressed in white, as Abhay Babu, but would be leaving dressed in saffron, a swami. In this matha, in Mathura Vrindavana, Prabhupada took Vaishnava renunciate vows, sannyasa, from his friend and godbrother Bhakti Prajnana Keshava Maharaja , and following this he single-handedly published the first three volumes covering seventeen chapters of the first book of Bhagavata Purana, filling three volumes of four hundred pages each with a detailed commentary. Introduction to the first volume was a biographical sketch of Chaitanya Mahaprabhu. He then left India, obtaining free passage on a freight ship called the Jaladuta, with the objective and a hope of fulfilling his spiritual master's instruction to spread the message of Chaitanya Mahaprabhu around the world. A suitcase, an umbrella, a supply of dry cereal, about eight dollars worth of Indian currency, and several boxes of books were his possessions.

Bhagawan Nityananda

As per the Indian Bhagawan Nityananda was an Indian guru. Several new religious movements (including Siddha Yoga and the Nityananda Institute) refer to him as the first Siddha guru in their lineages. His teachings are published in the Chidakash Gita. Nityananda was born in Quilandy (Pandalayini) Kerala, South India. Details about Nityananda's birth are sketchy but most accounts agree that Nityananda's mother abandoned him as an infant. He was adopted by a woman who worked as a maid working as a servants for Mr. Ishwar Iyer, a lawyer. Upon the woman's death Mr. Iyer adopted Nityananda. Even in childhood, Nityananda seemed to be in an remarkably advanced spiritual state, which gave rise to the belief that he was born enlightened. He was eventually given the name Nityananda (always in bliss). Before the age of twenty, Nityananda became a wandering yogi, spending time on yogic studies and practices in the Himalayas and other places. By 1920 he was back in southern India, where he had a fleeting encounter with a boy who would later become Swami Muktananda.

Settled in southern India, Nityananda gained a reputation for affecting miracles and wonderful cures. He then started building an ashram near Kanhangad, Kerala state. The local police thought he must be producing counterfeit money to pay for the building, so Nityananda took them to a crocodile-infested pool in the jungle. He dived in and then produced handfuls of money, which was obviously enough to satisfy the police.

By 1923, Nityananda had wandered to the Tansa Valley in Maharashtra state. There, his reputation as a miracle worker attracted people from as far away as Mumbai, though he never claimed credit for any miracles. He said, "Everything that happens, happens automatically by the will of god" Nityananda gave a great deal of help to the local adivasis, who were despised by the population at large.

Nityananda set up a school for them, as well as providing food and clothing. As a guru, Nityananda gave relatively little by way of verbal teachings. Starting in the early 1920s, devotees would sit with him in the evenings. Most of the time he was silent but occasionally he would give teachings. Some of the devotees starting writing down his words. Later these notes were compiled and published in the Kannada language.

Nityananda had the power to transmit spiritual energy (shaktipat) to people through non-verbal means. He could also be extremely fiery and intimidating in his behaviour, even to the point of throwing rocks on occasion. This was his way of deterring people who were not serious in their spiritual aspirations, or who came to him with ulterior motives.

In 1936 he went to the Shiva temple in the village of Ganeshpuri and asked if he could stay there. The family that looked after the temple agreed and built a hut for him. As his visitors and followers increased, the hut expanded and became an ashram. To the people around him, he was an avadhuta: one who is absorbed in the transcendental state.

Nityananda died on August 8, 1961. There is a shrine to him in the Gurudev Siddha Peeth ashram at Ganeshpuri. His ashram, tourist hostel and other buildings associated with his life in Ganeshpuri are preserved by the Shree Bhimeshwar Sadguru Nityanand Sanstha Ganeshpuri. This trust is also responsible for his samadhi shrine in Ganeshpuri, which is a pilgrimage site.

Maharishi Mahesh Yogi

The Hindu saint Maharishi Mahesh Yogi established and developed the Transcendental Meditation technique and related programs and initiatives, including schools and universities with campuses in India, the United States, Mexico, the United Kingdom, and China. In approximately 1939, Maharishi became a disciple of Swami Brahmananda Saraswati who, from 1941 to 1953, was the Shankaracharya (spiritual leader) of Jyotir Math, located in the Indian Himalayas. Maharishi credits the Shankaracharya with inspiring his teachings.

The first global tour of Maharishi Mahesh Yogi's began in 1958, from which time his techniques for human development have been taught worldwide. He became known in the Western world in part due to interactions with The Beatles and other celebrities. By 1990, Maharishi had commenced to coordinate his global activities from his residence in Vlodrop, the Netherlands. On January 11, 2008, he announced his retirement from all administrative activities and went into Mauna (spiritual silence). He was born Mahesh Prasad Varma, in the Panduka area of Raipur, India, to a Hindu family living in the Central Provinces of British India (although the Allahabad University list of distinguished alumni calls him "M. C. Shrivastava"). He earned a degree in physics at Allahabad University. Place of birth given in his passport is Pounalulla, India. The name of his father is was Sri Ram Prasad.

Jay Randolph Coplin says that, the name "Mahesh" indicated that Maharishi came from a Hindu family that worshipped Shiva. Cynthia Anne Hume writes that his family was of the Kayastha caste. Contrary to some reports, caste rules allow the honorific terms "yogi" or "maharishi" to be applied to those of the Kayastha caste.

In 1941 he became a secretary to Swami Brahmananda Saraswati, who gave him the name Bal Brahmachari Mahesh. Besides indicating his family faith, Coplin says the conferred title "identified him as a dedicated student of spiritual knowledge and life-long celibate ascetic." Maharishi remained with Brahmananda Saraswati until the latter died in 1953. Although Maharishi was a close disciple, he could not be the Shankaracharya's spiritual successor since he was not of the Brahmin caste.

In 1953, Maharishi moved to Uttarkashi, in the Valley of the Saints, in the Himalayas, where his own Master had lived in previous decades with his Master, Swami Krishanand Saraswati. In 1955, Maharishi left Uttarkashi, and began publicly teaching what he states is a conventional meditation technique that he later renamed Transcendental Meditation. He began The Spiritual Regeneration Movement in 1957, in Madras, India, on the concluding day of the Seminar of Spiritual Luminaries.

Just after establishing the Spiritual Regeneration Movement in the United States, Maharishi continued his world tour. He travelled to Europe in early 1960, stopping first in London. During the next two years, he returned to India and the Far East, before revisiting the U.S., Europe, and Africa. He lectured about, and taught the Transcendental Meditation technique, and also established administrative centers where practitioners could meet in his absence. Eventually the more experienced practitioners were trained to become teachers of the technique. In 1961, he conducted his first international Teacher Training Course near Rishikesh, India. Over 60 meditators from India, Canada, Denmark, Germany, Britain, Malaya, Norway, the United States, Australia, Greece, Italy and the West Indies attended.

Paramahansa Yogananda

Swami Paramahansa Yogananda born in Mukunda Lal Ghosh, was an Indian yogi and guru who introduced a number of westerners to the teachings of meditation and Kriya Yoga through his book, Autobiography of a Yogi. Yogananda was born in Gorakhpur, Uttar Pradesh, India into a devout Bengali family. As per the his younger brother, Sananda, from his earliest years young Mukunda's awareness and experience of the spiritual was far beyond the ordinary. In his youth he sought out a number of India's Hindu sages and saints, hoping to find an illuminated teacher to guide him in his spiritual quest. Yogananda's seeking after various saints mostly ended when he met his guru, Swami Sri Yukteswar Giri, in 1910, at the age of 17.

After passing his Intermediate Examination in Arts from the Scottish Church College, Calcutta, he did his graduation in religious studies from the Serampore College, a constituent college of the University of Calcutta. This allowed him to spend time at Yukteswar's ashram in Serampore. In 1915, he took formal vows into the monastic Swami Order and became 'Swami Yogananda Giri'. In 1917, Yogananda founded a school for boys in Dihika, West Bengal that combined modern educational techniques with yoga training and spiritual ideals. A year later, the school relocated to Ranchi.

This school would later become Yogoda Satsanga Society of India, the Indian branch of Yogananda's American organization. In 1920, he went to the United States aboard the ship City of Sparta, as India's delegate to an International Congress of Religious Liberals convening in Boston. That same year he founded the Self-Realization Fellowship to disseminate worldwide his teachings on India's ancient practices and philosophy of

Yoga and its custom of meditation. For the next several years, he lectured and taught on the East coast and in 1924 embarked on a cross-continental speaking tour. Thousands came to his lectures. The following year, he established in Los Angeles, California, an international headquarters for Self-Realization Fellowship, which became the spiritual and administrative heart of his growing work. Yogananda was the first Hindu teacher of yoga to make his permanent home in America, living there from 1920-1952.

He returned in 1935to India to visit Yukteswar and to help establish his Yogoda Satsanga work in India. During this visit, as told in his autobiography, he met with Mahatma Gandhi, the Bengali saint Anandamoyi Ma, Nobel winning physicist Chandrasekhara Venkata Raman, and several disciples of Yukteswar's Guru Lahiri Mahasaya. While in India, Yukteswar gave Yogananda the monastic title of Paramhansa.

Ramakrishna Paramahamsa

Sri Ramakrishna Paramahamsa born as Gadadhar Chattopadhyay was a Bengali religious ecstatic who practiced Vaishnava and Shakti bhakti, Vedanta, Tantra, and other spiritual disciplines. At the time of end of his life, he became a guru to Anglicized Bengalis, including Narendranath Dutta—the future Swami Vivekananda—and also became an influential figure in the Bengal Renaissance. He was regarded an avatar or incarnation of God by a number of his disciples, and is regarded as such by a number of his devotees today. Though recent academic scholarship has concentrated on, among other things, .aspects of his sexuality, the Ramakrishna Mission and other scholars have criticized the work of these scholars.

When Gadadhar started worshipping the deity Bhavatarini, he began to question if he was worshipping a piece of stone or a living Goddess. Gadadhar, however, unsatisfied, prayed to Mother Kali for more religious experiences. He especially wanted to know the truths that other religions taught. Strangely, these teachers came to him when necessary and he is said to have reached the ultimate goals of those religions with ease. Soon word spread about this remarkable man and people of all denominations and all stations of life began to come to him.

Around the 1870s, Ramakrishna had established a reputation as a mystic and had attracted a large number of male devotees from the emerging urban Bengali bourgeoisie class, most of whom including Narendranath Dutta, had been educated at English schools. He came to be known among his devotees as Sri Ramakrishna Paramahansa. The name Ramakrishna is said to have been given him by Mathur Babu, the son-in-law of Rani Rasmani. A number of prominent people of Calcutta like Pratap Chandra Mazumdar, Shivanath Shastri and Trailokyanath Sanyal began visiting him during this time (1871-1885). He also met Swami Dayananda.

Through his meetings with Keshab Chandra Sen of the Brahmo Samaj, he had become known to the general populace of Calcutta. After fifteen years of teaching, in April 1885 the first symptoms of throat cancer seem ed and in the beginning of September 1885 he was moved to Shyampukur. But the illness showed signs of aggravation and he was moved to a large garden house at Cossipore on December 11, 1885 on the advice of Dr. Sarkar, who was treating him. On August 15, 1886 his health deteriorated, and at 01:02 a.m. on the 16th he attained mahasamadhi. At noon, Dr. Sarkar pronounced that life had departed not more than half an hour before.

He left behind a devoted band of 16 young disciples headed by Swami Vivekananda. The key concepts in Ramakrishna's teachings were the oneness of existence; the divinity of all living beings; and the unity of God and the harmony of religions. Ramakrishna stressed that God-realisation is the supreme goal of all living beings. Religion, for him, was simply a means for the accomplishment of this goal. Ramakrishna's mystical realisation, classified by Hindu custom as nirvikalpa samadhi (literally, "involuntary meditation", thought to be assimilation in the all-encompassing Consciousness), led him to know that the several religions are various ways to reach The Absolute, and that the Ultimate Reality could never be expressed in human terms.

Sri Aurobindo

As per the Hindu religious scripts Sri Aurobindo was an Indian nationalist, scholar, poet, mystic, evolutionary philosopher, yogi and guru. After a short political career in which he became one of the leaders of the early movement for the freedom of India from British rule, Sri Aurobindo turned to explore spiritual realms of human existence and, as a consequence, developed a new path which he termed integral yoga.

Sri Aurobindo grew as a result of his spiritual pursuits into a visionary of new evolution, a poet of the plentitudes and profundity of the hidden realities of man and life, a seer-philosopher of the ascent of human life to the next higher level of its existence on earth. Apprecating his vision,

Times Literary Suppliment, London, wrote "In fact, he (Sri Aurobindo) is a new type of thinker, one who combines in his vision the alacrity of the West with the illumination of the East. To study his writings is to elaborate the limits of one's knowledge... He is a yogi who writes as though he were standing among the stars, with the constellations for his companions." On most aspects of human life as well as on India's past, present and future possibilities, Sri Aurobindo gave deeply original and comprehensive views that can guide India and mankind towards a new civilization and a higher equilibrium in human life.

The major writings of Sri Aurobindo contain poetry, his epic poem Savitri, and the Collected Poems and, in prose, in a number of highly acclaimed books such as The Life Divine, Synthesis of Yoga, Secret of Veda, Essays on the Gita, The Human Cycle, The Ideal of Human Unity, Renaissance in India and other essays, Supramental Expression upon Earth, The Future Poetry, Thoughts and Aphorisms, and several volumes of his letters.

In his vision of new evolution, Sri Aurobindo even foresees the seem ance of a totally new species on earth, which shall be as or even more advanced from man as man is from the ape, and he also elaborated on the process that could accelerate this evolution! Thus, the central theme of Sri Aurobindo's vision is the evolution of life into life divine. His central message:"Man is a transitional being. He is not final. The step from man to superman is the next nearing accomplishment in the earth's evolution. It is destiny because it is at once the intention of the inner spirit and the logic of Nature's process".

Swami Dayananda Saraswati

As per the Swami Dayananda Saraswati was an significant Hindu religious scholar born in a town called Tankara Gujarat, India. He is best known as the founder of the Arya Samaj, "Society of Nobles", a Hindu reform movement, founded in 1875. He was a sanyasi (one who has renounced all worldly possessions and relations) from his boyhood. He was an original scholar, who believed in the infallible authority of the Vedas. Dayananda advocated the doctrine of karma, skepticism in dogma, and emphasised the ideals of brahmacharya. The Theosophical Society and the Arya Samaj were united for a certain time under the name Theosophical Society of the Arya Samaj.

Swami Dayananda's creation, the Arya Samaj, is a unique component in Hinduism. The Arya Samaj unambiguously sentences idol-worship, animal sacrifices, ancestor worship, pilgrimages, priestcraft, offerings made in temples, the caste system, untouchability, child marriages and discrimination against women on the grounds that all these lacked Vedic sanction. The Arya Samaj discourages dogma and symbolism and encourages skepticism in beliefs that run opposite to common sense and logic. To a number of people, the Arya Samaj objectives to be a universal church based on the authority of the Vedas.

Among Swami Dayananda's immense contributions is his championing of the equal rights of women - such as their right to education and reading of Indian scriptures - and his translation of the Vedas from Sanskrit to Hindi so that the common man may be able to read the Vedas. The Arya Samaj is rare in Hinduism in its acceptance of women as leaders in prayer meetings and preaching.

Swami Dayananda set about the hard task with dedication despite attempts on his life. He traveled the country challenging religious scholars and priests of the day to discussions and won repeatedly on the strength of his arguments. He believed that Hinduism has been corrupted by difference from the founding principles of the Vedas and misled by the priesthood for the priests' self-aggrandisement. Hindu priests discouraged common folk from reading Vedic scriptures and encouraged rituals (such as bathing in the Ganges and feeding of priests on anniversaries) which Dayananda pronounced as superstitions or self-serving. He was interested with classical Hinduism (current Hindu practices) and became a wandering monk. He learned Panini's Grammar to understand and learn Sanskrit texts, and learnt from them that God can be seen. For over two decades after wandering in search of God, he found Swami Virjananda near Mathura who became his guru and told him to throw away all his books, as their motive was solved.

Apart from adopting concepts from other religions, as Raja Ram Mohan Roy had done, Swami Dayananda was quite critical of Islam and Christianity as may be seen in his book Satyartha Prakash. He was against what he regarded to be the corruption of the pure faith in his own country. Unlike a number of other reform movements within Hinduism, the Arya Samaj's appeal was addressed not only to the educated few in India, but to the world as a whole as evidenced in the 6th principle of the Arya Samaj.

Arya Samaj is a rare stream in Hinduism that allows and encourages converts to Hinduism. Dayananda's concept of Dharma is succinctly set forth in his Beliefs and Disbeliefs. He said, "I accept as Dharma whatever is in full conformity with impartial justice, truthfulness and the like; that which is not opposed to the teachings of God as embodied in the Vedas.

He was among the first great Indian stalwarts who popularised the concept of swaraj - the right to self-determination vested in an individual - when India was ruled by the British. His philosophy inspired nationalists in the mutiny of 1857 as well as champions such as Lala Lajpat Rai and Bhagat Singh. Dayananda's Vedic message was to emphasize respect and reverence for other human beings, supported by the Vedic notion of the divine nature of the individual - divine because the body was the temple where the human essence (soul or "Atma") could possibly interface with the creator. In the ten principles of the Arya Samaj, he enshrined the idea that "All actions should be performed with the prime objective of benefitting mankind" as opposed to following dogmatic rituals or revering idols and symbols.

Dayananda's back-to-the-Vedas message shaped a number of thinkers. The ideology presented in the works of Dayananda has been used to support the Hindutva movement of the 20th century. In his own life, rather calling to emancipate others he interpreted Moksha to be a lower calling (due to its benefit to one individual).

Swami Vivekananda

As per the Hindu custom Swami Vivekananda, whose name was Narendranath Dutta was an Indian Hindu sage and one of the most famous and influential social reformers of the 19th century. A redoubtable spiritual leader, he was an exponent of Vedanta and Yoga. He was the most eminent disciple of Ramakrishna Paramahamsa and the founder of the Ramakrishna Math and the Ramakrishna Mission. He is a major figure in the history of the Hindu reform movements. While he is widely credited with having uplifted his own nation, India, Vivekananda simultaneously introduced Yoga and Vedanta to America and England with his seminal lectures and private discourses on Vedanta philosophy.

He was the first known Hindu sage to travel to the West, where he introduced Eastern thought at the World's Parliament of Religions, in relation with the World's Fair in Chicago, in 1893. Here, his first lecture, which started with the opening line "Sisters and Brothers of America," made the audience clap for two minutes in appreciation, for prior to this seminal speech, they were always used to the usual address of "Ladies and Gentlemen."

It was this speech that catapulted him to fame by his wide audiences in Chicago and then later everywhere else in America, including far-flung places such as Memphis, Boston, San Francisco, New York, Los Angeles, and St. Louis. Narendra met Ramakrishna for the first time in November

1881. Though Narendra could not accept Ramakrishna and his visions, he could not neglect him either. It had always been in Narendra's nature to test something exhaustively ahead he would accept it. He tested Ramakrishna to the maximum, but the master was patient, forgiving, humorous, and full of love. He never asked Narendra to abandon fact, and he faced all of Narendra's arguments and examinations with patience.

In time, Narendra accepted Ramakrishna, and when he accepted, his acceptance was whole-hearted. While Ramakrishna predominantly taught duality and Bhakti to his other disciples, he taught Narendra the Advaita Vedanta, the philosophy of Sankara. During the course of five years of his training under Ramakrishna, Narendra was transformed from a restless, puzzled, impatient youth to a mature man who was ready to renounce everything for the sake of God-realization. In August 1886, Ramakrishna's end came in the form of throat cancer. After this Narendra and a core group of Ramakrishna's disciples took vows to become monks and renounce everything, and started living in a purportedly haunted house in Baranagore. They took alms to satisfy their hunger and their other needs were taken care of by Ramakrishna's richer householder disciples.

Vivekananda was a renowned thinker in his own right. One of his most significant contributions was to demonstrate how Advaitin thinking is not merely philosophically far-reaching, but how it also has social, even political, consequences. One significant lesson he claimed to receive from Ramakrishna was that "Jiva is Shiva " (each individual is divinity itself). This became his Mantra, and he coined the concept of daridra narayana seva - the service of God in and through (poor) human beings. If there truly is the unity of Brahman underlying all phenomena, then on what basis do we regard ourselves as better or worse, or even as better-off or worse-off, than others? This was the question he posed to himself. Ultimately, he concluded that these differentiations fade into nothingness in the light of the oneness that the devotee experiences in Moksha. What arises then is compassionateness for those "individuals" who remain unaware of this oneness and a decision to help them.

Swami Vivekananda belonged to that branch of Vedanta that held that no one can be truly free until all of us are. Even the desire for personal salvation has to be given up, and only tireless work for the salvation of others is the true mark of the enlightened person. He founded the Sri Ramakrishna Math and Mission on the principle of Atmano Mokshartham Jagadhitaya cha (for one's own salvation and for the welfare of the World).

However, Vivekananda also pleaded for a strict separation between religion and government, a value found in Freemasonry which as a Freemason he had been exposed to. Although social customs had been formed in the past with religious sanction, it was not now the business of religion to interfere with matters such as marriage, hereditary pattern and so on. The ideal society would be a mixture of Brahmin knowledge, Kshatriya culture, Vaisya efficiency and the egalitarian Shudra ethos. Domination by any one led to various sorts of lopsided societies. Vivekananda did not feel that religion, nor, any force for that matter, should be used forcefully to bring about an ideal society, since this was something that would evolve naturally by individualistic change when the circumstances were right.

He made a strict demarcation between the two classes of Hindu scriptures : the Sruti and the Smritis. The Sruti, by which is meant the Vedas, consist of eternally and universally valid spiritual truths. The Smritis on the other hand, are the dos and donts of religions, applicable to society and subject to revision from time to time. Vivekananda felt that existing Hindu smritis had to be revised for modern times. But the Srutis of course are eternal - they may only be re-interpreted. In one of the conversations with his childhood friend Sri Priya Nath Sinha he attributes his physical and mental strengths, eloquence to the practice of Brahmacharya. He advised his followers to be holy, unselfish and have shraddha (faith). He encouraged the practise of Brahmacharya (Celibacy).

REFERENCES

Beck, Brenda E. F.: "*Colour and Heat in South Indian Ritual*", 1969.

Berreman, Gerald D.: "*Brahmans and Shamans in Pahari Religion*" Journal of Asian Studies, 1964

Carstairs, Morris G.: *The Twice-Born: A Study of High Caste Hindus*, Bloomington, Indiana University Press, 1961

Census Operations: *Superintendent 1961 District Census Handbook: Raipur District*, Bhopal, Govt. of Madhya Pradesh, 1964.

Cunningham: *Alexander: "Report on a Tour in the Central Provinces and Lower Gangetic Doab in 1881-82"* Archaeological Survey of India, 1884.

Danielou: *Alain, Hindu Polytheism*, New York: Pantheon Books, 1964.

De E. A. Brett: *Chhattisgarh Feudatory States*, Bombay, Times Press, 1909.

Dubey, K. C. and M. G. Mohril: *Fairs and Festivals of Madhya Pradesh*, Delhi, Manager of Publications, 1965

Dumont, Louis, and David Pocock: "*On the Different Aspects or Levels in Hinduism.*" Contributions to Indian Sociology, 1959

Dumont, Louis: *"World Renunciation in Indian Religions"* Contributions to Indian Sociology, 1960.

Evans-Pritchard, E.: *Nuer Religion*. London, Oxford University Press, 1956

Harper, Edward B.: "*A Hindu Village Pantheon*" Southwestern Journal of Anthropology, 1959

Homo Hierarchicus: *An Essay on the Caste System*, Mark Sainsbury. Chicago, University of Chicago Press, 1970

Jagadisvarananda: *The Devi-Mahatmyam or Sri Durga-Saptasati*, Mylapore, Sri Ramakrishna Math.

Jay, Edward J.: "*Bridging the Gap Between Castes: Ceremonial Friendship in Chhattisgarh*" Contributions to Indian Sociology, 1973.

Kavyopadhyaya, Hira Lal: *A Grammar of the Chhattisgarhi Dialect of Eastern Hindi*, Calcutta, Baptist Mission Press, 1921.

6

Scriptures

The world literature regarded that the Hindu literary custom were predominantly composed in Sanskrit, indeed, much of the morphology and linguistic philosophy inherent in the learning of Sanskrit is inextricably linked to study of the Vedas and other Hindu texts. Hindu literature is divided into two categories: Shruti – that which is heard (i.e. revelation) and Smriti – that which is remembered (i.e. custom, not revelation). The Vedas constituting the former category are regarded scripture by a number of Hindus. A sort of cross-over between the religious epics and Upanishads of the Vedas is the Bhagavad Gita, regarded to be revered scripture by almost all Hindus today. The post-Vedic Hindu scriptures form the latter category: the various Shastras and the itihaases, or histories in epic verse.

In general Hindu texts are typically seen to revolve around a number of levels of reading, namely the gross or physical, the pernicious, and the supramental. Hindu literature refers to a composite of literary works in the form of prose, poetry, philosophical discussions, epics, and novels which have been created around the central themes of Hinduism, which are as follows:

- Doctrine of Karma (The Karmic Chakra)
- Temple and idol worship
- Observation of Sacraments
- Significance of Dharma
- Presence of an all-pervasive Divinity
- Worship of manifold Deities
- Compulsion and Certainty of re-birth and reincarnation

The ancient oral literary custom prevails over and influences a large section of early Hindu literature. Thus, texts in Hindu literature form only a part and not the whole. The seminal and basic creations of Hindu literature are in form of oral customs, termed as Shruti which were founded on heard compositions, without identification of the teller and Smriti which were only based on memory of listeners. The oral transmission of the original literary content for many centuries has resulted in countless modifications of the original text before these have been ultimately written down and the contents have been settled. Hindu literature encompasses the vast collection of works spanning over more than 5,000 years. The periodization of the Hindu literature is as under;

- Ancient Period: Sanskrit scripture, philosophical pieces, general poetry and prose, Sanskrit novels
- Medieval Period: Sanskrit and Dravidian literary works of the Medieval period in India
- Modern Period: Modern literary creations in all Indian languages, including in major Indian languages of Hindi, Tamil, Oriya, Bengali etc., while in Sanskrit to a very small extent
- Post-Modern Contemporary Period: Literature based on major themes of Hinduism as well as pieces work related to clarification/elucidation of Hindu motifs in present scenario.

The Hindu scriptures written that time were massive, and were written between 1400 B.C. and A.D. 500. The oldest of the Hindu scriptures is the Veda, which literally means "wisdom" or "knowledge." The Vedas contain hymns, prayers, and ritual texts composed from about 1400 to about 400 B.C. The Upanishads are a collection of writings composed between 800-600 B.C. Over one hundred of them still exist. These writings marked a definite change from the sacrificial humans and magic formulas in the Vedas, to the mystical ideas about man and the universe – specifically the Brahman, and the atman (the self or soul).

Among the tow major epic tales Ramayana is one tales of India, the other being the Mahabharata. A sage-poet named Valmiki wrote the Ramayana. The work consists of 24,000 couplets based upon the life of Rama, a righteous king who was supposedly an incarnation of the God Vishnu. The Mahabharata is the second epic. It is an the story of the deeds of Aryan clans, and consists of some 100,000 verses and was composed over an 800-year period beginning about 400 B.C. Contained within this work is a great classic, the Bhagavad Gita, or the "Song of the Blessed Lord." The Bhagavad Gita is not only the most sacred book of the Hindus, but it is also the best known and the most read of all Indian works in the entire world, despite the fact it was added late to the

Mahabharata, sometime in the first century A.D. The story revolves around duty of man, which, if carried out, will bring nothing but sorrow. The significance this story has on Hindu belief is its endorsement of bhakti, or devotion to a particular god, as a means of salvation, since Arjuna, the story's chief character, decides to put his devotion to Vishnu above his own personal desires.

DIVINE WORDS

Almost all the Hindu literary works say the same thing that God and His words are one and the same. Life in modern society is all work and no spirituality. Ignorance is the mother of all sins. All negative qualities such as lust, anger, and greed are nothing but a expression of ignorance only. The giving of the gift of knowledge is the best charity. It is equivalent to giving the whole world in charity. The best welfare is to help others discover their real nature that is the origin of eternal happiness rather than furnish material goods and comforts for temporary happiness. The affairs of the world run by the first precept of the creator. The sacred knowledge of doing one's duty without looking for a reward is the original teaching that alone can lead to salvation.

All the human beings living in this material world gains the knowledge of stones, cement, steel and iron. That which is born shall die, but the Atman (soul) is neither born nor shall it die. Then what is the fact to be sad? If you do not do your natural duty, do not follow your own dharma (religion), do not fight in a religious war as a Kshatriya (warrior) should do, then dishonour will come to your door which shall be worse than death. The body is transient, but the soul is deathless and indivisible. None can cause the destruction of soul. This Atman is not born, nor does it ever die. It is unborn, eternal, changeless, ancient and inexhaustible. The embodied self casts off worn out bodies, and enters others which are new in the same mannner as a man casts off worn out clothes and puts on new ones.

Hence, every one should attain the knowledge of imperishable Self, while performing the natural duties that have been assigned to him. The person who performs his duties honestly and with sincere efforts disregarding the fruit of action becomes even minded. Your right is to work only but never with its fruits. Let not the fruit of action be your motive, nor let your attachment be for inaction. Perform action being steadfast in Yoga, deserting attachment, and equilibrated in success and failure. Evenness of mind is Yoga. Such a person is liberated from the slavery of birth and death with time, and he becomes a man of steady wisdom. The Supreme Reality is then realized by him.

RELIGIOUS SCRIPTURES

Four Vedas

In Hindu religion there are four Vedas, the Rig Veda, Sama Veda, Yajur Veda and Atharva Veda. The Vedas are the primary texts of Hinduism. They also had a vast influence on Buddhism, Jainism, and Sikhism. Customally the text of the Vedas was coetaneous with the universe. Scholars have determined that the Rig Veda, the oldest of the four Vedas, was composed about 1500 BC., and codified about 600 BC. It is unknown when it was at last committed to writing, but this probably was at some point after 300 BC. The Vedas contain hymns, conjurations, and rituals from ancient India. They are between the most ancient religious texts still in existence. Besides their spiritual value, they also give a unique view of everyday life in India four thousand years ago. The Vedas are also the most ancient wide texts in an Indo-European language, and as such are invaluable in the study of relative linguistics.

Vedas in original are a large corpus of texts originating in Ancient India. They form the oldest layer of Sanskrit literature and the oldest sacred texts of Hinduism. As per the Hindu custom, the Vedas are not of human agency, being supposed to have been directly revealed, and thus are said to be the shruti (what is heard). At all the Hindu prayers, religious functions and other auspicious occasions these Vedic mantras are recited.

The class of Vedic texts is combined around the four canonical Samhitas or Vedas proper, of which three (trayi) are related to the carrying into action of yajna (sacrifice) in historical (Iron Age) Vedic religion:

- The Rigveda, containing hymns to be recited by the hotr or reciting priest;
- The Yajurveda, containing formulas to be recited by the adhvaryu or officiating priest;
- The Samaveda, containing formulas to be sung by the udgatr or chanting priest.
- The fourth is the Atharvaveda, a collection of magical spells and healing or apotropaic charms and some speculative hymns used by the Brahmin priest.

The Hindu Philosophies and sects that arose in the Indian subcontinent have taken differing positions on the Vedas. Schools of

Indian philosophy which cite the Vedas as their scriptural authority are classified as orthodox (astika). Other customs, notably Buddhism and Jainism, though they are (vedanta) likewise concerned with liberation did not regard the Vedas as divine ordinances but rather human expositions of the sphere of higher spiritual knowledge, hence not sacrosanct.

These groups are referred to by customal Hindu texts as "heterodox" or "non-orthodox" (nastika) schools. In addition to Buddhism and Jainism, Sikhism also does not accept the authority of the Vedas. The Yajurveda, Samaveda and Atharvaveda are independent aggregations of mantras and hymns intended as manuals for the Adhvaryu, Udgatr and Brahman priests respectively.

The fourth Veda is Atharvaveda. Its status has occasionally been ambiguous, probably due to its use in sorcery and healing. However, it comprises very old materials in early Vedic language. Manusmrti, which often speaks of the three Vedas, calling them trayam-brahma-sanatanam, "the triple eternal Veda". The Atharvaveda like the Rigveda, is a collection of original incantations, and other materials adopting relatively little from the Rigveda. It has no direct relation to the solemn Shrauta sacrifices, except for the fact that the for the most part silent Brahman priest observes the procedures and uses Atharvaveda mantras to 'heal' it when mistakes have been made. Its recitation also produces long life, cures diseases, or effects the ruin of enemies.

All the the four Vedas comprises the metrical Mantra or Samhita and the prose Brahmana part, giving discussions and directions for the detail of the ceremonies at which the Mantras were to be used and explanations of the legends connected with the Mantras and rituals. Both these portions are termed shruti (which custom says to have been heard but not composed or written down by men). Each of the four Vedas seems to have passed to numerous Shakhas or schools, giving rise to various recensions of the text. They each have an Index or Anukramanika, the main work of this kind being the general Index or Sarvanukramanika.

Rigveda

Some historians believe that the Rig Veda must have been composed more or less in the period 1450-1350 BC., in the Greater Punjab, before the onset of the Iron Age. The Rigveda Samhita is the oldest significant existent Indian text. It is a collection of 1,028 Vedic Sanskrit hymns and 10,600 verses in all, organized into ten books (Sanskrit: mandalas). The hymns are dedicated to Rigvedic deities.

The books of Vedas were composed by poets from various priestly groups over a period of some 500 years, which Avari dates as 1400 BC. to 900 BC., if not earlier. As per the Max Müller, based on internal evidence, the Rigveda was composed roughly between 1700–1100 BC. (early Vedic period) in the Punjab (Sapta Sindhu) region of the Indian subcontinent.

There are strong lingual and cultural laws of similarity between the Rigveda and the early Iranian Avesta, deriving from the Proto-Indo-Iranian times, often associated with the Andronovo culture; the earliest horse-drawn chariots were found at Andronovo sites in the Sintashta-Petrovka cultural area near the Ural mountains and date back to 2000 BC. Till this day these Vedas are similary valuable and authentic as they were at the time of their writing.

Yajurveda

The next veda is Yajur-Veda which comprises archaic prose mantras and also in part of verses borrowed and adapted from the Rig-Veda. Its motive was practical, in that each mantra must accompany an action in sacrifice but, unlike the Sama-Veda, it was compiled to apply to all sacrificial rites, not merely the Soma offering. There are two major recensions of this Veda known as the "Black" and "White" Yajur-Veda. The origin and meaning of these designations are not very clear. The White Yajur-Veda comprises only the verses and formulas (yajus) necessary for the sacrifice, while their discussion exist in a different work, the Shatapatha Brahmana. It differs widely from the Black Yajurveda, which incorporates such discussions in the work itself, often immediately following the verses. Of the Black Yajurveda four major recensions survive (Maitrayani, Katha, Kapisthala-Katha, Taittiriya), all showing by and large the same arrangement, but differing in a number of other respects, notably in the individual discussion of the rituals but also in matters of syntax and choice of words phonology, accent and grammatical forms.

Samaveda

The next to Yajur Veda is the Sama-Veda (Sanskrit samaveda) is the Veda of melodies or Knowledge of melodies. The name of this Veda is from the Sanskrit word saman which means a melody applied to metrical hymn or song of praise. It consists of 1549 stanzas, taken entirely from the Rig-Veda. Like the Rigvedic stanzas in the Yajurveda, the Samans have been changed and adapted for use in singing. Some of the Rig-Veda verses are repeated more than once. Including repetitions, there are a total of 1875 verses numbered in the Sama-Veda recension translated by

Griffith. The Kauthuma/Ranayaniya and the Jaiminiya are the two major recensions which exist even today.

To serve as a songbook for the "singer" priests who took part in the liturgy, its motive was liturgical and practical. A priest who sings hymns from the Sama-Veda during a ritual is called an udgatr, a word derived from the Sanskrit root ud-gai (to chant). A similar word in English might be cantor. The hymns were to be sung As per the certain fixed melodies; hence the name of the collection. The styles of chanting are significant to the liturgical use of the verses.

Atharvaveda

The last of these vedas is Artharva-Veda and it is the Knowledge of the atharvans and angirasa. The Artharva-Veda or Atharvangirasa is the text belonging to the Atharvan and Angirasa poets. Apte defined an atharvan as a priest who worshipped fire and Soma. However, the etymology of Atharvan is unclear, but it is related to Avesta athravan; he denies any connection with fire priests. Atharvan was an ancient term for a certain Rishi even in the Rigveda. The Atharva-Veda Samhita has 760 hymns, and about 160 of the hymns are in common with the Rig-Veda. Most of the verses are metrical, but some sections are in prose. It was compiled around 900 BC., although some of its material may go back to the time of the Rig Veda, and though not in linguistic form some parts of the Atharva-Veda are older than the Rig-Veda.

Atharva-Veda has been preserved in two recensions, the Paippalada and Œaunaka. As per the Apte it had nine schools (shakhas). The Paippalada text, which exists in a Kashmir and an Orissa version, is longer than the Saunaka one; it is only partially printed in its two versions and remains largely in its original form.

The Atharvana-Veda has less connection with sacrifice unlike the other three Vedas. Its first part comprises chiefly of spells and incantations, concerned with protection against demons and disaster, spells for the healing of diseases, for long life and for various desires or objectives in life.

Gavin Flood discusses the relatively late acceptance of the Atharva-Veda as follows:

"There were originally only three priests associated with the first three SaChitas, for the Brahman as overseer of the rites does not seem in the Rig Veda and is only incorporated later, thereby showing the acceptance of the Atharva Veda, which had been somewhat distinct from the other Samhitas and identified with the lower social strata, as being of equal standing with the other texts."

The second part of the text comprises speculative and philosophical hymns. In its third section, the Atharvaveda comprises Mantras used in marriage and death rituals, as well as those for kingship, female rivals and the Vratya (in Brahmana style prose).

Upanishads

After the Vedas the Upanishads were written. The Upanishads are a continuation of the Vedic philosophy, and were written between 800 and 400 B.C. They elaborate on how the soul (Atman) can be united with the ultimate truth (Brahman) through contemplation and mediation, as well as the doctrine of Karma— the cumulative effects of person's actions. The Upanishads are looked upon as part of the Vedas and as such form part of the Hindu scriptures. They form the core spiritual thought of Vedanta. The Upanishads are known as Vedânta ("the end/culmination of the Vedas"). The Upanishads do not belong to a particular period of Sanskrit literature. The oldest, such as the Brhadaranyaka, Chandogya Upanishads and Jaiminiya Upanisadbrahmana, date to the late Brahmana period (roughly around the mid first millennium BC., that is well before the Gita was composed), while the youngest were composed in the medieval or even the early modern period.

The scholars and researchers of the Vedic books consider the four Vedas as poetic liturgy, collectively called mantra or samhita, that is as adoration and supplication to the deities of Vedic religion, in parts melded with henotheist notions, and an overarching order (Rta) that transcended even the gods. The Brâhmanas are a collection of ritual discussions, detailing the meaning of the mantras, ritual actions, priestly functions as well as that of complete rituals. They are later than the Mantras. Vedanta, is chiefly composed of Âranyakas and Upanishads. The Aranyakas ("of the wilderness") are composed in Brahmana style and deal with the more secret Vedic Shrauta rituals. The Upanishads realized monist ideas, some of which are hinted at in earlier texts, and have maintained an significant influence on the rest of Hindu and Indian philosophy.

Shankra, the philosopher and commentator is thought to have composed commentaries on eleven Upanishads. These mukhya Upanishads are in general regarded as the oldest ones, spanning the late Vedic and the Mauryan periods. By the 17th century, there were a large number of Upanishads: The Muktika Upanishad (predates 1656) lists 108 Upanishads. The number of Upanishads translated into Persian by Dara Shikoh (d.

1659) is 50. There are also counts that give a total number of Upanishads in excess of 108: Max Müller (1879) is aware of 170, and there are other counts in excess of 200 or even 300. The category of Upanishads has remained somewhat permeable, with the later additions being highly sectarian, perhaps representing "one of the strategies used by sectarian movements to legitimate their own texts through granting them the nominal status of Shruti." The Upanishads hold information on basic Hindu beliefs, including belief in a world soul, a universal spirit, Brahman, and an individual soul, Atman.

In Sanskrit, the word Brahman has two genders (masculine, Brahmâ, the creator-god or Brahma, neuter, the Absolute). Custom sees a form of lesser gods as aspects of this one divine ground, Brahman (altogether different from Brahma). Brahman is the ultimate, both transcendent and immanent, the absolute infinite existence, the sum total of all that ever is, was, or ever shall be. Shankara's exegesis of the Upanishads describes Brahman not as God in the monotheistic sense; he ascribes to it no limiting characteristics, not even those of being and non-being. Thus, Shankara's philosophy is named advaita, "not two." Dvaita philosophy is a distinct interpretation.

Founded by Madhvacharya, this school holds that Brahman is ultimately a personal God, Vishnu, or Krishna (brahmano hi pratisthaham, I am the Foundation of Brahman Bhagavad Gita 14.27). Vishishtadvaita, founded by Ramanujacharya is the third major school of Vedanta, and it has some aspects in common with the other two. The sages of the Upanishad try to solve these mysteries and seek knowledge of a Reality beyond ordinary knowing.

Philosophy of Upanishads: Because of their mystical nature and intense philosophical bent that does away with all ritual and completely embraces principals of One Brahman and the inner Atman (Self), the Upanishads have a universal feel that has led to their explication in numerous manners, giving birth to the three schools of Vedanta. The Upanishads are summed up in one phrase "Tat Tvam Asi" (That thou art) by the Advaita Vedanta. However, Vedic interpretation of this phrase varies. Vedantins believe that in the end, the ultimate, formless, inconceivable Brahman is the same as our soul, Atman. We only have to realize it through discrimination. The Upanishads also contain the first and most definitive explanations of Aum (om) as the divine word, the cosmic vibration that underlies all existence and comprises multiple trinities of being and principles colligated into its One Self.

List of Upanishads

The eleven principal (mukhya) Upanishads that were commented upon by Shankara, and that are accepted as shruti by most Hindus are as follows.

1. Ishavasyopanishad
2. Kenopanishad
3. Kathopanishad
4. Mandukyopanishad
5. Mundakopanishad
6. Prashnopanishad
7. Taittiriyopanshid
8. Aiteryopanishad
9. Brihadaranyopanishad
10. Chhandogyopanishad
11. Shwetashvataropanishad

The Jaiminiya Upanishad brahmana that comprises the Kena Upanisad is as old as the Brhadaranyaka Upanisad. All these 15 Upanishads are the oldest ones, all of them dating to before the Common Era. From linguistic evidence, the oldest among them are the B[hadâraGyaka, Chândogya Upanishads and the Jaiminîya UpanisadbrâhmaGa, belonging to the late Vedic Sanskrit period; of nearly the same age are the Aitareya, Kausîtaki and Taittirîya Upanisads, while the remaining ones date to the transition from Vedic to Classical Sanskrit.

Shakta Upanishads

The canonical Shakta Upanishads are sectarian tracts reflecting doctrinal and interpretative differences between the two principal sects of Srividya upasana (a major Tantric form of Shaktism). As a result, a number of surviving listings of "authentic" Shakta Upanisads are highly variable as to content, inevitably reflecting the sectarian bias of their compilers:

"Past efforts to construct lists of Shakta Upanisads have left us no closer to understanding either their 'location' in Tantric custom or their place within the Vedic corpus. At stake for the Tantric is not the authority of sruti per se, which remains largely undisputed, but rather its correct interpretation. For non-Tantrics, [it is a text's] Tantric contents that brings into question its identity as an Upanishad. At issue is the text's classification as sruti and thus its inherent authority as Veda." The list excludes several notable and widely used Shakta Upanishads, comprising the Kaula Upanishad, the Úrîvidyâ Upanishad and the Œrichakra Upanishad.

The Smritis

In contrast to the Shruti literature, which comprises revelations, the Smriti literature is a product of human intellect. It comprises the works of various individuals who base their information and interpretations upon the Vedas. Smriti means that which is based upon memory. It is the literature produced out of human intellect. It is a sacred literature that is intellectual in origin and meant for the motive of human welfare. Strictly speaking all scriptures which are not shruti or divine in origin come under this classification.

However, standard classification comprises only those works that are based upon the knowledge contained in the Vedas. These are the law books known as Dharma shastras. They deal with various aspects of human life and social organization. They instruct how an individual should conduct himself or herself in society in the light of the caste to which the individual belongs. They define the rules and roles for various groups of individuals in the society. The topics range from such issues as the status, duties and responsibilities prescribed for the four chief castes, remedies against possible transgression of the prescribed laws and also remedies for divine retribution.

From the presently remaining Dharmashastras four are regarded to be very significant: They are the works of Manu, Yagjnavalkya, Sankha, and Parasara. Of these the first one known as Manusmriti is the most popular. Known as Manavadharma shastra, or the scripture of human laws, Manusmriti was regarded in ancient Hindu society as the ultimate guide book for human conduct and social and religious behavior. It provided guidelines for the Hindus to conduct themselves in line with their social order and religious duties.

However, it is also said that these four works were supposed to provide guidance to people during the four great ages called the Maha Yugas: the Manu-smriti for the first great age called Sat Yug, the Yagnavalkya-smriti for the second great age called Treta Yug, the Sankha-smriti for the third great epoch called Dvapar Yug and the Parasara-smriti for the present and the last great epoch called Kali Yug. In recent times the Hindu law books have drawn widespread criticism from a number of quarters due to their preferential treatment of certain castes against the others and their narrow minded and one-sided approach to such sensitive subjects as the status of women and the process of creation.

Even after everything and having quite good knowledge we cannot deny the fact that the Law Books were particularly unkind and insensitive to the lower castes and women, it is however significant to remember that the dharma shastras do not enjoy the same status as the Vedas. They need not inevitably be accepted as final authority on any issue, unless your own sense of justice agrees with them. Unlike the Vedas they are neither eternal nor fallible since they are products of human intellect and social and political circumstances. They are not derived from the Divine directly. They are developed in a particular age, As per the demands and general awareness of that age. Due to this they are prone to be defective and controversial. Hence in the event of any doubt or dispute regarding any information contained in these scriptures, one should check whether the data is line with the tenets of the Vedas and if it is not we can safely set it aside. The Vedas do not discriminate between man and woman. Nor do they suggest any caste discrimination. A Hindu is just Hindu in all forms.

BHAGAVAD GITA

The most sacred text of the Hindu religion Bhagavad Gita is a self-contained episode of seven hundred verses embedded in one book of the great Sanskrit epic, the Mahabharata. It is also the archetype of that necessarily modern phenomenon, the classic of world spirituality. Over the same period the Gita has assumed for a number of Hindus a universal status, so that it is regarded not only as the quintessential Hindu religious text, but also as a charter for all types of frequently contravening social and political action.

One fact for the Gita's universality is its capacity to bear almost any shade of interpretation, because of the variegated nature of its contents. While this shows the fact that the Gita is and always has been a live religious text, with an obviously limitless capacity to inspire new and necessarily valid meanings, from the perspective of the custom in which they are coined, it does not imply that all interpretations are equally convincing from the historical and philological perspectives; far from it. Nevertheless, it is often easier for scholarly exegetes and historians (themselves not always immune to bias) to reject other interpretations than to provide completely convincing substitutes.

In original Gita is a religious text, not a philosophical tract. Its motive is to engender and consolidate certain attitudes in its audience, in much the same way as the 'Lord' of the title, Krishna, attempts in a number of ways to lead his interlocutor, Arjuna, from perplexity to understanding and correct action. Although, in the context of the Mahabharata the problem is faced by one of the protagonists, Arjuna, and its resolution allows the action to proceed, for most Hindus the Gita is not simply part of the epic story but a religious teaching, transmitted to them personally by the guru-God Krishna.

The problem hence is not remote or fictional but imminent, and the solution, through the grace of God, is equally accessible. That it is thought to be the word of God and also part of a narrative encompassing, in the words of a Western theatrical adaptation of the Mahabharata, 'the poetical history of mankind', helps us to understand what seems to be a paradoxical fact about the Gita, in the light of its recent history.

Although it has been revered and the object of much exegesis from early in its existence, detailed knowledge of its contents seems not to have penetrated beyond scholarly circles in India until the last hundred years. One fact for this is that the original language of the Gita, Sanskrit, was known only to a relatively small number of pandits; moreover, translations into modern Indian languages, even if regarded desirable, would have necessitated a readership, which in turn necessitated education. Literacy of that kind commenced to come out in India on a significant scale only in the nineteenth century, initially through the medium of English. Moreover, it was not until this period that printing presses were introduced, creating the possibility of the widespread distribution of written material. Before this change, it seems likely that most Indians, if they knew the Gita at all, knew it as part of an orally transmitted and flexible narrative custom, as an adjunct to various rituals, and as material for recitation in a devotional context.

In other words, they might have known and been able to recite certain verses, but they would have had no theological overview of the text. Indeed, for a number of Hindus the situation may not be so very various today: what the Gita is (the word of God) or what it is perceived to represent (the values inherent in Hindu culture) may be more significant than its literal, verse by verse meaning. Moreover, its primary meaning may not be in its metaphysical or philosophical content at all, but in the story it tells, and in the relationship it dramatizes between God and human beings. This is not intended as a denial of the evident fact that some of the Gita's teachings have, in a generalized form, become cornerstones of belief for a number of, if not most Hindus.

But it may serve as a warning to the modern Westerner, catching a book called The Bhagavad Gita and reading it from cover to cover, not to assume that she or he is using, understanding, or valuing the text in ways that are necessarily like to those employed in the custom from which it derives.

Even within scholarly Sanskritic circles, there have been almost as a number of interpretations as interpreters or schools of thought. The history of the meaning of the text, so far as we can trace it, has hence always been that of its commentaries and interpretations, whatever their level of sophistication. Before the modern period, any systematic study of the Gita would always have been from within a particular commentarial custom. This method of approaching the text has been to some extent obscured by recent attempts to present the Gita 'as it is'. But for all their claims, the 'fundamentalists' responsible are of course no freer of interpretative frameworks and presuppositions than their forerunners, who were usually their superiors in rigour and sophistication.

Due to its role in the history of modern Indian culture and its pivotal position in the interaction which has taken place between Indian religions and the West in the last two centuries, study of the Gita continues to be instructive. But there are other, perhaps more significant reasons for the impartial reader to engage with it. (I leave aside what for some may be the most compelling consideration—the question of whether it has some universally valid spiritual or religious value.) Even in translation, even cut loose from a specific custom of commentary, the Gita touches on and develops in its own way a number of key themes from the history of Indian religions, and raises questions that are still debated.

As we shall see, it is the product of a time of transition, and it attempts to reconcile diverging world views. Maybe in that—in Arjuna's predicament, if not the solution to it—lies some of the Gita's appeal to our own age. The Mahabharata, the great epic which provides the Gita with its literary context, has no single author (if one discounts the mythical Vyasa). It belongs to an oral custom that may have its origins in the eighth or ninth century BC. Succeeding generations of reciter-poets added to, expanded on, and elaborated the basic material, which tells of a cataclysmic war between two branches of the same family and their followers. Like a snowball, the epic picked up and incorporated all the significant religious, philosophical, and social changes through which it passed, often juxtaposing layers with little or no attempt at reconciliation.

Nevertheless, certain themes, because they had come to preoccupy Indian religion and culture generally, began to dominate its 'poetical history': the question of what makes up Dharma or the Law (the way things really are and hence the way they should be), how men and women can assume knowledge of that truth, and how they should act in relation to it. By the time the Gita had been incorporated into or crystallized out of the epic (scholars are divided on which is the correct description)—perhaps in some form in the third century BC.

A number of these questions had become acutely significant for what we have come to call the 'Hindu' custom. In fact for this period that custom is more accurately termed 'Brahminical', after the hereditary priestly class or estate which had founded itself and its sacred body of knowledge, the Veda, as the arbiters of orthoprax and orthodox socio-religious conduct and values. This dominance is reflected both in the epic as we now have it and in the Gita.

The fact that the chief protagonists of the Gita are not brahmins at all but members of the equally hereditary warrior or ruling class should not blind us to this. To refer to the Brahminical custom is perhaps misleading, unless it is realized that by the time of the Gita there were a number of movements or tendencies within that custom, not all of them evidently compatible. This led to tensions, the most significant being between those (portrayed as customalists) who enjoined the fulfilment of one's prescribed social and religious duties as a member of the class into which one had been born, and those who recommended resigning that ascribed status altogether in favour of a life of homelessness and spiritual discipline.

In the context of Brahminical texts this divergence had first come to formal light in the early Upanishads (a category of late Vedic texts). It was there too that the essentials of the well-known doctrine of karma and rebirth made their initial seem ance. It is easy to suppose that such a doctrine developed naturally out of the ritualists' world view. The sacrifice is a mechanism for producing a result. Sacrificial action (the Sanskrit word for 'action' is karman), if performed correctly, produces future benefits for the sacrificer. It is hence possible to sacrifice in order to attain a place in another world after death. The responsibility for the correct performance of the ritual lies with the brahmins, the technicians of the sacrifice, who perform the ritual on behalf of the person who desires the result. The effects of the sacrifice are, however, finite, and it has to be continually renewed. So it is not hard to infer that the sacrificially created merit (or food), which was supposed to sustain life in the other world after death, would eventually run out.

At that point one would die again, returning through several natural stages to be reborn in this world, not necessarily as a human being. The cycle is potentially endless, and from this it is a relatively short step to the conclusion that action (karma) pursued for a motive of whatever kind results in a relatively better or worse rebirth, life after life. At about the same time there arose the perception that since embodied existence in this world, or any other, was necessarily impermanent and subject to various ills, then even if some individuals were not suffering now they soon would be, and death was both inevitable and unpleasant.

To be caught in the cycle of death and rebirth was hence not viewed positively, as a form of immortality, but negatively as suffering, and the object was to find a way to escape it. This was not annihilationism, for against continual rebirth was postulated a goal of permanent liberation and bliss, free of physical imperfection and impermanence. The way to this new goal was first formulated in the late Vedic texts in terms of knowledge of the inner meaning of the sacrifice—what holds it together and enables it to work. Presently this was extended to everything that exists: the same principle informs and underlies all things, including the embodied or essential self. The term that was eventually settled on to designate this principle was 'Brahman'.

As per this line of thought, there was essentially no difference between the essence of the individual and Brahman, the principle underlying all things. Consequently, liberation from the cycle of death and rebirth was a matter of gnosis, for by knowing or realizing Brahman (one's own true nature) one would go to Brahman, a permanent, unchanging, and blissful state—a line of thought reiterated in the Gita. Motiveful sacrificial action, indeed, motiveful action of any kind could not help in this; on the contrary, because such actions were linked with a personal desire for specific results, they merely bound one more firmly to the cycle of death and rebirth.

In line with this, the Gita itself defines Yoga as 'evenness of mind', the cultivation of an attitude of non-attachment, based on knowledge of the way things really are, which leads to 'skill in actions', that is, the ability to act without desire. As per the Brahminical orthodoxy, to fulfil one's duty in one of the three higher estates it was necessary to be a sacrificer, and to be a sacrificer it was necessary to be married and take a full part in the social world, the world of desire and motiveful action. Yet as we have seen, as per the Upanishadic analysis this was not conducive to liberation from rebirth and suffering. Only renunciation of the sacrificial and social world would enable the individual to approach that goal. Brahminical orthodoxy came to terms with this challenge by attempting to institutionalize renunciation as an alternative way of life that one could choose to follow after one had served one's apprenticeship as a Vedic student.

This later hardened into a compulsory progression from stage to stage, with renunciation taking place only after one had fulfilled one's duties as a householder and sacrificer. When the Gita was formulated, however, there was clearly still an element of choice. In the broader Indian context, neither was it a matter of a simple choice between orthodox Brahmanical renunciation and life as a ritually bound householder. Other routes, other modes of life were also available to those seeking personal liberation, chief among them the heterodox systems of Jainism and Buddhism, with their rival views of what constituted Dharma (correct behaviour in the light of the way things really are).

Indeed, it was in these heterodox systems that the doctrine of karma first became fully ethicized as a moral law that was universally applicable, regardless of birth, social status, or occupation. And whether to conform to it or not was a matter for the individual alone to decide. A cornerstone of this renunciatory morality was that deliberate injury done to other living beings was wrong and had bad karmic effects for the person doing the injury. This is an ethical stance which provides a direct challenge to Brahminical values for, as we have seen, Brahminical society is divided into four classes or estates, and members of each estate have their own inherent dutyor Dharma.

Persons born into a particular estate follow the inherent duty of that estate. By doing so they help to maintain the natural order of existence and automatically accrue good results; should they deviate from their inherent duty, however, the results will be bad for them personally and for society as a whole. One of the four estates is that of the warrior or ruler, and it is a warrior's duty to fight. This is clearly antithetical to the renunciatory ideal of nonviolence.

From one perspective, therefore, to refrain from violence will bring bad results, but from the other, to engage in it will be similarly disastrous. We are brought back to the Gita, for this is precisely Arjuna's dilemma: to conform to his inherent duty as a warrior and fight, and by doing so slaughter his enemies who are also his kinsmen, or to lay down his arms and disrupt the natural and social order. In other words, the Gita, through Arjuna, addresses the problem of the age: the problem of choice—of how to choose rightly. One of the Gita's chief projects, therefore, is to reconcile or synthesize the discordant ideologies of orthodox Brahminism and renunciation—a discord that is dramatized and personified in the person of Arjuna, who finds himself caught, like Hamlet, between two world-views and two sets of values.

The answer of this difference of opinion is put into the mouth of Krishna, Arjuna's charioteer, comrade-in-arms, teacher, and, as revealed in the Gita, God omnipotent. Krishna offers the distraught warrior what seems like a tier or nest of solutions. What they have in common is that they are all presented as justifications for fighting—hat is to say, for acting in the world, conforming to one's inherent duty, and perpetuating the socioreligious status quo. From the social perspective this is deeply conservative, although what Krishna is Offering in fact is a compromise. He tells Arjuna to act, but to do so without attachment to the results or fruits of his actions. In other words, he must act without desire, and that will ensure that, whatever its immediate physical consequences, the action will have no karmic repercussions for him as the apparent agent of the action. In this way it is possible to experience the soteriological benefits of renunciation without leaving society or abandoning one's inherent duty.

In fact, as per the Krishna, this internal renunciation is really the only way one can renounce, for the nature of material existence is such that it is impossible not to act. Yet, in rejecting the way of the renouncer, Krishna is not thereby necessarily fully endorsing mainstream ritual Brahminism, His prescription to act without attachment to the fruits of action devalues the Brahminical soteriological goal of heaven, which for the orthodox is something to be attained through motiveful ritual. In other words, sacrifice as a means to personal salvation, as opposed to cosmic and social regulation, is rejected by the Gita.

Acting with desire and attachment to the results of action is hence not merely deluded but meaningless. Where does this leave the person seeking liberation from suffering, or salvation? Krishna has already said that those who make over the results of their actions to God go to Him, and indeed that all actions should be sacrificed to Him. But beyond that, one should make such offerings with devotion to God: 'whoever shares in me with single-minded devotion, they are in me and I am in them.' No devotee of Krishna's, regardless of social status or gender, is lost. (Again there is a change in soteriological perspective without the kind of threat to orthodox Brahminical supremacy that external, social renunciation offers.) By thinking on God, by sacrificing one's actions to Him in a spirit of ego-less non-attachment, one can earn God's grace, and through that grace one will attain supreme peace. In effect it is possible to please God by conforming to one's class duty and doing the things one has always done; yet such a strategy can only be theologically effective if accompanied by a radical change of attitude towards those same duty-bound actions, so that they come to be regarded not as one's own but as God's. The last chapter of the Gita spells this out for us, and adds a new, more personal note—one which in various forms came to dominate the relation between God and human beings in later Hindu religion. Even many Hindu says that Gita have all the answers to the problems and worries of the people. If someone is tensed he should read Gita and he will find the answer to his question which is making him tensed and worried.

NON-RELIGIOUS SCRIPTURES

Ramayana

In a broader context Ramayana is an ancient Sanskrit epic attributed to the poet Valmiki and an significant part of the Hindu canon (smrti). The name Ramayana is a tatpurush compound of Ram and ayan "going, advancing", translating to "the travels of Ram". The Ramayana consists of 24,000 verses in seven cantos and tells the story of Raam, whose wife Sita is abducted by the demon (Rakshas) king of Lanka, Ravan. Verses are written in thirty two syllable sex meter called Anustubh.

In its current form, the Valmiki Ramayan is dated from 500 BC. to 100 BC., or about co-eval to early versions of the Mahabharat. As with most customal epics, it has since gone through a long process of interpolations and redactions and thus is impossible to date it accurately. The Ramayan is part of the Itihaas. Valmiki's version is the oldest written form and the most authentic. Customally the epic belongs to the Treta Yug, one of the four eons of Hindu chronology. Ram is said to have been born in the Treta Yug to King Dasharath. The Ramayan had an significant influence on later Sanskrit poetry, primarily through its establishment of the Slok meter. But, like its epic cousin Mahabharat, the Ramayan is not just an ordinary story. It comprises the teachings of ancient Hindu sages and presents them through allegory in narrative and the interspersion of the philosophical and the devotional.

The characters of Ram, Sita, Lakshman, Bharat, Hanuman and Ravana are all fundamental to the cultural consciousness of India. One of the most significant literary works on ancient India, the Ramayan has had a profound impact on art and culture in the Indian subcontinent and Southeast

Asia. The story of Raam also inspired a large amount of latter-day literature in various languages, notable among which are the works of the sixteenth century Hindi poet Tulsidas, Tamil poet Kambar of the 13th century and the 14th century Kannada poet Narahari Kavi‘s Torave Ramayan.

The Ramayan became popular in Southeast Asia during the 8th century and demonstrated itself in text, temple architecture and performance. This is an epic poem of courage, magic and humour, containing 18 books and 24,000 verses divided into 500 songs. Set in India, Rama and his wife Sita have been banished from their kingdom of Kosala for fourteen years, due to a plot by the mother of one of Rama's four brothers to keep Rama from the throne. Rama's brother, Laksmana, accompanies the couple. King Rawana of Ceylon spies the beautiful Sita and creates a plan to abduct her. He sends one of his minions, magically disguised as a golden deer to entice Rama and Laksmana away from Sita. Rama goes after the deer, instructing Laksmana not to leave Sita. Rama brings down the golden deer with his bow and arrow.

The golden deer returns to its original shape and with its dying breath calls out "Help, help, help" in Rama's voice. Sita, hearing Rama's voice, entreats Laksmana to go and help Rama. When he refuses, she goads him into leaving. Laksmana draws a magic circle around Sita and tells her that she must stay inside it until he and Rama return. When Sita is alone, Rawana seem s, disguised as an ailing old man, who begs Sita for help. When Sita steps out of the magic circle to aid the old man, the old man changes into Rawana and abducts Sita, telling her that Rama is dead. He rises in the air with her and flies to his Kingdom. Jatayu, King of the Birds, (also known as Garuda) spies Rawana carrying off Sita and they battle in the air. Rawana delivers a fatal wound to Jatayu who falls to the ground, where he is discovered by Rama and Laksmana. Jatayu is near death and manages to tell Rama of his failure to rescue Sita.

Both Lord Rama and Laksmana travel onward and enlist the aid of the army of wanaras, a race of huge monkeys. Sugriwa, King of the wanaras, agrees to help Rama rescue Sita in return for Rama's support of Sugriwa's attempt to regain his rightful throne in the land of Guakiskenda. When Sugriwa meets his nemesis, Subali, Rama saves Sugriwa's life with a magic arrow which kills Subali. After Sugriwa is crowned King of Guakiskenda, the white monkey general, Hanuman, is sent to Alengka (Ceylon) to scout the defences and to deliver Rama's ring to Sita, so that she would know that Rama was alive. After a narrow escape from the stomach of Wikateksi, the enormous sea monster which guarded the approaches to Alengka, Hanuman kills Wikateksi and flies to the capital of Alengka, the kingdom of the giants. Luckily, there are a number of monkeys living among the giants, which provide cover for Hanuman, who reduces his size. He looks everywhere in the city for Sita. Finally Hanuman finds Rawana's palace and the women's quarters. Hanuman meets Sita in the garden and gives her Rama's ring, which she recognizes at once, and tells her that Rama is on his way to saving her.

In order to test the power of the city, Hanuman resumes his normal size, climbs to the top of a tall building and hurls a challenge to the awestruck crowd below. He begins to destroy the buildings around him by using an uprooted palm tree as a club. He is felled by an arrow shot by the crown prince of Alengka, Hindrajit. Hanuman is shackled in chains and sentenced to die by slow fire. Hanuman appeals to Agni, the god of fire, to save him. A wall of flame springs up between Hanuman and the watching crowd. With a burst of strength, Hanuman breaks his bonds, and swinging a glowing torch picked up from the fire, goes on a rampage which ends in the burning of a large part of the city. Assuring himself that Sita's pavilion is safe, Hanuman leaps into the air and flies back to Guakiskenda. After hearing of Hanuman's exploits, Rama adopts him as his own son.

The army then heads for Alengka, which they find surrounded by a boiling sea. By hurling huge boulders into the sea, the monkey soldiers build a causeway to the island. Rawana learns of the invasion and assembles his generals. Some of the generals resent Rawana's evil rule, but heretofore have lacked the courage to oppose him. Wibishana, Rawana's brother, as spokesman, points out that it was because Rawana abducted Sita that Alengka is now beset by enemy armies. He suggests that Rawana release Sita and avoid bloodshed and loss of life and property. Angered, Rawana strikes Wibishana, who then deserts to Rama's army. Rawana is tempted to murder Sita, but is thwarted by Trijata, Wibishana's beautiful daughter, who has grown to love Sita as a sister. Rawana turns to another brother, the giant Kumbhakarna, who although rejecting of Rawana's crimes and baseness, decides to help because they are of the same blood. After a number of guerilla attacks by the monkey soldiers, the two armies ultimately face each other.

Two opponent generals, Kumbakarna and Laksmana challenge each other. Kumbhakarna is killed by Laksmana's magic arrow. Other duels take place on the battlefield. Rama spots Rawana and pursues him, shooting showers of arrows, which seem to have no effect on Rawana other than to make him back off. Rawana backs in between two unusually formed rocks which snap together and hold him in an inescapable grip. These rocks are inhabited by the souls of two of his daughters, who Rawana had murdered, and who are at last able to avenge themselves on their father. Rawana's army surrenders and Rama gives the throne of Alengka to Wibisana. Rama and Sita are joyfully united. The fourteen years of exile being over, Rama, Sita and Laksmana return to Kosala, where they are welcomed by all.

However, rumors circulate about Sita's virtue. She offers to test her virtue by fire. She enters the ring of fire and emerges unscathed, her faithfulness confirmed. When the rumors persist, she leaves the palace for the spiritual life. The Ramayana story is especially significant to Hindus because it is possible for ordinary people to identify with the characters and situations. The heroes and heroines are emulated for their positive qualities of honesty, devotion, perseverance, fidelity, and bravery. Strongly apparent in this story is the portrayal of pure evil and those who have the courage to resist and overcome that evil. So the moral of the Ramanaya is that truth always wins over the evil.

Mahabharat

Just like Ramanaya, Mahabharata is another Sanskrit epics of ancient India, the other being the Ramayana. With more than 74,000 verses, long prose passages, and about 1.8 million words in total, the Mahabharata is one of the longest epic poems in the world. Including the Harivamsa, the Mahabharata has a total length of more than 90,000 verses. It is of immense significance to the culture of India and Nepal, and is a major text of Hinduism. Its discussion of human goals (artha or wealth, kama or pleasure, Dharma or duty/harmony, and moksha or liberation) takes place in a long-standing custom, attempting to explicate the kinship of the individual to society and the world (the nature of the 'Self') and the workings of karma. The title may be translated as the great tale of the Bharata Dynasty, as per the Mahabharata's own testimony extended from a shorter version simply called Bharata of 24,000 verses The epic is part of the Hindu itihasa, literally "that which happened", which includes the Ramayana and the Puranas.

Customally, Hindus ascribe the Mahabharata to Vyasa. Because of its immense length, its philological study has a long history of attempts to unravel its historical growth and composition layers.

Its earliest layers date back to the late Vedic period (5 BC.) and it probably reached its final form in the early Gupta period (4 AD.). Mahabharat, (or Mahabharata as it is known in English), is the longest poem in the world, made up of 220,000 lines divided into 18 sections. It was written in Sanskrit, the ancient sacred language of India and it tells the story of a great battle that occurred about 3000 years back. It was on the banks of river Saraswati that saint Ved Vyas wrote Mahabharat, approximately in 900 BC. Lord Krishna preached 'Bhagvad Gita', the gospel of duty, to Arjun at the on set of the great battle of Mahabharat. Since then, this profound philosophy of the supremacy of duty has became the foundation of Hinduism, Indian culture and thought.

Dhritarashter and Pandu were born to Bhisham's brothers. Dhritarashter was born blind and though the elder, he had to forfeit his claim to the throne due to this physical defect. Pandu became king. Of the two brothers Dhritarashter married Gandhari, whereas Pandu, the younger had two wives, Kunti and Madri. Gandhari was so devoted to her husband that she bandaged her eyes, not to enjoy anything that she could not share with her royal husband, and thus remained voluntarily blind for life. She became the mother of the Kouravs, 100 in total, whereas Kunti got three sons and Madri two. One day while hunting, Pandu accidentally killed the wife of a sage, who got enraged and cursed Pandu that if ever he had intercourse with a woman, he would die instantly.

Pandu resigned his crown to become a hermit and went to the jungle with his two wives, Kunti and Madri. But one day, Pandu couldn't resist himself and had intercourse with Madri and thus died. Madri immolated herself and walked into her husband's funeral fire leaving behind her two sons Nakul and Sahadev in custody of Kunti who already had three sons Yudhishthir, Bheem and Arjun. On Pandu's death Dhritarashter became the king and the five sons of Pandu, known as the Pandavs grew up in the guardianship of Kunti. The five Pandav princes were educated along with Kourav boys under the supervision of Bhisham and the patronage of Dhritarashter. Drone, though a Brahmin was a very skilful and efficient teacher, who taught them the art of archery and the various techniques of warfare.

Yudhishthir, the eldest of the Pandavs, was so righteous that he gained the name Dharamputr. Bheem was a giant in physical strength. Arjun was handsome and the most skilful archer. Dharamputr was the beloved of the people and being the eldest among the 105 princes, was naturally, and by his right too, the heir to the throne. Duryodhan, the eldest of the Kouravs, however was jealous of the Pandavs and tried every means to destroy them. When Yudhishthir was proclaimed king, Duryodhan could not sit quiet and watch. Dhritarashter loved all the 105 princes alike, and there was no partiality in his mind between his own sons and the nephews, the Pandavs. The great blind royal father, came under the bad influence of Duryodhan and, though directly not an evil-doer, was in sympathy with his son's letdowns and sorrows.

Duryodhan's plan to kill the Pandavs cunningly giving poison to Bheem, burning down the lac-house etc., failed miserably. Bheem was strong enough to digest the poison. The Pandavs were warned in time by their uncle Vidur and so in the darkness of the night the five brothers along with their mother escaped into the jungle from the burning lac-house. After their miraculous escape from the lac-house, they did not return to the palace. They roamed about in the guise of Brahmins with their mother. Every one including the Kouravs believed them to be dead.

While wandering in the guise, they heard of the Swayamvara of Droupadi. The qualification to marry her lay in the extraordinary skill of archery in hitting a moving target. Arjun easily won. Everybody congratulated the winner, and discovered that it was Arjun. Thus the Pandavs were found out, He took his bride to their hut and called to his mother to come outside and see what he had brought. Instead of doing so, she answered back "My dear children, whatever it be, you share it among yourselves". Therefore, Droupadi became the common wife of all the five Pandavs. Krishna, who was also present, at the marriage ceremony became a great friend of the Pandavs from then onwards.

On Bhisham's advice, the kingdom was divided into two parts. Naturally the better half was taken away by the Kouravs. Still, the others built a wonderful city in their own half and called it Indraprastha. Duryodhan watching the increasing prosperity of the Pandavs and could contain himself no longer. He openly challenged Dharamputr for a game of dice, Sakuni, deceit in human form, was the uncle of the Kouravs. He played for them. Inevitably Dharamputr lost everything - his kingdom, his brothers and also his wife. Not satisfied with this gain, Duryodhan tried to insult Droupadi in public. By Lord Krishna's grace, nothing disastrous happened. Dhritarashter, fearing that this might bring unforeseen calamities begged Droupadi to take whatever she wanted. She asked for the freedom of her husbands. It was granted. Dhritarashter due to his excessive love for the eldest son was blind to what is right and what is wrong.

So again Duryodhan invited Dharamputr for another game of dice, and the bet was that the losers would live in the forest for 13 years without any claim to the kingdom, the last year however to be spent incognito. But if in the thirteenth year, they were detected, again a round of 13 years' exile; and this would go on forever. Dharamputr lost again.

During the twelve years in the forests, the Pandavs visited a number of holy places. They had a number of interesting adventures at this time. One of them led to Hanuman's friendship and grace. Arjun is called Kapidhvaja as he keeps on his flag the emblem of Hanuman. Krishna visited them now and then. Arjun, at the advice of Vyasa, practiced penance, propitiated Siva and got from Him the mighty weapon, the Pasupatastra. He propitiated also the other gods Indra, Agni, Varuna and others and got from all of them very powerful weapons.

Thus the twelve years were not wasted but spent in securing the divine weapons, which would become useful later on. In the 13th year, hiding all their weapons in the hollow of a tree in a burial ground, all the Pandavs with Droupadi went to the palace of the king of the Viratas and stayed there as servants. Duryodhan was making frantic efforts to discover them. When he heard about the strange murder of Kichaka the brother-in-law of the king, he concluded that the Pandavs must be in the Virata country. So the Kouravs attacked the Viratas, with evident motive of carrying away its cattle-wealth. Of course the Pandavs took part in the battle, but when they were recognized as Pandavs the time limit of thirteen years had already passed.

Dharamputr was fond of peace, and was ever against any quarrel, much less war. So he sent Krishna as a messenger to Hastinapura to claim his kingdom back from Duryodhan. But Duryodhan had by this time come to regard Indraprastha as his own. He not only refused to give their kingdom back, but refused to give even 5 houses for the five brothers to live! War had to be declared. This is the great war fought at Kurukshetra to decide the right of claim. The hundred Kouravs, Bhisham, Drone, Asvathama, etc., were on one side and the Pandavs, Krishna, Drupada, etc., were on the other. Krishna did not in realfight. He was the charioteer of Arjun and hence He is called Parthasarathy. Krishna was very impartial. He gave his army to the Kouravs and himself offered to serve the Pandavs.

The Kourav and the Pandav armies arrayed themselves for the war. The Kouravs planned their attacks under the supervision of Bhisham, and under Bheem's management the Pandava army marched into formation. This is the point at which Arjun has second thoughts about fighting in the battle. Krishna gives Arjun good advise that brings back his war-spirit. This advice is known as: The Bhagvad-Gita. All the Kourav princes died in this battle, and Yudhishthir became king. He continued to reign until he felt that he had completed his life's work. Then he renounced the throne and set out for heaven with the other Pandavs and their wife, Droupadi. With them also went a dog which represented Dharma, the god of duty and moral law. After more adventures, the Pandavs were ultimately united in heaven.

The whole story, which forms the chief theme of the Mahabharat, makes up only about a quarter of the poem. The Mahabharat comprises a number of other popular stories, including the tales of Nala and Damayanti, Savitri and Satyawan, Rama, and Shakuntala. The battle of Kurukshetra offers an opportunity to discuss military strategy, there is also a mention of a board game Chaturanga, from which the modern day Chess originated. But the underlying theme of the Mahabharat concerns moral duty and right conduct.

The long and complex dispute that divides the royal family of Bharat affords an opportunity to explain the duties and conduct expected of a king. It also shows the ideals of behaviour for subjects, soldiers, religious hermits, and people suffering misfortune. Sage Ved Vyasa is customally regarded as the author of the Mahabharat, but he is more likely to have been its compiler. The epic seems to be a collection of writings by several authors who lived at various times. The oldest parts are probably about 3,000 years old, while others can be traced to as late as AD 500.

The significance of Krishna as the chief god of this epic developed in Hindu thought between 200 BC and AD 200. As a result, the Mahabharat can be used to trace the spread and development of Vaishnavite thought in Hinduism. The god Vishnu became a very personal deity for his worshippers through his seem ance as Krishna, the adviser and friend of Prince Arjun in the Mahabharat. About 1,300 greatly varying manuscripts of the Mahabharat survive today. All of them show the poem in its later form because the earliest of them goes back only to the 1400's. The most famous addition to the Mahabharat is the Bhagvad-Gita. It occurs in the sixth book and is now the most widely recognized of Hinduism's sacred texts.

The Bhagavad Gita tells how Arjun, the third of the Pandav princes, has misgivings about whether he should be fighting his cousins, the Kouravs. Krishna, speaking with the authority of the god Vishnu, persuades him that his action is just, and then Arjun's military skill becomes a deciding factor in the ensuing Pandav victory. The teachings of the Bhagavad-Gita are fundamental to Hinduism. As already mentioned Gita is most sacred text of the Hindus and it comprises such verses and explanations which can bring a man out of his everyday worries.

The Puranas

According to the Hindu custom Puranas, part of Hindu Smriti, are religious scriptures that confer devotion and mythology. They are the richest collection of customal stories and teachings based on the spiritual philosophy of the Vedas and the Upanishads. These ancient books teach Hinduism in an easy and interesting way and provide information of all kinds. Purana means 'old' and were compiled by Sage Vyasa.

As per the Amara Simha, an ancient Sanskrit lexicographer, Purana must have five distinguishing topics - 1) Creation of Universe, 2) Its destruction and renovation, 3) The genealogy of gods and patriarchs, 4) The reigns of Manus and 5)The history of the solar and lunar races of kings.

Basically focusing on Vishnu, Shiva, Lord Brahma and Shakti there are eighteen major Puranas and some minor ones, known as Upa Puranas. A large portion of each Purana deals with the incarnation of Lord Vishnu and his glorification. Apart from this, stories of Gods and Goddesses, hymns, an outline of ancient history, cosmology, rules of life and rituals, holy places, and instructions on spiritual knowledge are the significant contents of the Puranas. Out of the 18 puranas, six are Sattvic Puranas and glorify Vishnu; six are Rajasic and glorify Lord Brahma; six are Tamasic and they glorify Lord Shiva. Vishnu Purana, Naradiya Purana, Padma Purana, Garuda Purana, Varaha Purana, Bhagavata Purana are Sattvic Puranas. Brahmanda Purana, Brahmavaivarta Purana, Markandeya Purana, Bhavishya Purana, Vamana Purana, Brahma Purana are Rajasic Puranas. Matsya Purana, Kurma Purana, Linga Purana, Shiva Purana, Skanda Purana and Agni Purana are Tamasic Puranas. Puranas chiefly inculcate the teachings of Vedas and Upanishads in a simple manner through concrete instances, myths, stories, legends, lives of saints, kings and great men, allegories and chronicles of great historical events. They mainly tell about the stories of Hindu Gods and Goddesses.

Brahma Purana: The Brahma Purana contains two parts- Purva Bhaag and Uttar Bhaag. Purva Bhaag comprises tales of creation, description of Lord Rama and Lord Krishna. Uttar Bhaag comprises a detailed description of Purshottam Tirtha prominent among all the holy places.

Padma Purana: The Padma Purana contains five parts. In the first part, sage Pulastya explains the essence of religion to Bheeshma. The second part comprises a description of the earth. Third part comprises tales of creation as well as geographical description of India. Fourth part describes the life of Lord Rama. In the fifth part, essential knowledge of religion has been discussed in dialogue style between Lord Shiva and Parvati.

Vishnu Purana: The Vishnu Purana also comprises five parts. First part narrates about the creation of the universe, Pralay and churning of the sea. Second part comprises geographical description of earth divided into seven islands. Third part describes about the origin of Buddhism. Fourth part comprises a description about the populating of the earth from the beginning. Fifth part is entirely devoted to the life and plays of Lord Krishna and his acts in Vrindavan.

Skanda Purana: The Skanda Purana is the largest Purana. It is mainly devoted to Kartikeya (Skanda), the son of Lord Shiva and Parvati. Besides, it comprises a lot of tales related to Lord Shiv and a number of holy places of pilgrimage devoted conspicuously to Shiv.

Shiv Mahapurana: The Shiv Mahapurana is also a huge compilation of tales devoted primarily to the life and plays of Lord Shiva. It is divided into seven Samhitas, which together contain more than twenty-four thousand stanzas.

Vamana Purana: The Vamana Purana is completely devoted to Vaman avtaar (incarnation) of Lord Vishnu narrated in dialogue style between the sage Pulastya and Narad.

Markandeya Purana: The Markandeya Purana commences with a question put forth by sage Jobjectiveini. In reply to this question, sage Markandeya narrates what constitutes the subject matter of this Purana.

Varaha Purana: The Varha Purana comprises the tale of rescue of the earth by 'Varaha' avtaar (boar incarnation) of Lord Vishnu.

Brahma Vaivat Purana: The Brahma Vaivat Purana comprises four parts. First part comprises the tale of creation. Second part comprises tales related to goddesses. Third part comprises tales related to Lord Ganesh. In the fourth part, tales related to the life and plays of Lord Krishna have been given.

Agni Purana: The Agni Purana is devoted to Agni. It is presented in preaching style by Agni to sage Vashishta. It comprises the description of various incarnations of God, Lord Rama and Krishna as well as of the earth and stars.

Bhavishya Purana: The Bhavishya Purana comprises five Parvas (parts). The first part comprises description of creation. Second, third and fourth parts contain detailed description of Lord Shiva, Lord Vishnu and Surya respectively. In the fifth part, description of heaven has been given.

Kurma Purana: It is said that Lord Himself has narrated this Purana in Kurma (tortoise) incarnation to Narad. Narad narrated it to Sutaji who in his term narrated it to an assembly of great sages.

Matsya Purana: The Tales of Lord's fish incarnation and preservation of Manu and the seeds of all life during Pralay by Matsya avtaar is the chief theme of this Purana.

Garuda Purana: In Garuda Purana, Lord Vishnu preaches his vehicle, Garuda about the subtleties of religion and life. Besides, trivial tales related to religion and moral, this Purana also contains description of diamond like jewels and the ways to identify best kind of jewels.

Brahmaand Purana: Brahamaand Puarana is the last of the eighteen Puranas. Presently it is available in various pieces and no connection seems to exist between them. Once, it had contained Aadhyatma Ramayana.

Shrimad Bhagwat Purana: Due to of its beautiful presentation style, Shrimad Bhagwat Purana has a high rank in Sanskrit literature. It comprises tales related to various incarnations of Lord Vishnu and mainly deals with the life and plays of Lord Krishna.

Linga Purana: Preaching about the glory of Lord Shiva and Linga Puja is the chief objective of this Purana. In two parts, this Purana comprises tales related to the creation of the universe, origin of Linga, and of all the Vedas, Brahma, Vishnu etc. from this Linga.

Narad Purana: It is a Vaishnav Purana presented in a style of dialogue between Narad and Sanat kumar. This Purana comprises detailed description of major places of pilgrimage.

In this way the whole Hindu religion its rules and laws, duties and ways of worshipping, do's and don't's all are well written in the books, its not just the word of mouth and told orally.

REFERENCES

Azad, A. K.: *India Wins Freedom*, London: Sangam Books, 1988.

Bacchetta, P.: '*Hindu Nationalist Women as Ideologues*' in Jayawardena and de Alwis eds, 1996.

Badrinath, C.: *Dharma, India and the World Order, Edinburgh*: Saint Andrew Press, 1993.

Banerjee, S.: '*The woman Shiv Sainik and her sister Swayamsevika*' in Sarkar and Butalia eds, 1995.

Basu, A: '*Feminism inverted: the gendered imagery and real women of Hindu nationalism*' in Sarkar and Butalia eds., 1995.

Basu, K. and Subrahmanyam, S.: *Unravelling the Nation: sectarian conflict and India's secular identity*, New Delhi: Penguin Books, 1996.

Braaten, C.: "*The Problem of the Absoluteness of Christianity*" Interpretation 40/4, October 1986.

Carman, J., and V. Narayanan: *The Tamil Veda: Pillan's Interpretation of the Tiruvaymoli*. Chicago, University of Chicago, 1989.

Chapman, M.: '*Theology as Vocation'- Ernst Troeltsch as Philosophical Theologian*" Ph.D. diss., Oxford University, 1988.

Clayton, J. P.: *Ernst Troeltsch and the Future of Theology. Cambridge*, Cambridge University, 1976.

Clooney, F. X.: "*The Tiruvaymoli of Shatakopan*, 1998.

DiNoia, J. A.: *The Diversity of Religions: A Christian Perspective*, Washington, D.C.: Catholic University of America, 1992.

Hume, R. E.: *The Thirteen Principle Upanishads*, Delhi: Oxford University, 1931.

J. Mascaró: *The Bhagavad Gita*, New York, Penguin, 1962.

7

Teachings

Some of the primary teachings of Hinduism contain elaborate explanations of the essence of life! Who is a human being, what is our relationship with the lower forms like insects, plants and animals, who is God Almighty, how is big bang created, why God Almighty produced the Cosmos, the doctrine of karma, meaning of Dharma, the importance of meditation and yoga, practicing absolute celibacy, moving on the path of absolute truthfulness, what is a soul atman, relationship between a soul atman and God Almighty etc. are some of the queries the answers of which can be found in Bhagavad Gita... the doctrine given to mankind by Lord Krishna in Mahabharata!

The Dharma in real according to Hinduism is a set of norms for people's behaviour, including that of the king. It is not made by kings, though kings are particularly responsible for enforcing it. Nor is it made by the gods, since the gods themselves are subject to dharma. An older form of the word, used in the hymns of the Rig-Veda, means 'support, decree, arrangement, order', and dharma is often explained as something which supports society as well as ordering it. Another meaning of the word is 'natural property'. It is the dharma of fire to burn, for example , and the dharma of water to extinguish fire. Animals also have their dharma, which is their natural behaviour: it is the dharma of the lion to kill and eat the deer, and it is the dharma of the deer to eat grass and to flee from the lion. Animals have little or no choice in their behaviour; like inanimate objects such as water and fire, they just follow their dharma. People, however, have a choice whether to follow their dharma or not, and in this context we may translate the word as 'morality' or 'law'. As we saw, because people have free will they earn merit or demerit - good or bad karma - by their actions, which animals do not.

Dharma tells us which actions are meritorious and which are not, and may also tell us what kinds of rebirth or other consequence will be their reward or punishment. In modern times the word dharma is often used to translate 'religion', and Hindus sometimes prefer to speak of 'Hindu dharma' rather than 'Hinduism'. In the context of the historical encounter of Hindus with Muslims, Christians and others, the differences that were most noticeable between these communities were differences of behaviour: how they dressed, what they ate, what patterns of marriage they followed, how they worshipped, and so on.

These are differences of dharma; in Western terms they are religious differences, so the word came to be translated 'religion'. However, it does not refer to religious belief, but only to behaviour, and includes matters that may be regarded outside the sphere of religion, such as the administration of justice in law-courts. While dharma applies to every human being, it is especially the concern of the king. The king's responsibility for the behaviour of his subjects is understood in terms of karma. A sixth share of everyone's merit belongs to the king who protects them, and a sixth share of their demerit belongs to the king who does not protect them. Whatever Veda-study, sacrifice, gifts, or worship a man executes, the king receives a sixth share of it as his due for protecting him.

However, this statement uses the analogy of the share of the produce of the land (often more than a sixth) which the king received as revenue. In the same way he receives a share of his subjects' good or bad karma, since whatever good they do is due in part to his protection, and whatever evil they do is due in part to his neglect. Dharma is one of the three worldly objectives, the other two being worldly power (artha, which includes wealth and political power) and pleasure (Kama). Though these objectives are often said to be those of everyone, or at least of every man, the discussions of them in ancient texts suggest that they are primarily the concerns of kings. They are listed in descending order of significance; the pursuit of pleasure is acceptable so long as it does not interfere with the pursuit of wealth and power, and these should not be sought at the expense of dharma. Beyond these three is the surpassing objective of salvation.

SPIRITUAL TEACHINGS

The Brahman supersedes all the Vedic devas in the Upanishads. Earlier texts had already deprived the gods of their ultimate superiority by making their existence dependent on creation. The gods came into existence after creation, and only gained their power and immortality through the sacrificial ritual. The supreme place now belonged to Brahman, conceptualized as a Supreme Deity in some texts and an impersonal Absolute in others. A passage in the Brihadaranyaka Upanishad identify the devas as the various powers of the Brahman. Here, the sage Yajnavalkya is asked how a number of gods there are. He says that there are 3306 gods. Asked again how a number of gods there are really, he says there are 33.

This process of reduction continues until he says there is only one god. Later he defines that One as Brahman. The term used for Brahman in this passage is sutra-atman, "thread-Self; the Self which passes like a thread through the universe." This name for Brahman emphasizes its role as the underlying fabric of the universe. But Brahman is also called the antaryamin, the "Inner Controller" that exists within each being. The Upanishads devote great energy to discussing the relationship between the external, cosmic aspect of Brahman and its internal aspect, usually called atman. The atman is the true Self within the individual person, the immortal, pure essence of each being.

One of the most famous passages describing the relation of Brahman and atman is a conversation between Shvetaketu and his father in the Chandogya Upanishad. Shvetaketu is instructed to break open the seed of a tree and describe what he sees. He finds nothing. His father points out that from the subtle essence of the seed which he cannot see, a great tree may grow. The whole world has this same subtle essence for its Self. The father then asks his son to dissolve salt in water and teaches him that just as the salt, which is not visible, pervades and cannot be separated from the water, so too the Brahman pervades the individual. The Brahman within the individual is called the atman. This teaching is punctuated with the refrain tat tvam asi, "You are That." In this equation, You means atman and That means Brahman. The concept of an individual, eternal atman that is identified with the universal Brahman changed the context and goals of religious practices. In the early Vedic hymns, the goal of the sacrifice was to procure the beneficence of the gods to ensure a good life on earth, and a safe trip to heaven after death. But in the Upanishads, the gods are no longer supreme and their heavenly abode is not a lasting, final goal. In this era, the belief in a single life span was replaced by a system of reincarnation called samsara, the cycle of rebirths. As per the this system, at death one would pass on to a life in heaven or hell, depending on the merits of one's activities in life. Then, after a certain amount of time, the individual would be reborn on earth once again.

The mechanism that governed this system was karman, a word that literally means "action." Every action must have an effect. So, the effects of one's actions in life determine what one will experience after death, and what kind of life one will have in the next birth. In this way, even if a person does not seem to receive all the rewards or punishments deserved in a particular life, the scales will be balanced in the future. The only way to stop this cycle of rebirths is to achieve moksha, "liberation" from samsara. This liberation is attained through knowledge. When one truly understands the nature of the Brahman, and hence the true nature of one's own self (the atman), then there is no more accumulation of karman and the individual is not reborn again. The Upanishads make it clear that this liberating knowledge of Brahman is separate from the old wisdom of the Vedas, which is now described as "lower knowledge" that only serves to prepare one for the "higher" knowledge of Brahman.

The descriptions of the principles and the nature of their relationships change, but the idea of a pair playing a role in the process of creation recurs, and the description of the universe as governed by the three qualities of purity, activity, and inertia becomes part of most Indian philosophies. Later customs elaborate and improve on the older cosmogonies in order to include various beliefs, but the idea that enlightenment necessitates the personal acquisition of knowledge about the true nature of the self and the cosmos remains constant. Yoga, as a system of discipline through which one can retrace the process of creation and gain higher knowledge, has an significant place in Hindu customs.

REDEMPTION

The liberation from the cycle of death and rebirth and attainment of the highest spiritual state is called Redemption. It is the ultimate goal, where even hell and heaven are temporary. This is called Moksha (liberation). Moksha is a final release from one's worldly conception of self, the loosening of the shackles of experiential duality and a re-establishment in one's own fundamental nature, though the nature is seen as ineffable and beyond sensation. The actual state of salvation is seen variously depending on one's beliefs. In Advaita, a monistic philosophy, which comprises most forms of Shaivism and some forms of Vaishnavism, it is oneness with Brahman, without form or being, something that essentially is without expression.

In dualist Hinduism, as found mostly in various forms of Vaishnavism, it is union or close association with God. In Hinduism, moksha occurs when the individual soul (human mind/spirit) or atman recognizes its identity with the Ground of all being - the Source of all phenomenal existence known as Brahman. The religion recognizes several paths to achieve this state, none of which is exclusive. They are the ways of selfless work (Karma Yoga), of self-dissolving love (Bhakti Yoga), of absolute discernment & knowledge (Jnana Yoga), and of 'royal' meditative immersion (Raja Yoga). Shiva swallowed the poison (halahala), so that it would not kill the creation. Shiva's act is celebrated at the Hindu festival Shivratri.

DEVOTION TO GOD

One of the Hindu beliefs which is most widespread is that a person's destiny is formed by his or her actions, so that each action we perform will have an effect on us in the future, and each thing that happens to us is the result of something we have done in the past. This belief does not enable us to define Hinduism, since it is also held by Buddhists and Jains, while even among Hindus it takes various forms. It is often referred to as karma (or karman; these are merely two English versions of the same Sanskrit word). This word (and related words in other Indian languages) means 'action, deed' in Sanskrit, but it is used in English to stand for the whole uninterrupted process whereby we shape our destiny through our actions, each action having its effect, or fruit as it is often called in Indian languages.

Karma

The process of karma does not cease at death: when we die we shall be born again in another body, to consume the fruit of our previous deeds. This other body may be a human one, but it may be the body of an animal or even a plant; it is even possible to be reborn as a god or goddess. (This is unlikely, since it necessitates an tremendous store of merit, and gods live far longer than we do, so that vacancies rarely occur.) In the same way, the body in which we now exist is the fruit of our actions in previous births. Thus our physical condition - strong or weak, whole or disabled, beautiful or ugly; our social condition - rich or poor, Brahmin or low caste; our sex; and the species we belong to - vegetable, animal, human or even divine, are all results of things we have done in the past. A man's destiny is shaped by their actions, and is not imposed by some higher power.

Sometimes Hindus or Hindu texts mention a deity who allots destinies as per the people's karma, but such a deity is merely following the system, and is not essential to it. Most people are not aware of their previous births; that feat of memory is achieved only through highly advanced meditation. It is said that the embryo in the womb remembers them, and is so distressed by the memory that it resolves never to be reborn again. However, the traumatic experience of birth wipes out the memory, so that the baby is born without knowledge of any kind. Nevertheless, there are stories which narrate the passage of particular living beings through a succession of bodies. There are also warnings of the punitive rebirths which await those guilty of particular sins. Manu has a list of them; for example :

Rebirth unites all living beings in one hierarchy, sometimes described as 'from Brahma [the ancestor of the gods] down to a tuft of grass'. This creates a moral bond between humankind and other species, which helps to explain the revulsion against meat-eating, slaughter and hunting which is frequently expressed, especially where brahmins and hermits are concerned. It also helps us to understand why there is no hard and fast line between people and gods.

It is believed that our conduct can be rewarded or punished in a heaven or hell besides rebirth; there are usually said to be seven hells. This belief is not inconsistent with rebirth, since the stay in a heaven or hell is not permanent, though it may be for hundreds of years. The passage in Manu from which the above instances are taken begins by saying that the various sinners spend a number of years in terrible hells before being reborn. Similarly, those who have won great merit go to heaven, but since their merit is finite, it can only keep them there for a finite time. After that, they return to this world to be reborn as per the their previous deeds.

Oftenly Karma is associated with rebirth, but the two are not the same concept. It is possible to believe in rebirth without karma; an ancient ascetic sect known as the Ajivikas did so, saying that each of us has to go through a predetermined series of bodies, which we can do nothing to change. On the other hand it would be hard to believe in karma without rebirth, since it is well known that those who do good deeds are not all rewarded, and those who do evil remain unpunished till they die, while a number of people's happiness or suffering seem s quite undeserved. Together, however, these two beliefs supply an intellectually acceptable answer to the old question, 'What have I done to deserve this?' I may not know what I have done to deserve a particular piece of good or bad fortune, since I probably did it in a previous life; but there is no doubt that I must have done something.

ETHICAL ACTIONS

Dharma: Norms of Conduct

In present time the word dharma is often used to translate 'religion', and Hindus sometimes prefer to speak of 'Hindu dharma' rather than 'Hinduism'. In the context of the historical encounter of Hindus with Muslims, Christians and others, the divergences that were most noticeable between these communities were differences of opinion or behaviour: how they dressed, what they ate, what patterns of marriage they followed, how they worshipped, and so on. These are differences of dharma; in Western terms they are religious differences, so the word came to be translated 'religion'. However, it does not refer to religious belief, but only to behaviour, and includes matters that may be regarded outside the sphere of religion, such as the administration of justice in law-courts.

According to the Hindu tradition Dharma is a set of norms for people's behaviour, including that of the king. It is not made by kings, though kings are particularly responsible for enforcing it. Nor is it made by the gods, since the gods themselves are subject to dharma. An older form of the word, used in the hymns of the Rig-Veda, means 'support, decree, arrangement, order', and dharma is often explained as something which supports society as well as ordering it. Another meaning of the word is 'natural property'. It is the dharma of fire to burn, for example , and the dharma of water to extinguish fire. Animals also have their dharma, which is their natural behaviour: it is the dharma of the lion to kill and eat the deer, and it is the dharma of the deer to eat grass and to flee from the lion. Animals have little or no choice in their behaviour; like inanimate objects such as water and fire, they just follow their dharma.

People, however, have a choice whether to follow their dharma or not, and in this context we may translate the word as 'morality' or 'law'. As we saw, because people have free will they earn merit or demerit - good or bad karma - by their actions, which animals do not. Dharma tells us which actions are meritorious and which are not, and may also tell us what kinds of rebirth or other consequence will be their reward or punishment. While dharma applies to every human being, it is especially the concern of the king. The king's responsibility for the behaviour of his subjects is understood in terms of karma:

A sixth share of everyone's merit belongs to the king who protects them, and a sixth share of their demerit belongs to the king who does not protect them. Whatever Veda-study, sacrifice, gifts, or worship a man performs, the king receives a sixth share of it as his due for protecting him.

This statement uses the analogy of the share of the produce of the land (often more than a sixth) which the king received as revenue. In the same way he receives a share of his subjects' good or bad karma, since whatever good they do is due in part to his protection, and whatever evil they do is due in part to his neglect. Dharma is one of the three worldly objectives, the other two being worldly power (artha, which includes wealth and political power) and pleasure (kama). Though these objectives are often said to be those of everyone, or at least of every man, the discourses of them in ancient texts suggest that they are primarily the concerns of kings. They are listed in descending order of significance; the pursuit of pleasure is satisfactory so long as it does not interfere with the pursuit of wealth and power, and these should not be sought at the expense of dharma. Beyond these three is the transcendent objective of salvation (moksha).

MESSAGE OF HARMONY AND LOVE

In the messege of Harmony and Love according to the Hindu tradition Peace is more than just a kind notion - it is a powerful action. The word itself will induce a sense of security and calm. Therefore, to merely think of peace or speak the word aloud or to yourself silently - begins to create the sense of peace you are looking for. Peace brings about love and harmony.

These three principals work in alignment with one another to create a very significant trinity or triangle. The triangle is a very powerful symbol and works wonders. So Peace, Love and Harmony are all intersected principals or "powers" working together. You cannot have peace without first having love and with love and peace comes harmony.

So when you meditate on peace, love and harmony, you are really bringing in the divine aspects of the universe. These three principals will transform all matter and situations. When you focus on peace you will deliver peace to not only yourself but to your immediate circle and the world as well. You will find that matters will flow more smoothly, situations will be easier, people will be kinder. Through peace you will find yourself closer to One, closer to your higher self. Peace elevates all emotions to the higher realms.

With Peace All is Well. Acceptance is a very nice outcome of peace. For peace transforms judgment and criticism into love, light -which brings about acceptance. The central truth as taught by Hinduism is that man has to transform his base human nature into the divine that is within him. In other words, he must reach the deeper strata of his being, wherein lies his unity with all mankind. And Hinduism can help us to reach and live that truth which spreads out our real nature — the divinity lying hidden in man.

Hinduism is not a particular religion but a philosophy which admits the basic truths of all religions. It teaches that man's real nature is divine; that it is the objective of man's life on earth to unfold and manifest the hidden Godhead within him; and that truth is universal...Thus Hinduism preaches a universal message, the message of harmony. In its insistence on personal experience of the truth of God, on the divinity of man, and the universality of truth it has kept the spirit of religion alive since the age of the Vedas (ancient scriptures). Even in our time there have been Ramakrishna, Vivekananda, and men like Gandhi.

In conclusion we easily can say that all religions does not mean that all people on earth have to come under the banner of one prophet or worship one aspect of God. If Christ is true, Krishna and Buddha are also true. Let there be a number of teachers, a number of scriptures; let there be churches, temples, and synagogues. Every religion is a path to reach the same goal. When the goal is reached the Christian, the Jew, the Sufi, the Hindu, and the Buddhist realize that each has worshiped the same Reality. One who has came upon this knowledge is no longer a follower of a particular path or a special religion he has become a man of God and a blessing to mankind. And such people are the good citizens of the society who spread peace and harmony in the society.

REFERENCES

Agrawala, Vasudeva: *Sparks from the Vedic Fire: A New Approach to Vedic Symbolism*. Varanasi, Banaras Hindu University, 1962.

Ainley, Alison: "*The Ethics of Sexual Difference.*" *In Abjection, Melancholia, and Love: The Works of Julia Kristeva*, London and New York: Routledge, 1990.

Alper, Harvey P.: *Understanding Mantras. SUNY Series in Religious Studies*, Albany, State University of New York Press, 1989.

Baartmans, Frans: *Aapaha, The Sacred Waters: an Analysis of a Primordial Symbol in Hindu Myths*, Delhi, B. R. Publishing Corporation, 1990.

Babb, Lawrence A.: *The Divine Hierarchy: Popular Hinduism in Central India*, New York, Columbia University Press, 1975.

Bailey, Greg.: *The Mythology of Brahma*, Delhi, Oxford University Press, 1983.

Banerjea, J. N.: *PauraGic and Tantric Religion (Early Phase)*, Calcutta, University of Calcutta, 1966.

Banerji, S. C.: *A Brief History of Tantra Literature*, Calcutta, Naya Prokash, 1988.

Coward, Harold G. Bhart: *Twayne's World Authors Series, no. 403. Boston*: Twayne Publishers, 1976.

Danielou, Alain.: *The Gods of India: Hindu Polytheism*, New York, Inner Traditions, 1985.

Das, S. K: *œakti or Divine Power*, Calcutta, University of Calcutta, 1934.

Das, Veena; *Structure and Cognition,* Delhi, Oxford University Press, 1982.

Heesterman, J. C.: "*Veda and Dharma.*" New Delhi: Vikas Publishing House, 1978.

Heimann, Betty: *Facets of Indian Thought. London*: George Allen and Unwin, 1964.

Holdrege, Barbara A.: "*Hindu Ethics." In The Berkely-Harvard Annotated Bibliography on Comparative Religious Ethics,* Cambridge and New York: Cambridge University Press, 1991.

Pandeya, R. C: *The Problem of Meaning in Indian Philosophy*, Delhi, Motilal Banarsidass, 1963.

Patni, B: *Shiv Purana: A Poetic Analysis*, Delhi, Ajanta Publications, 1980.

Payne, Ernest A.: *The Saktas: An Introductory and Comparative Study*, 1933.

Pfleuger, Lloyd William: "*God, Consciousness, and Meditation: The Concept of Iúvara in the Yogasutra.*" University of California, Santa Barbara, 1990.

8

Moral Value System

Although all religions have their different and varied features and characteristics and they all preaches a few things to their followers similarly Hinduism puts great emphasis on the necessity for ethical and moral behavior. As per the one scripture, a Hindu must observe moral and ethical laws from his birth till his death. Some scholars have rightly described Hinduism as a way of life.

Every significant event in Hindu life is directly influenced by religion. Marriage, birth, naming of babies, giving the first hair-cut, a baby's first intake of solid food, a child's first introduction to studies, eating habits, duties of married life, death, and post-mortem rituals - all are sanctified and made into sacraments. Moral values are the standards of good and evil, which govern an individual's behavior and choices. Individual's morals may derive from society and government, religion, or self. When moral values derive from society and government they, of necessity, may change as the laws and morals of the society change. Most religions have built-in lists of do's and don'ts, a set of codes by which its adherents should live. Individuals who are followers of a special religion will in general make a show of following that religion's behavioural code. It is interesting to note that these codes may widely vary; a person whose religion provides for polygamy will experience no guilt at having more than one spouse while adherents to other religions feel they must remain monogamous.

But, Hinduism goes beyond all other religions in that it is more than just a system of do's and don'ts; it is a relationship with the living God. A Hindu's set of moral values go beyond society's mores and selfish instincts. Hindus ideally behave correctly because they love God and want to please Him. This is at once a high calling and a low position. Moral values are things held to be right or wrong or desirable or undesirable. While morality is sometimes described as 'innate' in humans, the scientific view is that a capacity for morality is genetically determined in us, but the set of moral values is acquired, through instance, teaching, and imprinting from parents and society.

Various cultures have very respective moral value systems. Moral values, along with customs, laws, behaviour patterns, and beliefs, are the defining features of a culture. In Evolutionary psychology, moral values are seen as part of cultural evolution. Nationalists believe that a society needs one set of values to hold it together, and that 'multiculturalism' is not desirable as it tends to lead to conflict. People enforce moral values by parenting, peer guidance, conscience, disapproval, shunning, and only in some instances by law. They were effective in small communities before laws were formalised. They can also be sustained by the concept of 'status', a concept which has a number of meanings in various societies. There is today significant disagreement over what role status plays in contemporary society and of what it in real consists. Moral values are imposed, for example , by parenting, peer guidance, conscience, disapproval, shunning, and only in some instances by law.

MORAL VALUES

In general morality has three chief meanings. In its first descriptive usage, morality means a code of conduct held to be authoritative in matters of right and wrong. Morals are created by and define society, philosophy, religion, or individual conscience. In its second, normative and universal sense, morality refers to an ideal code of conduct, one which would be espoused in preference to alternatives by all rational people, under specified conditions. To deny 'morality' in this sense is a position known as moral skepticism. In its third usage, 'morality' is synonymous with ethics, the systematic philosophical study of the moral domain.

Ethics attempts to address questions such as how a moral outcome can be achieved in a specific situation (applied ethics), how moral values should be determined (normative ethics), what morals people in realabide by (descriptive ethics), what the fundamental nature of ethics or morality is, letting in whether it has any objective justification (meta-ethics), and how moral capacity or moral agency develops and what its nature is (moral psychology). In applied ethics, for example , the prohibition against taking human life is disputable with respect to capital punishment, abortion and wars of invasion.

In normative ethics, a typical question might be whether a lie told for the sake of protecting someone from harm is justified. In meta-ethics, a key issue is the meaning of the terms "right" or "wrong". Moral realism would hold that there are true moral statements which report objective moral facts, whereas moral anti-realism would hold that morality is derived from any one of the norms prevalent in society (cultural relativism); the edicts of a god (divine command theory); is merely an expression of the speakers' sentiments (emotivism); an implied imperative (prescriptive); falsely presupposes that there are nonsubjective moral facts (error theory).

Some thinkers are of the view that there is no correct definition of right behavior, that morality can only be judged with respect to particular situations, within the standards of particular belief systems and socio-historical contexts. This perspective, known as moral relativism, often cites empirical evidence from anthropology as evidence to support its claims. The opposite view, that there are universal, eternal moral truths is known as moral absolutism. Moral absolutists might concede that forces of social conformity significantly shape moral decisions, but deny that cultural norms and traditions define morally right behavior.

Religious people frequently claim religion is essential because without it there would be no absolute moral values. They explain by saying things like, "without absolute moral values mankind would be morally rudderless," and "without absolute moral value mankind has no fixed direction by which to set its moral compass." While such expressions result in mixed metaphors, there is an significant truth in them. Without absolute moral principles mankind truly is morally more mixed up than religion's metaphors. The special thing is, while it is primarily the religious, in our day, who are clamouring for a return to higher moral standards and true moral values, what the religions provide as absolute moral principles is neither moral nor absolute.

MORALITY IN LIFE

Morality or ethics is the science of conduct. Ethics is the study of what is right or good in conduct. Ethical science shows the way in which human beings should behave towards one another, as well as towards other creatures. It comprises systematised principles on which a man should act. Ethics is right conduct or Sadachara. The symbol of Dharma is good conduct (Achara). Dharma enhances life.

Man attains prosperity and fame, here and hereafter, through the practice of Dharma. Good conduct is the highest Dharma. It is the root of all austerities. Righteousness, truth and good works, power and prosperity, all originate from conduct. Man wills to obtain his objects of desires. Willing results in action. This is called conduct. Conduct is behaviour. The will that is expressed becomes conduct. Man has various sorts of desires. Sometimes, there is conflict of desires. That desire which obtains victory is termed - will -. The inner disposition which makes the will possible is called character. Character is the aggregate of peculiar qualities which constitute personal individuality. External behaviour is not always a sure guide in judging the character of a man.

We have human morality, family morality, social morality, national morality, professional morality, etc. A doctor has his professional ethics. He should not divulge to others the secrets of his patients. It is his duty to take all precautionary hygienic measures to stop the spread of an epidemic disease and direct his earnest attention towards public health and hygiene.

Ethics is a relative science. What is good for one man may not be good for another man. What is good at one time and at one place may not be good at another time and at another place. Ethics is relative to the man himself and to his surroundings. Without ethics, you cannot have progress in the spiritual path. Ethics is the foundation of Yoga. Ethics is the corner-stone of Vedanta. Ethics is the strong pillar on which the edifice of Bhakti Yoga rests. Ethics is the gateway to God-realisation.

Without ethical perfection, no spiritual progress or realisation is possible. A Yogic student or aspirant must be strictly ethical. He must be truthful and pure in thought, word and deed. He must possess excellent conduct. He must not injure any living being in thought, word and deed. He must practise rigidly right thought, right speech and right action. Morality is the gateway to religion. He who leads a moral or virtuous life attains freedom, perfection or Moksha.

Practice of ethics will help you to live in harmony with your neighbours, friends, your own family members, fellow-beings and other people. It will confer on you lasting happiness and Moksha. It will purify your heart. It will keep your conscience ever clean. A moral man who follows strictly the principles of ethics will not deviate even a fraction of an inch from the path of Dharma or righteousness. Yudhishthira had earned an undying reputation for his practice of ethics. He was an embodiment of Dharma. Hence he still lives in our hearts. Good conduct is the root of material and spiritual prosperity. Conduct increases fame. It is good conduct which prolongs life and destroys all calamities and evils and brings eternal happiness. It is good conduct that begets virtue.

Hinduism lays great emphasis on ethical discipline. Yama (self-restraint) and Niyama (religious observances) are the foundations of Yoga and Vedanta. Undeveloped persons cannot think for themselves. Hence rules of conduct have been laid down by great sages or seers like Manu and Sage Yajnavalkya.

The first thing you learn from religion is the unity of all selves. The Upanishads says: - The neighbour is, in truth, the very Self and what separates you from him is mere illusion. - One Atman or Self abides in all beings. Universal love is the expression of the unity. Universal brotherhood has its basis in the unity of Self. All human relations exist because of this unity. All are dear, because the one Self is in all. If you injure another man, you injure yourself. If you help another person, you help yourself. There is one life, one common consciousness in all beings. This is the basis of right conduct. This is the foundation of ethics.

In India, dinner is prepared for five hundred persons even when two hundred persons are invited. Feeding is worship of Narayana or the Lord, for a Hindu. It is Atithi-Yajna or sacred sacrifice. A Hindu regards every creature as the Lord. A philanthropist donates big sums to social institutions. He regards this as some kind of social service only. That is all. He has not got the Bhava or mental attitude, that the whole world is a expression of the Lord and that he is serving the Lord. He has not got the Bhava that the Lord is working through his instruments or senses, that every act is an offering unto the Lord, and that every deed is a Yogic activity.

Hindus in general and according to their custom and tradition are very generous, noble, large-hearted, charitable, God-fearing, sympathetic, merciful and hospitable. If they see a hungry man in the street, they will take him to their house, treat him as Atithi-Narayana (God in the form of guest), feed him first and then take their food. Nowhere in the world you will hear of such a treatment. You cannot get even a morsel of food free in other countries.

Ethics or morality and doing good to others, is the expression of this oneness. A Hindu believes that if he feeds a single sage or a Mahatma, he is feeding the whole world, because he has realised that a realised sage is identical with the whole Virat or Brahman and is one with all beings of the entire universe. Hindu ethics is based on the sublime philosophy of Vedanta which propounds the doctrine of oneness of life and unity of consciousness. A Hindu distributes food to the crows, dogs, cows and fish first before he takes his food. He tries to recognise the one Atman that is hidden in all these forms. He endeavours to become one with the Universal Being. He knows that in loving others he loves himself and in injuring others he injures himself. Through the practice of cosmic love he feels that all bodies are his, all hands are his, all feet are his and that the whole world is his home (Vasudhaiva Kutumbakam). Gradually he becomes one with the soul of the universe and one with the Oversoul also. Hindu ethics leads eventually to Self-realisation. Ethics is a means to Yoga.

MORAL VALUES FOR LEADER

The Leaders have a clear sense of where they want to go and how they intend to get there. Leaders aren't afraid to make hard or unpopular decisions because they have confidence in themselves and in their abilities. Leaders have the courage to act in situations where results aren't assured. Leaders can articulate their vision and ideals to others, convincing them of the value of their ideas. They can inspire people to work toward common goals and to achieve things they never thought they could do.

Leaders know their own strengths and weaknesses and are able to view their behavior objectively. They recognize their shortcomings, open themselves to feedback, and are willing to make alterations when necessary. Leaders must be trustworthy before others will follow them. Leaders have a desire to continually learn and grow and are open to new ideas. Leaders can convey their ideas to diverse individuals and adjust their styles to meet the needs of the people they lead. Leaders authorise others and go out of their way to help them achieve their full potential.

Religious leaders honour personal integrity. They teach others that one can negotiate the tensions that necessarily exist within a truly diverse community without compromising oneself and without asking others to compromise themselves. Good religious leaders model for the rest of us the preservation of one's integrity in a fashion that does not necessitate that one be judgmental of others who make various choices.

Religious leaders are not afraid of imprecision. They acknowledge and appreciate the ambiguities of communal life. Communities that are as internally diverse as our own cannot be led by leaders who insist upon uniformity, unanimity or the logical coherence of all communal positions and policies. Capable leaders will cultivate their capacity to tolerate ambiguity.

Religious leaders are willing to take unpopular stands and to advocate on behalf of unpopular positions. They accept that this means that they will sometimes feel as if they are out of sync – or unpopular — with the communities they lead. They accept that as leaders they must sometimes bear the burden of being "the heavy," of being the "bad guy" rather than the "good guy," of leading by being out in front of the community even when the community is lagging behind. Their commitment to the community is a long- term commitment and this helps them to avoid the temptation of being overly concerned with short-term popularity.

Religious leaders are committed to serious Torah study and scholarship – both for themselves and for their communities. Leaders are learners and they help communities to educate themselves. They work to build community by offering people a vision of religious possibilities and then work together with them to help them to become the Hindus they want to be. They never pander to Hindus by presenting Hinduism as a product that Hindus can "buy" and completely customize to fit their own preferences. Leadership means helping communities to learn from Hindu customs and teachings.

Religious leaders lead through vital personal relationships. Religious leaders know and care about the people in their community and share in their trials, their tragedies, their triumphs. Religious leaders do not lead from "on high," but are down in the trenches with the members of their community, talking with them, arguing with them, celebrating with them and suffering with them. Because they are there with them, religious leaders are there for them as well. Strong communities depend on strong connections between members and between members and leaders. Religious leaders embrace these connections and are embraced by their communities in turn.

MORAL DUTIES OF SUBJECTS

The values of a society derive over its spiritual and moral foundations. When those foundations are destroyed a vacuum exists and people can be manipulated as per the ideology and power ambitions of ruling elites. Customal morality is inestimably significant. Without it, all kinds of injustices and oppressions against individual persons are sanctioned; not the distorted and imaginary oppressions of Marxist theory but the real oppressions which arise when men forget the golden rule: love your neighbour as yourself. The abandonment of customal morality leads to expropriation of private property, heavy taxation, theft, waste, compulsory association, totalitarian thought control, sexual exploitation, homeless children, fraud and dishonesty, disloyalty to family, ever increasing government power and control, envy, indiscipline, laziness, individual irresponsibility, indecency, rudeness, impoliteness, social engineering and genocide, not to mention impiety.

The Morality is essential for the future of a civilisation. Morality includes such values as honesty, the pursuit of truth, responsibility, duty, fairness in interpersonal relations, concern for one's immediate neighbours, respect for property, loyalty and duty to one's spouse and children, the work ethic and keeping one's word. The emphasis is upon the duty and responsibility of the individual. No society can function efficiently or humanely and no civilisation can endure without these values. The failure to assume responsibility for one's actions and the tendency to look to government for everything are among the consequences of the break down of customal morality

All religions emphasise the significance of duties and responsibilities as distinct from rights. There is an emphasis on rights to the near exclusion of duties and responsibilities in modern society. There is a grave danger in the push towards legislative recognition of subjective rights (so called) in response to the demands of politically influential pressure groups.

A duty-centred society is preferable to a right-centred society. If individuals are concerned about their duties, responsibilities and obligations, they cannot but be concerned about the rights, needs and freedoms of others. A right-centred society is one in which individuals assert their rights. People are encouraged by individuals, organisations and Commonwealth and State departments and instrumentalities, to demand rights, with no consideration for the effect of these demands on other people.

There is no end to the so called rights which can be demanded. A right-conscious society in effect recognises a few rights and neglects a number of others. The rights that are recognised are those which are demanded by the powerful, the aggressive and the nasty.

MORAL VALUES IN SOCIETY

Hindu society is the only significant society in the world today, which presents a continuity of cultural existence and functioning since times immemorial. Most other societies known to human history-East and West, North and South-have suffered a sudden interruption and undergone a traumatic transformation due to the invasion and victory of latter-day ideologies-Christianity, Islam, Communism. The pre-Christian, pre-Islamic and pre-Communist cultural creations of these societies are now to be met only in libraries and museums, thanks to the labors of antiquarian scholars.

Hindu culture can meet the same frightful fate if there were no Hindu society to sustain it. This is the point, which is not always remembered even by those who take pride in Hindu culture. There are a number of

Hindus who cherish the great spiritual customs of Hinduism and its scriptures like the Gita and the Upanishads in which that custom is enshrined. But they do not cherish with an equal enthusiasm the Hindu society, which has honored and preserved these customs and scriptures down the ages.

Again, there are a number of Hindus who proclaim with great confidence that Sanatana Dharma that is Hinduism can never die. This is true in a sense. There will always be individuals in non-Hindu societies who will recover the mystique of Sanatana Dharma through their efforts at self-discovery. But Sanatana Dharma will surely suffer an eclipse and no more inform mankind at large with its message, if there is no Hindu society to sustain it.

Lastly, there are a number of Hindus who are legitimately proud of Hindu art, architecture, sculpture, music, painting, dance, drama, literature, linguistics, lexicography, and so on. But they seldom take into account the fact that this great wealth of artistic, literary and scientific heritage, will die if Hindu society, which created it, is no more there to preserve, protect and perpetuate it.

But the death of Hindu society is no longer an eventuality which cannot be envisaged. This great society is now besieged by the same dark and deadly forces which have overwhelmed and obliterated a number of ancient societies. Suffering from a loss of its élan, it has become a house divided within itself. And its beneficiaries no more seem to be interested in its survival because they have fallen victims to hostile propaganda. They have developed towards it an attitude of utter indifference, if not downright contempt. Let no Hindu worth his salt remain complacent. Hindu society is in mortal danger as never before.

At one time the dominant school of Western historians and their Indian disciples, for whom Hindu history commenced with Alexander's invasion, presented this history as a series of successful foreign invasions to which Hindu India invariably succumbed. They even invented an Aryan invasion of India in the second millennium BC to round up their cherished image of this country as some sort of a free for all into which any adventurer could descend and dwell at will.

It is little use crossing swords with the stalwarts inspired by Mecca and Moscow. It has been seen again and again that whatever be the facts, their conclusions remain the same. Their conclusions remain the same because their motives are the same. The motives are to malign and misrepresent Hindu history in order to denigrate and destroy Hindu society. Now a number of Indians too have joined the game.

Western historians also concede that the theory of an Aryan invasion of India is at best a conjecture for which there is no positive evidence, literary or archaeological. They admit further that the account which the Hindus gave of themselves in the face of foreign invaders has been quite creditable and by no means dishonorable. And they agree that whenever the Hindus suffered a defeat it was largely due to their neglect of and consequent inferiority in the art of warfare rather than any serious defect or deficiency in their social system or cultural milieu.

There was a time, not very long ago, when Hindu culture was a revered culture throughout the civilized world. Its seers and sages, its mystics and monks, its scholars and scientists, its missionaries and merchants took its message to the farthest corners of world-East Africa, Egypt and Ethiopia; Sumeria, Assyria, Babylonia, Chaldea and Iran; Burma, China, Japan, Korea and Mongolia; Indochina, Indonesia, Malaysia and Thailand; Pacific Islands, West Indies, Mexico, Peru and Columbia; Asia Minor, Central Asia, Greece and Rome. The history of a hundred cultures and nations provides evidence of this hoary heritage in their religions and philosophies, languages and literatures, sciences and technologies, manners and mores.

True, the Hindus never constructed a strong, centralised state, like that of ancient Iran and Rome, which could tyrannies over its constituent units and invade the neighbouring countries. Yet their society was a strong, steadfast and stupendous creation based on a highly decentralized yet a cohesive social fabric made of organic units such as the clan (kula), caste (jati), village (grama), town (nigam), metropolis (nagar), country (janapada) and empire (samrajya). Imperial systems rose and fell. But the infrastructure survived the test of time and remained vigorous and vibrant till very recent times.

Thus Hindu society not only presents itself as a prey to these exclusive, intolerant and imperialist ideologies but also acts as a buffer between them. India is secular because India is Hindu. It can be added as a corollary that India is a democracy also because India is Hindu. If Hindu society permits this free for all any further, the days of Secularism and Democracy in this country are numbered. Let the Hindus unite and save themselves, their democratic polity, their secular state, and their Sanatana Dharma for a new cycle of civilization, not only for themselves but also the world.

PRACTICAL ASPECTS

Moral culture is a reflex product of man and society. It is also the moral rules which correct the mutual relations between people, their consciousness, psychology, acts and vital activities. Among the factors and criteria of social progress, moral culture holds a special place, for it is the system of self-determination in society. It includes the notions and concepts of person and society, good and evil, the motive and meaning of life, honour and duty, freedom and responsibility, justice and dignity, love and friendship, customs, rituals, customs, norms, rules, principles, models of conduct, ideals and national and common values which were transformed in conformity with the values, emotions, senses, persuasions, views, acts, vital activities, models of life and personal qualities. These are also the chief support of the moral culture whose principal function is the regulation of mutual relations of man with nature, society and other peoples.

The beginning of morality, its imperatives and taboos at the dawn of human history, reflect an understanding that man lives not by himself without other people, but must have some rules for social life. Upon that thesis, we draw the following conclusions:

First, morality commenced at the same time as human society and before moral culture. Second, the concepts of morality and moral culture are interconnected, but are not identical, the latter being more liberal than the former. Third, at the present time moral culture is developing and improves human life through individual forms of activity and social-historical practice. Fourth, the essence of moral culture is to become aware of every man as necessarily related to other people. Fifth, the subjects of a moral culture must include everyone in order to improve persons and society in their indissoluble and versatile connections and interconnections.

Moral culture is a measure of moral values and their practical realization in all the spheres of social activity by persons, groups, communities or society. An significant characteristic of the subject of moral culture is an alignment of national and common values, with priority given to common values in consciousness, action, communications and practice. It is the formed self-awareness of man as a member of an ethnos, group, social stratum, society and, of course, his civic, social, human duties and responsibilities.

Moral culture is founded on the historical, moral ethics of a custom and at the same time is oriented on present and future values. It unites such factors of development as change and stability. As a dynamic system of society it has the chance and the means to secure its stableness, development and progress. The spiritual-cultural values of the past attract our attention because we can see in them the predilection and foundation of our moral search for the motive and meaning of life, social activity, happiness and goodness. In the new historical, social, economic and cultural situation it is essential to understand this. The highest social value of the culture is its unity. The acquisition of moral culture is founded upon the education of the intellect, emotions, senses and will.

The brain is the basis of human actions; but one's emotions constitute the internal, spiritual world of a person as a moral force confirming goodness, truth, beauty, responsibility, achievement, knowledge, patriotism, honour, duty, justice, friendship, love and dignity. Moral culture, therefore, concerns the formation, development and expression of the creative essence of man. The process of reforming society, its change, development and progress, are instances of the creative activity of man. At the same time the stability of society is a condition and foundation of social development. This cannot be described without its subject which is oriented by social, spiritual-moral values. In the process of such activity, one changes oneself and at the same time improves social relations, assisting in both their stabilization and their progress. Orienting life on moral norms, ideas and principles manifests moral culture and strengthens the interconnections and interactions between people and their improvement.

A human being has only the potential or possibility to be a "whole subject"; for its formation and development moral culture plays a great role, together with other components of culture and social-historical factors. Man and the world are connected and interact on the basis of moral values. The experience and practice of totalitarian society showed the communist moral to be erroneous both in the sphere of morality and in economics. Moral culture is the complex of social and individual moralities.

Individual morality is the means, method and form for the realization of the moral value of man and society. It is a condition and factor of the moral cultural development and the self-improvement of every person. The actions of the morally cultured person follow the norms, rules and principles of society. They do not contradict the chief interests of man and society, but coordinate one's activity with the interests of other people and subordinate one's own interests to those of society.

Therefore, individual and social morality, professional ethics and moral culture are significant factors in the development of personality and social progress. This necessitates the highest development of social and individual consciousness and of the self-awareness, self-education and self-improvement of the person. By it one becomes aware of one's needs and interests, and of one's civil, professional, human duty, dignity and responsibility.

One of the chief characteristics of personality is to be self-critical, that is to say, the ability to relate to oneself as to another person, the objective analysis of one's own actions and the correction of one's own mistakes. Self-improvement takes place through the connection between a self-critical personality and his or her sense of responsibility.

Moral culture is the creative activity of people and its result. Conditions change and new tasks seem as people look for new activities, ways and methods of self-improvement. These are connected with the characteristics of the subject of moral activity and one's spiritual and emotional experience. This culture plays a great role in the realization of a society in which objective social relations, laws, standards and the moral atmosphere give persons the possibility and right to choose for oneself their convictions, profession, place and mode of life and self-improvement, thereby enabling one to transform one's relations to oneself, to other people, to nature and to society.

Moral norms, rights, principles, values and criteria are the basis of such transformations and moral culture is the chief factor in the education of a personality and the promotion and progress of a society. As the subject of moral culture the person has special needs which conform with norms of morality as with his or her motive, tasks and characteristics. The person respects laws and has rights shared by all members of society; one fulfils one's duties as per the demands of morality and the progressive development of society. Moral culture is manifested in human desires as one lives in accord with his group, society and nation.

Here the human is always the end, never the means. The development and self-improvement of the person and of society is the end. This is the task and foundation of moral culture because social progress has the improvement, self-improvement and development of persons as its chief goal. For the development of modern civilization, moral culture is the chief factor. Only this is able to safeguard positive achievements and exclude negative tendencies. Every epoch needs a special moral culture for the person and society. The great significance of moral culture lies in its specific but non-coercive method of overcoming the negatives.

These methods are: the system of education, information, self-education and self-improvement, social opinion, awareness of law and self-awareness, and, as per the this, the methods, activity and practice of goodness. Moral culture is specific to a nation, but is a common and universal method of mutual understanding and collaboration between people as ethnicities, nations and countries. It is the chief source and factor of social progress, because it has a great influence on social and individual consciousness and their activities and on the characteristics of social relations.

The human person has his or her own national and common values; one knows one's place, role and responsibility before society and before oneself. It is a special state of emotions, consciousness, will, needs, wishes, interests, forms and methods manifest in all spheres of personal activity. The significance of the person depends upon one's character, the level of knowledge and of the development of one's consciousness, and upon the measure of one's self-education and self-improvement. These are engaged in social practice as defining the motive and meaning of one's life.

REFERENCES

F. Edgerton: *The Bhagavad-Gita*, Cambridge, Mass, Harvard University Press, 1944.

G. Buhler: *The Laws of Manu*, Oxford, Clarendon Press, 1886.

G. Buhler: *The Sacred Books of the East*, Oxford: Clarendon Press, 1882, 1897.

H. Oldenberg: *The Grhya-Sutras*, Oxford: Clarendon Press, 1886.

J. Eggeling: *The Uatapatha-Brahmana*, Oxford, Clarendon Press, 1900.

J. Jolly: *The Institutes of Vishnu*, Oxford, Clarendon Press, 1900.

M. Winternitz: *A History of Indian Literature*, Calcutta, University, 1927.

Ortner, Sherry B.: "*Is Female to Male as Nature Is to Culture?" In Women, Culture, and Society*, Stanford, Calif. Stanford University Press, 1974.

Padoux, André. Vac: T*he Concept of the Word in Selected Hindu Tantras*, State University of New York Press, 1990.

Ramanujan, A. K. "*On Folk Mythologies and Folk PuraGas.*" *In PuraGa Perennis: Reciprocity and Transformation in Hindu and Jaina Texts*, State University of New York Press, 1993.

Regnaud, Paul: "*La Maya et le Pouvoir Createur Des Divinitiés Védiques.*" Revue de L'Histoire Des Religions, 1885.

Renou, Louis: "*Les Connexions entre le Rituel et la Grammaire en Sanskrit.*" Cambridge, Mass.: MIT Press, 1972.

Sharma, Chandradhar: *A Critical Survey of Indian Philosophy*, Delhi, Motilal Banarsidass, 1987.

Shastri, P. D.: *The Doctrine of Maya in the Philosophy of the Vedanta,* London, Luzac and Co., 1911.

Sheridan, Daniel P.: *The Advaitic Theism of the Bhagavata Puraga,* Delhi: Motilal Banarsidass, 1986.

Shulman, David: *Tamil Temple Myths: Sacrifice and Divine Marriage in the South Indian,* N.J.: Princeton University Press, 1980.

Siddhantashastree, Rabindra Kumar: *VaicGavism Through the Ages.* New Delhi, Munshiram Manoharlal, 1985.

Singh, Renuka: *The Womb of Mind: A Sociological Exploration of the Status Experience of Women in Delhi*, New Delhi, Vikas Publishing House, 1990.

Sircar, D. C.: *Foreigners in Ancient India and Lakcmi and Sarasvati in Art and Literature*, Calcutta, University of Calcutta, 1970.

9

Movements

Hinduism is a religion that originated in the Indian subcontinent. The scholars refer to it more as Sanâtana Dharma (the eternal path/law) than a religion, as it is believed to be a virtuous way of life. It is the oldest practised religion in the world and has the third largest following after Christianity and Islam. Having originated in the Indian subcontinent, it has spread selectively to other parts of the world owing to migration, as the ideas of conversion and evangelisation are absent in Hinduism.

As a religion Hinduism has gone through a phase of regeneration and reform through various movements. Although these movements are very individual in their exact philosophies they in general stress the spiritual, secular and logical/scientific aspects of the Vedic customs, creating a form that is egalitarian that does not discriminate based on Jati (caste or subcaste), gender, or race. There are groups in India that are actively engaged in getting women and those from socially disadvantaged jâtis to become priests of Vedic ritual. One of the foremost movements in breaking the caste system and educating the downtrodden was the Lingayat movement spearheaded by Basavanna in the 12th century in Anubhava Mantapa in Kalyani of Karnataka. The less accessible Vedas were rejected and parallel Vachanas were compiled.

The new movements look up to Swami Vivekananda; Rabindranath Tagore; Ramana Maharshi; Shri Aurobindo (for his Integral Yoga); A.C. Bhaktivedanta Swami Prabhupada (founder of the modern Hare Krishna movement); Swami Sivananda, Swami Rama Tirtha; Narayana Guru, Paramhansa Yogananda; Shrii Shrii Anandamurti and for inspiration. More recently, the work of Maharishi Mahesh Yogi, Sathya Sai Baba, Shirdi Sai Baba, Swami Muktananda, Swami Chinmayananda, Dayananda Saraswati, Sri Sri Ravi Shankar, and Mata Amritanandamayi has inspired millions to create new centers of spiritual development. In the intellectual field, the writings of Ananda Coomaraswamy, Ram Swarup, Stephen Knapp, Sita Ram Goel, Subhash Kak and David Frawley have been influential.

In social work, Mahatma Gandhi, Vinoba Bhave, Pandurang Shastri Athavale, Baba Amte and Shrii Shrii Anandamurti have been most significant. Sundarlal Bahuguna created the chipko movement for the preservation of forestlands As per the Hindu ecological ideas. The Rashtriya Swayamsevak Sangh or RSS was founded Keshav Baliram Hegdewar in 1925. The aim was to unite Hindus, make them rise over their caste differences and work to achieve a Hindu Rashtra; the ideology of the Sangh, closely associated with political Hinduism, came to be known as Hindutva.

There have been an increasing number of Western devotees of various Hindu lineages and practices since the counter-culture revolution of the 1960s. These have come about not only through the Hare Krishnas, but also through the Universalist teachings of such Hindu figures as Sri Ramakrishna, and the yoga teachings of B.K.S. Iyengar. The growing number of Indian immigrants relocating into the West, and the subsequent building of Hindu temples to meet the spiritual needs of these newly founded Hindu communities, has also resulted in Westerns having ready access to customal teachings. A number of Western converts were introduced to Hinduism after attending the Western temples and then embracing the custom.

There can also be no doubt that the fitness revolution's ecstatic love-affair with yoga in the 1990s has helped spur on new interest in the teachings of Hinduism in the West. More and more texts are being written by Western-born Hindu converts specifically for a new Western audience, the vast bulk of which have little to no experience with Sanskrit which renders customal literature all but useless.

RELIGIOUS MOVEMENTS

Bhakti Movement

The Bhakti Movement was essentially founded in South India and later spread to the North during the late medieval period.The notion of Bhakti (devotional love to God) is of antiquity. An emergent consciousness of what Bhakti constitutes is already to be found in the earliest Vedas, especially in relation to deities such as Varuna. A clearer expression of Bhakti began to be formed during the so-called Epic Period and the Puranic periods of Hindu history. Texts such as the Bhagavad Gita and the

Bhagavata Purana clearly explore Bhakti Yoga or the Path of Devotion as a means to salvation. Bhakti movement was Hindu a religious movement in which the chief spiritual practice was the fostering of loving devotion to God, called bhakti. They were monotheistic movements generally devoted to worship of Shiva, Vishnu, Murukan or Shakti.

The Bhakti Movement itself is a historical-spiritual phenomenon that crystallized in South India during Late Antiquity. It was spearheaded by devotional mystics (later revered as Hindu saints) who extolled devotion and love to God as the chief means of spiritual perfection. The Bhakti movement in South India was spearheaded by the sixty-three Nayanars (Shaivite devotees) and the twelve Alvars (Vaishnavaite devotees).

Among the earliest Shaivite mystics was Karaikkal Amaiyar, who probably lived around the late 5th century AD or perhaps the early 6th century. She was said to be a contemporary of the Vaishnavaite saints Bhuttalwar and Peialwar. Kannapa Nayanar was also an early Shaiva Bhakti saint. But most famous among the Shaiva Bhakti saints were the Nalvar (The Four Eminent Ones), Sundarar, Appar, Sambandar and Manikkavasagar. Their devotional hymns are ecstatic, lyrical and moving.

The Vaishnavaite Bhakti movement was coetaneous with the Shaiva Bhakti movement. The hymns of the twelve alvars are held together as the Nalayira Divya Prabandham and recited (as are the Shaiva texts) in temple rituals. While all the saints are held in great reverence, Aandaal (or Goda-devi) in particular holds a special place among the Vaishnava saints. Not only is she the only female Vaishnava saint but also her hymns are among the best expressions of bridal mysticism in the Hindu religion.

The twelve Alvars and the sixty-three Nayanars nurtured the incipient bhakti movement in South India under the Pallavas and Pandyas in the fifth to seventh centuries AD. They constitute South India's 75 Apostles of Bhakti and were greatly influential in determining the expression of faith in South India. The path of devotion as expounded by these mystics would later be incorporated into Ramanuja and Madhva philosophical systems.

The Virashaiva movement during the 12th and 13th centuries A.D. and, during the rule of the Vijayanagar Empire in South India, the Haridasa movement spread from present-day Karnataka. The Virashaiva movement spread the philosophy of Basavanna, a Hindu reformer. The seeds of Carnatic music were sown, and the philosophy of Madhvacharya was propagated by the Kannada Haridasas. The Haridasa movement presented, like the Virashaiva movement, another strong current of bhakti, pervading the lives of millions. The Haridasas presented two groups – Vyasakuta and Dasakuta. The former were necessitated to be proficient in the Vedas, Upanishads and other Darshanas, while the Dasakuta merely conveyed the message of Madhvacharya through the Kannada language to the people. The philosophy of Madhvacharya was preserved and perpetuated by his eminent disciples like Vyasatirtha or Vyasaraja Naraharitirtha, Vadirajatirtha, Sripadaraya, Jayathirtha and others. In the fifteenth century, the Haridasa movement took shape under Sripadaraya of Mulbagal; but his disciple Vyasatirtha provided it a strong organizational base. He was intimately associated with the Vijayanagar Empire, where he became a great moral and spiritual force. His eminent disciples were Purandaradasa and Kanakadasa. Yakshagana, as a theater form emerged as an offshoot of this movement in Karnataka.

The Bhakti movement in later years led to the proliferation of regional poetic literature in the various vernacular languages of India. The Bhakti movement in what is now Karnataka resulted in a burst of poetic Kannada literature in praise of Vishnu. Some of its leaders include Purandara Dasa and Kanaka Dasa, whose contributions were essential to Carnatic music. The later Carnatic Trinity is also no doubt a product of this long Bhakti Movement.

The Bhakti movement started to spread to the North during the late medieval ages when North India was under Muslim domination. There was no grouping of the mystics into Shaiva and Vaishnava devotees as it was in the South. The movement was spontaneous and the various mystics had their own version of devotional expression. Unlike in the South where devotion was centered on both Shiva and Vishnu (in all his forms), the Northern devotional movement was more or less centered on Rama and Krishna, both of whom were incarnations of Vishnu. Though this did not mean that the sect of Shiva or of the Devi went into decline. In fact for all of its history the Bhakti movement co-existed peacefully with the other movements in Hinduism. It was initially regarded unorthodox as it rebelled against caste distinctions and made disregarded Brahmanic rituals which as per the Bhakti saints not necessary for salvation. In the course of time however, owing to its immense popularity among the masses (and even royal patronage) it became 'orthodox' and continues to be one of the most significant modes of religious expression in modern India.

A great bhakti movement swept through Central & Northern India in the period between the 14-17th centuries, initiated by a loosely associated group of teachers or 'Sants'. Chaitanya, Vallabha, Meera Bai, Kabir, Tulsi Das,Dnyaneshwar, Namdeo, Tukaram and other mystics spearheaded the Bhakti movement in the North. Their teachings were that people could cast aside the heavy burdens of ritual and caste and the subtle complexities of philosophy and simply express their overwhelming love for God. This period was also characterized by a spate of devotional literature in vernacular prose and poetry in the ethnic languages of the various Indian states or provinces.

Shri Madhvacharya (1238-1317) identified God with Vishnu. His view of reality is purely dualistic, in that he understood a fundamental variation between the ultimate Godhead and the individual soul, and the system is hence called Dvaita (dualistic) Vedanta. Madhva is regarded one of the influential theologians in Hindu history. His influence was profound, and he is one of the fathers of the Vaishnava Bhakti movement. Great leaders of the Vaishnava Bhakti movement in Karnataka like Purandara Dasa, Kanaka Dasa, Raghavendra Swami and a number of others were influenced by Dvaita customs.

Vallabhacharya (1479 — 1531) called his system of thought Shuddhadvaita (pure monism). As per the him, it is by God's grace alone that one can obtain release from bondage and attain Krishna's heaven. This heaven is far above the "heavens" of Brahma, Vishnu and Shiva, for Krishna is himself the eternal Brahman.

Chaitanya Mahaprabhu (1486 - 1534) defined his system of philosophy as Achintya Bheda Abheda (inconceivable and simultaneous oneness and difference). It synthesizes elements of monism and dualism into a single system. Chaitanya's philosophy is taught by the contemporary International Society for Krishna Consciousness, better known as the Hare Krishna movement.

Srimanta Sankardeva (1449 - 1568) named his religion ek sarana naam dharma and propagated it in Assam. An instance of dasa bhakti, in this form there was no place for Radha. The most significant symbol of this religion is the naamghor or prayer hall, which dot Assam's landscape. This form of worship is very strong in Assam today, and much of the customs are maintained by the monasteries called Satras.

Beyond the confines of such formal schools and movements, however, the development of bhakti as a major form of Hindu practice has left an indelible stamp on the faith. Philosophical speculation was concern for the minority, and even the great Advaitist scholar Adi Shankaracharya, when questioned as to the way to God, said that chanting the name of the lord was essential. The philosophical schools changed the way people thought, but Bhakti was immediately accessible to all, calling to the instinct emotion of love and redirecting it to the highest pursuit of God and self-realization. In general a liberal movement, its denouncement of caste offered recourse for Hindus from the orthodox Brahaminical systems. Of course Bhakti's message of tolerance and love was not often heeded by those ensconced in the societal construct of caste. Altogether, Bhakti resulted in a mass of devotional literature, music and art that has enriched the world and gave India renewed spiritual impetus, one eschewing unnecessary ritual and artificial social limits.

Ananda Marga

India in 1955 by Prabhat Ranjan Sarkar (1921-1990) founded Ananda Marga, officially known as Ananda Marga Pracharaka Samgha meaning "the organization for the propagation of the path of bliss" is a social and spiritual movement founded in Jamalpur, Bihar, known by his spiritual name of Shrii Shrii Anandamurti. Ananda Marga followers describe their belief system as a practical philosophy for personal development and social service to the community. The meaning of the Sanskrit term Ananda Marga is "path of bliss"; ananda or "bliss", and marga or "path". Through its meditation centers and service projects around the world, Ananda Marga offers instruction in meditation, yoga and other self-development practices on a non-commercial basis.

Tantra tantra yoga, as understood by Shrii Shrii Anandamurti is the foundation of Ananda Marga, or the Path of Bliss. Tantra in the customal Western sense meaning sexual practices is not a part of the Ananda Marga tantra custom. The practitioner of Ananda Marga tantra yoga sees the mind as a "trapped monkey" striving to escape from its cage. The tantra path is the path of the brave, because it necessitates the practitioner to follow strict rules as to their spiritual practice.

Meditation is the chief practice of this tantric custom, and through the meditation the practitioner struggles to overcome weaknesses and imperfections. Through daily meditations the practitioner faces their minds deepest secrets, and to proceed in the practice he must manage to overcome whatever one faces in the deepness. Because the path is regarded so hard a number of people stray from the path and reject the teachings afterwards.

The basis of Ananda Marga practice is covered in a set of rules called the sixteen points. The sixteen points guides the practitioner of the tantric path on both spiritual and social aspects. In the tantric custom of Ananda Marga the spiritual aspirant is called a sadhaka, and he practices sádhaná. Sádhaná comes from the Sanskrit root word sadh which means "to control". Sádhaná signifies the effort through which a person becomes completely realized.

In the tantric custom the spiritual master, the guru plays a special role. The guru, or dispeler of darkness, guides and leads students on the spiritual path that is likened to be razor sharp. It is also stated in the tantric custom that the student doesn't find the teacher, but the teacher finds the student.

When the student decides to aspire on the path of bliss he will be initiated by a qualified meditation teacher called acarya, Sanskrit for teacher. An acharya is most commonly a monk or nun, but there are also family acaryas in the Ananda Marga custom. In the initiation the aspirant makes a commitment to practice meditation, and is then taught the technique itself. The aspirant is then necessitated to keep all his practices secret and not discuss them with others.

Anandamurtiiji taught a number of systems of meditation such as Pra'rambhika Yoga, Sa'dharana Yoga, Sahaja Yoga and Vishesha Yoga.[citation needed] In addition, he also taught Kapalika meditation to a number of sanyasiins. His system of yoga can be termed as Rajadhira'ja Yoga or Tantra Yoga or just Ananda Marga Yoga. The Ananda Marga meditation system is called Sahaja Yoga, meaning 'easy yoga', in the sense that everyone can do the practice. The sahaja yoga system consists of 6 meditation proficiencies called lessons.

The lessons are taught one by one, on a personal basis. There is no specific system as to when one can learn a new technique, but is rather taught on a personal basis depending on the level of interest and dedication of the student. Thus some students learn all six lessons in a year or two, while some complete all lessons in over 20 years. There is also a higher set of meditation lessons taught by Ananda Marga and advanced practitioners are ever taught them.

Brahma Kumaris

The Brahma Kumaris or Prajapita Brahma Kumaris is a monastic, renunciate, millenarian new religious movement of Indian origin whose teachings are based on practises involving both mediumship and channelling. It encourages a form of meditation called Raja Yoga, which differs from classical Raja Yoga as described by Patanjali. As a neo-Hindu sect, the Brahma Kumaris pre-date the New Age movement but have developed characteristics that link them to its thinking.

The beginning can be traced to the group Om Mandali, founded by Lekhraj Kripalani in Hyderabad, Sindh in the 1930s. Lekhraj Kripalani, known as "Dada Lekhraj", "Om Baba" or "Brahma Baba" to his followers, was a Bhaibund merchant and follower of the Vaishnavite Vallabhacharya Sect. Dada Lekhraj retired from his business in 1932 with assets of 1,000,000 Indian rupees to turn to spirituality. Their original spiritual knowledge was obtained through divine revelations and divine visions of women who had the gift of trance-vision.

Lekhraj began holding satsangs which attracted a number of people and the group became known as Om Mandali. One of his chief visions concerned the establishment of a perfected paradise after a kind of universal destruction of the cosmos, a destruction necessary for an ideal world to be founded. In 1937, he named some of his followers as a managing committee, then reportedly transferred his fortune to the committee. Several women joined Om Mandali and contributed their wealth to the association as well.

Members of the local Bhaibund community reacted unfavourably to his movement. A number of young married Sindhi women attended his ashram and were being encouraged to take vows of celibacy, so the Om Mandali was accused of breaking up families including that of his own daughter who he had married into the family of the leader of what was to become the Anti-Party. Om Mandali was denounced as disturber of family peace and some of the Brahma Kumari wives were mistreated by their families. Lekhraj Kripalani was accused of sorcery, lechery, accused of forming a cult and controlling his community through the art of hypnotism.

After the Partition of India in April 1950, the Brahma Kumaris moved to Mount Abu in India saying that they had been instructed by God to do so. After Dada Lekhraj's death in 1969, his followers expanded the movement to other countries. In 1952, after a 14 year period of retreat during which the Brahma-kumaris published numerous pamphlets, newspaper articles and wrote letters to significant national and international figures, a more structured form of teaching started to be offered to the public by way of a seven lesson course. The movement does not associate itself with Hinduism but projects itself as a vehicle for spiritual teaching rather than a religion.

Brahma Kumaris are monotheistic in their doctrine. God, addressed as "Shiv Baba", is regarded to be an eternal soul, a personality like human souls but the Supreme one (Paramatma) and "knowledgeful". His motive is to awaken humanity and restore harmony, giving power through the Brahma Kumaris' practise of Raja Yoga, eliminating negativity. He is not the creator of matter which is itself regarded to be eternal. He is said to have spoken in person through the mouth of the organization's primary medium Lekhraj Kripalani and to be the destroyer of evil.

The Brahma Kumaris teach a form of meditation through which members are encouraged to purify their minds and 'burn away' the Karmic effects of past misdeeds. This may be done by sitting tranquilly in front of a screen on to which Dada Lekhraj's image is projected, then making affirmations regarding the eternal nature of the soul. Lawrence Babbs described another practise where "the student or students sit in a semi-darkened room facing the teacher (usually a woman). Just above and behind the teacher's head is a red plastic ovoid that glows from a lightbulb within, in its center is a tiny hole which seem s as an intense whitelight against the red glow. This device represents the Supreme Soul (known as Shiv Baba) who is the presiding deity of the universe.

With devotional songs playing softly in the background, student and teacher gaze intently at each other, either in the eyes or at the forehead. While doing this the student is supposed to imagine him or herself as a soul and not as a body. The student is told to think of themselves as separate from the body, as bodiless, as light, as power, as bathed in the love and light of the Supreme Soul, and so on. This might continue for fifteen or twenty minutes". Babb also states that while staring (gazing into the eyes of an adept) at the teacher, a number of students experience visual hallucinations involving lights.

Swaminarayan Sampraday

Bhagwan Swaminarayan or Sahajanand Swami is the central figure in a modern form of Hinduism known as the Swaminarayan Faith and is the founder of the Swaminarayan Sampraday in which followers offer devotion to Bhagwan Swaminarayan as the last expression of god. In this particular custom, Sahajanand Swami is respectfully addressed as Bhagwan Swaminarayan by his followers.

Sahajanand Swami was born in Chhapaiya, Uttar Pradesh, India. He settled in the West Indian state of Gujarat, where he then preached his doctrine until his death in 1830. Sahajanand Swami is also known as Lord Swaminarayan, Ghanshyam Pande, Ghanshyam Maharaj, Shreeji Maharaj, HariKrishna Maharaj and Shri Hari. The Basic Principle of Swaminaryan Bhagawan is Vishista-advaita (qualified non-dualism) propounded by Ramanujacharya.

- Dharma (Religion): Virtuous conduct as defined in the Shrutis and Smrutis is known as Dharma.

- Bhakti (Devotion): Supreme love of the soul combined with the consciousness of the glory of Supreme God is known as Bhakti.
- Jnâna (Enlightenment): Correct awareness about the forms of the soul, illusion, and God is known as 'Jnyana'.
- Vairagya (Renunciation): Detachment from all material possessions and absolute attachment towards God is known as Vairagya.
- Mâyâ (Illusion): It is regarded Tri-Gunatmika i.e. illusion prevails in all three qualities viz. Satva, Rajas and Tamas; To be possessed by Maya is to be caught in darkness; God is the Lord of Maya who acts as the power of God; It breeds ego in one for his body and for the relatives of the body.
- Mukti (Moksha): Loving worship of God.
- Âtman (Self): Recognition of the âtman, after which one experiences a transcendental bliss, is achieved through bhakti-yoga as outlined in the Bhagavad Gitâ, as per the teachings of Lord Swaminarayan. It is the source of energy and is the real knower; It pervades the entire body and is the essence that variousiates matter and life; in character it is inseparable, impenetrable, indestructible and immortal.
- Paramâtman (The Supreme Soul): It is omnipresent within the souls, just as soul is present in the body; it is independent and is the one whom rewards the fala (fruits) to the souls. It is the source of infinite material universes and the First Cause.

International Society for Krishna Consciousness

The International Society for Krishna Consciousness (ISKCON), also known as 'the Hare Krishna' movement, is one of several Vaishnava groups. It was founded in 1966 in New York City by A.C. Bhaktivedanta Swami Prabhupada. While some classified it as a new religious movement, its core philosophy is based on scriptures such as the Úrîmad Bhâgavatam and the Bhagavad-gîtâ, both of which date back more than two millennia. The classifiable visual aspect of the movement and its culture come from the Gaudiya Vaishnava custom, which has had adherents in India ever since the late 1400s. Early converts to the movement were dated to early 1930s.

Non-sectarian in its ideals, ISKCON was formed to spread the practice of bhakti yoga (devotion to God), in which aspirant devotees (bhaktas) dedicate their thoughts and actions towards pleasing the Supreme Lord, Krishna (seen as non-various from God). ISKCON today is a worldwide confederation of more than 400 centres, including 60 farm communities some objectiveing for self-sufficiency, 50 schools and 60 restaurants. In recent decades the movements most rapid expansions in terms of numbers of membership have been within Eastern Europe and India.

Although Krishna is described as the eighth avatara of Vishnu, some Hindus believe that he is the avatari, or the source of all the other avatars. Thus devotees in ISKCON worship Krishna as the highest form of God, svayam bhagavan, and often refer to him as the Supreme Personality of Godhead in writing, which was a phrase coined by Prabhupada in his books on the subject. Devotees consider Radha to be Krishna's divine female counterpart, the embodiment of love. An significant aspect of their philosophy is the belief that the individual soul is an eternal personal identity which does not at last merge into any formless light or void as suggested by the monistic (Advaita) schools of Hinduism. Prabhupada himself never declared ISKCON to be a Hindu organisation, because he regarded it to be a 'material designation' and not an appropriate name. Prabhupada most frequently offers Sanatana-dharma and Varnasrama-dharma as righter names for the religious system which accepts Vedic authority. Also referred as Gaudiya Vaishnavism it is a monotheistic custom that has its roots in the theistic Vedanta customs. These are also other branches of Gaudiya Vaishnavism, of which ISKCON is the largest branch.

Hare Krishna devotees specifically follow a disciplic line of Gaudiya, or Bengali, Bhagavata Vaishnavas which comes under the general description of Gaudiya Vaishnavism. Vaishnavism means 'worship of Vishnu', and Gau

a refers to the area where this particular branch of Vaishnavism is practiced and is widespread, among other places, such as Rajastan and Vrindavana. Gaudiya Vaishnavism has had a uninterrupted following in India, particularly West Bengal and Orissa for the past five hundred years. Srila Prabhupada disseminated Gaudiya Vaishnava Theology in the Western world through extensive writings and translations, including Bhagavad Gita, Srimad Bhagavatam (Bhagavata Purana) and Chaitanya Charitamrita and other scriptures. These works are now available in more than seventy languages and serve as the canon of ISKCON.

Early western conversions to monotheistic Krishna vaisnavism or Bhagavata Vaishnava line, that forms the basis of ISKCON philosophy, were recorded by the Greeks and survived as archeological monuments.

ISKCON is actively evangelistic. Members try to spread Krishna consciousness, primarily by singing the Hare Krishna mantra in public places and by selling books written by A. C. Bhaktivedanta Swami Prabhupada. Both of these activities are known within the movement as Sankirtan. As per the doctrine of Chaitanya Mahaprabhu, one does not need to be born in a Hindu family to take up the practice of Vaishnavism.

This philosophy places ISKCON in strong contrast to a number of other branches of Hinduism, which may stress hereditary lineage and are non-missionary by nature. There are ISKCON communities around the world with schools, restaurants and farms. In general, funds collected by ISKCON are treated as communal property and used to support the community as a whole and to promote the preaching mission. A number of temples also have programs to provide meals for the needy. Also, ISKCON has recently brought the academic study of Krishna into western academia as Krishnology.

Lingayatism

The history of the Lingayat faith goes back to Basavanna (1134 - 1196 AD). Lingayatism or Veerashaivism is a Hindu religious sect in India. The adherents of this faith are known as Lingayats or Veerashaivas. The term is derived from Lingavantha in Kannada. This religion represents a reform movement attributed to Basavanna and others in the 12th century AD.

It is said that Basavanna, though born a Brahmin, rebelled against the rigid practices of the caste system then prevalent, and eventually began expounding his own philosophy with a casteless society at its core. Soon, his philosophy began attracting large numbers of people into the fold. Saints like Allama Prabhu, Akka Mahadevi, Channabasavanna also played pivotal roles in founding and spearheading the sect.

Basavanna lived and taught in the northern part of what is now Karnataka State. This movement found its roots during the brief rule of the southern Kalachuri dynasty in those parts of the state. Customally, Basavanna is believed to be an incarnation of Nandi, Shiva's greatest devotee.

Another school of thought maintains that Basavanna only brought about a renaissance in an already existing sect. They attribute the founding of the sect to the mythological Panchacharyas (Five Teachers). The Panchacharyas consisted of Sri Revanaradhya or Revanasiddha, Marularadhya or Marulasidhdha, Ekoramaradhaya or Ekorama, Panditaradhya and Vishwaradhya. This theory however, is not historically attested and Basavanna is widely held as having founded this sect.

Lingayats believe in a monotheistic world where Shiva the supreme god and self are one and the same. This form of monotheism is called Shakti Vishishtadvaita. Unlike other Hindus, Lingayats don't place significance on the Vedas but rather focus more on the Hindu Agamas, specifically, the Shaivite Agamas. Some Lingayats view the Vedas to be polytheistic in nature while the Agamas are held as being strictly monotheistic and devotional in nature. Veera Shaivism's means of attainment depend on the concepts of Panchâchâra (five codes of conduct), Ashtâvarana (eight shields) and Shatsthala which are central to Lingayat theosophy. The Shatsthala refers to the various levels of attainment that the devotee can achieve to protect the body as the abode of the Lord.

REFORM MOVEMENTS

Arya Samaj

Arya Samaj is a Hindu reform movement founded in India by Swami Dayananda in 1875. He was a sannyasi (renouncer) who believed in the infallible authority of the Vedas. Dayananda advocated the doctrine of karma and reincarnation, and emphasized the ideals of brahmacharya (chastity) and sanyasa (renunciation).

The Vedic Schools represented the first practical application of Swami Dayanand's vision of religious and social reform. They enjoyed a mixed reception. On the one hand, students were not allowed to perform customal murtipuja at the school, and were instead expected to perform sandhya (a form of meditative prayer using mantras from the Vedas) and participate in agnihotra twice daily. Also, disciplinary action was swift and not infrequently severe. On the other hand, all meals, lodging, clothing and books were given to the students free of charge, and the study of Sanskrit was opened to non-Brahmins. The most noteworthy characteristic of the Schools was that only those texts which accepted the authority of the Vedas were to be taught. This, in the opinion of Swami Dayanand, was critical for the spiritual and social regeneration of Vedic culture in India.

While travelling Swami Dayanand came into close and extended contact with several of the leading Indian intellectuals of the age, including Raj Narayan Bose, Debendranath Tagore and Keshab Chandra Sen, all of whom were actively involved in the Brahmo Samaj. This reform organization, founded in 1828, held a number of views similar to those of Swami Dayanand in matters both religious (e.g. a belief in monotheism and the eternality of the soul) and social (e.g. the need to abolish the hereditary caste system and uplift the masses through education). Tagore had written a book entitled Brahmo Dharma, which serves as a comprehensive manual of religion and ethics to the members of that society, and Swami Dayanand is said to have studied it thoroughly while in Calcutta.

Although Sen tried on more than one occasion to persuade Swami Dayanand to join the Brahmo Samaj, there existed various points of contention which the Swami simply could not overlook, the most significant being the position of the Vedas. Swami Dayanand held the Vedas to be divine revelation, and refused to accept any suggestions to the contrary. Despite this difference of opinion, however, it seems that the members of the Brahmo Samaj and Swami Dayanand parted on good terms, the former having publicly praised the latter's visit to Calcutta in several journals and the latter having taken inspiration from the former's activity in the social sphere.

Swami Dayanand made several changes in his approach to the work of reforming Hindu society after having visited Calcutta. The most significant of these changes was that he began lecturing in Hindi. Prior to his tour of Bengal, the Swami had always held his discourses and debates in Sanskrit. While this gained him a certain degree of respect among both the learned and the common people alike, it prevented him from spreading his message to the broader masses. The change to Hindi allowed him to attract increasingly larger crowds, and as a result his ideas of reform began to circulate among the lower classes of society as well.

From June to September 1874, Swami Dayanand dictated a comprehensive series of lectures to his scribe, Pundit Bhimsen Sharma, which dealt with his views and beliefs regarding a wide range of subjects including God, the Vedas, Dharma, the soul, science, philosophy, childrearing, education, government and the possible future of both India and the world. The resulting manuscript was edited by Sharma and others, and was eventually published under the title Satyarth Prakash or The Light of Truth in 1875 at Varanasi. This voluminous work would prove to play a central role in the establishment and later growth of the organization which would come to be known as the Arya Samaj.

The 10 Principles of the Arya Samaj was agreed on unanimously (including Swami Dayanand, the founder of the Arya Samaj) at the formation of the Lahore Arya Samaj on 24 June 1877. This replaced the original list of 28 rules and regulations drafted by Dayanand for the Rajkot

Arya Samaj. This simplified the principles, while the bylaws were removed to a different document.

Of the ten, the first three principles are seen as comprising the doctrinal core of the Arya Samaj, as they summarize the member's beliefs in regard to God, the nature of Divinity and the authority of the Vedas. The remaining seven principles reflect the reformative ambitions of the Samaj in regard to both the individual and society at large. The 10 Principles of the Arya Samaj are:

1. God is the original source of all true knowledge and all that is known by the physical sciences.
2. God is existent, intelligent and blissful. He is formless, almighty, just, merciful,unborn, endless, unchangeable, incomparable, the support and master of all. He is omnipresent, immortal, fearless, eternal, holy and the maker of the universe. He alone is worthy of worship.
3. The Vedas are the scriptures of all true knowledge. It is the duty of all Aryas to read them, hear them being read and teach them to others.
4. One should always be ready to accept truth and give up untruth.
5. All acts should be performed in accordance with Dharma, after deliberating what is right and wrong.
6. The primary object of Arya Samaj is to do good to the world, by promoting physical, spiritual and social good of everyone
7. Our conduct towards all should be guided by love, righteousness and justice.
8. We should dispel ignorance and promote knowledge.
9. One should see one's own greatest welfare as residing in the welfare of others.
10. One should regard oneself under restriction to follow the rules of society calculated to promote the well being of all, while one should be free in matters of individual welfare.

Sri Aurobindo Ashram

Sri Aurobindo's Ashram was founded by Sri Aurobindo on the 24 November 1926 At the time there were no more than 24 disciples in the Ashram. In December of that year, Sri Aurobindo decided to withdraw from public view, and appointed his co-worker Mirra Alfassa, thenceforth known as The Mother in charge of the ashram. In the early history of the ashram there was a regular routine. At 6:15 every morning The Mother seem ed on the ashram balcony to initiate the day with her blessings. Sadhaks (spiritual aspirants), who got up at 3AM, finished their own meditations and a good portion of the day's work, and then assembled under the balcony to receive her blessings.

As the ashram grew, a number of departments sprang up: the office, library, dining room, press, workshops, playground, art gallery, dispensary, farms, dairies, flower gardens, guest houses, legal department, audit department, and a number of others, too. The heads of the departments met The Mother in the morning and took her blessings and orders. Again at 10 a.m. she used to meet all the sadhaks individually. Once again, in the evening at 5:30 PM, she conducted meditation and met each sadhak once more.

In addition, four times a year she used to give public Darshans (a spiritual gathering where the guru bestows blessings) at which a few thousand devotees gathered and received her Grace. A complete method of Yoga that would transform human nature to divine life. In Sri Aurobindo's system, the highest objective is the being of one, without the renunciation of life in the world. Such a fulfillment of the consciousness, the urge for perfection, must not be confined to few individuals but must extend to the masses, leading to a new type of being that is "eternal, self-existing, and inalienable".

Sri Aurobindo lays the foundation of his inquiry by focusing on the contradiction between the mundane human existence and the human desire to acquire a divine perfection in life. By introducing the category of evolution, he wants to resolve the paradox of the human being's delimited consciousness and his desire to be identical with a divine form. Apart from study of Sri Aurobindo's and The Mother's books, there are no specific disciplines recommended, but rather the practice of Integral Yoga means that every sadhak should follow whatever spiritual methods they feel guided to.

Anyone can join at any time. There's no method, no period and no training as such. It's the only self-practice to reach the higher mind, eternal state and the continuous help will be sourced only from Divine and no one else. Sri Aurobindo's teachings have influenced not just Indian thought, but also is founded throughout the West, thanks to books and regional centers. It is also a contributing element in Integral philosophy.

Brahmo Samaj

Brahmo Samaj is the societal component of Brahmoism. It is without doubt the most influential socio-religious movement in the evolution of

Modern India. It was conceived as reformation of the prevailing Bengal of the time and began the Bengal Renaissance of the 19th century pioneering all religious, social and educational advance of the Hindu community in the 19th century. From the Brahmo Samaj springs Brahmoism, the most recent of legally recognised religions in India and Bangladesh, reflecting its non-syncretic "foundation of Rammohun Roy's reformed spiritual Hinduism and scientifically invigorated by inclusion of root Hebraic - Islamic religious doctrine and practice."

The Brahmo Samaj is a community of people assembled for orderly public meeting, discussion or worship of the Eternal, Immutable Supreme Being, Author and Preserver of the Universe. The Brahmo Samaj, represents a body of men who are struggling, in India, to establish the worship of the Supreme Being in spirit as opposed to the prevailing idolatry of the land. Although the Brahmo Samaj movement was born in Kolkata, the idea soon spread to the rest of India. That happened to be the period when the railways were expanding and communication was becoming easier. Outside Bengal presidency some of the prominent centres of Brahmo activity were: Punjab, Sind, and Bombay and Madras presidencies. Even to this day, there are several active branches outside West Bengal.

In all fields of social reform, including abolition of the caste system and of the dowry system, emancipation of women, and improving the educational system, the Brahmo Samaj reflected the ideologies of the Bengal Renaissance. Brahmoism, as a means of discussing the dowry system, was a central theme of Sarat Chandra Chattopadhyay's noted 1914 Bengali language novella, Parineeta. After controversies, including the controversy over Keshub Chunder Sen's daughter's child marriage rituals wherein the validity of Brahmo marriages were questioned and split the Brahmo Samaj of India, the Brahmo Samaj Marriage Bill of 1871 was enacted as the Special Marriages Act of 1872 and set the age at which girls could be married at 14. All Brahmo marriages were thereafter solemnised under this law which necessitated the affirmation "I am not Hindu, nor a Mussalman, nor a Christian". The Special Marriages Act 1872 was repealed by the new Special Marriages Act in 1954 which became the secular Marriage law for India. The old Special Marriages Act of 1872 was allowed to live on as the Hindu Marriage Act 1955 for Hindus - Brahmo Religionists are barred from this Act; which is applicable, however, to Hindus who follow the Brahmo Samaj. It also affirmed social reform movements of people not directly attached to the Samaj, such as Pandit Iswar Chandra Vidyasagar's movement which promoted widow re-marriage.

Ramakrishna Mission

The Ramakrishna Mission is a philanthropic, volunteer, organization founded by Sri Ramakrishna's chief disciple Swami Vivekananda on May 1, 1897. The Mission conducts extensive work in healthcare, disaster relief, rural management, tribal welfare, elementary and higher education and culture through its 114 centers spread across India. It uses the combined efforts of hundreds of ordered monks and thousands of householder disciples. The Mission claims to draw inspiration from the karma yoga. The Mission, which is headquartered at Belur Math near Kolkata, India, subscribes to the ancient Hindu philosophy of Vedanta. It is affiliated with the monastic organization Ramakrishna Math, with whom it shares members. The Mission also manages nearly 50 centers outside India.

The Mission is a registered Society laying emphasis on rendering welfare services undertaken with a spiritual outlook. The service activities are rendered looking upon all as veritable expression of the Divine. The Motto of the organisation is Atmano Mokshartham Jagad-hitaya Cha (For one's own salvation, and for the good of the world). Strictly speaking, the Ramakrishna Math is a monastic order, and the Ramakrishna Mission is the part of the organization that carries on activities such as disaster relief, operation of schools and charitable hospitals, and other work. However, because the humanitarian activities of the movement are more well-known than the monastic order, and because the monks of the order perform a great deal of the humanitarian work, "Ramakrishna Mission" is popularly used to refer to both institutions.

REVIVALIST MOVEMENTS

Gayatri Pariwar

Shriram Sharma was an Indian seer, sage, a visionary of the New Golden Era and the Founder of the All World Gayatri Pariwar. He devoted his life to the welfare of people and the refinement of the moral and cultural environment. He pioneered the revival of spirituality, creative integration of the modern and ancient sciences and religion relevant in the challenging conditions of the present times. His personality was a harmonious blend of a saint, spiritual scientist,freedom fighter , proponent of scientific spirituality, yogi, philosopher, psychologist, writer, reformer, scholar and visionary.

Pt. Shriram Sharma founded Gayatri Tapobhumi at Mathura, India in 1953. On the completion of the 24 Mahapurashcharans, he organized a grand 1008 Kundi Yagya in 1958, which served as a base to launch the Yug Nirman Yojna, a global movement for moral, cultural, intellectual and spiritual refinement and reconstruction. The objectives of this movement are to reform the individual, the family and social values of mankind and to change the current ideologies and concepts of morality and social structure for a better tomorrow.

Through various activities at Mathura, including the performance of yagnas on large scale, Acharyaji gathered a team of dedicated men and women. Thus the organization called "Gayatri Pariwar" was born. As per the plans projected under the Yug Nirman Yojna, the mission has contributed to the upliftment of the personal, familial and social aspects of human life. Its major activities include mass awareness and education on cultural values through small and large scale Gayatri Yojnas and collective projects of social transformation with people's voluntary participation. Propagation of ideal marriages without dowry and extravagant shows has been a significant and trend-setting achievement, especially in the Indian context. Other accomplishments include upliftment of the social status of women and an integrated and self-reliant development of villages.

Art of Living Foundation

The Art of Living Foundation, is a non-profit, volunteer based organization founded by Sri Sri Ravi Shankar. A non-denominational, educational and humanitarian non-profit organization, The Art of Living Foundation (AOLF)'s stated mission is to uplift society by strengthening the individual through programs that create a sense of belonging, repair human values, develop life to its full potential, and encourage people from all backgrounds, religions, and cultural customs to come together in celebration and service. As per the Foundation, it has programs in more than 140 countries around the world, and offers several courses to bring individuals knowledge and techniques to unlock their deepest potential and bring fullness to life.

The Art of Living Foundation (AOLF) has its international headquarters in Bangalore, India at Veda Vignan Manahvidyapeeth or VVM campus (usually referred to as the Bangalore Ashram)and has regional centers in more than 140 countries. The foundation was founded by His Holiness Sri Sri Ravi Shankar. AOLF has been a non profit educational and humanitarian organization in the U.S. since 1989. Accredited as a United Nations Non-Governmental organization in 1996, it is now one of the UN's largest volunteer-based NGOs. It works in special consultative status with the UN's Economic and Social Council, participating in a variety of committees and activities relating to health, education, sustainable development, conflict resolution, and disaster relief.

The Foundation operates as a social business and its chief activity is to organize Art of Living courses, yoga and meditation workshops, and education and trauma relief in areas of trauma and disaster.. The majority of the officers of the organization, along with most of its teachers and staff, are volunteers. All humanitarian programs, disaster relief efforts and training programs are conducted through, or in conjunction with its sister organization, the International Association for Human Values (IAHV). Some of the key world-wide chapters include the Art of Living Foundation (U.S.A.), Vyakti Vikas Kendra (India), Die Kunst des Lebens (Germany), Art of Living Center (Canada), Art of Living South Africa, Art of Living Israel, Art of Living Brazil, and Art of Living Argentina. All told, there are international centres in 140 countries.

Chinmaya Mission

Chinmaya Mission was founded in 1953 by Swami Chinmayananda. It is administered from Central Chinmaya Mission Trust, Mumbai. There are over 300 mission centres all over India and Abroad. His Holiness Swami Chinmayananda, founder of Chinmaya Mission, taught spirituality as the art of living. Through jnana yoga (the Vedantic path of spiritual knowledge), he emphasized the balance of head and heart, pointing out selfless work, study, and meditation as the cornerstones of spiritual practice.

Not gratified by worldly aspirations or his degrees in literature and law, Balakrishna Menon pursued spiritual studies for nine years in the Himalayas, under the guidance of Swami Sivananda (Divine Life Society) and the tutelage of Swami Tapovanam. He eventually came to share this Vedantic knowledge with the masses, in the form of the dynamic teacher known as Swami Chinmayananda.

Swamiji is famous worldwide as a spiritual master and one of the foremost teachers of Shrimad Bhagavad Gita. He is credited with the renaissance of spirituality and cultural values in India, and with the spreading of the ageless wisdom of Advaita Vedanta, as expounded by Adi Shankaracharya, throughout the world. Mission's objective is to provide to individuals, from any background, the wisdom of Vedanta and practical means for spiritual growth and happiness, enabling them to become a positive contributor to the society and to give maximum happiness to maximum number for the maximum time is our religion.

Divine Life Society

The Divine Life Society was founded by Swami Sivananda Saraswati at Rishikesh, India in 1936.

In 1936, after returning from a pilgrimage, Swami Sivananda took residence in an old kutir on the banks of the Ganges in Rishikesh. Other disciples seeking to live in his company also took up residence in the surrounding area, often in less than ideal conditions. In order to better serve the growing tide of disciples, he founded The Divine Life Society Trust. A grant of land from the ruler of Tehri-Garhwal eventually helped to provide space for new buildings and the continuing growth of the new ashram.

Its objective is to disperse spiritual knowledge in the following ways:

- through publication of books, pamphlets and magazines on the subjects of Yoga and Vedanta.
- holding and arranging spiritual conferences and discourses (Satsang)
- establishing training centers for the practice of Yoga.
- enabling aspirants to develop their spiritual lives via systematic training in yoga and philosophy.
- establishing charitable organizations.
- through the preservation of the ancient customs and cultural practices of India.

Rashtriya Swayamsevak Sangh

The Rashtriya Swayamsevak Sangh also known as the Sangh or the RSS, is a Hindu nationalist organization in India. It was founded in 1925 by Dr. K.B. Hedgewar. The RSS is active throughout India, whilst it operates abroad by a number of names. Their general philosophical outlook is cultural nationalism known as integral humanism, objectiveed at revitalizing the spiritual and moral customs of India. RSS believes that Hinduism is not simply a religion but a way of life. The proclaimed need of the organization is serving the nation and its people in the form of - Bharata Mata (Mother India) and protecting the interests of the People who treat India as their motherland. RSS has never directly contested elections, but they support parties that support its outlook on key issues of swadeshi and cultural nationalism. Even though the RSS usually supports the Bharatiya Janata Party it has at times refused to support it due to difference of opinion with the party.

Most of the organisational work of the RSS is done through the coordination of shakhas, or branches. These shakhas are run every morning (prabhat shakha), evening (sayam shakha) or night (ratri shakha) for 1 hour in public places and are open to people of all castes, religious doctrines or social and economic status. Currently more than 60,000 shakhas are run throughout India. Apart from 42,000 daily gatherings, there are about 5,000 weekly and 2,000 monthly gatherings conducted throughout the length and breadth of the country.

These shakhas are the core building blocks of RSS structure. During a Shakha, the activities consist of yoga, games, discussions on broad range of social topics, prayer to Bharat Mata and an inspirational session (baudhik). The RSS uniform consists of a black cap, white shirt and khaki-coloured shorts. On the day of 'Guru Poornima' the RSS volunteers pay tributes to the 'Bhagwa Dhwaj (the saffron flag), which has considerable symbolic significance.

As per the RSS its primarily goal is the revival of national consciousness or national renaissance as it feels that centuries of foreign rule has led to self-oblivion overtaking the society. RSS believes in a "burning devotion to the Motherland (India), a feeling of fraternity among all citizens, intense awareness of a common national life derived from a common culture and shared history and heritage", as well as to "activise the dormant Hindu society (of India), realise its past mistakes, to instill in it a firm determination to set them right, and ultimately to make it bestir itself to reassert its honour and self-respect". RSS claims that its core ideology is based on Integral humanism and Cultural Nationalism.

Vishva Hindu Parishad

Vishva Hindu Parishad (World Hindu Council), widely recognized by its initials 'VHP', is a Hindu organization in India, an offshoot of the Rashtriya Swayamsevak Sangh. It was founded in 1964. Its slogan is "Dharmo raksati raksitah", which means "Dharma protects those who protect Dharma." Its symbol is a banyan tree.

The VHP says Bharat has historically been a Hindu nation, in culture, heritage and history. Islam was brought by foreign invaders who imposed and coerced it upon millions of Hindus (corroborated by a number of historic acts of temple destruction, pogroms and mass conversions); Christian missionaries brought in Christianity when the Portuguese, French and the British colonized the land. It is a fact that Christian missionaries often denigrated and demonized the Hindu religion to coerce native peoples into converting. While working to convert Christians, tribal peoples (native

Hindus) and Muslims to Hinduism, the VHP states that all Muslims and Christians were Hindus in the first place, and that all citizens of Bharat are naturally Hindus.

The VHP has recently engaged in several programs to reconvert Hindus who had previously converted to Christianity. VHP has advanced that conversion to Christianity had earned them no significant benefits and so their return to Hinduism was relatively straightforward. The law enforcement authorities have reported that the conversion processes have largely been peaceful and voluntary. However, there has been some aggressive altercations associated concerning this issue, the subject of religious conversions being very controversial in a number of parts of India.

In addition, the VHP has spoken out against Islamic Fundamentalism and the rise of Islamist terrorism in various parts of India in recent years. The VHP has organized awareness programs to educate people about Islamic terrorism and have criticized the central government for being soft on terror in order to cultivate Muslim votes. They have also protested against Islamism by organizing business shutdowns (Bandhs) as a gesture of civil disobedience. The VHP has been a prime backer of the World Hindu Conference in which issues such as casteism, sectarianism, and the future of Hindus were discussed. Prior Conferences have included Hindu Groups such as Parisada Hindu Dharma.

REFERENCES

Balslev, A.N.: *A study of time in Indian philosophy*, Wiesbaden, Otto Harrassowitz, 1983.

Barnett, S.A.: *Coconuts and gold: relational identity in a South Indian caste*, 1976.

Clothey, F.W.: *Chronometry, cosmology and the festival calendar in the Murukan cult.*, New Delhi: Manohar, 1982.

Courtright, PB.: *Ganesa: Lord of obstacles, Lord of beginnings*, New York, Oxford University Press, 1985.

Daniel, E.V.: *Fluid signs: being a person the Tamil way*, Berkeley, University of California Press, 1984.

Durkheim, E.: *The elementary forms of the religions life*, London, George Allen & Unwin, 1915.

Fuller, C. J.: *Gods, priests and purity: on the relation between Hinduism and the caste system*, 1979.

Gale, R.M.: *The language of time*, London, Routledge & Kegan Paul, 1968.

Gell, A.: *The anthropology of time*, Berg, Oxford, 1992.

Gopinatha Rao, T.A.: *Elements of Hindu,* Delhi, Motilal Banarsidass. 1997.

Gough, E.K.: *Brahman kinship in a Tamil village*, Am. Anthrop, 1956.

Handelman, D. & D.D.: *Shulman Cod inside out: Siva's game of dice*, New York, Oxford University Press, 1997.

Kalynasuntaram, N.: *Tiruccentur Murukankoyil varalaru.: Tiruchendur*: *Tirukkumaran Patippakam*, 1980.

Kane, P.V.: *History of Dharmasastra, 5,* Poona, Bhandarkar Oriental Research Institute, 1958.

McTaggart, J.M.E.: *The nature of existence 2*, Cambridge, University Press, 1927.

Mellor, D.H.: *Real time*, Cambridge, University Press, 1981.

Merrey, K.L.: *The Hindu festival calendar*, New Delhi: Manohar, 1982.

Moreno Arcas: *M. Murukan: a God of healing poisons; the physics of worship in a South Indian center for pilgrimage*, University of Chicago, 1984.

O'Flaherty, W.D.: *Women, androgynes, and other mythical beasts*, Chicago, University Press, 1980.

Paktavatsalam, K.: *Kalukumalaittala varalaru: Kovilpatti: Selvarajan*, 1972.

Pocock, D.F.: *The anthropology of time-reckoning*, Contrib, Ind. Social, 1964.

Trautmann, T.R.: *Indian time, European time*, Ann Arbor: University of Michigan Press, 1995.

10

Reformers

In India, whenever religion and philosophy were perceived to be in danger of getting distorted at the hands of a few, reformers emerged to steer the faith away from distortions. They were concerned with the protection of the essence of religion, which is devotion to God; they did their best to rid religion of unwanted fringe elements who tampered with its true nature and practice.

The first thing the reformers did was to carry off the dominance of the Sanskrit language in Hinduism and certain modes of worship. They used the native language of the people to teach the truths of religion through songs and simple poems. To make religion common man-friendly, they played down the significance of erudition in the sastras and stressed the significance of bhakti or devotion to God. They also strove to remove the impression that God, religion and devotion are exclusive domains of the Brahmins. These reformers also decried ostentation and hypocrisy.

The Azhwars and Nayanmars of Tamil Nadu, and saint-poets like Thyagaraja, Annamacharya, Narayanateertha, Meera Bai and Narsi Mehta were reformers who evoked the God-loving nature inherent in people. The dasas of Karnataka promoted religion and bhakti through devotional songs composed in Kannada.

REFORMERS IN EARLY PERIOD

Azhwars

The twelve Azhwars flourished in south India somewhere between the fifth and ninth centuries of the first millenium . The Bhakti movement in India got a great boost from their Tamil hymns, which are profound and spontaneous outpourings of their bhagavath anubhavam (the enjoyment of the Divine being). Their hymns add up to 4000 in number and are revered as " the sacred collect" (Dhivya Prabhandham). They house a rich vein of philosophical and theological ideas central to the Visishtadvaitha Vedantham: Tattva (ultimate reality), Hitha (the means for attainment of that reality) and the Purushartha (the supreme goal of life). In the second millenium, Acharya Raamanuja developed further the theory of Supreme reality expounded by Azhwars into a clear doctrine with all its philosophical implications and underpinnings.

The Bhakti literature that sprang from these Azhwars has contributed to the establishment and sustenance of a culture that broke away from the ritual-oriented Vedic religion and rooted itself in devotion as the only path for salvation. In addition they helped to make the Tamil religious life independent of a knowledge of Sanskrit. As part of the legacy of the Azhwars, five Vaishnava philosophical customs (sampradayas) has developed at the later stages.

The twelve Azhwars were all inspired and ardent devotees who transmitted their divine infatuation to millions. They have left behind an imperishable legacy of devotional Tamil poetry - naalaayira Divya Prabhandham (regarded to be the essence of the Vedas, in Tamil, and all in praise of Lord Vishnu). These have been rarely equalled either in quantity or in quality ever after. The one held in greatest esteem among the Azhwars is NammAzhwar. He lived during the seventh century AD. His contribution to the four thousand prabandhams is as many as 1352. His hymns are believed by the Vaishnavites to contain the essence of the Vedas. His works - Thiru Aasiriyam, Thiru Virudham, Periya Thiruvandhadhi correspond to the Yajur, Rig and Atharva Vedas respectively. His other work Periya Thirumozhi (Divine words) is the one of the key works of Vaishnavism.

PeriyAzhwar delighted in worshipping Vishnu as mother, nurse, devotee and lady love. Andal, who grew up in PeriyAzhwar's home, is assigned the Tiruppaavai, a most beautiful collection of 30 verses giving expression to the purest love of God. Thirumangai Azhwar has done mangalasasanam (sung in praise) of maximum number of Divya Desams.

Nayanmars

Nayanmars were Saivite saints from Tamil Nadu, who were active between the fifth and the tenth centuries AD. As per the Tamil Saiva hagiography Periyapuranam written during the thirteenth century AD, there were 63 Nayanmars. Periyapuranam narrates the history of each of these Nayanmars. The Jain hagiography Mahapurana, a ninth century

Sanskrit work by Jinasena, which lists 63 Jain saints, probably formed the basis of Periyapuranam as well as the number of Nayanmars.

Sundarar's eighth century work Tiruttondar tokai lists 60 Saiva saints. But it does not give any of the legends linked with them. In the 10th century, Nambiyandar Nambi composed the Tirrutontar Antati, in which he added Sundarar and his parents to the list, thus creating the canonical list of 63 saints. The composition also contained brief sketches of their legends. Nayanmars were from varied backgrounds. They ranged from kings to soldiers to the untouchables. The Nayanmars who were regarded as the foremost among the 63 are Appar, Sundarar and Sambandar.

Saint-poet Thyagaraja

Tyagaraja was born on 4th May 1767 in Tiruvarur at the residence of his maternal grandfather, Sri Giriraja Kavi who was attached to the Tanjore court. He was the third son of Sri Rama Brahmam and Sitamma, who were then living in a house gifted by Tulajaji of Tanjavur on Tirumanjana Veethi in Tiruvayyaru. Tyagaraja had his early tutelage under his father, Sri Ramabrahmam, a scholar by his won right and later Sri Ramakrshnananda. It is recorded that Tyagaraja had come under the determine of Saint Narada about whom he gained a wide knowledge from the palm leaf manuscripts preserved by his grandfather and later, a treatise called 'Svaranava.' The magnitude and the quality of Tyagaraja's later achievements reveal an effort possible only with the blessings of saints like Sri Narada. Hence his compositions: "Narada Guru Swami" in Darbar, "Sri Narada" in Kanada, and "Vara Narada" in VijayaSri extolling Narada are seen as acknowledgment of his feeling.

Tyagaraja at some stage in his early life, came under the influence of Rama yahna and what followed was a period of undivided devotion to Sri Rama, a movement of tidal proportions in the field of music and spirituality that vies comparability with Ramadasa and Tulasidasa, especially the latter whose picturesque depictions of Sri Rama on the Suvela mountain, Ehi Vidhikrpa Rupa Gunadhama Ram...(Lanka, Doha Ila, Ramacharita Manasa), as per the scholars, finds and echo in Tyagaraja's "Giripai Nelakonna" in Sahana and "Paritapamu" in Pratapa Varali, two of his last pieces associated with salvation, where he narrates the experience of the divine presence.

Tyagaraja's fame and the popularity of his songs brought him a number of disciples. Three branches of his Sishya parampara need specific mention, namely: Umayalpuram, Tillaisthanam and Walajapet, headed by Sundara Bhagavatar and Krshna Bhagavatar, Rama Iyengar, and Valajapet

Venkataramana Bhagavatar respectively, who imbibed all that was Tyagaraja and, in turn, propagated his kritis.

An invitation from his far flung disciples and admirers took Tyagaraja on a pilgrimage which extended unto Tirupati where the drawn curtain at the sanctum sanctorum moved him to compose "Tera Tiyagarada" in Gaulipantu. His next move was to the neighbourhood of Madras where at the insistence of Kovur Sundara Mudaliar, he visited his village Kovurr and composed five songs on Lord Sundaresa. At Tiruvotiryur, he was drawn by Goddes Tripurasundari to sing five kritis. A srimukham from the noble sanyasin and Ramabhakta, Upanishad Brahmam took Tyagaraja to Kanchipuram where he sang in praise of Lord Varadaraja and Goddess Kamakshi. At Nagapatnam he composed two pieces on Goddess Nilayatakshi.

Tyagaraja's visit to Srirangam is commemorated by five kritis. The next shrine he visited was Lalgudi, known then as Tapastirthapura, where he composed three pieces on Goddess Mahita pravrddha Srimati and two pieces on Saptarshisvara. Besides these kshetra pancaratna kirtanas, Tyagaraja also composed Utsava sampradaya and Divyanama kirtanas and Operas like Nauka caritra and Prahlada bhaktivijaya.

Annamacharya

Sri Tallapaka Annamacharya, the mystic saint composer of the 15th century is the earliest known musician of South India to compose songs called sankeertanas in praise of Lord Venkateswara, the deity of Seven Hills in Tirumala, India. Annamacharya was born on May 9, 1408 in Tallapaka, a remote village in Kadapa district of Andhra Pradesh, India. He lived immaculately for 95 years until February 23, 1503. His wife, Thimmakka was also a poet and had written Subhadra Kalyanam and regarded as the first Telugu women poet. His Son PeddaTirumalacharya was also a well known poet.

Annamacharya was one of the first few who opposed the social stigma of "untouchable castes" in his era with his sankeertanas explaining the relationship between God and human is same irrespective of their color, caste and financial status in beautiful yet powerful usage of words in his songs. Usage of words in the sankeertanas have a mellifluous effect on any listener. Writing 32,000 songs in a life time with highest quality of language can be regarded the greatest achievement of any era and most significantly they are woven beautifully around the god he believed.

Annamacharya regarded his compositions as floral offerings to God. In the poems, he praises Venkateswara, describes his love for him, argues and quarrels with the Lord, confesses the devotee's failures and apprehensions, and surrenders himself to Venkateshwara. His songs are classified into Adhyaatama (spiritual) and Sringaara (romantic) sankeertanas.

Mirabai

Mirabai was a Hindu mystical poetess whose compositions are popular throughout India. Mirabai is held to have been a disciple of Ravidas. Mirabai composed between 200 to 1300 prayerful songs called bhajans. These bhajans are in the bhakti custom, and most passionately praised Lord Krishna. The extant version of her poems are in a Rajasthani dialect of Hindi and in Gujarati. A number of the details of Mirabai's life are pieced together from her poetry and the stories later recounted by members of her community. Mirabai's life history is held as truth by followers of the Bhakti custom.

Saguna class of worshippers of Brahman. Theologically, they believed that between Atman and Paramatma (here the Sanskrit Parama- carries approximately the same meaning as Latin Trans-), this physical body is the only wall, and upon death the Atman and Paramatman will combine just as a pot filled with water is placed in pond and if the pot breaks the water inside (Atman) will combine with the water outside (Parama Atman).

Mirabai's poetry holds love for Krishna closer to her heart than the love for friends and family. She perceived Krishna to be her husband, lover, lord and master. The unique characteristic of Mirabai's poetry is the use of complete surrender to her love for Krishna. Her longing for union with Krishna is predominant in Mira's poetry who says she wants to be coloured with the colour of dusk (dusk being the symbolic colour of Krishna). She believed that in her previous life she was one of the several gopis in Vrindavan, in love with Krishna. Much like the gopis, as mentioned in the life of Krishna, Mirabai looked upon Krishna as her lover, seeking spiritual and physical union with him. Her writings were at the same time, spiritual and highly devotional. Mirabai's songs portray a personal universe where the only existence was that of Krishna - her sole object of desire.

A Mirabai poem is customally called a pada, a term used by the 14th century preachers for a small spiritual song. This is usually composed in simple rhythms and carries a refrain within itself. Her collection of songs is called the Padavali. The typicality of Indian love poetry of those days was used by Mirabai but as an instrument to express her deepest emotions felt for her ishta-devata. Her typical medium of singing was Vraja-bhasha, a dialect of Hindi spoken in and around Vrindavan (the childhood home of Krishna), sometimes mixed with Rajasthani.

Narsi Mehta

Narsi Mehta was the first Vaishnava poet saint of Gujarat. He was a contemporary of Namdev. The autobiography of Namdev consists of eight pads. This Gujarati poet saint speaks about his conversion to Krishna Bhakti in its opening pads. As per the a popular belief, Narsi Mehta was deeply affected by his sister-in-law's mockery. He went and meditated before Siva for seven days, as a result of which Siva granted him darshan. Then Siva told him, 'Your Bhakti delights me' and placed his hand on Narsi's head. Thus Narsi was purified from his sins and his sleeping speech was awakened. Narsi then asked for a boon saying, 'O Lord, give me something agreeable to you and easy to attain: have pity on me'.

Narsi Mehta considers Siva as his guru. Siva granted him a boon to his humble devotee the boon was the joy of singing Krishna's praise forever. It shows that Siva himself frees his bhaktas to become Hari bhaktas. Narsi has referred Siva as Gopinath (Lord of the cowherds) in his Gujarati pad. In a number of his writings, the Vaishnava names of God alternating with Saiva or Vedantic names such as Jagadguru, Jagadis, Atmaram and Parabrahman can be seen. Apart from these three names, the name Vitthala has seem ed most frequently in Narsi's pad, who is referred to the Pandharpur deity.

REFORMERS IN MEDIEVAL PERIOD

Raja Ram Mohan Roy

Raja Ram Mohan Roy (1772-1833) in 1828 founded an organization called Brahmo Samaj. Indian historians consider this organization forerunner which paved the way for reformation in India and its establisher as the 'father of modern India'. Raja Ram was a Brahman from Bengal. He was a British civil servant in India. He saw in British rule of India the best things that were benefical to India. He adored the west European philosophy of democracy, liberalism and humanism. He had a great interest in non- Indian cultures and religions. He was especially impressed by Christianity and other religions which preached the existence of one Almighty God.

Raja Ram tried to produce a new Hindu religion philosophy and enfolded in it the existence of one God and other beliefs, which were then not the predominant features in Hinduism. He attacked some Hindu customs and features among them caste system, child marriages, Sati - burning of the live wife over her dead husband's pyre, idolatry and other beliefs. He tried to change the popular Hindu customs and claimed that the popular Hindu customs were various from the real Hindu beliefs.

Raja Ram and his organization 'Brahmo Samaj' tried to alter the social order of India. He founded newspapers and schools all around India. He convinced the British in 1829 to outlaw Sati. But during that period there wasn't yet an Indian ethos among the Indians. Indians were never one nation but always a collection of various entities. They were used to various rulers including non- Indians. From their point of view the British were just another ruler over them. But the chief contribution of the Brahmo Samaj to the society of India was that it evoked issues that were common to people all around the Indian sub-continent. The notions of this organization were the inspiration for other organizations and various secular political parties, like the Indian National Congress, which were later on created in India.

Dayanand Sarawati

Arya Samaj was a Hindu nationalist religious organization. It was founded by Dayanand Sarawati in Bombay in 1875. This organization saw in the holy books of Hinduism, the Vedas, infallible and as books that hold in it all the necessary knowledge the human race needs. In the Vedas one can find the past and the future, and, with the correct reading also sciences like engineering, chemistry, military science and other sciences.

This organization believed that the Hindu/Indian society was varied than it was suppose to be as per the Hindu holy books. They opposed idolatry and the monopoly Brahman priest had over Hinduism. They supported giving education to all including women and the untouchables. They even founded schools all over India. They were for equal rights between men and women. This organization wanted to change the Indian society into a more open and equal society, but their slogan was not modernizing India or westernizing India instead it was 'back to the Vedas'.

This organization's objectives were social and religious reforms in the Hindu society. This organization tried to establish Hindu pride among the Hindus. Because of its references to the Hindu religion this organization attracted only Hindus in India but it deterred Muslims and also secular Hindus. Later on in India's history the ideas expressed by this organization inspired a number of Indian nationalist leaders, who, for some period, were also the dominant leaders in the Indian National Congress. It also inspired establishing Hindu nationalist parties outside the Indian National Congress.

Ramakrishna Paramhansa

Sri Ramakrishna Paramhansa represents the very core of the spiritual realizations of the seers and sages of India. His whole life was an uninterrupted contemplation of God. He reached a depth of God-consciousness that transcends all time and place and has a universal appeal. Seekers of God of all religions feel irresistibly drawn to his life and teachings.

One of the leading Hindu spiritual leaders in 19th century Bengal, nay entire India, Ramakrishna Paramhansa was born as Gadadhar Chattopadhyay on February 18, 1836 in Kamarpukur, in Hooghly district of West Bengal. Born into a poor family who lived a hand to mouth existence, Ramakrishna was neither interested in going to school nor in business. He was a non-conformist and questioned existing beliefs and conventions.

Ramakrishna's elder brother Ramkumar began a Sanskrit school in Kolkata and sometimes also served as a priest. During this time, a rich lady of Kolkata, Rani Rashmoni, founded a temple at Dakshineswar. She approached Ramkumar to serve as priest in that temple. Ramkumar agreed and the mantle passed on to Ramkrishna when Ramkumar retired. As Ramakrishna started worshipping the deity Bhavatarini, a number of a question started to trouble him. He started praying to Goddess Kali to reveal Herself to him and one fine day, Ramkrishna is said to have seen light coming from the deity. This incident changed his life overnight and began to flock to him from far and wide.

Ramakrishna stressed that the realization of the existence of God is the supreme goal of all living beings. For him, various religions were only a means to reach the Absolute. This great saint passed away on August 16, 1886. Among his most famous disciples was Swami Vivekananda, who became famous across the world in his own right.

Swami Vivekananda

Swami Vivekananda was born Narendranath Dutta, son of a well-known lawyer in Calcutta, Biswanath Dutta, and lady Bhuvaneswari Dewi, in the year 1863. Naren learnt the Epics and Puranas from his mother, who was a good story-teller. He also inherited her memory among other qualities. He, in fact, owed much to her as he used to say later. Naren passed Entrance Examination from the Metropolitan Institute and F.A.

and B.A. Examinations from the General Assembly's Institution (now Scottish Church College). Hastie, Principal of the College, was highly impressed by Naren's philosophical insight. It was from Hastie that he first heard of Sri Ramakrishna. As a student of Philosophy, the question of God was very much in his mind.

A relation of his used to advise him to visit Ramakrishna at Dakshineswar, who, he said, would be able to remove all his doubts about religion. He happened to meet Ramakrishna at the house of a neighbour, but there is nothing on record about the impression that he created on Naren's mind. He, however, invited Naren to visit him at Dakshineswar some day. As the days passed, Naren began to grow restless about the various riddles that religion presented to him. He particularly wanted to meet a person who could talk about God with the authority of personal experience. Ultimately, he went to Ramakrishna one day and asked him directly if he had seen God. He said he had, and if Naren so wished, he could even show God to him. This naturally took Naren by surprise. But he did not know what to make of it, for though his simplicity and love of God impressed Naren, his idiosyncrasies made him suspect if Ramakrishna was not a 'monomaniac'. He started to watch him from close quarters and after a long time he was left in no doubt that Ramakrishna was an extraordinary man. He was the only man he had so far met who had completely mastered himself. Then, he was also the best illustration of every religious truth he preached. Naren loved and admired Ramakrishna but never surrendered his independence of judgment. Naren gradually came to accept Ramakrishna as his master. Naren also would sometimes go travelling. It was while he was thus travelling that he assumed the name of Swami Vivekananda.

Vivekananda travelled widely through India, sometimes on foot. He was shocked to see the conditions of rural India-people ignorant, superstitious, half-starved, and victims of caste-tyranny. If this shocked him, the callousness of the so-called educated upper classes shocked him still more. In the course of his travels he met a number of princes who invited him to stay with them as their guest. He met also city-based members of the intelligentsia-lawyers, teachers, journalists and government officials. He appealed to all to do something for the masses. No one seemed to pay any heed to him-except the Maharaja of Mysore, the Maharaja of Khetri and a few young men of Madras. Swami Vivekananda impressed on everybody the need to mobilize the masses.

A number of young people assembled round him drawn by his bright and inspiring talks. They begged him to go to the USA to attend the forthcoming Parliament of Religions in Chicago to represent Hinduism. They even started raising funds for the motive. Swamiji was first reluctant but later felt some good might come of his visit to the West, for if he could make some impression there, his people back at home, who always judged a thing good or bad according as the Western critics thought of it, would then give him a respectful hearing. That is exactly what happened : Swamiji made a tremendous impression, first in the USA and then also in England. This was the starting point of the Indian renaissance one hears about. A long successful of national leaders starting from Tilak have drawn inspiration from Swami Vivekananda. They 'discovered' India-her strong and weak points-through him. 'If you want to know India, study Vivekananda', was Tagore's advice to Romain Rolland. This holds true even today, indeed no one has studied India's body and mind so thoroughly as Swamiji did.

It was Swamiji's hope that India would create a new social order and a new civilization by combining her best spiritual customs with the latest advancements in science and technology. She would be rich both materially and spiritually. He knew affluence was not enough, man had to be human, too. He wanted India to set an instance in this.

REFORMERS IN MODERN PERIOD

Sri Aurobindo

Sri Aurobindo (1872-1950) was born in Calcutta on 15 August, and educated at a christian convent in Darjeeling. At the age of seven, along with his two brothers, he was sent by his Anglophile father to England in order to receive a British Education. Returning to his homeland at age 21, he worked for some years in the public service, while learning from scratch the languages and customs of his own culture.

He was prominent in the struggle for independence against the British, and spent a year in prison. Whilst in prison he had a vision of the Divine, which assured him that India would attain its independence and that he could leave the movement to devote himself to the spiritual task. He retreated to the French colony of Pondicherry, where he would be safe against the British, and set up an ashram. There he became an significant philosopher, yogi, and teacher and developed he called Integral Yoga, the yoga of the whole being. He was joined by his co-worker and fellow Adept Mirra Alfassa, who later became known as The Mother. For the remainder of his life Sri Aurobindo worked tirelessly for the transformation of the world, the yoga of the earth. A prolific writer, he produced a total of twenty-nine volumes, including such classics of spirituality as Savitri, The Life Divine, and the Synthesis of Yoga. He spent a number of hours each day writing replies to letters from disciples, some of which were later collated and published.

Sri Aurobindo's teachings are interesting, indeed unique for a major Indian philosopher, in that he presents a very theosophical-anthroposophical cosmology, involving specific planes of existence, subtle psychic faculties, spiritual entities, and long processes of evolution. In a real sense he represents more the theosophical-gnostic stream in Indian guise, rather than a specifically Indian (Advaitan or Tantric) approach; the very real contributions of the latter notwithstanding. So if Western spiritul philosophy aquires an Indian-Tibetan flavour with Blavatskian Theosophy, India conversely aquires a Western (esoteric and exoteric) flavour with Aurobindo.

Of course, Theosophy itself had a strong influence on Indian politics. Madam Blavatsky's successor Annie Besant was outspoken in her struggle on behalf of Indian independence (swaraj or "self-rule") from the British; and Gandhi was chosen, educated, and primed by Theosophical people in London. And the Vegetarian Society he founded there was strongly Theosophical.

Swami Prabhupada

Swami Prabhupada was the founder of the International Society for Krishna Consciousness, a movement to propagate Gaudiya Vaishnavism of Hinduism, not only in India, but also throughout the whole world, a devotional yoga custom that is popularly known as the "Hare Krishna". Born as Abhay Charan De, in Calcutta, he was educated at the prestigious local Scottish Churches College.

Before adopting the life of a pious renunciate, vanaprastha, in 1950, he was married with children and owned a small pharmaceutical business. He later took a vow of renunciation, sannyasa, in 1959 and started writing commentaries on Vaishnava scriptures. In his later years, as a traveling Vaishnava sadhu, he became an influential communicator of Gaudiya Vaishnava theology to India and specifically to the West through his leadership of the International Society for Krishna Consciousness (ISKCON), founded in 1966. As the founder of ISKCON, he has "emerged as a major figure of the Western counterculture, initiating thousands of young Americans."

Despite attacks from the anticult groups, he received a favourable welcome from a number of religious scholars, such as J. Stillson Judah,

Harvey Cox, Larry Shinn and Thomas Hopkins, who praised Prabhupada's translations and defended the group against distorted media images and misinterpretations. In respect to his achievements, religious leaders from other Gaudiya Vaishnava movements have also given him the credit. He has been described as a charismatic leader, in the sense used by the sociologist Max Weber, as he was successful in acquiring followers in the United States, Europe, India and elsewhere.

After his death in 1977 his ISKCON, an authentic form of Hindu Krishnaism based on Bhagavata Purana, continues to grow, and is respected in India, but there have been a number of squabbles about leadership among the followers. His Hare Krishna movement is accepted by the academics as the most genuinely Hindu of all the a number of Indian movements in the West.

Swami Rama Tirtha

Rama Tirtha was born in Murariwala, Gujranwala district, in Punjab (now in Pakistan. Swami Rama Tirtha was an Indian teacher of the Hindu philosophy of Vedanta. He was among the first notable Hindu swamis to lecture and teach in the west, traveling to the United States in 1902, preceded by Swami Vivekananda in 1893, and followed by Paramahansa Yogananda in 1920. During his lecture tours in the U.S. he spoke frequently on his concept of practical Vedanta and on education of Indian youth. He proposed bringing young Indians to American universities, and helped founded several scholarships for Indian students

When he was a few days old his mother died, and he was raised by his elder brother Gossain Gurudas. After receiving his Masters degree in mathematics from Government College of Lahore, he became Professor of Mathematics at Forman Christian College in Lahore. A chance meeting with Swami Vivekananda in 1897 in Lahore inspired his later decision to take up the life of a sannyasi.

In the late 19th century, he became well known in Punjab for his speeches on worship of Krishna and later through lectures and essays on Advaita Vedanta. He eventually entered the monastic swami order in 1901, leaving his life as a math professor, husband, and father. A maharaja sponsored a trip by Rama Tirtha to Japan to teach Hinduism. From Japan he traveled in 1902 to the United States, where he spent two years lecturing on the essence of Hinduism and other religions, a philosophy he called practical Vedanta.

His talks also included denunciation of the caste system in India. Regarding the significance of education for women and the poor, he said, "Neglecting the education of women and children and the labouring classes is like cutting down the branches that are supporting us, nay, it is like striking a death-blow to the roots of the tree of nationality." He began an organization to aid Indian students in American universities, arguing that India needed educated young people and not missionaries. To solve the problem of poverty in India, he suggested bringing young Indian students to American universities, and helped to establish a number of scholarships for Indian students during his tour of America.

Upon his return to India in 1904, he received acclaim for his tour of America, with large crowds thronging to his public lectures. In 1906, he withdrew from public life, weary of the public adoration and large crowds, moving to the foothills of the Himalaya. There he prepared to write a systematic presentation of his 'practical Vedanta.' His book was not finished, as he drowned while bathing in the Ganges on October 17, 1906.

Paramahansa Yogananda

Paramahansa Yogananda is recognized as one of the greatest emissaries to the West of India's ancient wisdom. His life and teachings continue to be a source of light and inspiration to people of all races, cultures and religious doctrines.

He was born Mukunda Lal Ghosh on January 5, 1893, in Gorakhpur, India, into a devout and well-to-do Bengali family. From his earliest years, he developed a depth of awareness and experience in the spiritual. In his youth he sought out a number of India's sages and saints, hoping to find an illumined teacher to guide him in his spiritual quest.

It was in 1910, at the age of 17, that he met and became a disciple of the revered Swami Sri Yukteswar Giri. In the hermitage of this great master of Yoga he spent the better part of the next ten years, receiving Sri Yukteswar's strict but loving spiritual discipline. After he graduated from Calcutta University in 1915, he took formal vows as a monk of India's venerable monastic Swami Order, at which time he received the name Yogananda.

Yogananda began his life's work with the founding, in 1917, of a "how-to-live" school for boys, where modern educational methods were combined with yoga and spirituality. In 1920, he was invited to serve as India's delegate to an international congress of religious leaders convening in Boston where he presented his discourse "The Science of Religion." Shortly thereafter, he founded the Self-Realization Fellowship (SRF) for the motive of disseminating his teachings. His founding and ongoing development of his society was at the heart of his mission for the more than 30 years that he lived and taught in the West.

In 1935, Yogananda started an 18-month tour of Europe and India. During his yearlong sojourn in his native land, he spoke in cities throughout the subcontinent and enjoyed meetings with Gandhi, C. V. Raman, Ramana Maharshi and Anandamoyi Ma, among others. In this year his guru, Swami Sri Yukteswar, bestowed on him the title of "paramahansa" (supreme swan - a symbol of spiritual discrimination), that signifies one who manifests the supreme state of unbroken communion with God.

During the 1930s, Yogananda began to withdraw somewhat from his nationwide public lecturing so as to devote himself to the writings that would carry his message to future generations. On March 7, 1952, Yogananda entered mahasamadhi. Yogananda's life story, "Autobiography of a Yogi", was published in 1946 and expanded by him in subsequent editions. A perennial best seller, the book has been in continuous publication since it first seem ed and has been translated into 18 languages. It is widely regarded as a modern spiritual classic.

Maharishi Mahesh Yogi

Maharishi Mahesh founded and developed the Transcendental Meditation technique and related programs and initiatives, including schools and universities with campuses in India, the United States, Mexico, the United Kingdom and China. In about 1939, Maharishi became a disciple of Swami Brahmananda Saraswati who was the Shankaracharya (spiritual leader) of Jyotir Math, located in the Indian Himalayas. Maharishi credits the Shankaracharya (Guru Deva) with inspiring his teachings.

Maharishi Mahesh Yogi's first global tour began in 1958, from which time his techniques for human development have been taught worldwide. He became known in the Western world in part due to interactions with The Beatles and other celebrities. By 1990, Maharishi had begun to coordinate his global activities from his residence in Vlodrop, the Netherlands. On January 11, 2008, he announced his retirement from all administrative activities and went into Mauna (spiritual silence).

Sri Sri Ravi Shankar

He was born in 1956 in Papanasam, Tamil Nadu. Even as a young child Sri Sri Ravi Shankar was of a spiritual disposition - often found in peaceful meditation at a very tender age. At the age of four, His parents discovered Him reciting verses from the Bhagavad Gita.

Throughout His teens, He studied with a number of renowned spiritual masters and became a scholar of Vedic literature, along with an advanced degree in modern science by age seventeen.

In 1982, Sri Sri Ravi Shankar began to teach the Sudarshan Kriya, a powerful breathing technique which eliminates stress and brings one completely into the present moment. Today this program is taught in over 140 countries as part of the Art of Living Course. Millions of people around the world have experienced physical and emotional healing from these programs which help eliminate stress and create a sense of belonging.

Today, Sri Sri Ravi Shankar travels and teaches internationally, reminding us that the great spiritual customs have common goals and values. His simple message of love, practical wisdom, and compassion continues to inspire people from all walks of life, and He encourages everyone to follow their chosen religious or spiritual path while honoring the path of others. Sri Sri is the founder of the Art of Living Foundation and the International Association for Human Values.

His Holiness Sri Sri Ravi Shankar founded the Art of Living Foundation in 1982, to spread the message of compassion, commitment to society, and a cosmic understanding of life. He has traveled extensively all across the globe, promoting global peace and development.

In 1997, Sri Sri Ravi Shankar founded the International Association for Human Values (IAHV), which implements development projects in remote villages.

It has undertaken relief efforts in a number of locations around the world like Afghanistan, Bosnia, New York after the 9/11 attacks, Gujarat and in Asia after the devastating Tsunami.

Swami Chinmayananda

Swami Chinmayananda was born as Balakrishna Menon (Balan) in Ernakulam district of Kerala, in 1916. Swami Chinmayananda is one of the most famous spiritual leaders in India. He was regarded as an authority on the ancient Indian scriptures, especially the sacred Bhagwad Gita and the Upanishads. He was the founder of the Chinmayananda Mission and also the author of more than 30 books, dedicated to the philosophical belief behind religion.

He completed his graduation from the Lucknow University and thereafter entered the field of journalism. Till that time, he felt that he could influence the political, economic and social reform movement through journalism.

Meeting Swami Sivananda at Rishikesh proved to be a turning point in the life of Balakrishna. He developed an interest in the path of spirituality. It was under Swami Sivananda only that Balakrishna took Sanyas (asceticism) and became Swami Chinmayananda. Seeing the enormous untapped potential of Swami Chinmayananda, Swami Sivananda sent him to study under Swami Tapovan Maharaj in the Himalayas. After studying for eight years under Swami Tapovan, Chinmayananda decided to spread his knowledge amongst people.

Swami Chinmayananda spent forty years of his life in helping others. He opened a number of ashrams, schools, hospitals, nursing homes and clinics throughout the world. Swami Chinmayananda was selected as the President of Hindu Religion by the Hindu Host Committee in the year 1993. The honor was given to him at the Meeting of the Parliament of World Religions in Chicago. He was also honored for serving humanity selflessly throughout his life at "World Vision 2000," a conference of religious leaders. Swami Chinmayananda left his body on August 3, 1993. Chinmayananda Mission was founded with an objective, to bring the timeless knowledge of Vedanta closer to people. At the same time, it teaches them to way to attain spiritual growth and contentment. He died in San Diego, California.

REFERENCES

Beck, B.E.F.: *The kin nucleus in Tamil folklore. In Kinship and history in South Asia*, Ann Arbor: University of Michigan, 1974.

Biardeau, M.: *Hinduism: the anthropology of a civilisation*, Delhi, Oxford University Press, 1989.

Bowker, J.: *Oxford dictionary of world religions*, Oxford, 'University Press, 1997.

Daniel, S.B.: *Marriage in Tamil culture*: *the problem of conflicting 'models'*, Syracuse, N.Y: Maxwell School of Citizenship & Public Affairs, 1980.

Davis, R.H.: *Ritual in an oscillating universe: worshiping Siva in medieval India*, Princeton, University Press, 1991.

Devasenapathi, V.A.: *Saiva Siddhanta. Madras*, University of Madras, 1974.

Dumont, L.: *The Dravidian kinship terminology as an expression of marriage*, Man, 1953.

Good, A.: *Law, legitimacy, and the hereditary rights of Tamil temple priests*. Mod. Asian Stud., 1989.

Kapadia, K.: *Siva and her sisters: gender, caste, and class in rural South India*, Boulder, Col: Westview Press, 1995.

Kersenboom, S.: *Word, sound, image: the life of the Tamil text,* Oxford: Berg, 1995.

Leach, E.R.: *Rethinking anthropology*, London, Athlone Press, 1961.

Long, J.B.: *Mahasivaratri: the Saiva festival of repentance*, New Delhi: Manohar, 1982.

Reynolds, H.B.: *The auspicious married woman,*. Syracuse, N.Y., Maxwell School of Citizenship & Public Affairs, 1980.

Sastri, H.K.: *South Indian images of Gods and Goddesses*, New Delhi, Asian Educational Services, 1986

Shulman, D.D.: *Tamil temple myths: sacrifice and divine marriage in the South Indian Saiva tradition*, Princeton, University Press, 1980.

Thapar, R.: *Time as a metaphor of history: early India*, Delhi, Oxford University Press, 1996.

11

Major Sects

A religious sect or denomination shares a common ground of beliefs but embraces a number of movements and schools inside its philosophical branches. Sect is a subgroup within a religion that operates under a common name, custom and identity.

A sect is in general a small religious or political group that has broken off from a larger group, for example from a large, well-founded religious group, like a denomination, usually due to a dispute about doctrinal matters. In its historical usage in Christendom the term has a pejorative connotation and refers to a movement committed to heretical beliefs and that often deviated from orthodox practices. A sect as used in an Indian context refers to an organized custom.

The term describes various Christian sects (for example , Eastern Orthodox, Catholicism, and a number of varieties of Protestantism or Restorationism). The term also describes the four branches of Judaism (Orthodox, Conservative, Reform and Reconstructionist), and describes the two chief branches of Islam (Sunni and Shia). In Hinduism, the major deity or philosophical belief identifies a sect, which also typically has distinct cultural and religious practices. The major sects include Shaivism, Shaktism, Vaishnavism, Halumatha and Smartism.

Denominations often form slowly over time for a number of facts. Due to historical accidents of geography, culture and influence between various groups, members of a given religion slowly begin to diverge in their views. Over time members of a religion may find that they have developed significantly various views on theology, philosophy, religious pluralism, ethics and religious practices and rituals. Consequently, various denominations may eventually form. In other cases, denominations form very rapidly, either resulting from a split or schism in an existing denomination, or if people share an experience of spiritual revival or spiritual awakening, and choose to form a new denomination based on that new experience or understanding.

Examples: An instance within Christianity is the Mennonite and the Church of the Brethren denominations. Both denominations are similar in their beliefs, yet they are unique because their customs were influenced by various founders (Menno Simons and Alexander Mack respectively). Their division is administrative, and there is much communication and interaction between them. Since its founding, the Mennonite denomination has split into a number of smaller Mennonite denominations, due to geography, social and theological differences.

Hinduism has no central doctrinal authority and a number of practising Hindus do not claim to belong to any particular denomination. However, academics categorize contemporary Hinduism into four major denominations: Vaishnavism, Shaivism, Shaktism and Smartism. The denominations differ primarily in the god worshipped as the Supreme One and in the customs that accompany worship of that god.

VAISHNAVISM

The most prominent community within the family of religions called Hinduism worships God under the name of Vishnu ("one who is all-pervading"). Vaishnavas are divided into a number of smaller divisions, often focussing on one form or avatar (descent) of Vishnu.There are also a number of prominent theologians, who founded their own sampradayas (preceptoral successions) teaching various forms of Vedanta and contesting the purely monistic doctrine of Shankara.

There are four chief branches of Vaishnavism and the various sampradayas often claim orthodoxy on the basis of belonging to one of these. The two chief focuses of veneration are Krishna and Rama, who are usually regarded God, with other deities in relatively subordinate positions. Vaishnavas tend to be personalists, associated with the devotional, bhakti customs.

History

Vaishnavism was founded by Ramanuja and claims to go back millions of years (in keeping with its own historical worldview). Worship of Krishna dates back at least 5,000 years, though Western scholars suggest it emerged more recently. Between the 6th and 9th centuries, the twelve Alvars (poet-mystics) laid the foundations for the Shri Vaishnavas based in Shri Rangam, South India. After him emerged three other sampradayas headed by Nimbarka (1125–1162), Vishnuswami (1200–1250) and Madhva (1238–1317).

From the twelfth century onwards a bhakti renaissance swept across India, bringing waves of devotional sentiment. Centres of devotion were rediscovered and revived in places such as Ayodhya and Vrindavana. The bhakti customs broke through caste barriers and attracted millions of followers. Among the a number of bhakti saints are a number of notable women such as Andal and Mirabai. Vaishnavas remain the largest Hindu community, both within India and the UK. The four sampradayas, each named after a specific deity shown below:

Ramanuja: The chief exponent of the Sri sampradaya, born in 1016, propagated the doctrine called visista-advaita. His school is probably the most famous in south India and has various branches, all characterized by a particular tilaka (a mark on the forehead made with sacred clay and natural colours).

Ramanuja was deeply influenced by the devotional poetry of the south Indian mystics known as Alvars, and resided as a pujari or priest in the temple of Ranganatha or Srirangam (near modern Tirucchirapalli).

This philosophy states that the jiva (the individual soul) and the jagat (the material universe) depend on Isvara (the Supreme sa-guna Brahman, or Bhagavan), the only Reality. As per the this philosophy, the individual soul can be either baddha (conditioned) or mukta (liberated). Jagat, the material world, is real and eternal, although manifested and withdrawn in cycles, meaning it is temporary.

This philosophical system is based on pramana ("epistemology, or evidence"), explained as pratyaksa (direct perception), anumana (deduction), and sabda (evidence from shastra or scripture, guru and sadhu). The eternal and natural knowledge (jnana svarupa) of the baddha soul is covered by ignorance, while the liberated soul resides in Vaikuntha. The difference is total surrender (prapatti) in bhakti (love and devotion) to God.

God manifests in five forms as Para (the transcendental form), Vyuha (the divine expressions that originate Reality), Vibhava (the avataras), Archa (the Deity form) and Antaryami (residing in the heart of each living entity and each atom).

Madhva: The chief exponent of Brahma sampradaya, born in 1238, propagated the philosophy called Dvaita or Visistha Dvaita ("duality with differences", or "various differences"). The center of the Madhva school is Udupi, the birthplace of Madhva. As per this philosophy, there is a substantial distinction between Isvara (God), jiva (individual soul) and jagat (material energy). Isvara is always independent (sva-tantra) while the jivas (souls), prakriti (material energy), kala (time), karma (reactions to activities), etc., are dependent realities (para-tantra). Such differences are elaborated in five categories (pancha-bheda) as between Isvara and jiva, Isvara and jada (prakriti), jiva and jiva, jiva and jada, jada and jada (or between an object and another).

These five differences are eternal, although jagat can be sometimes manifest (vyakta) and sometimes not manifest (avyakta). Jivas are also eternally categorized in three groups as sattvik (who can attain mukti or liberation), rajasik (destined to remain in samsara or cycles of birth and death, but with the possibility of making progress) and tamasik (hopelessly destined to hell or darkness).

Another perspective on the various differences explained by Madhva is the sajatiya, vijatiya and svagata: respectively the differences between several categories of objects, the differences between objects in the same category, and the differences amongst the parts of one specific object.

Nimbarka: The chief exponent of the Kumara or. Chatuhsana sampradaya (this knowledge was transmitted to the four Kumaras by the Hamsa avatara), who lived in the 13th century and propagated the doctrine called dvaita advaita, "simultaneous oneness and duality". Nimbarka presents himself as a disciple of Narada Muni and says that for a period of his life he lived in Nobjectiveisharanya.

This philosophical school has centers in the area of Mathura-Vrindavana (Nimbarka was born near Govardhana from a family of Telugu brahmanas), Rajasthan and Bengal, and identifies the Supreme Brahman as the divine couple of Radha and Krishna.

The identification between the savisesha (with form) and nirvisesha (without form) aspects of Bhagavan (the Supreme Person) is called svabhavika-bheda-abheda, "natural difference and oneness", as he sees no contradiction. The two categories of jivas as baddhas (materially conditioned) and muktas (liberated) are temporary as a baddha jiva can become a mukta through the path to realization or sadhana, which is bhakti (the path of devotion) that includes both karma (the knowledge of action and reaction and becoming free from karma) and jnana (cultivated knowledge). The first stage is karma (the ritualistic process), the second is jnana (the cultivation of knowledge), the third is dhyana (meditation), the fourth is prapatti (surrender), and the fifth is guru prapatti (complete dedication to the instructions of the guru).

Vishnuswami: The fourth Vaishnava acharya, Vishnusvami, representative of the Rudra sampradaya (who worship the avatara of God known as Narasimhadeva) is less known than the other three. In real there is some confusion about him, as it seems there have been three Vishnu Svamis: Adi Vishnu Svami (3rd century BC.), Raja Gopala Vishnu Svami (9th century AD.), and Andhra Vishnu Svami (14th century).

The emphasis of this school, called suddha-advaita ("pure monism"), is on the concept of lila or the pastimes by which God can be transcendental and immanent As per the His will. Thus everything is pure, including the material universe, that is created by God and intimately related to Him. In his method of worship, Vishnusvami gives preeminence to Rama, the previous avatara before Krishna. Vishnusvami visited Puri and founded there the Jagannatha Vallabha Math in the gardens of the temple, where Ramananda Raya also founded his spiritual school.

SHAIVISM

Shaivism is the second largest religious community in cotemporary India. It has several distinct and significant branches, and is commonly associated with asceticism. Lord Shiva himself is often depicted as a yogi sitting in meditation in the Himalayas. Shaivism includes the principle of avatar, but the concept is less developed than in Vaishnavism. Shiva has significant forms as Rudra (in a fierce and angry mood), Nataraja (the King of Dance), and the Linga. Shiva's followers often consider him the Supreme deity, above all others.

History

The roots of Shaivism are anchored in pre-historic India. Evidence of the worship of Shiva has been found in ancient archaeological sites, such as Harappa and Mohenjo Daro. In the Rig Veda, he is referred to by the name Rudra.The oldest story about Shiva concerns his destruction of the sacrificial arena of Daksha after Shiva's wife (Sati) voluntarily gave up her life upon being insulted by her father, Daksha.

Between 700 and 1000 AD. there lived sixty-three Nayanmars (singer-saints) whose poems are still recited today. Thereafter, Shaivism became the prominent religion of India, particularly in the South. The rulers of a number of major kingdoms became Shaivites and patronised its representatives. Magnificent temples were built in Shiva's honour and a number of impressive sculptures were inspired by him. Shiva is mentioned in the four Vedas, and particularly the Svetashvatara Upanishad, the Shaivite equivalent to the Vaishnava Bhagavad-gita. There are numerous references to Shiva in the epics and Puranas. Most Shaivite theology though, derives from later scriptures, particularly the Agamas.There are five chief customs, shown below.

SHAKTISM

The Shaktism focusses on the goddess generically called "Devi." She is worshipped most often as the consort of Shiva, but has also been raised to the status of the Supreme. Although some books equate Shaktism with all major female deities (the "shaktis" of their respective consorts), the Shakta custom specifically worships Shiva's consort, in her various forms such as Parvati, Durga, Kali, etc. The worship of Sita (with Rama) or of Radha (with Krishna) is not strictly part of Shaktism, but does point to the ubiquitous role that the female deity plays within Hinduism.

Within Shaktism, there is little emphasis on doctrinal sampradayas, and much ideology comes from Shaivism. Since Shiva embodies the male principle and Shakti embodies the female, the two principles of Shaivism and Shaktism are complementary. Shakti doctrine tends to emphasise the non-difference between matter and spirit, and looks to the creative impetus of matter rather than its ability to delude and entangle. For this fact, Shaktas worship for material benefit as well as final liberation. A notable aspect of Shaktism is animal sacrifice and even documented accounts of human sacrifice.

The findings of the Archaeological department suggest that Shaktism goes back to prehistoric times. The Goddess does feature in the Vedas themselves, but scholars suggest that mainstream worship comes from other sources. She seem s in the Epics and Puranas, especially the Markandeya Purana. It is in the Tantras that she seem s to take the role of the Supreme.

There seem to be no strong sampradayic links, and Shaktism may have been passed down in a broader fashion, largely through local and village customs, and through connections with other schools such as Shaivism. Shaktism has greatly influenced modern thinkers such as Ramakrishna and Aurobindo. Not surprisingly Devi in her fiercer forms has become the patron deity of women's liberation movements. Wherever Hindus have settled throughout the world, there are now a number of prominent Devi temples.

SMARTA SAMPRADAYA

There is a fourth mainstream Hindu community. For its emphasis on smriti, its followers are known as Smartas. They are customal, very strict about rules and regulations, and emphasise the universality of Hinduism by distancing themselves from the exclusive worshippers of Vishnu, Shiva or Devi.

They worship five main deities – Vishnu, Shiva, Devi, Ganesh, and Surya, as introduced by Shankara. The ten orders of sannyasa (dasanam), founded by Shankara, also follow the same system of panchopasana (five types of worship). Some of these sannyasis (renunciates) tend towards special veneration of Shiva, of whom Shankara is regarded an incarnation.

The Smarta tradition is a relativiely new development in Hinduism. A number of Hindus may not strictly identify themselves as Smartas but, by adhering to Advaita Vedanta as a foundation for non-sectarianism, are indirect followers. Nonetheless, other customs dispute the claim that the notion of an impersonal God is the only basis for non-sectarianism. These controversies over the nature and identity of the Absolute were spearheaded by prominent theologians.

HALUMATHA

Halumatha is a denomination of the Hindu religion mainly followed by Kurubas and Other Backward Classes. The majority of members of Halumatha are followers of Advaita and Nature Worship. Halumatha or Palamatha means beliefs of the protectors of the society. In Sanskrit Pal means protect, defend, rule, govern etc. Matha means group view, belief, doctrine etc.

Worshiping developed from Halumatha. Stone is the source for the soil. Soil is the source for the plants. Plants are the source for the animals. This may be the fact for worshiping Almight in Stone. Through the ages, this stone worship custom might have lead to worshiping Shiva as Beeralingeswara, Mailara Linga, Malladevaru, Mahadeshwara, Nanjundeswara, Mallappa, Mallara, Mallikarjuna etc. Even the worshiping of shakti as Yellamma, Renuka, Chowdamma, Kariyamma, Chamundi, Bhanashankari, Gullamma etc might have come from this custom. Even today, ancestoral worship as deities is very common. The worship of ancestors like Revanasidda, Rama, Hanuman, Krishna,Keshava, Ranganatha, EeraThimmanna, Tirupati Thimmappa, Venkateswara,

Kalidasa, Siddarama, Kanakadasa etc as Devaru very much exists in Kuruba customs. Kurubas worship Shiva and Vishnu concept of the Almighty with the equal devotion. Kuruba Sangama Dynasty of Vijayanagara Empire disseminated this concept during their ruling. Even the founder of Vijayanagara Empire Hakkaraya is also called Harihara-I.

AGAMA HINDU DHARMA

Agama Hindu Dharma is the conventional name of Hinduism in Indonesia. It is practised by 93% of the population of Bali, but also in Sumatra, Java (especially by the Tenggerese people on the east), and Kalimantan. Although, officially, only about 3% of Indonesian population is Hindu, those following Hindu customal beliefs together with their nominal religion is more than 30%. This group lives mainly in Java, which forms the majorty of the Javanese Muslims, are known as Abangan or Santri which means " Easy-going muslims".

The coming of Soeharto's new order resulted in an increasing Indonesianisation of both Hindu Dharma and Parisada Hindu Dharma , partly due to the fact that every Indonesian citizen was now necessitated to be a registered member of one of the five acknowledged religious communities (Islam, Christianity [i.e. Protestantism], Catholicism, Hinduism and Buddhism). Inspired by the glorious Hindu Javanese past, a large number of Javanese converted to Hinduism in the 1960s and 1970s. When the adherents of the ethnic religions Aluk To Dolo (Sa'dan Toraja) and Kaharingan (Ngaju, Luangan) claimed official recognition of their customs, the Ministry of Religion classified them as Hindu variants in 1968 and 1980. Due to Hindu missionary work by Balinese and Indians living in Medan, several members of the Karo in North Sumatra started to embrace Hinduism in 1977. Having become a truly national representative of Hinduism, the Parisada Hindu Dharma changed its name to Parisada Hindu Dharma Indonesia in 1984.

Practitioners of Agama Hindu Dharma share a number of common beliefs, which include:

- A belief in one supreme being (Ida Sanghyang Widi Wasa).
- A belief that all of the gods are expressions of this supreme being.
- A belief in the Tri Murti, consisting of Brahma (the creator), Vishnu (the preserver) and Shiva (the destroyer)
- A belief in all of the other Hindu gods and goddesses (Dewa and Bharata)

The sacred texts detected in Agama Hindu Dharma are the Vedas. Only two of the Vedas reached Bali in the past, and they are the basis of Balinese Hinduism. Other sources of religious information include the PuranasHindu mythology bases more on its eighteen Puranas six each are rendered to each of the Hindu Trinity, Brahma, Vishnu and Shiva.

It is interesting to study changeover to Hinduism in two close and culturally similar regions, the Yogyakarta. Yogyakarta is located in the south-central part of the island of Java, and is surrounded by the province of Central Java (Jawa Tengah). The sultanate of Yogyakarta was for region, where only sporadic conversions to Hinduism had taken place, and the Klaten region, which has witnessed the highest percentage of Hindu converts in Java. It has been argued that this dissimilarity was related to the difference in the perception of Islam among the Javanese population in each region. Since the mass killings of 1965-1966 in Klaten had been far more awful than those in Yogyakarta, in Klaten the political landscape had been far more politicized than in Yogyakarta. Because the killers in Klaten were to a large extent identified with Islam, the people in this region did not convert to Islam, but preferred Hinduism (and Christianity).

REFERENCES

Census of India: *Data from the 2001 Census, including cities, villages and towns,* Census Commission of India, 2001.

Hill, John E.: *The Peoples of the West from the Weilue by Yu Huan: A Third Century Chinese Account Composed between 239 and 265 AD*, Draft annotated English translation, 2004.

Legge, James: *A Record of Buddhistic Kingdoms: Being an account by the (1886): Chinese Monk Fa-Hien of his travels in India and Ceylon (AD. 399-414) in search of the Buddhist Books of Discipline.* Oxford, Clarendon Press. Reprint: New York, Paragon Book Reprint Corp, 1965.

Thomas, F. W.: "*Sandanes, Nahapana, Cacmana and Kanicka : Tung-li P'an-ch'i and Chinese Turkestan.*" New Indian Antiquary, 1944.

Watters, Thomas: *On Yuan Chwang's Travels in India. Thomas Watters*. London. Royal Asiatic Society. Reprint: Delhi. Mushiram Manoharlal. 1973.

12

Demographic Propagation

Hinduism is an umbrella term to draw the overall beliefs and practices of India rather than an organized religion. Today there are around 930 million Hindus in the world. The beliefs and even the gods in India have changed drastically over the years with each new invasion. Hinduism is like a river into which new streams are constantly flowing and absorbed. No one agrees on the exact dates but there were fertility rites taking place around rivers and phallic symbols since around the 8th century BC.

Then the Aryan invaders came from the Baltic Sea and they brought their own nature beliefs with them. Over time the two mingled and the world's oldest religious scripts, the Vedas, were told in an oral custom that was eventually put in print around the 3rd century BC. The Aryans also brought the caste system.

Hinduism gave birth to Jainism and Buddhism which could be seen as breakaway movements from the former in 600-44 BC. Buddhism in particular spread far and wide for a few centuries but eventually a Hindu revival absorbed it. Buddha was declared to be an incarnation of Vishnu, a god gaining in popularity.

Hinduism continued to change, evolve and mutate with changing social conditions and new migrations though none challenged it as much as the arrival of Islam. The Turks invaded in the 17th century and perceived the Hindus to be polytheistic and idolatrous. They wouldn't have that but found the Indians too slippery to convert. They built mosques on top of temples and sewed the seeds of discord for conflicts in Kashmir and elsewhere continue until the present day.

Hinduism spread with Indian migrants to Bali, Java and even England and the US in recent days. However it's essentially an Indian thing. Hindus often refer to Vedic culture as being their own. This derives from the Vedas, the oldest Indian sacred books, and from which a number of the essential tenets of Indian religious and social life derive. Hindus often talk about their faith as Sanatana Dharma (Eternal Truth), one of its ancient names. There continue to be hundreds of various ways that this "foundation of all life and reality" is expressed, the two chief forms being Vaishnavita (special devotion to Vishnu) and Shaivite (special devotion to Shiva).

Hindu philosophy is ancient and abiding, and adherents over time have dwelled alongside devotees of countless other religions (Jains, Buddhists, Parsees, Muslims, Sikhs, and Christians). Buddhist roots are in India, and the Jains are a distinct religious group whose founder broke away from the prevailing norms of Hinduism in the 5 century BC.

The spread of Hindu ideas elsewhere has been considerable throughout Europe and North America as well as Asia and Australia. Hindu gurus have travelled west in response to the coming of Christian missionaries to India, and Westerners have been profoundly affected by visiting India and by translations of Hindu classics. Hindu belief, imagery and philosophy offer a very various form of religious understanding from that practiced in the West. It has created waves of groups inspired by Hindu philosophy and practice—ranging from overtly religious movements to yoga and Hindu meditation. This has led to a revival of devotional Hinduism among a number of Hindus as well as attracting converts from other faiths and cultures.

ORIGIN

The word Hindu originated, not as the name of a religion, but as a geographical marker. Hindu derives from the Sanskrit word for river, sindhu, from which the Indus River received its name. Sometime in the first millennium B.C., the Persians, who were then South Asia's closest neighbours, mispronounced sindhu, and designated the land around the Indus River as hindu. Over a thousand years later, in AD. 712, the Muslims invaded the Indus Valley. To separate themselves, they called all non-Muslims hindus; the name of the land became, by default, the name of the people and their religion. Christians, upon entering Hindustan, committed the same error of reduction. Thus the name hindu originally was given by outsiders to denote a geographic territory, but through the encroachment of various other religious groups it came to encompass all native religions in South East Asia.

As the history of its name evidences, unity in Indian religion has been superimposed by outsiders, first by the Muslims, then the Christians, and much later by the British colonialists who through their censuses unintentionally reified the South Asian peoples under that banner. It has only been in the last couple of centuries that the Indian people have embraced the name Hindu as their own, though two Indians rarely use the word with the same meaning. Some scholars suggest that it is more appropriate to speak of "Hinduisms" than to risk giving off a false sense of unity.

The genesis of Hinduism is almost as elusive as its contemporary definition. Unlike Islam, which began with Mohammed, or Judaism, which began with Moses, Hinduism has no founder, nor any customal time or place of origin; it emerges from the jungle as a continually evolving religious system. Scholars debate the primary source of what would become the Hindu religion, though all agree that several cultures had an influence. Ancient Hinduism evolved from at least three antecedents: "an early element common to most of the Indo-European tribes; a later element held in common with the early Iranians; and an element acquired in the Indian subcontinent itself ".

The oldest of these influences are the symbols and deities indigenous to the Indus valley, part of the ancient and abstruse Dravidian culture. Archaeologists date this glorious society to the third millennium BC., making it one of the oldest known civilizations. This early date also places the religion of the Indus over a thousand years before the writing of the Old Testament, in the time of the Patriarchal Age. If the archaeologists' dating is correct, the Indus civilization was founded soon after the Tower of Babel incident. The archaeological sites along the Indus have revealed a number of terra-cotta figures resembling gods and goddesses in the Vedic literature, some of which are still worshipped. Though religious figurines abound, temples inexplicably are absent from the Indus cities. Because the Indus valley script has yet to be decoded, much of the Dravidian culture and religion remains a mystery.

EARLY RISE

Every religion except Hinduism and Christianity has their origin from some other religion. Islam grew out of Judaism and Christianity, and Buddhism derived from Hinduism; Hinduism is the only major religion lacking an adequate explanation as to its origin. No substantial texts exist beyond 1000 BC., and the texts after 1000 do not contain narrative. The earliest of these is the Rig Veda, which is nothing but a collection of praise hymns to the gods rather than the record of a people as in the Bible. Unlike western cultures, which tend to view time as a linear progression, the eastern religions generally reckon time to be cyclical. As a result, they emphasize the eternal over the transient and historical. Scholars are able to piece together the earliest Indian religion only through archaeology, clues in the later texts, and by extrapolating from existing customs. Using these same resources, Christian scholars can reinterpret the available data so that the Hindu religion fits into a biblical scheme of world history. Reconstructing the ancient history of any civilization is tentative, however, and all such projects are educated speculations at best.

The earliest Hindu literature, the Rig Veda, speaks often of the Creator, of the One, a Great God over all the other gods. He is called Varuna, and is closely related to the Zoroastrian god Ahura Mazdâ (Wise Lord) and the Greek god Uranus. Though an insignificant sea god in the current pantheon, Varuna was a prominent god in the ancient system, and the subject of a number of hymns in the Rig Veda. Zwemer writes that Varuna is the most impressive of the Vedic gods. He is the prehistoric Sky-god whose nature and attributes point to a very early monotheistic conception. This god is an ethical god, capable of great wrath or merciful forgiveness of sins.

Varuna is already on the decline by the time the Vedas were committed to writing; Indra, a warrior god, takes prominence in the later Vedic period. Yet even then, Varuna is qualitatively various from Indra and all the other gods that follow him in the Vedic literature; he is less anthropomorphic and more majestic (cf. Zwemer, p. 88). Other Hindu deities act like humans in the same way as the Greek gods, yet Varuna is above that. It would seem that this god embodies a number of the qualities of Jehovah, albeit diluted and removed by a number of hundreds of miles and years.

The bear witness from India's earliest literary customs reveals that Hinduism is a corruption of true religion. Though for most of its existence Hinduism has been an extremely pluralistic religion—being influenced by several cultures originally, and later by surrounding religions (Islam, Buddhism, and Christianity)—it seem s to have grown out of monotheism.

FACTORS RESPONSIBLE FOR RISE

The Gupta dynasty ruled India (what was India then, the north of the Vindhyas), between fourth and sixth centuries of the common era.

Though not as vast as Mauryan empire, Gupta rule has left a deep and wide cultural impact not only in the subcontinent but on the adjacent Asian countries as well. The practice of dedicating temples to various deities came into vogue followed by fine artistic temple architecture and sculpture. Books on medicine, veterinary science, mathematics, astronomy and astrophysics were written. The famous Aryabhata and Varahamihira belong to this age. The Gupta founded a strong central government which also allowed a degree of local control. Gupta society was ordered in accordance with Hindu beliefs. This included a strict caste system, or class system. The peace and prosperity created under Gupta leadership enabled the pursuit of scientific and artistic endeavours.

At the time of Shankara's life, Hinduism had lost some of its appeal due to the influence of Buddhism and Jainism. Shankara stressed the significance of the Vedas, and he travelled extensively to restore the study of the Vedas.

He wrote commentaries on the Upanishads, Vishnu sahasranama, Brahma Sutras, and the Bhagavad Gita. He engaged in a series of debates with Buddhist scholars, and with scholars of the Purva Mimamsa school. One of the most famous of these debates was with the famed ritualist Mandana Mishra. During the 1st century, the trade on the overland Silk Road tended to be restricted by the rise in the Middle-East of the Parthian empire, an unvanquished enemy of Rome, just as Romans were becoming extremely wealthy and their demand for Asian luxury was rising.

This demand revived the sea connections between the Mediterranean and China, with India as the intermediary of choice. From that time, through trade connection, commercial settlements, and even political interventions, India started to strongly influence Southeast Asian countries. Trade routes linked India with southern Burma, central and southern Siam, lower Cambodia and southern Vietnam, and numerous urbanized coastal settlements were founded there. For more than a thousand years, Indian influence was hence the major factor that brought a certain level of cultural unity to the various countries of the region. The Pali and Sanskrit languages and the Indian script, together with Theravada and Mahayana Buddhism, Brahmanism, and Hinduism, were transmitted from direct contact and through sacred texts and Indian literature such as the Ramayana and the Mahabharata.

From the 5th to the 13th century, South-East Asia had very powerful empires and became extremely active in Buddhist architectural and artistic creation. The Sri Vijaya Empire to the south and the Khmer Empire to the north competed for influence. Langkasuka was an ancient kingdom Hindu located in the Malay Peninsula. The kingdom along with Old Kedah are probably the earliest kingdom founded on the Malay Peninsula. As per the custom the founding of the kingdom happened in the 2nd century. Malay legends claim that Langkasuka was founded at Kedah, and later moved to Pattani. Pan Pan is a lost Hindu Kingdom believed to be exist around 3rd-5th Century AD. somewhere in Kelantan or Terengganu, Malaysia.

Gangga Negara was believed to be a lost Hindu kingdom somewhere in the state of Perak, Malaysia, ruled by Raja Gangga Shah Johan. Researchers believed that the kingdom collapsed after an attack by King Rajendra Chola I of Coromandel, South India, between 1025 and 1026.

From the 5th-15th centuries Sri Vijayan empire, a maritime empire centered on the island of Sumatra in Indonesia, had adopted Mahayana and Vajrayana Buddhism under a line of rulers named the Sailendras. The Empire of Sri Vijaya declined due to conflicts with the Chola rulers of India, before being destabilized by the Islamic invasion of India from the 13th century.

The Majapahit Empire succeeded the Singhasari empire. It was one of the last and greatest Hindu empires in the Malay Archeipeilago. Funan was a pre-Angkor Cambodian kingdom located around the Mekong delta, probably founded by Mon-Khmer settlers speaking an Austro-Asiatic language. As per the reports by two Chinese envoys, K'ang T'ai and Chu Ying, the state was founded by an Indian Brahimin named Kaundinya, who in the first century AD.was given instruction in a dream to take a magic bow from a temple and defeat a Khmer queen, Soma. Soma, the daughter of the king of the Nagas, married Kaundinya and their lineage became the royal dynasty of Funan. The myth had the advantage of providing the legitimacy of both an Indian Brahmin and the divinity of the cobras, who at that time were held in religious regard by the inhabitants of the region.

The kingdom of Champa kept in line what is now south and central Vietnam from approximately 192 through 1697. The dominant religion of the Cham people was Hinduism and the culture was heavily influenced by India. A number of Cham towers still stand in central Vietnam. The most significant instance of Cham architecture is My Son near the Vietnamese city of Hoi An.

Later, from the 9th to the 13th century, the Mahayana Buddhist and Hindu Khmer Empire dominated much of the South-East Asian peninsula. Under the Khmer, more than 900 temples were built in Cambodia and in neighbouring Thailand. Angkor was at the center of this development, with a temple complex and urban organization able to support around one million urban dwellers.

Modern Hinduism is the reflection of continuity and progressive alterations that occurred in various customs and institutions of hinduism during the 19th and 20th centuries. This continuity and adaptation to modern ideas is still a continuing process.

Modern Hinduism has as its values rational thought, modern education and the ideals of humanism, rationalism and religious universalism. This has meant battling the conservative and obscurantist elements, imbibing modernity, modern education contrasted withclassical sanskritic education system, and countering Christian missionary criticism. The positive consequences of modernity in Hinduism is most visible in the status of women and the dalits. Also, ritualism has declined.

Brahmo Samaj is a social and religious movement founded in Kolkata, India in 1828 by Raja Ram Mohan Roy. He was influenced by western thought and was one of the first Indians to visit Europe. He died in Bristol, England. The Brahmo Samaj movement thereafter resulted in the Brahmo religion in 1850 founded by Debendranath Tagore — better known as the father of Rabindranath Tagore.

Arya Samaj is a Hindu reform movement in India that was founded by Swami Dayananda in 1875. He was a sannyasin (renouncer) who believed in the infallible authority of the Vedas. Dayananda advocated the doctrine of karma and reincarnation, and emphasised the ideals of brahmacharya (chastity) and sanyasa (renunciation).

Modernity has led to infusion of newer ideas into the Hindu religion, thereby making it more open, so that we find a number of non-South Asians taking on Hinduism. This is particularly interesting when there is no organised proselytising effort in the Hindu religion.

An significant aspect of 20th century modern Hinduism has been its spread among foreigners, who have accepted the religion voluntarily. This can be traced most prominently to the sojourn of Vivekananda to the World Parliament of Religions in Chicago in 1893, where he made a huge impact on the people. He founded the Ramakrishna Mission. In our times, this has also been facilitated by emergence of sects like Transcendental Meditation, or the International Society of Krishna Consciousness. Similar are other modern day Gurus like Rajneesh, also known as Osho (he started his career as a lecturer in philosophy at

Jabalpur). An interesting fact of such movements is that these are often inspired by Bhakti, more particularly the Vaishnavite strand. Of late, Pandurang Shastri Athavale a Social reformer, philosopher, spiritual teacher from Western India, state of Maharashtra, Guru of Swadhyay Movement is also a Modern Hinduism Spiritual teacher.

The revitalisation of Hinduism in Indonesia is occurring in all parts of the country. In the early seventies, the Toraja people of Sulawesi were the first to be identified under the umbrella of 'Hinduism', followed by the Karo Batak of Sumatra in 1977 and the Ngaju Dayak of Kalimantan in 1980.

The growth of Hinduism has been driven also by the famous Javanese prophesies of Sabdapalon and Jayabaya. A number of recent converts to Hinduism had been members of the families of Sukarno's PNI, and now support Megawati Sukarnoputri. This return return to the 'religion of Majapahit' (Hinduism) is a matter of nationalist pride.

The new Hindu communities in Java tend to be focused around recently built temples (pura) or around archaeological temple sites (candi) which are being reclaimed as places of Hindu worship. An significant new Hindu temple in eastern Java is Pura Mandaragiri Sumeru Agung, located on the slope of Mt. Semeru, Java's highest mountain. Mass conversions have also occurred in the region around Pura Agung Blambangan, another new temple, built on a site with minor archaeological remnants attributed to the kingdom of Blambangan, the last Hindu polity on Java, and Pura Loka Moksa Jayabaya (in the village of Menang near Kediri), where the Hindu king and prophet Jayabaya is said to have achieved spiritual liberation (moksa). Another site is the new Pura Pucak Raung in East Java, which is mentioned in Balinese literature as the place from where Maharishi Markandeya took Hinduism to Bali in the fifth century AD.

Started by Arya Samaj in early 20th century to bring back to Hinduism people converted to Islam and Christianity. Dayananda claimed to be rejecting all non-Vedic beliefs altogether. Hence the Arya Samaj unequivocally condemned idolatry, animal sacrifices, ancestor worship, pilgrimages, priestcraft, offerings made in temples, the caste system, untouchability and child marriages, on the grounds that all these lacked Vedic sanction. It objectiveed to be a universal church based on the authority of the Vedas. Dayananda stated that he wanted 'to make the whole world Aryan'. That is, he wanted to develop a missionary Hinduism based on the universality of the Vedas.

To this end the Arya Samaj set up schools and missionary organisations, extending its activities outside India. It now has branches around the world. It has a disproportional amount of adherents among people of Indian ancestry in Suriname and the Netherlands, in contrast with India.

HINDUISM IN OTHER PARTS OF WORLD

Hinduism in its minuter sense, is the conglomeration of religious beliefs and practices existing in India that have grown out of ancient Brahminism, and which stand in sharp contrast to orthodox, customal Brahminism to-day. Hinduism is the popular, distorted, corrupted side of Brahminism. In its broad sense, it comprises those phases of religous, social, and intellectual life that are generally recognized in India to-day as the legitimate outgrowth of ancient Brahmin institutions, and hence are tolerated by the Brahmin priests as compatible with Brahmin customs. Far from being a uniform system of worship, Hinduism, in this large sense, comprises, besides orthodox Brahminism, the numerous sectarian developments of cult in honour of Vishnu, Siva, and their associates, in which for centuries the great mass of the people have found satisfaction for their religious cravings.

In Hinduism, as distinguished from the heretical sects of India, it is of minor significance what sort of worship is adopted, provided one recognizes the supremacy of the Brahmins and the sacredness of Brahmin customs and customs. In the pantheistic all-god Brahma, the whole world of deities, spirits, and other objects of worship is contained, so that Hinduism adapts itself to every form of religion, from the lofty monotheism of the cultivated Brahmin to the degraded nature-worship of the ignorant, half savage peasant. Hinduism, to quote Monier Williams, "has something to offer which is suited to all minds. Its very strength lies in its infinite adaptability to the infinite diversity of human characters and human tendencies.

It has its highly spiritual and abstract side suited to the metaphysical philosopher151its practical and concrete side suited to the man of affairs and the man of the world—its esthetic and ceremonial side suited to the man of poetic feeling and imagination—its quiescent and contemplative side suited to the man of peace and lover of seclusion. Nay, it holds out the right hand of brotherhood to nature-worshippers, demon-worshippers, animal-worshippers, tree-worshippers, fetish-worshippers. It does not scruple to permit the most grotesque forms of idolatry, and the most degrading varieties of superstition. And it is to this latter fact that yet another remarkable peculiarity of Hinduism is mainly due—namely, that in no other system in the world is the chasm more vast which separates the religion of the higher, cultured, and thoughtful classes from that of the lower, uncultured, and unthinking masses" (Brahmanism and Hinduism, 1891, p. 11).

Hinduism is thus a national, not a world religion, it has never made any serious effort to proselytize in countries outside of India. The occasional visits of Brahmins to countries of Europe and America, and their lectures on religious metaphysics are not to be mistaken for genuine missionary enterprises. Not to speak of its grosser phases, Hinduism, even in its highest form known as Brahminism, could not take root and flourish in countries where the caste system and the intricate network of social and domestic customs it implies do not prevail. Nor has Hinduism exercised any notable influence on European thought and culture. The pessimism of Schopenhauer and his school is indeed very like the pessimism of Buddhism and of the Vedanta system of philosophy, and seems to have been derived from one of these sources. But apart from this unsignificant line of modern speculation, and from the abortive theosophic movement of more recent times, one finds no trace of Hindu influence on Western civilization. We have nothing to learn from India that makes for higher culture. On the other hand, India has much of value to learn from Christian civilization.

As per the census of 1901, the total population of India is a little more than 294,000,000 souls, of which 207,000,000 are adherents of Hinduism. The provinces in which they are most numerous are Assam, Bengal, Bombay, Berrar, Madras, Agra, and Oudh, and the Central Provinces. Of foreign religions, Mohammedanism has, by dint of long domination, made the deepest impression on the natives, numbering in India today nearly 62,500,000 adherents. Christianity, considering the length of time it has been operative in India, has converted but an insignificant fraction of the people from Hinduism. The Christians of all sects, foreign officials included, number but 2,664,000, nearly one-half being Catholics.

It was not till towards the end of the eighteenth century that Europeans—excepting Father de Nobili and a few other early missionaries—acquired any knowledge of Sanskrit and allied tongues in which the sacred literature of India was preserved. The extensive commerce which the English developed in Bombay and other parts of

India gave occasion to English scholars to make extensive studies in this new field of Oriental research. Sir William Jones was one of the first European scholars to master Sanskrit and to give translations of Sanskrit texts. He translated in 1789 one of Kalidasa's classic dramas, the "Sakuntalã", and in 1794 published a translation of the "Ordinances of Manu". He founded, in 1784, the Royal Asiatic Society, destined to prove a powerful means of diffusing the knowledge of Indian literature and institutions.

An able, but less famous, contemporary was the Portuguese missionary, Father Paulinus a Sancto Bartholomeo, to whom belongs the honour of composing the first European grammar of the Sanskrit tongue, published at Rome in 1790. The first significant study of Indian literature and rites was made by Henry T. Colebrooke. His "Miscellaneous Essays on the Sacred Writings and Religion of the Hindus", first published in 1805, became a classic in this new field of research. The collection was reedited in 1873 by Professor E. B. Cowell, and is still a work of great value to the student of Hinduism. Other distinguished scholars of England who contributed to the knowledge of Brahminism and Hinduism were Horace H. Wilson, author of a Sanskrit dictionary and of a translation of the Vishnu Purana (1840) and other Hindu texts; John Muir, author of the great work "Original Sanskrit Texts on the Origin and History of the People of India, their Religions and Institutions" (5 vols., London, 1858-70), and Sir Monier Williams, whose work "Brahmanism and Hinduism, Religious Thought and Life in India" (4th ed., London, 1891), is a masterly exposition of Hinduism. With these may be associated Professor Max Müller, though whose exertions the most significant sacred texts of India as well as of other Oriental lands have been made accessible to English readers in the well-known collection, "The Sacred Books of the East".

More than 95% of all Hindus reside in India and approx. 98% in South Asia. Besides, Hindus in most countries outside South Asia are emigrants from India and other countries of the region. Only the Hindus of South Asia, Vietnam and Indonesia are indigenous. In contrast, Christians dominate countries of the entire Western hemisphere, Europe, Oceania and southern half of the African Continent while Islam dominates in scores of countries in North Africa, West Asia besides Albania in Europe, Pakistan, Afghanistan, Maldives and Bangladesh in South Asia and Malaysia, Brunei and Indonesia in the Far East. The two paramount facts for the geographical confinement of Hinduism are:

Traditionally, Hinduism is a non-proselytizing religion i.e., Hindus do not normally convert people of other faiths to their own. Forcible conversions have never been carried (except in a solitary instance around the Independence of India) and even peaceful methods have not been employed on any significant scale. This contrasts totally with the record of Semitic faiths like Christianity and Islam.

In the last few centuries, Hindus in a number of countries have suffered severe reverses due to absorption by or conversion to other religions or massacres and persecution leading to migrations to India or conversion to other faiths.

It is appropriate here to point out, however, that various fundamental tenets of Hinduism have been accepted whole heartedly by Non-Hindus all over the world. For example , one in four residents of the United States believes in the doctrine of rebirth. The Hindu-Buddhist spiritual discipline of Yoga has been gaining popularity in the West for quite some time and has even been granted recognition by certain churches.

DEMOGRAPHICS

Total population of Hindus is approximately 850 million in the world. This makes Hinduism the third largest religion in the world, after Christianity and Islam.

Country Approximate Percentage ofTotal Hindu Population Number of Hindus in Millions

India	82	800
Nepal	89	19.69
Sri Lanka	15	2.67
Bangladesh	11	16
Bhutan	20	0.17
Pakistan	1.3	2.2
Malaysia	7.1	1.2
Indonesia	2.3	3.8
Singapore	6	0.09
Vietnam	-	0.05
Hong Kong	<1.0	0.04
Burma	2.0	0.24
South Africa	2	0.7

Mauritius	50.6	0.58
Kenya, Uganda	<1.0	0.2
Kuwait, Oman, UAE	15	0.17
Fiji	41	0.3
Trinidad and Tobago	24	0.36
Guyana	38	0.25
Surinam	30	0.1
Jamaica	3	
Canada	0.5	0.22
USA	0.4	1
UK	0.5	0.4
Netherlands	1	0.16

***(Source:** Encyclopaedia Britannica)*

REFERENCES

Balslev, A.N.: *A study of time in Indian philosophy*, Wiesbaden, Otto Harrassowitz, 1983.

Barnett, S.A.: *Coconuts and gold: relational identity in a South Indian caste*, 1976.

Clothey, F.W.: *Chronometry, cosmology and the festival calendar in the Murukan cult*, New Delhi: Manohar, 1982.

Courtright, PB.: *Ganesa: Lord of obstacles, Lord of beginnings*, New York, Oxford University Press, 1985.

Daniel, E.V.: *Fluid signs: being a person the Tamil way*, Berkeley, University of California Press, 1984.

Durkheim, E.: *The elementary forms of the religions life*, London, George Allen & Unwin, 1915.

Fuller, C. J.: *Gods, priests and purity: on the relation between Hinduism and the caste system*, 1979.

Gale, R.M.: *The language of time. London: Routledge & Kegan Paul*, 1968.

Gell, A.: *The anthropology of time*, Berg, Oxford, 1992.

Handelman, D. & D.D.: *Shulman Cod inside out: Siva's game of dice*, New York, Oxford University Press, 1997.

Kalynasuntaram, N.: *Tiruccentur Murukankoyil varalaru.: Tiruchendur*: Tirukkumaran Patippakam, 1980.

Kane, P.V.: *History of Dharmasastra* 5, Poona: Bhandarkar Oriental Research Institute, 1958.

McTaggart, J.M.E.: *The nature of existence 2*, Cambridge, University Press, 1927.

Mellor, D.H.: *Real time,* Cambridge, University Press, 1981.

Moreno Arcas, M.: *Murukan: a God of healing poisons; the physics of worship in a South Indian center for pilgrimage*, University of Chicago, 1984.

O'Flaherty, W.D.: *Women, androgynes, and other mythical beasts*, Chicago, University Press, 1980.

Paktavatsalam, K.: *Kalukumalaittala varalaru: Kovilpatti: Selvarajan*, 1972.

13

Socio-Political Influence

Hindu politics announces the political movements conceding to absorb guidance from Hinduism. Hindu nationalism is the numerically most significant among the current political movements claiming to be inspired by Hinduism. Mahatma Gandhi, the leader of the Indian independence movement, claimed that Hinduism, among other religions and philosophies, was a source of his political ideas. Hindu revivalism started with a mild reassertion of Hinduism in British India,mainly in its largest province, Bengal.

Hindus were trying to incorporate things from the West, but while some were trying to make a clean break from their past, others tried to preserve their heritage in an adopted form. Swami Dayananda Saraswati, Bankim Chandra Chatterjee and Swami Vivekananda were the earliest to formulate a political vision and a social reform program for India on the basis of Hinduism. Later, Aurobindo, Vinayak Damodar Savarkar and Golwalkar formed much of the political direction of the Hindus in India. Hinduism is an significant source of political discourse in India. Hindu minorities have played significant roles in Bangladesh, Pakistan and Sri Lanka.

Hindu symbols are frequently used in political campaigns of Indian politicians. For example , the Ram Janmabhoomi issue in Ayodhya was brought up as a national issue by the Bharatiya Janata Party before the Babri Mosque demolition in 1992

SOCIO-POLITICAL IDENTITY

Modern Hindus seem to be unable to discriminate between how to deal with other religions on a political level, on one hand, versus how to deal with them on a religious level, on the other. They have confused political tolerance with religious acceptance, thinking that they must accept all religions as true in order to create political harmony with their followers. This has led to a situation in which Hindus do not defend their religion so as not to politically offend other religious groups, even though other religions do not reciprocate and continue their criticism and missionary efforts against Hindus.

The result of this confusion is that Hinduism is losing any clear identity for itself and failing to counter the forces that are assailing it. One does not need to sacrifice one's religious beliefs at the altar of political exigency, particularly when other religious groups hold their own ground. One can be clear and strong in one's religion, including defending it against missionary attacks and media distortions, without having to lose one's political tolerance.

Unfortunately most political leaders in India, including some who claim to be staunch Hindus, don't seem to understand how to do this. They have chosen to hide their religion in this age of the clash of cultures and instead give their public praise to the beliefs of others. This has been done mainly out of political accommodation but there is a pretence that there is something deeply spiritual about it.

In attempts to create political tolerance in India Hindus have tried to make all religions the same, calling them all equally valid paths to God, and this even though other religions may not define themselves as paths to God (Paramatman) in the Hindu sense at all. Modern India has built its politics of dealing with minority religions on this idea of Sarva Dharma Samabhava.

Yet it has gone beyond the idea that all religions should be given equal respect by the law. The further idea has arisen that the majority religion should stoop down to help minority religions and should not do anything to offend them, including not questioning the foreign missionary elements working within them, even if these forces are antinational in nature. This has led Hindus to ignore the missionary element in religions, even when active in their own neighbourhood.

From fear of losing the favour of minority religious support in the political sphere, Hindus in India have failed to defend themselves from the onslaught of these same missionary religions. Hindus are hence confronted with a dichotomy or at least dilemma to consider. This is the balance between political tolerance of religions and acceptance of all religions on a spiritual level. Hindus have confused the two issues to their own detriment.

HINDUISM AND POLITICS

In a free society people must be allowed to follow whatever religion they like as long as long as it does not become a means of antisocial or antinational activities. The government should not officially endorse any religious belief as the ultimate truth. Yet this does not mean that political leaders cannot demonstrate any religious activity or show any concern for the majority religion of their land.

In Western countries secularism, or a free society, does not prevent political leaders from extolling or espousing their majority religion of Christianity, but only that they should not use it as a political plank. It is part of their personal lives, which they can demonstrate in public, but it should not be used to create religious favouritism by law or policy.

A secular based society has not prevented Western countries from supporting or defending their religious groups in their international policy. Western countries commonly defend Christian groups on an international basis. For example , when Russia recently tried to ban the Mormons, a unique American form of Christianity that they regarded as a cult, the American government issued a protest. Yet the government of Hindu majority India has not similarly defended overseas Hindu groups from such charges, like the cases against the Hare Krishna movement (ISKON), a Hindu movement in the United States, which has been the object of attack by American religious groups as a cult.

In creating a country in which all religions are tolerated Hindus, alone of all people, have felt the additional need to make all religions the same on a spiritual level. Hindus have chosen not merely to accept all religions but to try to exalt them all. In order to remain secular and tolerant Hindus have felt that they should not criticize or try to counter inimical religious groups and their activities to undermine Hinduism.

Naturally this has led to a weakening of the ability of Hindus to defend their religion even in their own country. That is why, in spite of so a number of ashrams built in India and so a number of spiritual books on Hindu gurus or sadhanas being published, there are few books in India in defence of Hinduism, Hindu critiques of other religions, or Hindu rebuttals to missionaries. The policy has been to ignore the aggression of the missionaries and emphasize that the spirituality and tolerance of Hinduism can endure all things.

This has often given the missionaries a free hand to prey upon the weaker elements of Hindu society and left such poorer Hindu groups feeling abandoned by Hindu society. We must remember that though Hinduism is the majority religion of India, during a thousand years of foreign rule, it was oppressed. Hindu temples were routinely destroyed and Hindu religious activities were either curtailed or looked upon with disfavour by the government. Present minority religions of India, Islam and Christianity, ruled over Hindus and objectiveed at conversion of Hindus as a government policy. After independence the socialist government of India has been anti-Hindu as well and missionary activity remains strong in the country.

FUNDAMENTALISM

Fundamentalism is an easily discernible phenomenon in belief-oriented religions like Christianity and Islam which have a simple and exclusive pattern to their faith. They generally insist that there is only One God, who has only one Son or final Prophet, and only one true scripture. They hold that belief in this One God and his chief representative brings salvation in an eternal heaven, and disbelief causes condemnation to an eternal hell. Muslims daily chant "there is no God but Allah and Mohammed is his prophet. " Most Christians recognize belief in Christ as one's personal saviour as the only true way to salvation.

Fundamentalists are literalists in these customs who hold rigidly to their beliefs and insist that since their religion alone is true that other religions should not be tolerated, particularly in the lands where members of their religion are in a majority. Fundamentalists also generally hold to their religion's older social customs, and refuse to integrate into the broader stream of modern society which recognizes the freedom of belief.

It is questionable whether fundamentalism, as it is usually defined relative to Christianity and Islam, can exist at all in the more open and diverse religious custom of Hinduism which has a number of names and forms for God, a number of great teachers and incarnations, a number of sacred books, and a pursuit of Self-realization which does not recognize the existence of any eternal heaven or hell. There is no monolithic faith called Hinduism with a set system of beliefs which all Hindus must follow that can be turned into fundamentalism.

Fundamentalist groups insist that theirs is the only true God and that all other Gods or names of God are wrong. Islamic fundamentalists insist that the only God is Allah, and will not accept Hindu names for God like

Brahman or Ishvara, even though these mean pretty much the same thing. Christian fundamentalists will not accept Allah or Brahman as names for God as they conceive Him to be. Hindus with their a number of names and forms for God don't mind accepting the Christian name God or even Islamic Allah as referring to the same reality. A belief in God is not even necessary to be a Hindu, as such non-theistic Hindu systems as Sankhya reveal.

Islamic fundamentalists consider that Islam is the only true religion, that no true new faith can be founded after Islam and that with the advent of Islam all previous faiths became outdated. Christian fundamentalists hold that Christianity alone is true, and that Islam and Hinduism are religions of the devil. Even orthodox people in these customs may hold these views to some degree.

Hindus are not of one faith only. They are divided up into Shaivites, Vaishnavas, Shaktas, Smartas and a number of other groups which are constantly being revised relative to modern gurus. Those called Hindu fundamentalists are also divided up into these various sects.

No Hindus insist that there is only one true faith called Hinduism and that all other faiths are false. Hinduism comprises too much plurality to allow for that. Its tendency is to not to coalesce into a fanatic unity like the fundamentalists of other religions, but to disperse into its various diverse components and fail to arrive at any common action, historically even one of self-defence against foreign invaders.

Fundamentalist groups insist upon belief in the literal truth of one book as the Word of God, which they base their behaviour on. Muslim fundamentalists insist that the Koran is the Word of God and that all necessary knowledge is contained in it. Christian fundamentalists say the same thing of the Bible. Again even orthodox or ordinary Muslims and Christians, not only fundamentalists, may believe this to some degree. Hindus have a number of holy books like the Vedas, Agamas, Gita, Ramayana and so on, which contain a great variety of teachings and a number of various points of view and no one of these books is necessitated reading for all Hindus. Hindus generally respect the holy books of other religions as well.

Fundamentalist groups are often involved in conversion activity wherein they are seeking to get other people to adopt their beliefs. They frequently promote missionary efforts throughout the world to bring the entire world to their views. This again is true of a number of ordinary or orthodox Muslims and Christians. Fundamentalists are merely more tearing in their practices.

CONTEMPORARY POLITICS

Hinduism is not only a religion. It is a vast culture, permeating all faces of life from household matters to the highest spiritual philosophies. As Hindu Dharma is an open and diverse rather than exclusive religious custom with a number of holy books, teachers and meditation practices, similarly Hindu or Bharatiya culture is a broad and open culture, encouraging, not trying to obstruct the development of art, science, philosophy and literature.

Because of this strong cultural component there are those who claim that Hinduism is not a religion but a way of life, the custom of India, and hence members of any religion including Muslims and Christians can become Hindus. They propose Hinduism or Hindutva as a form of cultural nationalism that is religiously neutral and can accommodate not only Buddhists, Sikhs and Jains, whose religions are native to India, but also Christianity and Islam, which have existed in India so long so as to almost be native as well.

Hinduism is not a dogmatic or exclusive religion to be sure, and can accommodate a number of beliefs, but does have its particular orientation, its way of Dharma. Though it is not simply a religion its religious element cannot be ignored. It has its particular beliefs of karma, rebirth and Self-realization, which however diversely formulated, cannot be set aside. Its chief concern is the realization of immorality, which is certainly an issue in the sphere of religion.

Of course one can classify Hindu culture from Hindu religion. One can define Hindu culture as Indian (Bharatiya). One can easily include Buddhist, Jain, and Sikh customs as Bharatiya because of the a number of common cultural elements of these native customs. In addition one can identify Bharatiya elements in Indian Islam or Christianity, with their devotional and mystical trends that reflect a Hindu religious influence, and their dress, food habits, and other outer aspects of life inherited from the local culture.

Yet one cannot pretend that there is no Hindu religious element in the field of Bharatiya culture. The Hindu religion permeates Bharatiya culture, whether it is the music, dance, poetry, mythology, or philosophy. A Hindu element permeates Indian culture more so than a Christian element does that of Europe. Europe had a Greco-Roman background for most of its art, law and philosophy that was pre-Christian in nature, but in India all of these cultural factors have a Hindu background.

Of course India is a big country and there are areas in which an Islamic culture or other non-Hindu or even non-Bharatiya cultures have prevailed, but this cannot be used to override a greater Hindu influence. Hence the idea that India is a composite culture of Hinduism and Islam, such as a number of scholars have proposed, is not really true. The dominant culture remains Hindu or Indian, while the Islamic influence is mainly on the religious practices of Indian Muslims. For this fact one cannot entirely separate Hindu religion and either Hindu or Indian culture. In recent years, partly as a backlash to this failed policy of accommodation of religions, more pro-Hindu political parties have come to prominence in India. They strive to defend Hindu causes and to reverse the policy of anti- Hinduism in the government. Naturally, to one unacquainted with India and its history, this at face value may look like a religious interference in politics.

But if we look at the matter carefully we see that such so-called Hindu parties are asking for the removal of anti-Hindu policies, eliminating the current pseudo-secularism that grants special favours to religious minorities and penalizes the majority religious community. They want Hinduism to be honored in India and to be recognized for its contribution to the culture. They are not asking, like Islamic countries, for a religious state, or for the imposition of religious law, but only for a common civil code, which India has yet to have.

Of course political groups should avoid criticizing religious beliefs whatever these may be. Only the political activity of religious groups should be their concern. However, Hindus are in a position in which rival nations, like Pakistan, are using religion against them, creating holy wars against India, and trying to encourage the Muslim minority of India to join these. There is not only an Islamic but a Christian agenda against Hindu majority India. Not only Hindus, any nationalist Indians, should be willing to criticize religious groups that encourage separatist and terrorist activities in their own country. In this case it is the political activities of these groups that is the issue, not their metaphysical beliefs.

One must remember that India was partitioned in favour of the Islamic State of Pakistan, which means that India was more or less left over for the Hindus. Muslims in the subcontinent of India decided that they could not share the same government with Hindus. This along with the militant nature of Islam makes it hard to separate religion from Hindu-Muslim or India-Pakistan relations.

We should note that it is mainly the Hindus in India who have tried to create a free society, not the Muslims of the subcontinent. There is little religious tolerance in Islamic countries, including Pakistan and Bangladesh, where Hindus are routinely oppressed and have been steadily diminishing in numbers. These countries pride themselves in being Islamic states or Islamic republics following customal Islamic law. Islamic law means that Muslims cannot convert to other religions, though members of other religious groups can convert to Islam.

It intends that no one can publicly criticize Islam, though other religions have no such protection. Hence Hindus must recognize the non-secular, exclusive and non-pluralistic nature of certain religions and their possible social ramifications. Hindus politically should not be against any particular religion, but they should not accept antinational policies, even these are done in the name of religion. Just as the United States will not tolerate Islamic terrorist actions, like the World Trade Center Bombing, India has to challenge antinational religious groups as well. Unfortunately missionary conversion in India often has an antinational component, with newly converted religious minorities, at the behest of their leaders, agitating for separate states along the lines of the formation of Pakistan. Hindus cannot ignore such activity merely because it is called religious.

Naturally other religious groups will not be happy if Hindus are more assertive politically because this will limit their influence. They will accuse Hindus of religious prejudice even if it has no real basis. But they cannot deny the power of the majority either. If Hindus assert themselves, not to control others, but to sustain their customs and national values against unjust attacks, such voices must become silent. Hindus must not bow down to the charge that they are intolerant, particularly if leveled by groups who have no real history of tolerance, but must remain firm in the truth of their Dharma.

REFERENCES

Balslev, A.N.: *A study of time in Indian philosophy*, Wiesbaden, Otto Harrassowitz, 1983.

Barnett, S.A.: *Coconuts and gold: relational identity in a South Indian caste*, 1976.

Clothey, F.W.: *Chronometry, cosmology and the festival calendar in the Murukan cult*, New Delhi: Manohar, 1982.

Courtright, PB.: *Ganesa: Lord of obstacles, Lord of beginnings*, New York, Oxford University Press, 1985.

Daniel, E.V.: *Fluid signs: being a person the Tamil way*, Berkeley, University of California Press, 1984.

Durkheim, E.: *The elementary forms of the religions life*, London, George Allen & Unwin, 1915.

Fuller, C. J.: *Gods, priests and purity: on the relation between Hinduism and the caste system*, 1979.

Gale, R.M.: *The language of time. London: Routledge & Kegan Paul*, 1968.

Gell, A.: *The anthropology of time*, Berg, Oxford, 1992.

Gopinatha Rao, T.A.: *Elements of Hindu iconography (2 vols). Delhi: Motilal Banarsidass. 1997*.Gough, E.K.: Brahman kinship in a Tamil village. Am. Anthrop, 1956.

Handelman, D. & D.D.: *Shulman Cod inside out: Siva's game of dice*, New York, Oxford University Press, 1997.

Kalynasuntaram, N.: *Tiruccentur Murukankoyil varalaru.: Tiruchendur*: Tirukkumaran Patippakam, 1980.

Kane, P.V.: *History of Dharmasastra* 5, Poona: Bhandarkar Oriental Research Institute, 1958.

McTaggart, J.M.E.: *The nature of existence 2*, Cambridge, University Press, 1927.

14

Religious Rituals and Traditions

The religious life of most of the Hindus is centered on the devotion to God. The interpretations of God may differ from person to person. A number of rituals are developed which help the man realize the divinity from the midst of daily life.

The more philosophically oriented Hindus will ignore the idea of gods and seek realization through various forms of meditation. Other Hindus will perform their duties towards society while keeping the moral values and seek the divine. In fact, there are three possible paths (margas) to liberation and all the recognized as equally valid. The three paths are:

- Path of work and action (Karmamarga)
- Path of knowledge (Jnanamarga)
- Path of devotion (Bhaktimarga)

RELIGIOUS RITUALS

Samskaras

Orthodox Hindu code of conduct places emphasis primarily on two qualities in a human being, which also distinguish him from the animals and the low life characters. They are education (vidya) and proper social and religious conduct (samskarah). Of the two, education is more significant because the other (samskarah) does not come without it. Samskarah is a personification or giving shape to such excellent qualities as inner balance, refinement and polished and civilized behavior. The word samskriti (culture or civilization) and Sanskrit (language) are closely linked to the word samskarah.

Samskarah also entails an obligatory sacred rite or a religious ceremony or a rite of passage. The closest English equivalent perhaps is sacrament. But it does not convey its full purport. Samskaras are the rites of passage a person is expected to perform during the various stages (ashramas) of his life, starting from his birth till his death. They are connected with his present and future, providing meaning, structure, motive and order to his life. Although meant for an individual, they are primarily social events in which a number of people participate, with or without the participation of the individual for whom they are meant.

There is a misconception that the samskaras are prescribed for men only. Custom proves to the contrary. They vary as per the caste. Certain castes are barred from the obligation of performing most or of them. They are performed at various times during the four stages (ashramas) of human life. There is no unanimous opinion as to the number of rites. The number varies between 13 and 40. The Gautama Dharmashastra prescribes 40 samskaras, the Grihya sutras between 12 and 18, where as the Manusmriti mentions only 13. The most customally accepted number is 16 and they are mentioned below.

Garbhadana: The rite of conception, a prenatal ceremony, performed at the time of conception.

Pumsavana: Ceremony performed seeking a male child or to increase the chances of the birth of a male child.

Simantam: The parting of hair ceremony seeking safe delivery. This is usually performed for women and celebrated by the women.

Jatakarman: At the time of birth and before severing the cord.

Namakaranam: Naming ceremony performed usually on the 10th or 12th day after birth.

Niskramana: Performed on the first outing of the baby and usually involves the first viewing of the sun.

Annaprasana: Performed on the occasion of the first feeding of the child with solid food such as rice, ghee and lentils. Now a days this ceremony is performed both for boys and girls.

Chudakarana: The tonsure ceremony performed usually in the first or third year of the child's birth

Karnavedha: The ear piercing ceremony performed during the third or fifth year. Now a days this ceremony is performed mostly for girls as boys are reluctant to get their ears pierced for fear of ridicule or looking feminine or orthodox.

Vidyarambha: Performed on the occasion of a child's initiation into education. Now a days this is executed on the first day a child goes to school and starts practicing the alphabet beginning with the letter AUM.

Upanayana: The ceremony necessitating the wearing of the sacred thread, which is confined to the upper three castes only and performed between the ages of 8 and 24.

Vedarambha: The ceremony marking the beginning of the study of the Vedas. Now a days not all children show interest in the study of the Vedas. The priestly profession is not very fetching. So this ceremony is performed in select cases only.

Kesantha: The ceremony marking the first shaving of the beard or the approach of manhood. In case of girls, in some regions, there is a corresponding ceremony to mark the commencing of menstruation or change in dress from a gown to a sari.

Samvartana: Performed when a student completes his education and returns home from the school. In olden days the schools existed in remote places. Once a student left home for education, he would return only after several years of study in the house of his teacher. So his return was a matter of joy and celebration for the family because the child not only survived the tough conditions of life in gurukulas but also acquired knowledge of the scriptures. Now a days the schools are located mostly in the same village or town where the child lives and the child is hardly separated from his or her parents during studies. So the ceremony is truly ceremonial.

SOCIAL RITUALS

Hinduism dictates both ritual and spiritual practices for the final liberation of men. The ritual aspect is meant to make man more spiritual in the end, not vice versa. Each and every significant event in the life a Hindu, who has chosen to lead a normal householder's life calls for the performance of certain rites. These rites are intended mainly to invoke the blessings of various gods and ensure success in the performance of his ordained duties. They are performed during various stages in his life for various ends. Some of the significant rites of Hinduism are described here.

1. Rites performed before the birth of an individual, invoking gods to make a woman of the household conceive.
2. Rites performed during the third month of pregnancy invoking gods for the birth of a male child. (Hindu women please take

note. The Aryans were chauvinistic and wanted more male children!)

3. Rites performed at the time of the birth of a child.
4. Rites performed at the time of name giving ceremony.
5. Rites performed six months after the birth of the child.
6. The hair cutting ceremony.
7. Rites performed at the time of "upanayana" to make the individual a "dvija" or twice born".
8. Rites associated with marriage ceremony, starting from the time the marriage is fixed till the ceremony is concluded.
9. Rites associated with marriage life involving both the couples.
10. Rites associated with entry into a new house or construction of a new house.
11. Rites associated with the death and funeral of an individual.

It must be noted that in the modern day world the texture of Hinduism is changing gradually. Ritualism is giving way spiritualism. It is the desire of a number of to look modern and spiritual, rather than conventional and ritualistic. Besides in ritualism casteism still plays its cruel role and ruptures the hurt sentiments of a number of, while in spiritualism doors are open for all Hindus.

So today a number of Hindus either do not perform these rites or perform them very selectively. Some ceremonies, such as the upanayana ceremony which are confined to the upper castes, are looked at with disdain by the remaining castes as they continue to remain barred from such privileges by the prejudices of the past.

The ceremonies linked with marriage, birth of a child, the naming ceremony and the death of an individual, are still practiced by a number of Hindus. But a lot of regional variations have come into them and each region and linguistic community follows them as per the their respective local customs. It is very true that today most of the Hindus perform these rites more as a social obligation rather than a religious duty.

CEREMONIAL RITUALS

Upanayanam

Now a days Upanayanam is more and more performed a day before the marriage ceremony. It is an elaborate ritual in which the boys are elevated to the twice born status by investing them with a sacred thread consisting of three strands of cotton worn over their left shoulders. It is renewed annually and worn till death. During the ceremony, they wear customal dress and necessitated to take the oath of celibacy. The boys are also given a secret name and taught to recite the Gayatri mantra. At the end of the ceremony, they feign to go to Kasi as a symbolic gesture to study the Vedas, but change their minds after being persuaded in a dramatic fashion by their (usually maternal) uncles.

It is a custom in Hindu society for a woman to move permanently to her husband's home after marriage and maintain a nominal or minimal relation with her parents whom she visits occasionally. However it is also a custom for a pregnant woman to go to her parents' home during her first pregnancy and stay their till the child is delivered. So usually simantam, jatakarman and namakaranam are celebrated in her parents' home. Because of the pressures of modern life, now a days it is not uncommon to see parents coming and staying with their pregnant daughters to take care of them during pregnancy instead of the other way round.

Marriage Ceremony

Marriage is an significant sacrament in Hindu society, celebrated mostly with pomp and gaiety, often resulting in debt and economic hardship for poor families. It is an opportunity for people to display their social status and significance among friends and relatives. From religious point of view, marriage onsets the beginning of householder's duties (grihastha ashrama) in the life of a person so that he can pursue the four objectives (purusharthas), namely dharma (religion), artha (wealth), kama (pleasures) and moksha (liberation).

The marriage ceremony calls for a number of rituals and customs, some of which vary from region to region, caste to caste and sect to sect. The most common form of customal marriage begins with the bride and bridegroom seeing each other in a prearranged place and agreeing for a marriage. Since most of the marriages are arranged marriages, this is usually done in the presence of elders who also finalize such sensitive issues as the amount of dowry, the place of marriage, gifts to family members, date and time of marriage, the list of invitees and so on. Marriage as per the Hindu custom is not just a relationship between two individuals but between two families. In matters of marriage most children obey their parents and elders and accept most of the decisions taken on their behalf.

In marriage the status of a bride is that of a piece of property owned by her father. This is in conformity with the notion suggested by the Dharmashastras that at no time a woman is to be left alone to live by herself. She should always be in the care of a male person, be it her father, brother, husband or son. The bride goes from her parents house to that of her husband as a gift from her father. Marriage is hence also referred as kanyadan (donation of a girl child) in which the girl is passed on by her father to the groom as a gift.

In marriage the groom and his family enjoy an upper hand. They get preferential treatment while the bride and her family have to be constantly on their toes to keep the groom and his family satisfied with the arrangements. Upon the arrival of the groom to the place of marriage, the bride's father and relatives receive the groom with a lot of fanfare. The bride's father or his son wash the feet of the groom. They house him and his family in a comfortable place with all the care and attention till the ceremony begins. Meals are served to the invited guests before the marriage begins. A number of guests pay attention to the food served and pass comments if the food served to them is not up to their expectations.

Usually one or two priests preside over the marriage to perform the rituals, which usually take hours. The Hindu marriage is a very elaborate and systematic affair. To an outsider not familiar with Hindu customs, it may look very boring and time consuming. But every aspect of Hindu marriage has a specific motive and hidden meaning. The bride is first offered to the gods, as a sacrifice, before she is handed over to the groom for his lifelong support and companionship. The marriage becomes officially confirmed either with the tying of mangalsutra (sacred thread) by the groom around the neck of the bride or by walking seven steps (sapta padi) around a sacred fire lit in the customal fashion or by both.

If the marriage is celebrated in the night, which is usually the norm in southern India, the priest takes the newly wedded couple under the night sky and shows them the star Arundhati. The occasion serves as a reminder for the bride to follow the shining instance of Arundhati who was steadfast in her devotion and loyalty to her husband. It is followed by meal sharing, where the husband and wife feed each other. After the marriage, either on the same day or after a day or two, the bride accompanies her husband to his house or to her in-laws' house where she begins a new life as the new bride. It is usual for the newly married couple to consummate their marriage in the house of the bride's parents. Honeymoon is a new practice introduced into Hindu custom due to western influence.

Family status and caste background matter a great deal in Hindu marriage with interesting ramifications. Marriages outside one's caste and religion are not appreciated and rarely celebrated in the customal manner by the elders of both families. Dowry is a big problem for parents having daughters of marriageable age and no property to backup. However, love marriages and live in couples are not unknown. It is hard to quantify how much acceptance and appreciation they enjoy in society. Gay marriages and same sex marriages are neither approved by the custom minded which constitute a majority nor recognized by law. In fact most homosexuals lead a double life, one for themselves and one for society and suffer from low self-esteem. In southern India marriage between certain cousins are legal and permitted.

Funeral Rites

Funeral is antyeshti or the last religious ceremony. Although a majority of Hindus believe in karma and rebirth, most of them consider death as an inauspicious and sad occasion. Upon the death of a person, wailing and crying are more common among close relations and especially women. The more unexpected and sudden the death is, the greater the bereavement and commotion. The general belief is that at the time of death a soul leaves the physical body through a small aperture in the skull and travels to other worlds. The souls of pious people with good merit (karma) go to the higher worlds and those with low merit and bad karma go to the lower worlds. In either case they would return to earth having exhausted their respective karma. So death is not a permanent solution for one's problems upon earth. It is a process in which the soul discards an old garment (body) to wear a new one.

Among common people; the imagery of death is associated more with the expectation of suffering and the negative feelings of fear and unpleasantness, coupled with the terrifying prospects of facing Yama and his dutas (servants), rather than the expectation of joy and the positive feelings of comfort and blessedness occasioned by the close proximity to such divinities as Indra, Vishnu, Siva and Shakti who rule their respective worlds of light and delight.

A Christian experiences assured of his place in heaven after death, whether he deserves it or not. But an ordinary Hindu, even if he has accumulated enough merit in his life through pious deeds or devotion to God, is not sure. He is not sure how his karma would work out eventually, because he hears a number of interpretations about it. He remains either confused or unsure of his path or approach for they often seem contradictory. As he approaches old age, he begins to experience fear and anxiety about his afterlife, for endless are the possibilities and numerous the worlds, both above and below, about which the scriptures are vague and descriptions few. Death is a very mysterious and serious situation for a number of Hindus, which they would prefer to avoid thinking about rather than confront it.

The funeral rites of Hindus are based on a very ancient custom of founded practices and core beliefs. They are in some ways contradictory, in the sense that the funeral rites remained more or less static over the centuries, except for some regional variations, while Hinduism underwent a great transformation incorporating a number of new customs, beliefs, practices and divinities. The funeral rites are centered mostly around two worlds, the astral world of the ghosts (preta-lok), where a departed soul stays temporarily till he builds an astral body and the more stable world of the ancestors (pitru-lok), where the soul enjoys the company of the souls of previously departed ancestors. In funeral rites we find no reference to either paradise (svarg) or hell (narak) but just two worlds. There is no clear affirmation of the belief that upon death a soul would travel farther to much higher worlds. There is no clarification as to why the ancestors languish in the ancestral world for so long neither moving into the higher worlds nor returning to the earth.

Death in the family is regarded inauspicious and cause of aural impurity. The bereaved family has to stay away from normal social contacts and engagements till the impurity caused by the death of a close relative is washed away through rituals and purification ceremonies. The restrictions last from a few days up to a year depending upon what is at stake. Celebration of festivals and marriages within the family are postponed up to a year from the date of the death of its family member.

Cremation is based on the vedic belief that Agni (fire god) receives all the offerings of a sacrifice on behalf of all the gods and that the body of a human being is an aggregation of the five great elements (pancha maha bhutas), triple qualities (gunas) and 24 principles (tattvas). Cremation is a kind of sacrifice in which whatever that is offered to Agni is shared by other gods through him. Blessed by the divinities, the sacrifice sanctifies the offering (the body) made in the sacrificial ceremony of cremation and ensures a place in heaven for the departed soul. Secondly the body is a handiwork of Prakriti or nature made up of the above mentioned elements, qualities and principles. When a person dies and his body is cremated, these constituent parts return to nature to be recycled and regenerated in other forms.

The place of cremation and the time of cremation are equally significant. Cremating a body in a place of pilgrimage or on the banks of a sacred river is regarded auspicious as it would ensure the soul a safe passage to the higher world. Cremation grounds are usually found outside the towns and villages or in secluded places. Unless warranted by the death of a close relation or friend, they are usually avoided by people for the impurity they are believed to cause upon mere visit. A lot of myth and superstition is associated with the cremation grounds as in other cultures. In some places the cremation grounds are maintained by a special class of people, but they are becoming a rare breed.

With increasing population and urbanization, it is becoming increasingly hard to maintain the exclusivity of the cremation grounds. In a number of urban areas they are gradually replaced by crematoriums, where the bodies are incinerated within a short time using high temperatures and the ashes are returned to the relatives for further rites.

The body of a deceased person is usually cremated on the same day. On occasions it is kept in the house till significant relations living in distant places arrive to have a last glimpse of the body. Once the time of cremation is decided, the body is washed with clean water, applied sandal paste and turmeric and decorated with ornaments or items with whom the deceased had known attachment. It is wrapped in a white cotton cloth of a particular kind, placed on a wooden mat or a similar contraption and carried to the cremation grounds by significant male relatives. The procession is led by the sons of the deceased, carrying a pot of burning incense emitting smoke, followed by other relatives and friends and on lookers. In urban areas the body is usually carried up to a distance and then transferred to a vehicle which is then led to the cremation place. At the cremation grounds the funeral pyre is made ready by using a variety of wood, depending upon the social and economic status of the deceased. It is not uncommon to see sandalwood being used in case of rich people, religious and political leaders. The body is usually placed on the top of the pyre and then lit either by the eldest son (in case of father) or the youngest son (in case of mother). There are caste based and regional variations about the manner in which the ceremony is performed.

After the body is cremated, depending upon the time and date fixed by the family priest, the sons of the deceased collect the ashes from the cremation ground in one or more urns. They are taken to specific places depending upon the wishes of the deceased or the customs of the family and scattered in water (a river or a lake), in the air and on earth. It marks the completion of the physical life of the departed being. For a few days, after the cremation, the family of the deceased is regarded highly impure (malinam) because of their coming into contact with the biomagnetic energy accumulated around the dead body. They remain secluded, avoiding social contacts and visits to friends and family for the fear of spreading the impurities. For the next ten days or so the family members of the deceased remain busy performing special rites called sraddha in which the deceased is offered rice balls. It is done with the belief that the rice balls would help the departed soul that is now residing temporarily in the world of pretas (ghosts) to construct a special body which would give him a right to enter the world of his ancestors (pitra-lokam). In the south, relatives carry some pindas or rice balls to the cremation grounds, place them in open and wait for the crows to come and eat them. If crows oblige and eat the rice ball or even peck at them, it is regarded as a positive sign that the deceased person is happy with the rites performed and is in the ancestral world.

The customal funeral rites focus on the soul's journey to the world of ancestors, neither to the Vaikuntah of the Vaishnavas nor to the Kailasa of the Saivites. The Bhagavadgita and other scriptures speak of the soul's journey to the world of the sun and the moon depending upon the time at which the soul leaves the body. In the Bhagavadgita Lord Krishna cautions his devotees to seek liberation through yoga instead of objectiveing for a place in heaven, because upon exhausting their good karma in the heaven souls have to return to the earthly world and continue their mortal existence. These are latter day concepts unknown in the early vedic period.

Modern spiritual masters like Swami Vivekananda and Rajneesh emphasized the significance of remaining detached and positive upon the death of person. As per the them death is a temporary interlude in the long journey of a soul and there is no fact for any one to be unhappy at all. Dying is not a tragedy but a transition. It is ignorance which makes people feel sad and unhappy about the death of a person, where as they should rejoice in the belief that soul is unaffected by all this and will take birth again somewhere to continue the learning process. Besides negative emotions will have a negative pull on the departed soul and interfere with its afterlife.

We have seen from the above discussion that the samskaras of Hindus are, mostly if not completely. based on the vedic custom. Over the centuries they have undergone little change. While Hinduism has evolved and integrated a number of customs into it, the samskaras carry within themselves an imprint of the original beliefs and practices of the Vedas and the early vedic people. To some degree they play an significant role in keeping the vedic custom alive.

OTHER RITUALS

Daily Rituals

In Hinduism, these rituals are always meant to infuse feelings of devotion and to bring about the divine orientation of human life. As a part of his householders responsibilities, a devout Hindu is expected to perform certain rituals every day starting from morning till evening.

These rituals include: making offerings to the gods, to all beings, and to the departed souls especially before partaking any food, showing hospitality to others and continuous remembrance of God through recitation of the Vedas or some holy scripture.

In addition, the householder is expected to perform oblations both in the morning and in the evening. The morning rituals include bathing or physical self-purification, offering prayers to the Sun, chanting the Gayatri mantra, applying certain specific religious marks on the body etc.

The marks would differ from person to person depending upon whether the individual belongs to Saivite or Vaishnavite sects. These rituals are meant to be performed by the householder who has chosen to lead a worldly life.

While it is a fact that most of these practices were confined to the upper castes of Hindu society in the past and a number of still follow them even today, though not with the same degree of devotion and enthusiasm, most of these rituals have been in recent times either discontinued or replaced by short and simple practices, reflecting the changing nature of Hindu society.

The new forms of daily rituals of present day Hinduism include performance of puja, practicing meditation and yoga, recitation of holy scriptures, reading religious books, participating in "satsang" or visiting the company of holy men, doing some charitable work, visiting temples and holy places, or chanting of some mantra or the name of a specific god.

The religious marks which the devout Hindus used to apply in the past on various parts of their body in a manner prescribed by the scriptures, have now become a rare sight and in some cases have been replaced by a simple mark called tilak either on the forehead or between the eye brows.

A number of modern Hindus do not wear any religious marks at all on their bodies, or are shy of wearing them, though the women still sport a tilak on their foreheads. It is however not entirely incorrect to say that a number of them do so out of habit and as a part of make up rather than out of any specific religious consideration.

Yajnas

These are the outer forms of worship in Hinduism, reminders of its direct connection with the Vedic religion of the ancient past. During the performance of the yajnas, offerings are made to various deities in a prescribed and systematic manner by qualified priests to supplicate them, so that they would assist the worshipper in achieving certain results in life.

The chanting of mantras while performing the sacrifices is expected to ensure fulfilment of specific desires, the overall welfare of an individual, a group of people or the entire society.

The simplest form of yajna is the domestic ritual performed by the householder who would offer simple oblation into the sacred fire lit in his house. A more complex version involves setting up of three to five fires and pouring offerings into them such as food grains, ghee or butter, and other vegetable substances by chosen and qualified priests, chanting mantras simultaneously, invoking various gods especially Agni, Indra, Varuna etc.

Some yajnas are performed on large scale for the general welfare of the entire community, to increase fertility of soil, to invite rains, to welcome peace and wealth etc. Depending upon the degree of complexity, these yajnas may last from a few hours to several days. The number of priests participating and conducting the ceremony would depend upon the nature and objective for which it is performed.

It is a fact that the incidence of performing the yajnas and other forms of sacrifices is slowly coming down in modern Hinduism, primarily because of the influence of western education, the complexity involved in performing them and the decreasing number of qualified priests who can perform yajnas effectively as per the full Vedic injunctions.

REFERENCES

Babb, Lawrence A.: *The Divine Hierarchy: Popular Hinduism in Central India*, New York, Columbia University Press, 1975.

Bacchetta, P.: '*Hindu Nationalist Women as Ideologues*' in Jayawardena and de Alwis eds, 1996.

Badrinath, C.: *Dharma, India and the World Order, Edinburgh*: Saint Andrew Press, 1993.

Bailey, Greg.: *The Mythology of Brahma*, Delhi, Oxford University Press, 1983.

Balslev, A.N.: *A study of time in Indian philosophy*, Wiesbaden, Otto Harrassowitz, 1983.

Banerjea, J. N.: *Pauragic and Tantric Religion (Early Phase)*, Calcutta, University of Calcutta, 1966.

Banerjee, S.: '*The woman Shiv Sainik and her sister Swayamsevika*' in Sarkar and Butalia eds, 1995.

Banerji, S. C.: *A Brief History of Tantra Literature*, Calcutta, Naya Prokash, 1988.

Barnett, S.A.: *Coconuts and gold: relational identity in a South Indian caste*, 1976.

Basham A. L.: *A Cultural History of India*, Oxford, 1975.

Basu, A.: '*Feminism inverted: the gendered imagery and real women of Hindu nationalism*' in Sarkar and Butalia eds., 1995.

Basu, K. and Subrahmanyam, S.: *Unravelling the Nation: sectarian conflict and India's secular identity*, New Delhi: Penguin Books, 1996.

15

Society

The Hindu society is the sole significant society in the world today demonstrating a link of cultural survival and working since ancient times. Most other societies have suffered a sudden interruption and undergone a painful shift due to the incursion of latter-day ideologies.

Hindu culture can meet the same atrocious fate if there were no Hindu society to sustain it. This is the point which is not always remembered even by those who take pride in Hindu culture. There are a number of Hindus who cherish the great spiritual customs of Hinduism and its scriptures like the Gita and the Upanishads in which that custom is enshrined. But they do not cherish with an equal enthusiasm the Hindu society which has honoured and preserved these customs and scriptures down the ages. Again, there are a number of Hindus who proclaim with great confidence that Sanãtana Dharma that is Hinduism can never die. This is true in a sense. There will always be individuals in non-Hindu societies who will recover the mystique of Sanãtana Dharma through their efforts at self-discovery. But Sanãtana Dharma will surely suffer an eclipse and no more inform mankind at large with its message, if there is no Hindu society to sustain it.

Lastly, there are a number of Hindus who are legitimately proud of Hindu art, architecture, sculpture, music, painting, dance, drama, literature, linguistics, lexicography, and so on. But they seldom take into account the fact that this great wealth of artistic, literary and scientific heritage, will die if Hindu society which created it is no more there to preserve, protect and perpetuate it. But the death of Hindu society is no longer an eventuality which cannot be envisaged. This great society is now besieged by the same dark and deadly forces which have overwhelmed and obliterated a number of ancient societies. Suffering from a loss of its elan, it has become a house divided within itself. And its beneficiaries no more seem to be interested in its survival because they have fallen victims to hostile propaganda.

They have formulated towards it an attitude of utter indifference, if not downright contempt. Let no Hindu worth his salt remain complacent. Hindu society is in mortal danger as never before. It would be relevant to recall the history of Hindu society in order to put the record straight. For, there is very little in that record which invites indifference or contempt, and a good deal which deserves honour and homage. A word about misunderstandings first. At one time the dominant school of Western historians and their Indian disciples, for whom Hindu history commenced with Alexander's invasion, presented this history as a series of successful foreign invasions to which Hindu India invariably succumbed. They even invented an Aryan invasion of India in the second millennium BC. to round up their cherished image of this country as some sort of a free for all into which any adventurer could descend and dwell at will.

HINDU SOCIAL ORDER

As per the Manu Dharma, the Hindu religious code of conduct, divides human persons into four Varnas (Varna means colour, the Caste). Over the generations, the origins were forgotten and the system became the stratification of a single society. People are born into the caste of their parents. There is no mobility across caste lines during one's lifetime. Each Varna is divided into a number of sub-castes, each of which is called a jati. Just as the varnas provide a social hierarchy in society at large, the various jatis provide a social hierarchy within a Varna.

This system of varnas and jatis serves two significant functions. First, it assigns occupations. The Varna and jati to which one belongs is usually identified with an occupation. Within the Vaishyas, for example , there are jatis of bakers, sheep herders, metal workers, and so on. Second, the system separates the members of the various the varnas and jatis by a complex system of purity and impurity. The higher a Varna or jati in the system, the higher a level of purity they must maintain. The lower, the more likely they are to transmit impurity. These purity restrictions seem most frequently in four areas: marriage, drink, food, and touch. Marriage is possible only between members of jatis closely related in the hierarchy, for example . A mere touch—if a shudra should accidently brush against a Brahmin—can necessitate the Brahmin to undergo extensive rites of purification.

The top three varnas have a status that excludes the fourth; this is the status of being "Twice-born." This means that the religion described in the Vedas applies to them only. The designation "twice-born" refers to the rite of initiation that the members of this caste go through upon reaching maturity. This rite brings them into the religion; they are reborn as a Hindu and not just as a caste member. The shudras, therefore, are barred from worship in the Vedic religion, and are not even permitted to hear the Vedas read outloud. They hence have their own priests and religious rites.

Associated with each varna, there is a customal colour. These sound suspiciously like skin colours; and, indeed, there is an expectation in India that higher caste people will have lighter skin — although there are plenty of exceptions (especially in the South of India). This all probably goes back to the original invasion of the Arya, who came from Central Asia and so were undoubtedly light skinned. The people already in India were quite dark, even as today a number of people in India seem positively black. Apart from skin colour, Indians otherwise have "Caucasian" features — narrow noses, thin lips, etc. — and recent genetic mapping studies seem to show that Indians are more closely related to the people of the Middle East and Europe than to anyone else. Because Untouchables are not a varna, they do not have a customal colour. I have supplied blue, since this is otherwise not found, and it is customally used for the skin colour of Vishnu and his incarnations. Chief among those is Krishna, whose name in realmeans "black" or "dark," but he is always shown blue rather than with some natural skin colour.

The first three varnas are called the twice born. This has nothing to do with reincarnation. Being "twice born" means that you come of age religiously, making you a member of the Vedic religion, eligible to learn Sanskrit, study the Vedas, and perform Vedic rituals. The "second birth" is thus like Confirmation or a Bar Mitzvah. As per the Laws of Manu (whose necessitatements may not always be observed in modern life), boys are "born again" at specific ages: 8 for Brahmins; 11 for Ksatriyas; and 12 for Vaishyas. A thread is bestowed at the coming of age to be worn around the waist as the symbol of being twice born. The equivalent of coming of age for girls is marriage. The bestowal of the thread is part of the wedding ceremony. That part of the wedding ritual is even preserved in Jainism. Ancient Iran also had a coming of age ceremony that involved a thread. That and other evidence leads to the speculation that the three classes of the twice born are from the archetype Indo-European social system — the theory of George Dumézil. Even the distant Celts believed in three social classes. The three classes of Plato's Republic thus may not have been entirely his idea. Although there must have been a great deal of early intermarriage in India, nowhere did such an Indo-European social system become as rigid a system of birth as there. The rigidity may well be due to the influence of the idea of karma, that poor birth is morally deserved.

HINDU SOCIAL CONDUCT

It is samaskars which ennoble a person. A person who has imbibed good samskars rises in stature in society. One who has allowed himself to be overtaken by wrong tendencies eventually destroys himself. A number of sections of society have stagenated because of negative tendencies. But they are out brethren too, and we have an obligation to lift them up.

To highlight the results of some of these endeavours is the objective of this chapter.

Adapting the Hindu custom of the three Rinas (obligations) emphasis has been laid on Deva-Rina (obligation towards the gods), Rishi-Rina (obligation towards the sages), Pitri-Rina (obligation towards the ancestors) and Samaja-Rina (obligation towards the society) as the tetrad forming the bedrock of material and spiritual progress.

It is through adherence to this path that our society achieved all-round progress in earlier timer. But because of social distortions it is now not easy to establish rapport with people in the lower rungs of society.

In principle, Hinduism incorporates all forms of belief and worship without necessitating the selection or elimination of any. It is axiomatic that no religious idea in India ever dies or is superseded—it is merely combined with the new ideas that arise in response to it. Hindus are inclined to revere the divine in every expression, whatever it may be, and are doctrinally tolerant, allowing others—including both Hindus and non-Hindus—whatever beliefs suit them best.

A Hindu may embrace a non-Hindu religion without ceasing to be a Hindu, and because Hindus are disposed to think synthetically and to regard other forms of worship, strange gods, and divergent doctrines as inadequate rather than wrong or objectionable, they tend to believe that the highest divine powers complement one another. Few religious ideas are regarded to be irreconcilable. The core of religion does not depend on the existence or nonexistence of God or on whether there is one god or a number of. Because religious truth is said to transcend all verbal definition, it is not conceived in dogmatic terms. Moreover, the tendency of Hindus to distinguish themselves from others on the basis of practice (orthopraxy) rather than doctrine (orthodoxy) further de-emphasizes doctrinal differences.

In the West, the so called life-negating aspects of Hinduism have often been overemphasized. The polarity of asceticism and sensuality, which assumed the form of a conflict between the aspiration to liberation and the heartfelt desire to have descendants and continue earthly life, manifested itself in Hindu social life as the tension between the various goals and stages of life. The relative value of an active life and the performance of meritorious works (pravrtti) as opposed to the forgoing of all worldly interests and activity (nivrtti) was a much-debated issue. While one-sided religious and philosophical works, such as the Upanishads, placed emphasis on renunciation, the dharma texts argued that the householder who maintains his sacred fire, procreates children, and performs his ritual duties well also earns religious merit.

Nearly 2,000 years ago, these dharma texts elaborated the social doctrine of the four ashramas (stages of life). This concept is an attempt at harmonizing the conflicting tendencies of Hinduism into one system. It held that a member of the three higher classes should first become a chaste student (brahmachari); then become a married householder (grihastha), discharging his debts to his ancestors by begetting sons and to the gods by sacrificing; then retire (as a vanaprastha), with or without his wife, to the forest to devote himself to spiritual contemplation; and ultimately, but not mandatorily, become a homeless wandering ascetic (sannyasin). The situation of the forest dweller was always a delicate compromise that remained problematic on the mythological level and was often omitted or rejected in practical life.

Although the status of a householder was often extolled, and some authorities, regarding studentship as a mere preparation, went so far as to brand the other stages as inferior, there were always people who became wandering ascetics immediately after studentship. Theorists were inclined to reconcile the divergent views and practices by allowing the ascetic way of life to those who are, owing to the effects of restrained conduct in former lives, entirely free from worldly desire, even if they had not gone through the customal prior stages.

This customal dharma applies theoretically to all Hindus, but it is replaced by the more particular dharmas that are appropriate to each of the four major varnas, or classes of society: Brahmans (priests), Ksatriyas (warrior kings), Vaisyas (the common people), and Sudras (servants).

These four rather abstract categories are further superseded by the more practically applicable dharmas appropriate to each of the thousands of particular castes (jatis). Thus, religion for Hindus is mainly a custom and a heritage, a way of life and a mode of thought. In practice, it is the right application of methods for securing both welfare in this life and a good condition in the hereafter.

TRADITIONAL VALUES IN SOCIETY

Hindutva is the Practical approach to the problems of Hindu Society, to the problems of Bharath. Hindutva has a definite goal and offers the methods to reach that goal. Hindutva Philosophy outlines the ultimate goal of all Hindus to be the Unity of all the Hindus. Its ultimate goal is to restore the grand status of Hindu Rashtra which it had enjoyed in the past. It objectives for the overall development of Hindus. But, setting a goal is not enough. We should work towards achieving it. This is where the practical part of the Hindutva ideology comes into picture.

To achieve the goals, the Hindutva suggests a multi-dimensional approach. Hindutva philosophy proposes that our approach should be political, social and religious. It suggests that the approach should be both Material and Philosophical.

No man can achieve Ananda-the spiritual Bliss without first satisfying himself with the material desires. Our Hindu Philosophy had summed up the objectives of human life in a very well thought-out pattern, of aspiration designated as Dharma, Artha, Kama and Moksha. Hinduism suggests that a person who has not fulfilled the first three cannot attain Moksha-Supreme Bliss.

In the same way a society in which the material needs are not fulfilled cannot achieve Social Peace and Tranquility. Such a society is filled with violence and disturbances.

So to achieve the overall development of Hindus, our first concern should be social enlistment. So, the social approach of Hindutva becomes very vital.

Hindu Society had been inherently Tolerant, Non-Aggressive, and peaceful and also very diverse. This diversity which is the unique heritage of Bharath had also been a root cause for the social problems.

Hindutva's basic goal of unification of Hindus itself says that Caste System has no place in Hindu society. Every Hindu should be identified has Hindu and not as a Brahmin or a Dalit. Hindutva clearly propagates that all the elements in the Hindu society which are a hinder the rising of Hindu Dharma should be discarded.

HINDU CASTE SYSTEM

The customal caste system consists of a hierarchy of four castes (varnas): Brahmins (priests and teachers), Kshatriyas (rulers and warriors), Vaishyas (merchants and cultivators), and Shudras (servants). The non-Aryans who were incorporated into the Aryan society belonged to the Shudra caste. Those who were rejected on the grounds of ritual impurity were treated as and called Untouchables because members of the four castes did not associate with them. With the expansion and spread of the Hindu worldview throughout India, the division, hierarchy, and names of the customal castes were not maintained, with the exception of the Brahmins, who claimed and were acknowledged as possessing a degree of ritual purity that retained their superiority above the other castes. The word dharma is central to Hindu belief. Hindus often refer to their religion as Hindu Dharma, basically stating that Hinduism is a way of life rather than a religion.

The key constructors and defenders of the caste system, the Brahmins, claimed that the presence of an organized caste system, with its elaborate rules and necessitated caste duty (dharma), prevented society from degenerating into chaos. The Brahmins thus devised rules for each caste (varna) in accordance with the four stages (ashramas) in the life of a man (the Vedic society was patriarchal): celibate student, married householder, retired forest dweller, and the ascetic stage. This whole system was called varnashrama dharma— the duties of each caste in the four stages of a man's life. In the first stage, a boy receives his education by studying under a guru, and in the second stage he marries and has children. In the third stage, he retires with his wife to the forest after handing over the responsibility of the household to his oldest son. In the final stage he sends his wife home to their son and renounces all contact with the society by becoming an ascetic, and attempting to pursue moksha with greater intention. Among the four stages of the ashramas, most people only completed the first three. Retired couples usually stayed with their oldest son, and very rarely did a man become an ascetic in his old age. Basically, the concept of the four ashramas sought to synthesize the necessity of order in society and the spiritual liberation (moksha) of the individual.

With the advent and expansion of modern industries and Western education in the postindependent (after 1947) cities of India, the significance and demands of the caste system has weakened. In the major cities, a person's professional and economic status often determines his or her social standing. The secular constitution of India also outlaws untouchability and recognizes all Indian citizens as equal. Almost all urban Hindus intermingle professionally and socially, and a number of marry outside their caste. However, in rural areas and smaller towns, the stringent nature of the caste system and its necessitatements continue to define society and the lives of its members.

STATUS OF WOMEN

In ancient India, women occupied a very significant position, In fact, a superior position, to men. "Sakhti" a feminine term means "power" and "strength". All male power comes from the feminine. Literary evidence suggests that kings and towns were destroyed because the rulers troubled a single woman.

For example , Valmiki Ramayana teaches us that Ravana and his entire kingdom were wiped out because he abducted Sita. Veda Vyasa's Mahabharata teaches us that all the Kauravas were killed because they humiliated Draupadi in public. Elango Adigal's Sillapathigaram teaches us Madurai, the capital of the Pandyas was burnt because Pandyan Nedunchezhiyan mistakenly did harm to Kannaki.

In Vedic times women and men were equal in a number of aspects. Women participated in the public sacrifices alongside men. One script mentions a female rishi Visvara. Some Vedic hymns, are attributed to women such as Apala, the daughter of Atri, Ghosa, the daughter of Kaksivant or Indrani, the wife of Indra.

Knowledge, intelligence, rhythm and harmony are all essential ingredients for any creative activity. These aspects are personified in Saraswati, the Goddess of Learning, Music and Fine Arts. Without the grace of Saraswati, or Saraswati Kataksham, as it is called, Brahma cannot do a worthwhile job as the Creator. Any maintenance activity needs plenty of resources, mainly fiscal resources. So Lakshmi, the Goddess of Wealth, is an essential companion to Vishnu. Siva, as Destroyer, derives power and energy from Parvathi, or Durga as she is called Sakhti. It is only the Hindu custom, which provides, even at the conceptual level, the picture of the male and female principles working together, hand in hand, as equal partners in the universe. This concept is carried further to its logical climax in the form of Ardhanareeswara, formed by the fusion of Siva and Sakhti in one body, each occupying one half of the body, denoting that one is not complete without the other.

Just the sloka that is commonly recited during daily prayers is enough to show the status of the Goddesses. A sloka on Devi comprises the following line: Yaa Brahma Achyuta Sankara Prabhrudibihi Devaissadaa Poojithaa, which means, 'O Devi! Brahma, Vishnu, Shiva and other Gods' always adore you.

In Hinduism, all power, Sakhti, is female. Sakhti is the fundamental strength of the feminine that infuses all life. Sakhti is the divine feminine power found in everything. She is the Goddess. So that, actually, in India, Kali is the great divinity.

Hindus hold rivers in great reverence. The rivers are female divinities, food and life bestowing mothers. As such, they are prominent among the popular divinities represented in the works of art of the classical period. The most holy of rivers, the best known and most honored, is the Ganga or Ganges. She is personified as Goddess Ganga. The river rises from an ice bed, 13,800 feet above the sea level in the Garhwal Himalayas. The river Saraswati is regarded as the mother god.

One of the most significant of all Vedic hymns, the Devisukta, is addressed to Vak (speech, revelation), the goddess who is described as the instrument that makes ritual efficacious: "I am the queen, the gatherer-up of treasures." It is not unsignificant, that Earth (prithivi) is regarded female, and the goddess who bears the mountains and who brings forth food that feed all.

Education for girls was regarded as quite significant. While Bramhavadani girls were taught Vedic wisdom, girls of the Ksatriya girls were taught the use of the bow and arrow. Patanjali mentions the spear bearers (saktikis). Megasthanese speaks of Chandragupta's bodyguard of Amazonian women.

Similarly, Kautilya in his Artha sastra, which is also taken to be a document of Mauryan history, refers to women soldiers armed with bows and arrows. Buddhism kept up the customs of Brahmanical religion in as per the womanhood an honored place in social life. Women were made eligible for admission to what was known as the Bhikshuni-Sangha, the Order of Nuns, which opened to them avenues of culture and social service and ample opportunities for public life.

In Gurukulas, the ancient Universities of India, boys and girls were educated together. Atreyi studied under Valmiki along with Lava and Kusa, the sons of Rama. Fine arts like music, dancing and painting was especially encouraged in the case of girls.

Girls had Upanayana performed for them and carried out the Sandhya rites. A young daughter who has observed brahmacarya should be married to a bridegroom who is learned like her. Seclusion of women was unknown in the Vedic times.

The Atharva Veda refers to daughters remaining with their parents until the end of their lives. A part of the ancestral property is given to them as dowry, which becomes their own property, and is called stridhana in later writings. "Home is not what is made of wood and stone; but where a wife is, there is the home."

It is significant to note that only Hindus worship God in the form of Divine Mother. In Hinduism the deities for knowledge, learning and material wealth are female and not male. The past social inconsistencies and injustices that did not arise from Hindu scriptures, but from humans who failed to correctly incorporate the teachings of the scriptures, such as the Upanishads and the Bhagavad Gita, into their social philosophy.

A father protects his daughter in childhood, a husband protects his wife in youth, and the sons protect their mother in old age. The father who does not give away his daughter in marriage at the proper time is censurable; censurable is the husband who does not approach his wife in due season; and after the husband is dead, the son, verily is censurable, who does not protect his mother. Even against the slightest provocations should women be particularly guarded; for unguarded they would bring grief to both the families.

Motherhood is regarded the greatest glory of Hindu women. The Taittiriya Upanishad teaches, "Matridevo bhava" - "Let your mother be the god to you."

In Hindusim four Vedas, Bhavad gita and the two puranas Ramayan and Mahabharath are regarded to be the supreme. All others are just commentaries, explanatory notes or stories written by individuals. As commentaries written on the Constitution of India cannot override the articles of the Constitution of India, similarly, commentaries or explanations on Vedas by individuals cannot supersede richas of Vedas or the Ramayana or Gita.

In the Ramayana, everyone knows that after the death of King Dasharatha, his wives were never asked to step into the pyre of Dasharatha. Rather, they lived in family with full honor and Rama always bowed his head before his widowed mothers with full respect. In the Mahabharata, Kunti, mother of the Pandavas did not commit sati. Thus, there is no command in the Ramayana, Mahabharata or in Gita to commit sati.

In ancient India, Hindu women enjoyed great respect and freedom in the society. But repeated attacks on Hindus in India by Muslims and the British through centuries changed the situation. During such aggressions the honor and chastity of women often became the casualties. There have been numerous cases when Hindu women killed themselves rather than yield to indignities inflicted by the aggressors.

The killing of men and enslaving of women and children was a standard practice in Islamic conquests. Thus when Mohammed bin Qasim conquered the lower Indus basin in AD 721, he entered Multan and, as per the Chach-Nama, "6,000 warriors were put to death, and all their relations and dependents were taken as slaves." This is why Rajput women took to immolating themselves en masse to save their honour in the face of the imminent entry of victorious Muslim armies, e.g. 8,000 women immolated themselves during Akbar's capture of Chittorgarh in 1568.

This custom is exemplified in a verse from "Bhihadara-nyakopanishad," which reads "Artha ya icched duhita me pandita jayeta," (a well-to-do Political instability and successive foreign invasions further made it hard for women to take up formal learning, which made it impossible for her to undertake Vedic studies and conduct Vedic rites.

Due to these factors, Hindu society became more protective about its women. The freedom of women was restricted. To protect themselves, Hindu women started to avoid public seem ance and started to stay home. Their participation in public life and their social contribution was greatly restricted.

Now that we are no more under aggression or invasion, we should allow the women community to regain their power, fame and name. It is we, who made Indira Gandhi, a woman as the prime Minister. It is we who placed the Mother before the Father in priority for reverence? Matr devo bhava was the first Upanishad exhortation to the young. Hinduism is the only religion whose symbolism places the Feminine on a par with the Masculine in the profound concept of Siva-Sakhti culminating in the image of Ardharnari-Isvara. We have honored our country as our Motherland "Bharat Mata" and our nationalism has grown up from the seed Mantra "Vande Mataram".

REFERENCES

Berreman, Gerald D.: "*Brahmans and Shamans in Pahari Religion*" Journal of Asian Studies, 1964

Biardeau, M.: *Hinduism: the anthropology of a civilisation*, Delhi, Oxford University Press, 1989.

Bowes Pratima: *The Hindu Religious Tradition*, A philosophical approach, London, 1978.

Bowker, J.: *Oxford dictionary of world religions*, Oxford, 'University Press, 1997.

Braaten, C.: "*The Problem of the Absoluteness of Christianity*" Interpretation 40/4, October 1986.

Brown W. N.: *Man in the Universe*, Some continuities in Indian thought, Berkeley, 1966.

Carman, J., and V. Narayanan: *The Tamil Veda: Pillan's Interpretation of the Tiruvaymoli*. Chicago, University of Chicago, 1989.

Carstairs, Morris G.: *The Twice-Born: A Study of High Caste Hindus*, Bloomington, Indiana University Press, 1961

Chapman, M.: '*Theology as Vocation'- Ernst Troeltsch as Philosophical Theologian*" Ph.D. diss., Oxford University, 1988.

Clayton, J. P.: *Ernst Troeltsch and the Future of Theology. Cambridge*, Cambridge University, 1976.

Clooney, F. X.: "*The Tiruvaymoli of Shatakopan*, 1998.

16

Festivals

India is known all over the world for its festivals and fairs. Every day of the year there is a festival celebrated in some part of the country. Some festivals welcome the seasons of the year, the harvest, the rains, or the full moon. Others celebrate religious occasions, the birthdays of divine beings, saints, and gurus (revered teachers), or the advent of the New Year. A number of these festivals are common to most parts of India. However, they may be called by various names in various parts of the country or may be celebrated in a various fashion.

DEEPAVALI

Diwali, or Deepavali is a major festival of India and Nepal and a significant festival in Hinduism, Sikhism and Jainism. A number of legends are associated with Diwali. Today it is celebrated by Hindus, Jains and Sikhs all over the world as the "Festival of Light," where the lights or lamps signify victory of good over the evil within every human being. The festival is also celebrated by Buddhists of Nepal, particularly the Newar Buddhists.

As per the one theory Diwali may have sprang up as a harvest festival, marking the last harvest of the year before winter. In an agrarian society this results in businessmen closing accounts, and beginning a new accounting year. The deity of wealth in Hinduism, goddess Lakshmi is hence thanked on this day and everyone prays for a good year ahead. This is the common factor in Diwali celebrations all over the Indian subcontinent.

In North India, it is the homecoming of King Rama of Ayodhya after a 14-year exile in the forest. The people of Ayodhya (the capital of his kingdom) welcomed Rama by lighting rows (avali) of lamps (deepa), thus its name, Deepawali, or simply shortened as Diwali. Southern India marks it as the day Lord Krishna overcame the demon Narakasura. In western India it is also in honor of the day King Bali went to rule the nether-world by the order of Vishnu.

Diwali comes in the month of October or November. In Jainism it marks the nirvana of Lord Mahavira, which occurred on Oct. 15, 527 BC. The Sikhs have always celebrated Diwali; however, its significance for Sikhs increased when, on this day, the Sixth Guru, Guru Hargobind Ji, was freed from imprisonment along with 52 Hindu Kings (political prisoners) whom he had arranged to be released as well. In India, Diwali is now regarded to be a national festival, and the aesthetic aspect of the festival is enjoyed by most Indians irrespective of faith.

Kidha is celebrated for a differing number of days by various communities. Though the core days are common and fall on just the same set of days across Nepal and India, they fall in various Gregorian months depending on the version of the Hindu calendar being used in the given region. The Amanta ("ending on the new-moon") version of the Hindu Calendar has been adopted as the Indian national calendar. As per the this calendar, which is prevalent in southern India and Maharashtra, the 6-day celebration is spread over the last four days of the month of Ashwin and the first two days of the new month of Kartika. As per the Purnimanta ("ending on the full-moon") version prevalent in northern India, it falls in the middle of the month of Ashwayuja/Ashvin. In the Gregorian calendar, it falls in general in the months of October or November. In Nepal, it is celebrated as per the Nepalese calendar. The festival marks the last three days and the first two days of Nepalese era.

The festival marks the victory of good over evil, and uplifting of spiritual darkness. Symbolically it marks the homecoming of goodwill and faith after an absence, as suggested by the story of Ramayana. On the day of Diwali, a number of people wear new clothes and share sweets and snacks. Some North Indian business communities begin their financial year on Diwali and new account books are opened on this day.

While Deepavali is popularly known as the "festival of lights", the most significant spiritual meaning is "the awareness of the inner light". Key to Hindu philosophy is the assertion that there is something beyond the physical body and mind which is pure, infinite, and eternal, called the Atman. Just as we celebrate the birth of our physical being, Deepavali is the celebration of this Inner Light, in particular the knowing of which outshines all darkness (removes all obstacles and dispels all ignorance), awakening the individual to one's true nature, not as the body, but as the unchanging, infinite, immanent and transcendent reality. With the realization of the Atman come universal compassion, love, and the awareness of the oneness of all things (higher knowledge). This brings Ananda (Inner Joy or Peace).

Diwali celebrates this by festive fireworks, lights, flowers, sharing of sweets, and worship. While the story behind Deepavali varies from region to region, the essence is the same - to rejoice in the Inner Light (Atman) or the underlying reality of all things (Brahman).

HOLI

Holi or Phagwa (Bhojpuri), also called the Festival of Colours, is a popular Hindu spring festival observed in India, Guyana, Trinidad, and Nepal. In West Bengal, it is known as Dolyatra (Doljatra) or Boshonto Utsav ("spring festival"). On the first day, burning of the demoness Holika, Hiranyakashipu's sister, in a huge bonfires at night. It is called as Kama dahanam in Andhra Pradesh. On the second day, known as Dhulhendi, people spend the day throwing coloured powder and water at each other.

The spring season, during which the weather changes, is believed to cause viral fever and cold. Thus, the playful throwing of the coloured powders has a medicinal significance: the colours are customally made of Neem, Kumkum, Haldi, Bilva, and other medicinal herbs prescribed by Âyurvedic doctors. A special drink called thandai (made up of Bhang) is prepared, sometimes containing bhang (Cannabis sativa). Rangapanchami occurs a few days later on a Panchami (fifth day of the full moon), marking the end of festivities involving colours.

Holi takes place over two days in the later part of February or March. As per the Hindu calendar, it falls on the Phalgun Purnima (or Pooranmashi, Full Moon), which will occur on March 22 in 2008. On the first day (22 March 2008 AD.), symbolic burning of evil takes place, while the fun part of playing with colours takes place on the second day. (In 2007, Holi was celebrated on 3 March, the burning of Holika was on 4 March and the Dhuleti on 5 March.)

In Vaishnava Theology, Hiranyakashipu is the king of demons, and he had been granted a boon by Brahma, which made it almost impossible for him to be killed. The boon was due to his long self-mortification, after which he had demanded that he not be killed "during day or night; inside the home or outside, not on earth or on sky; neither by a man nor an animal; neither by astra nor by shastra". Accordingly, he grew arrogant, and attacked the Heavens and the Earth. He demanded that people stop worshipping gods and start praying to him.

Despite this, Hiranyakashipu's own son, Prahlad, was a devotee of Lord Vishnu. In spite of various threats from Hiranyakashipu, Prahlad kept offering prayers to Lord Vishnu. He was poisoned but the poison turned to nectar in his mouth. He was ordered to be trampled by elephants yet remained unharmed. He was put in a room with hungry, poisonous snakes and survived. All of Hiranyakashipu's attempts to kill his son failed. Ultimately, he ordered young Prahlad to sit on a pyre on the lap of his sister, Holika, who could not die by fire by virtue of a shawl which would prevent fire affecting the person wearing it. Prahlad readily accepted his father's orders, and prayed to Vishnu to keep him safe. When the fire started, everyone watched in amazement as the shawl flew from Holika, who then was burnt to death, while Prahlad survived unharmed, after the shawl moved to cover him. The burning of Holika is celebrated as Holi.

Afterwards Lord Vishnu came in the form of a Narasimha (who is half-man and half-lion) and killed Hiranyakashipu at dusk (which was neither day nor night), on the steps of the porch of his house (which was neither inside the house nor outside) by restraining him on his lap (which is neither in the sky nor on the earth) and mauling him with his claws (which are neither astra nor shastra).

In Vrindavan and Mathura, where Lord Krishna grew up, the festival is celebrated for 16 days (until Rangpanchmi in remembrance of the divine love of Radha for Krishna). Lord Krishna is believed to have popularized the festival by playing pranks on the gopis here. Krishna is believed to have complained to his mother about the contrast between his dark colour and his consort Radha's fair colour. Krishna's mother decided to apply colour to Radha's face. The celebrations officially usher in spring, the celebrated season of love.

RAMNAVMI

Ramanavmi is celebrated in the name of Lord Rama, an Incarnation of Lord Vishnu, who is measureless, who is of the nature of pure Consciousness and bliss, who is the consort of Sita, Master of Sri Hanuman, and the Lord of the three worlds, who took His birth at His own will in order to establish righteousness, destroy the wicked and protect His devotees. Ramnavami or the birthday of Lord Rama falls on the 9th day of the bright fortnight of the month of Chaitra (March-April).

Rama was the Lord Hari Himself, incarnate on earth for the destruction of Ravana. He was well accomplished, beautiful and endowed with royal marks. His glory and prowess were inexhaustible. He was peerless on earth. He was free from malice. He was gentle. He was the protector of all His people. He always addressed them in gentle words. He never used any harsh words even when somebody evoked Him. He held sway over the whole world.

Ramnavmi is one of the most significant festivals of the Vaishnava sect of the Hindus. However, even those who adore Lord Shiva celebrate the occasion. Some observe a strict fast on the day. Temples are decorated and the image of Lord Rama is richly adorned. The holy Ramayana is read in the temples. At Ayodhya, the birthplace of Sri Rama, a big fair is held on this day. In South India the Sri Ramnavmi Utsavam is celebrated for nine days with great fervour and devotion. Those talented in the art of story-telling narrate the thrilling episodes of the Ramayana. The Kirtanists chant the holy Name of Rama and celebrate the wedding of Rama with Sita on this great day. It is an highly colourful ceremony, highly inspiring and instructive, too. At the Sivananda Ashram, Rishikesh, Ramnavmi is celebrated for nine days.

DURGA POOJA

Durga puja is celebrated in the name of Divine Mother, Durga, who exists in all beings in the form of intelligence, mercy, beauty, who is the consort of Lord Shiva, who creates, sustains and destroys the universe. This festival is observed twice a year, once in the month of Chaitra and then in Aswayuja. It lasts for nine days in honour of the nine expressions of Durga. During Navaratri (the word literally means "nine nights") devotees of Durga observe a fast. Brahmins are fed and prayers are offered for the protection of health and property.

The commencing of summer and the beginning of winter are two very significant junctions of climatic and solar influence. These two periods are taken as sacred opportunities for the worship of the Divine Mother. They are indicated respectively by the Rama-Navaratri in Chaitra (April-May) and the Durga Navaratri in Aswayuja (September-October). The bodies and minds of people undergo a considerable change on account of the changes in Nature. Sri Rama is worshipped during Ramnavmi, and Mother Durga during Navaratri.

The Durga Puja is celebrated in several parts of India in various styles. But the one basic objective of this celebration is to propitiate Shakti, the Goddess in Her aspect as Power, to bestow upon man all wealth, auspiciousness, prosperity, knowledge (both sacred and secular), and all other potent powers. Whatever be the particular or special request that everyone may put before the Goddess, whatever boon may be asked of Her, the one thing behind all these is conciliation, worship and linking oneself with Her. There is no other objective. This is being regarded consciously or unconsciously. Everyone is blessed with Her loving mercy and is protected by Her.

Durga Puja or Navaratri begins on the first and ends on the tenth day of the bright half of Aswayuja (September-October). It is held in commemoration of the victory of Durga over Mahishasura, the buffalo-headed demon. In Bengal Her image is worshipped for nine days and then cast into water. The tenth day is called Vijaya Dasami or Dussera (the "tenth day"). Processions with Her image are taken out along the streets of villages and cities.

The mother of Durga (that is, the wife of the King of the Himalayas) longed to see her daughter. Durga was permitted by Lord Shiva to visit her beloved mother only for nine days in the year. The festival of Durga Puja marks this brief visit and ends with the Vijaya Dasami day, when Goddess Durga leaves for Her return to Mount Kailas. This is the view of some devotees. In Bengal, Durga Puja is a great festival. All who live away from home return during the Puja days? Mothers reunite with their sons and daughters, and wives with their husbands. The potter shows his skill in making images, the painter in drawing pictures, the songster in playing on his instrument, and the priest in reciting the sacred books. The Bengalis save money throughout the year only to spend everything during the Puja days.

The Bengali women welcomes the Goddess with a mother's love and sends away the image on the last day, with every ceremony associated with a daughter's departure to her husband's home and with motherly tears in her eyes. This signifies the parting of Durga from Her beloved mother. Durga Puja is the greatest Hindu festival in which God is adored as Mother. Hinduism is the only religion in the world which has emphasised to such an extent the motherhood of God. One's relationship with one's mother is the dearest and the sweetest of all human relations. Hence, it is proper to look upon God as mother.

VIJAYADASHAMI

Vijayadashmi or dussehra is celebrated on the tenth day, which follows nine days of Durga Pooja, some time in September / October. The Tenth day of the bright half of the lunar month of Aashwayuja.

This is among the most fortunate days in the Hindu calendar and comes as the finale of the nine-day festival, Navaraatri. This festival of victory is preceded by worship of Saraswati the Goddess of Learning and of Durgaa the Goddess of Strength. This is among the most auspicious days in the Hindu calendar and comes as the finale of the nine-day festival, Navaraatri. This festival of victory is anteceded by worship of Saraswati the Goddess of Learning and of Durgaa the Goddess of Strength. Several have been the names of the Goddess of Strength - Durgaa, Mahaa Kaali, Mahishasura Mardini etc., under which that supreme protectress of the good and the holy put to rout, time and again, the demoniac forces and established the supremacy of the righteous.

The story of how Mahishaasura Mardini took birth is striking for its unique message. At one stage the Gods felt powerless against the onslaughts of the demoniac forces headed by Mahishaasura. In answer to their prayers for protection, they were ordered to part with a portion of their divine powers to form into a new Goddess. It was thus that Mahishaasura Mardini took on a physical form as the combined might of 33 crores of Gods. The dreaded demon Mahishaasura was slain by Chaamundeshwari after a ceaseless fight of nine days and nights.

The lesson of this legend is so beautifully clear. Even the good and the moral can succeed against the evil forces only when they come together in an organized endeavour. Could there be a more telling message to the present-day disorganized Hindu people - A number of them individually good and pious but who have stayed incapable of overcoming the forces inimical to them and their culture? Truly has it been said, 'Sanghe shaktih kalau yuge' - Organization holds the key to strength in Kaliyuga. And this is the one single, most significant lesson which the Hindu people have to learn today.

Every page of our past history bears testimony to the shocking phenomenon of how the Hindus, though vastly superior in culture, wealth, armies, territory and sheer numbers to the foreign aggressors, were defeated and enslaved. And all this tragedy because of their fatal drawback of disorganization. Now, it is high time the Hindus learnt the bitter lesson of the past and realize that "Organization is life and disorganization is death".

The unique concept of worship of strength in the Hindu custom is far, far removed from that of accumulation of aggressive power. This strength is termed nigrahaanugraha shakti, i.e., while on the one hand it destroys the wicked, on the other it protects the good and the holy. That is how we find that the rise of Hindu power was never attended by aggression and exploitation of other countries. Probably the only nation on the face of the earth to display this rate restraint has been the Hindu Nation. The world history is replete with the blood curdling stories of nation after nation, whenever they became powerful, embarking upon barbaric invasions of other countries and liquidating whole native races. It was given to the Hindu Nation alone to live up to the famous saying of Jesus Christ, "I have come to fulfil, and not to destroy".

Vijaya Dashami is splendid with a number of an inspiring episode reflecting the victorious culmination of deeds of valour of our illustrious ancestors. The custom in southern parts depicts Sri Rama's triumphant return to Ayodhya after fourteen years of banishment entailing endless hardships, dangers and mental anguish like separation from Sita and ultimately the slaying of Raavana, as coinciding with this day. Symbolic of the victorious occasion, Raama-Leela is observed with great enthusiasm and eclat in the northern parts.

Shree Raama, it is said, worshipped Shami tree before proceeding to Ayodhya. On the same day, the Paandavas too, took out their arms hidden in the Shami tree and revealed their identity after their one year of Agyatavaasa (living incognito) after twelve years of exile to a forest. That marked their preparation for the victorious war of Kurukshetra. Invoking these inspiring memories the Shami is worshipped on this day and the holy leaves are distributed by one another as an auspicious omen for the coming year.

KRISHNA JANMASHTAMI

Krishna Janmashtmi is the birthday of Lord Krishna, the eighth Divine Incarnation. It falls on the 8th day of the dark half of the month of Bhadrapada (August-September). This is one of the greatest of all Hindu festivals. Lord Krishna was born at midnight. A twenty-four hour fast is observed on this day, which is broken at midnight. Temples are decorated for the occasion. Kirtans are sung, bells are rung, the conch is blown, and Sanskrit hymns are recited in praise of Lord Krishna. At Mathura, the birthplace of Lord Krishna, special spiritual gatherings are organised at this time. Pilgrims from all over India attend these festive gatherings.

The Lord seem ed when the moon entered the house of Vrishabha at the constellation of the star Rohini, on Wednesday, the 8th day of the second fortnight of the month of Sravana, which corresponds to the month of Bhadrapada Krishnapaksha as per the Barhaspatyamana, in the year of Visvavasu, 5,172 years ago (from 1945), which means 3227 BC. The eighth Avatara, Krishna, who has become the Beloved of India and the world at large, had a threefold objective: to destroy the wicked demons, to play the leading role in the great war fought on the battlefield of Kurukshetra (where he delivered His wonderful message of the Gita) and to become the centre of a marvellous development of the Bhakti schools of India.

Krishna has played various roles during His stay in the world. He was Arjuna's charioteer. He was an excellent statesman. He was a master musician; he gave lessons even to Narada in the art of playing the veena. The music of His flute thrilled the hearts of the Gopis and everyone else. He was a cowherd in Brindavan and Gokul. He exhibited miraculous powers even as a child. He killed a number of demons. He revealed His Comic Form to His mother, Yasoda. He performed the Rasa Lila, the secret of which can only be understood by devotees like Narada, Gauranga, Radha and the Gopis. He taught the supreme Truth of Yoga, Bhakti and Vedanta to Arjuna and Uddhava. He had mastered every one of the sixty-four fine arts. For all these facts He is regarded as a full and complete expression of God. There is no true science except devotion to Lord Krishna. That man is wealthy indeed who loves Radha and Krishna. There is no sorrow other than lack of devotion to Krishna. He is the foremost of the manumitted who loves Krishna. There is no right course, except the society of Sri Krishna's devotees. The Name, virtues and Lilas (divine pastimes) of Krishna are the chief things to be remembered. The Lotus Feet of Radha and Krishna are the chief objects of meditation.

The ladies in South India decorate their houses beautifully, ready to welcome the Lord. They prepare various sweetmeats and offer them to the Lord. Butter was Krishna's favourite, and this is also offered. From the doorway to the inner meditation room of the house the floor is marked with a child's footprints, using some flour mixed with water. This creates the feeling in them that the Lord's own Feet have made the mark. They treat the day as one of very great rejoicing. There is recitation of the Bhagavatam, singing and praying everywhere.

The Janmashtami is celebrated at the Sivananda Ashram, Rishikesh, with the following programme of intense spiritual activity:

GURU PURNIMA

The full moon day in the month of Ashad (July-August) is an extremely auspicious and holy day of Guru Purnima. On this day, sacred to the memory of the great sage, Bhagavan Sri Vyasa, Sannyasins settle at some place to study and discourse on the thrice-blessed Brahma Sutras composed by Maharishi Vyasa, and engage themselves in Vedantic, philosophical investigation. Sri Vyasa has done unforgettable service to humanity for all times by editing the four Vedas, writing the eighteen Puranas, the Mahabharata and the Srimad Bhagavata.

We can only repay the deep debt of gratitude we owe him, by constant study of his works and practice of his teachings imparted for the regeneration of humanity in this Iron Age. In honour of this divine personage, all spiritual aspirants and devotees perform Vyasa Puja on this day, and disciples worship their spiritual preceptor. Saints, monks and men of God are honoured and entertained with acts of charity by all the householders with deep faith and sincerity. The period Chaturmas (the "four months") begins from this day; Sannyasins stay at one place during the ensuing four rainy months, engaging in the study of the Brahma Sutras and the practice of meditation.

Mark fully the deep implication of this great day. It heralds the setting in of the eagerly awaited rains. The water drawn up and stored as clouds in the hot summer now manifests in plentiful showers that usher in the advent of fresh life all over. Even so, all begin seriously to put into actual practice all the theory and philosophy that have been stored up in them through patient study. Aspirants commence or resolve to intensify with all earnestness, their practical spiritual Sadhana right from this day.

SANKRANTI

Sankranti means to go from one place to another place (to change direction). It also means one meets another. When the sun changes direction from one constellation (of the zodiac) to another is known as Sankranti. Transition of the Sun from Sagittarius to Capricorn during the winter solstice in the northern hemisphere (Uttarayana) is known as Makar sankranti. There are 12 signs of the zodiac. There are 12 Sankrantis as well. They are given names as per the position of the sun in relation to the signs of the zodiac. Each of the 12 Sankrantis has its relevant significance but two of these are most prominent.

These two are Mesh Sankranti and Makar Sankranti (Aries and Capricorn).The solar year commences when the sun is in Aries (the first sign of the zodiac). From the point of view of mathematical calculations, the solar year is more scientific than the lunar year. One lunar year has 354 days only and lunar days (or nights) increase or decrease as per the phases of the moon. Compare this to the solar year which has 365 ¼ days and remains the same. A number of astrological books are based upon solar calculations. The sun is the most significant and the most outstanding of our stars and the undisputed lord of our planetary system. The sun always comes first. First day of the week commences with Sunday (Ravi).

Science attaches great significance to the sun. The sun is the inexhaustible storehouse and the source of light and energy. Without sunlight creatures and vegetation would cease to exist. People will lose their life sustaining vitality. Lack of nourishing substances would lead to the end of creation. This is why the sun's existence, movements and positions in the cosmos are so significant and that is why the sun earns our respect, admiration and reverence.

The solar year commences when the sun is in Aries (the first sign of the zodiac). During this auspicious period, great deal of merits are acquired by performing Havan (Yajna or Sacred Fire ceremony), Japa (repetition of Mantra or God's name), Shraddha, Charity etc. Householders top up their grain jars and families start wedding preparations for their sons and daughters of marriageable age. The second Sankranti of great significance is Makar. Transition of the Sun from Sagittarius to Capricorn during the winter solstice in the northern hemisphere (Uttarayana) is known as Makar sankranti. The sun and journeys northward. The days are step by step lengthening in the northern hemisphere.

Makar Sankranti is also known as khichadi (Indian dish made from rice and lentils) Sankranti because on this day the injunction to eat Khichadi, is in general observed by people. Seasonal crops become available. Ghee, and spices are used for making tasty nourishing Khichadi. Winter loosens its grip on shiver producing cold, admitting springtime that brings with it the chance for all round health improvement. In addition to Khichadi, great significance is attached to the use of Til (Sesame seeds) during Makar Sankranti. Therefore, this Sankranti is also called Til Sankranti. People make Laddoos (round balls) from Til. Til oil is used for massaging.

Six types of usage of Til are described. Til is used for Bathing, for Massaging, for Havan (sacred fire ceremony), Tarpan with Til (oblations of water with Til), Til used as food, and Til is donated in charity. It is said that Til emanates from Vishnu's body and that the above described usage wash away all kinds of sins. Sankranti period is held to be very auspicious and any good deeds during this time will produce merits. Gifts of clothing, blankets etc., on this day are productive of merits in both this life and in the next life.

VASANTA PANCHAMI

Vasanta means the spring season, which is very compatible for doing vigorous Yoga Sadhana. Men, women and girls wear yellow cloth. The yellow colour is a sign of auspiciousness and spirituality. It represents the ripening of the spring crops. Even the food is coloured yellow by using saffron. All the folk get together and sing songs connected with spring. All get up in the early morning, take bath and worship the sun, Mother Ganga, the Deity of the sacred river Ganges, and the earth.

On this unforgettable day, Lord Shiva burnt the god of love, Cupid. The gods had sent Cupid to tempt the Lord while he was absorbed in Samadhi, in order to beget a powerful son who would be able to destroy the wicked demon Tarakasura. Cupid discharged an arrow at Lord Shiva from behind a tree. Shiva turned very greatly enraged. He opened His third eye and reduced Cupid to ashes. The Bengalis call this festival Saraswathi Puja. They worship the Goddess Saraswathi on this day. The image of the Goddess is taken in progress and immersed in the holy Ganges.

GANESH CHATURTHI

Ganesh Chaturthi is one of the most popular of Hindu festivals. This is the birthday of Lord Ganesha. It is the day most sacred to Lord Ganesha. It falls on the 4th day of the bright fortnight of Bhadrapada (August-September). It is observed throughout India, as well as by devoted Hindus in all parts of the world. Clay figures of the Deity are made and after being worshipped for two days, or in some cases ten days, they are thrown into water.

Lord Ganesha is the elephant-headed God. He is worshipped first in any prayers. His Names are repeated first before any auspicious work is set out, before any kind of worship is begun. He is the Lord of power and wisdom. He is the eldest son of Lord Shiva and the elder brother of Skanda or Kartikeya. He is the energy of Lord Shiva and so He is called the son of Shankar and Umadevi. By worshipping Lord Ganesha mothers hope to earn for their sons the sterling virtues of Ganesha.

The story given below is narrated about His birth and how He came to have the head of an elephant:

Once upon a time, the Goddess Gauri (consort of Lord Shiva), while bathing, created Ganesha as a pure white being out of the mud of Her Body and placed Him at the entrance of the house. She told Him not to allow anyone to enter while she went inside for a bath. Lord Shiva Himself was returning home quite thirsty and was stopped by Ganesha at the gate. Shiva became angry and cut off Ganesha's head as He thought Ganesha was an outsider. When Gauri came to know of this she was sorely grieved. To console her grief, Shiva ordered His servants to cut off and bring to Him the head of any creature that might be sleeping with its head facing north. The servants went on their mission and found only an elephant in that position. The sacrifice was thus made and the elephant's head was brought before Shiva. The Lord then joined the elephant's head onto the body of Ganesha.

The great Lord Shiva made His son worthy of worship at the outset of all undertakings, marriages, expeditions, studies, etc. He ordained that the annual worship of Ganesha should take place on the 4th day of the bright half of Bhadrapada. Without the Grace of Sri Ganesha and His help nothing whatsoever can be achieved. No action can be undertaken without His support, Grace or blessing. In his first lesson in the alphabet a Maharashtrian child is initiated into the Mantra of Lord Ganesha, Om Sri Ganeshaya Namah.

HANUMAN JAYANTI

Sri hanuman is worshipped all over India—either alone or together with Sri Rama. Every temple of Sri Rama has the murti or idol of Sri Hanuman. Hanuman is the Avatara of Lord Shiva. He was born of the Wind-God and Anjani Devi. His other names are Pavanasuta, Marutsuta, Pavankumar, Bajrangabali and Mahavira. He is the living embodiment of Ram-Nam. He was an ideal selfless worker, a true Karma Yogi who worked desirable and dynamically. He was a great devotee and an exceptional Brahmachari or celibate. He served Sri Rama with pure love and devotion, without expecting any fruit in return. He lived to serve Sri Rama. He was humble, brave and wise. He possessed all the divine virtues. He did what others could not do—crossing the ocean simply by expressing Ram-Nam, burning the city of Lanka, and bringing the sanjeevini herb and repairing Lakshmana to life again. He brought Sri Rama and Lakshmana from the nether world after killing Ahiravana.

He had devotion, knowledge, spirit of selfless service, power of celibacy, and desirelessness. He never boasted of his bravery and intelligence. His birthday falls on Chaitra Shukla Purnima (the March-April full moon day). On this holy day worship Sri Hanuman. Fast on this day. Read the Hanuman Chalisa. Spend the whole day in the Japa of

Ram-Nam. Sri Hanuman will be highly pleased and will bless you with success in all your undertakings.

SHIVARATRI

This falls on the 13th or 14th day of the dark half of Phalgun (February-March). The name means "the night of Shiva". The ceremonies take place chiefly at night. This is a festival observed in honour of Lord Shiva. Shiva was married to Parvati on this day.

People observe a strict fast on this day. Some devotees do not even take a drop of water. They keep vigil all night. The Shiva Lingam is worshipped throughout the night by washing it every three hours with milk, curd, honey, rose water, etc., whilst the chanting of the Mantra Om Namah Shivaya goes forward. Offerings of bael leaves are made to the Lingam. Bael leaves are very sacred as, it is said, Lakshmi resides in them.

Hymns in praise of Lord Shiva, such as the Shiva Mahimna Stotra of Pushpadanta or Ravana's Shiva Tandava Stotra are sung with great fervour and devotion. People repeat the Panchakshara Mantra, Om Namah Shivaya. He who utters the Names of Shiva during Shivaratri, with perfect devotion and concentration, is freed from all sins. He reaches the abode of Shiva and lives there happily. He is liberated from the wheel of births and deaths. A number of pilgrims flock to the places where there are Shiva temples.

THE CHHATH FESTIVAL

A week after the festival of lights, Diwali, is the festival Chhath. For one night and day, the people of Bihar literally live on the banks of the river Ganga when a ritual offering is made to the Sun God. The word chhath denotes the number six and thus the name itself serves as a admonisher of this auspicious day on the festival almanac. The venue for this unique festivity is the river bank and since the being Ganga transverses the countryside of Bihar like a lifeline it is but appropriate that the rising and setting sun as witnessed on the banks of this river should be the ideal prayer propitiation locale. Having paid homage to the setting sun, the next day, one must make ready for the daybreak obeisance.

This is the crucial part of the ritual and the journey towards the river begins when not even the slightest hint of sunlight is visible. It is a mahogany black sky outside as the festival falls during the dark phase of the moon. One can tell when the river bank is near from the smell of dew soaked grass and the inky waters can only be decoded by the sound of a soft lapping. This time the faces turn eastwards and instead of just standing on the river bank, they enter the water for the customary holy dip. In the meantime, the precious baskets are left securely under a temporary canopy, made of freshly harvested sugar cane stalks. The four sided platform is made special with its corners beautified with terra-cotta lamps shaped like elephants or birds. The attendants of sandalwood paste, vermilion, wet rice, flowers and fruits, covered over with red dyed cotton cloth, to ward off evil designs and spirits, adds the right note of sanctity.

The milling crowd of priests in the medley of worshippers readily oblige devotees with chantings and prayers as the family stand around their altar with folded hands closed eyes and devoted hearts to offer their prayers to the giver of all life in the world. Once the first streaks seem on the horizon, men and women, dressed in their saris and dhotis (loin cloth) plunge into the shallow waters. Having found a foothold and entirely oblivious of the chilling waters, they begin the timeless mantra of the Rig Veda, specific to the Sun—the Gayatri Mantra. It is this unquestioned faith, a reminder about the basics of human existence, a conscious upkeep of the environment in its benefaction and bounty that becomes integral to the currency of living and conceiving.

ONAM

Onam or Thiruonam grew as a joyous annual reminiscence of the golden rule of King Mahabali, a mythical king, who ruled Kerala a very long time ago. It recalls the sacrifice of the great king, his true devotion to God, his human pride and his ultimate redemption. Onam welcomes the spirit of a great king, and assures him that his people are happy and wish him well. Facts and fables blend as Kerala celebrates this royal return, year after year with the festivities of Onam. Legend has it that the gods plotted against Mahabali to end his reign. For this they sent Lord Vishnu to earth in the form of a dwarf Brahmin. But before being trampled down to the netherworld, Vishnu granted the king's sole wish: To visit his land and people once every year.

A flower carpet called 'Pookalam' is laid in front of every house to welcome the advent of the vanquished king, and earthen mounds representing Mahabali and Vishnu are placed in the dung-plastered courtyards. Customal rituals are performed followed by a lavish feast called 'Sadhya'. Onam also means new clothes for the whole family, sumptuous home-cooked delicacies on plantain leaf and the lingering aroma of the sweet Payasam.

Spectacular parades of caparisoned elephants, fireworks and the famous Kathakali dance are customally associated with Onam. It's also the season of a number of cultural and sport events and carnivals. All this makes Onam-time a perfect period to visit this coastal state, touted as "Gods Own Country". No wonder the Government of Kerala has declared this time every year as Tourism Week.

Pongal is the first festival beginning off each new year in the South Indian states. As the dates for this festival are calculated by the solar calander (ie. Western), the dates of January 13-16 rarely change. Each day of this festival has a special significance, however, it is celebrated more grandly in the villages, while the city folk mainly celebrate on the second day only. The first day of the festival, which falls on the last day of the Tamil month, Margazhi, is called Bhogi. On Bhogi all people clean out their homes from top to bottom, and collect all unwanted goods.

In the evening, people will light bonfires and burn what can be burnt. The porches of these homes was fully covered by the thatch material, but somewhat elevated from the ground. This part of the home was taken apart and reconstructed on this day along with the front section of the walkway in front of their home. Both the porch and ground in front of their home was solid mud which had dried. So, to undo this, they put in water to soften it, and dug it out and rebuilt it. After rebuilding it, they took cow dung and added water to make a paste and spread this mixture evenly over the new fixtures to coat and sanitize them. This mixture was also spread on the floor of the hut, on which we slept at night. The second day of the festival which falls on the first month of the Tamil month Thai is called, Surya Pongal (or Thai Pongal), is the day on which the celebrations in realbegins, is the first day of the Tamil month Thai. On this day, Surya, the sun God is worshipped and women will wake early on this day to create elaborate kolum on the grounds in front of their doorway or home. Kolums are created with colored rice flour placed on the ground carefully by using one's hand. All people will wear their new dresses and use the new utensils or household items which replace the ones discarded the previous day.

On this day the new rice is gathered and cooked in pots with milk until it overflows. It is this overflowing which means Pongal. This overflowing of rice is a joyous occasion, and the children and adults as well will shout out 'Pongal-o Pongal!' Children will dance and make music to the tune of these words. The rice is cooked and prepared as a dish called Pongal, which is rice with dhal and sugar. This Pongal variety is called venpongal, ven meaning white. Another variety is also prepared with dhal and jaggery (sweet), called chakraipongal, chakrai meaning sweet. To accompany the venpongal, people eat brinjal (eggplant) sambar (stew), vadai, idli, and spicy accompaniments.

The third day is called Maatu Pongal, maatu meaning cattle. This day is devoted to paying homage to cattle. Cows and Bulls are decorated with paint and bells and people pray to them. In some villages in south India, there are bull fights of varying types. These are not so common as they once were. The fourth day is termed as Kaanum Pongal. On this day, people travel to see other family members. On this day, the younger members of the family pay homage to the elders, and the elders thank them by giving token money.

REFERENCES

Cunningham: *Alexander: "Report on a Tour in the Central Provinces and Lower Gangetic Doab in 1881-82"* Archaeological Survey of India, 1884.

Daniel, E.V.: *Fluid signs: being a person the Tamil way*, Berkeley, University of California Press, 1984.

Daniel, S.B.: *Marriage in Tamil culture: the problem of conflicting 'models'*, Syracuse, N.Y: Maxwell School of Citizenship & Public Affairs, 1980.

Daniélou Alain: *Hindu Polytheism*, London, 1964.

Danielou, Alain.: *The Gods of India: Hindu Polytheism*, New York, Inner Traditions, 1985.

Das, S. K: *Shakti or Divine Power*, Calcutta, University of Calcutta, 1934.

Das, Veena; *Structure and Cognition,* Delhi, Oxford University Press, 1982.

Davis, R.H.: *Ritual in an oscillating universe: worshiping Siva in medieval India*, Princeton, University Press, 1991.

De E. A. Brett: *Chhattisgarh Feudatory States*, Bombay, Times Press, 1909.

Devasenapathi, V.A.: *Saiva Siddhanta. Madras*, University of Madras, 1974.

DiNoia, J. A.: *The Diversity of Religions: A Christian Perspective*, Washington, D.C.: Catholic University of America, 1992.

Dubey, K. C. and M. G. Mohril: *Fairs and Festivals of Madhya Pradesh*, Delhi, Manager of Publications, 1965

Dumont, L.: *The Dravidian kinship terminology as an expression of marriage*, Man, 1953.

Dumont, Louis, and David Pocock: "*On the Different Aspects or Levels in Hinduism.*" Contributions to Indian Sociology, 1959

Dumont, Louis: "*World Renunciation in Indian Religions*" Contributions to Indian Sociology, 1960.

Durkheim, E.: *The elementary forms of the religions life*, London, George Allen & Unwin, 1915.

17

Religious Places

In the Hindu culture there is a great significance of pilgrimage. In India there are numerous pilgrimage centres in different places wide across the country. In religion and spirituality, a pilgrimage is a long journey or search of great moral significance.

Sometimes, it is a journey to a sacred place or shrine of significance to a person's beliefs and faith. Members of every major religion participate in pilgrimages. A person who makes such a journey is called a pilgrim. Unlike some other religions, Hindus are not necessitated to undertake pilgrimages during their lifetime.

However, most Hindus who can afford to go on such journeys travel to numerous iconic sites. Pilgrimage is another major ritual in Hinduism practiced by both householders and sadhus. Because the transcendent has become immanent at certain locations, these places have become tirthas, "fords" or "crossing places," where divine grace is localized. The pilgrim travels to these tirthas to experience the manifest Divine. Pilgrimages are governed by complex rules including fasting, celibacy', and taking up ascetic practices like sleeping on the floor instead of a bed as preparation for the journey. Ideally the pilgrim should walk all the way to his or her destination, but modern public transportation and even private cars have become acceptable alternatives. The destination may be a temple, wherein resides the deity to whom one has made a vow asking for aid, or one of the sacred rivers. Usually the pilgrim journeys to the tirtha during a festival season.

Millions of pilgrims, both layfolk and sadhus, will meet on Allahabad (Prayaga) for the Kumbha Mela festival. Allahabad is one of the most sacred places in India, because three rivers, the Ganges, the Yamuna, and the invisible Sarasvati, come together there. The Ganges is the holiest river in India; bathing in her waters purifies the pilgrim and his or her family back through seven generations. A bath at the confluence of the three rivers at the auspicious hour of sunrise on special days of the calendar ensures the soul freedom from the cycle of rebirth. Such freedom may also be gained further along the Ganges at Benaras (also called Varanasi and Kashi), one of the most popular pilgrimage sites in India. Benaras is considered the centre of the cosmos, a place where all the gods are gathered and all pilgrimage places are united. To die there ensures liberation so the city has extensive cremation grounds for those who make this holy place the culmination of their final pilgrimage.

RELIGIOUS PLACES IN INDIA

Allahabad

A great Hindu pilgrimage Allahabad also called Prayag is where river Ganga and Yamuna meet. It is one of the ancient pilgrimage centers of India. Prayag is venerated in the hymns of the Rig Veda. As per the Hindu mythology the region between the Ganga and the Yamuna is the most fertile region on earth. Prayag is also referred to as Triveni Sangam- the confluence of the subterranean river Saraswati, Ganga and Yamuna. The name Allahabad (the city of God) was given to Prayag by the Mughal Emperor, Akbar.

As per the legends Prayag remains intact at the time of the great deluge and Vishnu resides here as a Yoga Murthy, on a banyan leaf in the form of a child. Vishnu is referred to as Veni Mahadeva, and Shiva is believed to be personified here as the immortal banyan tree or the Akshaya Vata Vriksham. Prayag is also associated with Amrit (nectar of immortality). Legends have it that Jupiter picked up the pot of the celestial nectar as it emerged from the milky ocean and made off with it (to prevent the demons from having access to it). The infuriated demons chased him and in the course of the chase the pot (Kumbh) overflowed and the nectar fell into four various places on earth, corresponding to Prayag, Nashik, Ujjain and Haridwar (all these four places are sites of Kumbh Mela).

The Hindu pilgrims make offerings to the departed souls at Prayag. Bathing at the confluence of the three rivers - Triveni Sangam is regarded sacred in the Hindu month of Magha - especially on Makara Sankranti, Ratha Saptami, the full moon and the new moon day. Prayag is also the seat of Kumbh Mela celebrations once in twelve years when the planet Jupiter resides in the zodiac sign of Taurus. Kumbh Mela is also held at Nashik, Ujjain and Haridwar.

Badrinath

The great Lord Shiva's temple Badrinath temple, sometimes called Badrinarayan temple, is situated along the Alaknanda river, in the hill town of Badrinath in Uttarakhand state in India. It is widely regarded to be one of the holiest Hindu temples, and is dedicated to Lord Vishnu. The temple and town are one of the four Char Dham pilgrimage sites. It is also one of the 108 Divya Desams, holy shrines for Vaishnavites. The temple is open only six months every year (between the end of April and the beginning of November), due to extreme weather conditions in the Himalayan region.

Several murtis (idols) are worshipped in the temple. The most significant is a one meter tall statue of Vishnu as Lord Badrinarayan, made of black Saligram stone. The statue is regarded by a number of Hindus to be one of eight swayam vyakta keshtras, or self-manifested statues of Vishnu. The murti depicts Vishnu sitting in meditative posture, rather than His far more typical reclining pose. In November each year, when the town of Badrinath is closed, the image is moved to nearby Jyotirmath. Badrinath was originally founded as a pilgrimage site by Adi Shankara in the ninth century. Shankara discovered the image of Badrinarayan in the Alaknanda River and enshrined it in a cave near the Tapt Kund hot springs. In the sixteenth century, the king of Garhwal moved the murti to the present temple.

Badrinath is mentioned in religious texts as far back as the Vedic period. Some accounts claim that the temple was built on a former Buddhist temple site. One legend explains the fact that Vishnu is shown sitting in padmasana, rather than reclining. As per the story, Vishnu was chastised by a sage who saw Vishnu's consort Lakshmi massaging his feet. Vishnu went to Badrinath to perform austerity, meditating for a long time in padmasana. To this day, the area around Badrinath attracts yogis who come for meditation and seclusion.

Another legend says that Shiva and Parvati were doing tapasya in Badrinath. Vishnu came in disguise as a small boy, crying loudly and disturbing them. Parvati asked the fact for his crying and he replied that he wanted Badrinath for meditation. Shiva and Parvati found that it was Lord Narayan in disguise. They then left Badrinath and moved to Kedarnath. As per the Srimad Bhagavatam, "There in Badrikashram the Personality of Godhead (Vishnu), in his incarnation as the sages Nara and Narayana, had been undergoing great penance since time immemorial for the welfare of all living entities." The Skanda Purana states that "There are several sacred shrines in heaven, on earth, and in hell; but there is no shrine like Badrinath." The area around Badrinath was also celebrated in Padma Purana as abounding in spiritual treasures.

Banaras

Another important Hindu pilgrimage center Varanasi also called Banaras or Kashi is one of the oldest living cities in the world. A number of names have been given to Varanasi, though its recently revived official appellation is mentioned in the Mahabharata and in the Jataka tales of Buddhism. It probably derives from the two rivers that flank the city, the Varana to the north and the Asi to the south.

A number of still use the anglicized forms of Banaras or Benares, while pilgrims refer to Kash, first used three thousand years ago to describe the kingdom and the city outside which the Buddha preached his first sermon; the "City of Light" is also called Kashika, "the shining one", referring to the light of Shiva. Another epithet, Avimukta, meaning "Never Forsaken", refers to the city that Shiva never deserted, or that one should never leave. Further alternatives include Anandavana, the "forest of bliss", and Rudravasa, the place where Shiva (Rudra) resides.

Varanasi's associations with Shiva extend to the beginning of time: legends relate how, after his marriage to Parvati, Shiva left his Himalyan abode and came to reside in Kashi with all the gods in attendance. Temporarily banished during the rule of the great king Divodasa, Shiva sent Brahma and Vishnu as his emissaries, but ultimately returned to his rightful abode protected by his loyal attendants Kalabhairav and Dandapani. Over 350 gods and goddesses, including a protective ring of Ganeshaa form a mandala or sacred pattern with Shiva Vishwanatha at its centre.

Varanasi is to Hindus what Mecca is to Muslims or Vatican to Catholics. Varanasi is the site of the holy shrine of Lord Kashi Vishwanath, one of the twelve revered Jyotirlingas of the Lord Shiva. Kashi Vishwanath Temple, which in its present shape was built in 1780 by Maharani Ahilyabai Holkar of Indore, is located on the banks of the Ganges. This temple makes Varanasi a place of great religious significance to the Hindus. Varanasi is regarded as the most sacred place of pilgrimage for Hindus irrespective of denomination.

It is believed that bathing in the river Ganges results in the remission of sins and that dying in the holy city of Kasi (Varanasi) circumvents rebirth. This belief has encouraged the establishment of innumerable geriatric homes and hospices in the city, and led to the disposal of half-burnt corpses into the river Ganges. This practice continues to cause immense damage to the river's ecology. The ministry of water resources has banned cremation on the city's ghats (ghats are the banks of a holy river, and often, as at Varanasi, steps are built to facilitate bathing).

In the neighbourhood of the city lies Sarnath, the site of a deerpark where Gautam Buddha is said to have given his first sermon about the basic principles of Buddhism. It is a major Buddhist pilgrimage center and also has a stupa built by the Mauryan emperor "Ashoka, the Great". The modern name Varanasi is derived from two tributaries of the Ganges, one in the north end of the city, called Varuna and the other in the south end, called Asi (now reduced to a water-drain). The city has an airport at Babatpur, 20 km from the city centre, and is also well-connected to all major cities in India by road and rail. Regions near the banks of river Ganges are extremely crowded and house various Hindu temples and road-side shops. The chief residential areas of Varanasi are situated in regions far from the Ghats, which are much more spacious and less polluted.

Devprayag

Devprayag is a city situated in the state of Uttaranchal in northern India. It is significant because it is the point where the Bhagirathi and the Alaknanda join to form the river Ganga. It is one of the five sacred confluences in the hills and is a great place of pilgrimage for devout Hindus. Devaprayag stands at an elevation of 2265 ft. on the side of a hill which rises above it 800 ft. On a terrace in the upper part of the village is the temple of Raghunath, built of huge uncemented stones, pyramidical in form and capped by a white cupola. Situated at the confluence of the Alaknanda and the Bhagirathi, the town of Devaprayag lies at an altitude of 472 m. on the metalled road running from Rishikesh to Badrinath and about 87 km. from Narendra Nagar. Near the town there are two suspension bridges, one each on the Bhagirathi and the Alaknanda. The metalled road to Badrinath crosses the former by a third bridge. The town is the headquarters of the tahsil of the same name and is one of the five sacred prayags (confluences) of the Alaknanda. Custom has it that the town is named after Deosharma, a sage, who led a life of penance here and succeeded in having a glimpse of God.

The Raghunathji temple is claimed to have been erected some ten thousand years ago and is built of massive uncemented stones. It stands upon a terrace in the upper part of the town and consists of an irregular pyramid capped by a white cupola with a golden ball and spire. Religious ablutions take place at 2 basins excavated in the rock at the junction of the holy streams - on the Bhagirathi known as the Brahm Kund and the other on the Alaknanda called the Vasisht Kund. The temple, along with the other Buildings of the town, was shattered by an earthquake in 1803 but the damage was subsequently repaired through the munificence of Daulat Rao Sindhia. Every year a large number of people visit this temple..

Dwarka

Dwarka derives its name from word dvar meaning door or gate in the Sanskrit language. Dwarka is regarded to be one of the holiest cities in Hinduism and one of the 4 chief "dhams" along with Badrinath, Puri, Rameshwaram. The city is especially respected by Vaishnavas. The temple of Lord Vishnu, the deitie of the deities is as high as the peak of the mountain 'Kailash' and as bright as the white clouds. A man who has divine sight of Dwarka is supreme. A man who gets down from his vehicle after seeing the flag and golden Kalash on top of the temple, gets liberated from the various kinds of sins- sins due to killing of insects and worms by trampling under the feet, having another's food and water etc.

The Dwarakadhish Temple: The Dwarkadhish temple has a five storey tower which was built by Sambha, who is the grandson of Lord Sri Krishna. The city is believed to be built by Vishwakarma, who is a celestial architect in Hinduism. The temple is made of limestone and sand. There is a flag hoisted in the temple tower four times each day, which waves in the air beautifully welcoming the pilgrims. The structure of the temple is quite complicated. There are two gateways: Swarga Dwar, where pilgrims enter, and Moksha Dwar, where pilgrims exit.

From the temple one can view the Sangam (confluence) of River Gomati flowing towards the sea. In Dwaraka, there are also shrines for Vasudeva, Devaki, Balarama and Revati, Subhadra, Rukmini Devi, Jambavati Devi and Satyabhama Devi. The Jagatmandir temple which houses the Dwarkadhish, a form of Krishna is also located in Dwaraka. Nageshwar Jyotirling, one of the 12 holy shrines of Lord Shiva, is located near Dwaraka. Dwarka is also the site of Dwaraka Pîtha (also known as Sharada Pîtha), one of the four cardinal mathas founded by Sri Adi Shankaracharya, the others being those at Sringeri, Puri and Jyotirmath.

Adi Sankara had visited Dwarakdish Shrine and had founded the Dwarka peeth. The Lord here is dressed in Kalyana Kolam where he seem s to be a Royal Wedding costume. The place is so sacred as Lord Shri Krishna himself had resided and his successors had built the temple. It is one of the 108 Divya desam.

Gangasagar

Gangasagar is the popular name given to the point where the Ganga drains out into the Bay of Bengal. Located on the western edge of the Sunderban delta, it is a part of the Sagar island. In an age gone by, these islands were part of the dense forest. Sometime in the late 19th century, the forest was cleared by the British and converted into settlements.

At the edge of Sagar town-adjacent to the beach-is the colourful temple dedicated to Kapil Muni, the sage responsible for initiating the chain of events that ultimately resulted in Ganga coming down to earth from heaven and giving mankind an opportunity to wash away its sins in her pure water. Inside the temple, a vermilion-smeared stone panel is the object of worship. Carved in the centre is an image of the saint holding a small pot of water in his left hand and a rosary in the right. Flanking this image are two others-of Ganga, the four-armed goddess with Bhagirath sitting on her lap and another one of Sagar, the bearded king.

Bathing in the sea and worshipping at the temple are the two objectives of the Gangasagar mela. Unlike the Kumbh mela-where successive days are regarded holy for bathing-at Gangasagar only the day of Makar Sankranti (14-15 January) is earmarked as the most significant day, with dawn being regarded the most auspicious moment.

Gangasagar Mela is the largest fair celebrated in West Bengal. This fair is held where the Ganga and the Bay of Bengal form a nexus. Hence the name Gangasagar Mela. The river Ganga which originates in the Gangotri glacier in the snow clad Himalayas, descends down the mountains, reaches the plains at Haridwar, flows through ancient pilgrimage sites such as Benares and Prayag, and drains into the Bay of Bengal. Sagar Island, at the mouth of the river Hooghly in Bengal (accessed from Diamond Harbor), where the Ganga breaks up into hundreds of streams, and drains into the sea, is honored as a pilgrimage site.

Having a dip in the ocean, where the Ganga drains into the sea is regarded to be of great religious significance particularly on the Makara Sankranti day when the sun makes a transition to Capricorn from Sagittarius and this town becomes home to vast fairs, drawing visitors and recluses from all over the state. There is a common belief among the locals that the girls who take the holy dip get handsome grooms and the boys get beautiful brides. When they are done with the ritual obligations, they head towards the Kapilmuni Temple situated nearby, to worship the deity as a mark of respect.

Gangotri

In the hinterlands of the Himalayas the picturesque pilgrimage is the most sacred spot where Ganga, the stream of life, touched earth for the first time. As per the mythology, Goddess Ganga - the daughter of heaven, manifested herself in the form of a river to absolve the sins of King Bhagirath's predecessors, following his severe penance of several centuries. Lord Shiva received into his matted locks to minimise the immense impact of her fall. She came to be called Bhagirathi at her legendary source.

On the right bank of Bhagirathi is situated the shrine of Gangotri dedicated to the Goddess. Perched at a height of 3042 mts., it was constructed in the early 18th century by a Gorkha Commander, Amar Singh Thapa. Every year, lakhs of pilgrims throng the sacred temple between May and October. By November, Gangotri is covered by snow. It is thought that the Goddess retreats to Mukhba, her winter abode (12 kms downstream). The physical source of the holy river is at Gaumukh, 18 kms. further uphill, along the Gangotri Glacier. Several pilgrims trek upto the source to offer prayers either on foot or on ponies.The verdant valleys, dense forests and towering peaks offer excellent trekking and mountaineering opportunities for adventure enthusiasts. The 18th century's temple dedicated to Goddess Ganga is located near a sacred stone where Kind Bhagirath worshipped Lord Shiva. Ganga is believed to have touched earth at this spot. As per the another legend, Pandavas performed the great 'Deva Yagna' here to atone the deaths of their kinsmen in the epic battle of Mahabharata.The temple is an exquisite 20 ft. high structure made of white granite.

The natural rock Shiva linga, submerged in the river, is an amazing sight reinforcing the power of the divine. As per the mythology, Lord Shiva sat at this spot to receive the Ganga in his matted locks. The linga is visible in the early winters when the water level goes down.

Haridwar

The holy city of Hindus, Haridwar lies in the state of Uttarakhand in India. In Hindi, Haridwar means "Gateway to God" (Hari means God and Dwar means Gate). Haridwar was also known as Mayapuri, Gangadwar, Mokhsadwar in the ancient Hindu scriptures. Haridwar is regarded as one of the seven holiest places of Hindus, as the Gods (devas) are said to have left their footprints there. Haridwar located in the foothills of the Himalayas, represents the point where river Ganga reaches the plains.

Haridwar is an ancient pilgrimage site, holds respect for centuries. Several sacred temples and ashrams are located in this town. A number of Hindus come here to immerse the ashes of their deceased in the river Ganga. As per the Hindu mythology, Haridwar is one of the four sites (among Ujjain, Haridwar, Nasik, and Allahabad) where drops of the Amrit (drink of immortality) were accidentally spilled over from a pitcher. This pitcher was being carried by the sacred bird Garuda (the vehicle of Vishnu). The place where the drops of Amrit fell is said to be the Brahma Kund at Har-ki-Pauri (footsteps of the Lord), the most sacred ghat of Haridwar. Thousands of devotees and pilgrims visit here from all over the world to take a holy dip in Ganga. This act of taking a holy dip in Ganga is said to completely wash away one's sins.

The most beautiful ceremony to see in Haridwar is the Aarti (evening prayer) at dusk which is offered to Goddess Ganga at Hari-Ki-Pauri. It is a charming experience for the visitors. In this ceremony, pilgrims float Diyas (floral floats with lamps) and incense on the river. This speaks its own beauty and wonderfully eye catching.

The great Kumbha Mela, which takes place once every twelve years and the Ardha Kumbha Mela, once every six years, are the chief festivals. One of the oldest living cities, Haridwar has occupied a prominent place from ancient times and now even in the 21st century. Besides being a religious place, it has served as the center for learning arts, science and culture. Haridwar has a rich and ancient religious and cultural legacy.

Jaganath Puri

According to the Hindu ancient texts Jagannath is a Sanskrit name used to describe a deity form of Krishna. The term means master (nath) of the universe (jagat). Jagannath is regarded amongst Vaishnavas to be a very merciful form of Krishna. The oldest and most famous Jagannath deity is in the city of Puri, in Orissa, India (the city is known to a number of as Jagannath Puri) where each year the famous Rath Yatra festival takes place.

Two interesting stories are associated with this deity. First is the story of how Krishna seemed to be a great devotee of the lord, King Indradyuma and ordered him to carve a deity from a log he would find washed up on the sea shore. King Indradruma found a mysterious old Brahmin carpenter to carve the deity, but the carpenter insisted that he not be disturbed while he was carving the deity. The king waited anxiously outside his room, but after some time, all sound stopped. The impatient Indradyumna worried what had happened and assuming the worst, opened the doors - only to find the deity half-finished and the carpenter gone! The mysterious carpenter was none other than Vishvakarma, the heavenly architect. The king was distraught as the deity had no arms and legs. Utterly repentant that he had interrupted the carving, the king was only pacified when the muni (sage) called Narada seem ed and explained that the form the king now sees is a legitimate form of the supreme personality of godhead. The second story here was narrated to further explain and remove any doubts and confusion.

The second fact for Lord Jagannath's depicts the story of how Krishna was earwigging on the gopis as they spoke amongst themselves of His pastimes, and how much they loved him. Sister Subhadra was instructed to keep watch and ensure Krishna wasn't nearby while the gopis spoke of Krishna. But after a while Subhadra was so overwhelmed by the gopis' devotion and their stories that she became completely engrossed in listening. She didn't see the brothers Krishna and Balarama approaching. As the brothers listened their hairs stood on end, their arms retracted, their eyes grew larger and larger, and they smiled broadly in ecstasy. That is why Jagannath, Balarama and Subhadra look like they do.

This form is worshiped by Vaishnavas as the abstract form of Krishna. The deities - Jagannath, Balabhadra (Balarama) and Subhadra (Krishna's sister) are normally worshipped in the temple, but once in every Asadha Masa (Rainy Season, usually June or July), they are brought out onto the chief high street of Puri and travel to the Mausimaa Temple, allowing the public to have Darshan (holy view) of the deities as they pass. This festival is known as Ratha Yatra. The Rath carts themselves are huge wooden structures built new every year and are pulled by the millions of pilgrims who turn up for the event from all parts of the Globe. The festival commemorates Krishna's return to His home in Vrindavan after a long period of separation from the people there.

The Temple of Lord Jagannath is one of the major temples in India. The worship of Lord Jaganatha is so ancient that there is no accurate record of how long it has been going on. It is strictly forbidden for non-Hindus to enter the Jaganatha temple. The temple known as Shrimandira to the devout is built in Kalinga style of architecture. It consists of a tall shikhara (dome) housing the sanctum sanctorum (grabhagriha). A pillar made of fossilized wood is used for placing lamps as offering. The lion gate (Singhadwara) is the chief gate to the temple, guarded by two guardian deities Jaya and Vijaya. A memorial column known as Aruna Stambha faces the chief gate.

Once a year Lord Jaganatha, along with his brother Baladeva, and sister Subhadra, are taken out of the temple and pulled on huge chariots through the streets of Puri. Millions of devotees attend this festival every year, including the King of Puri, who sweeps the path in front of Lord Jaganatha cart.

Joshimath

Joshimath is situated in the state of Uttaranchal. When Badrinath closes during the winter, the priests from the Badrinath Temple come to Joshimath and continue worship at the Narasimha Temple. The utsava-murti (moving deity) of Badri Vishal is brought to Pandukeswar for worship. There is the ancient Vasudeva Temple, which is dedicated to Lord Krishna.

One of the four chief Sankaracharya mutts (maths) is located here. It is said that Adi Sankaracharya meditated in a cave here and attained samadhi (enlightenment) about 1,200 years ago under the Kalpavriksa tree (Shahtoot/Mulberry). In the lower part of the town is the Gauri Shankar Siva and Nava Durga temples.

Narasimhadeva Temple: There are many legends about this temple. In this temple is a Deity of Lord Narasimha, which is self-manifested from a shalagram-shila. He is about 25cm (10 in) high and remarkably detailed, sitting in a lotus position. To the right of Lord Narasimha are Sita, Rama, Hanuman, and Garuda. Against the left wall is a deity of Chandika, which is another name for Kali. On the altar to the right of Lord Narasimha are deities of Kubera, Uddhava, and Badri Vishal. There is an altar for Lakshmi Devi just outside the door of the temple.

Vasudeva Temple: This temple is one of the 108 Divya Desams, recognized by the Tamil Nadu Vaishnava saints as being very significant Vishnu temples. The black carved stone Deity of Lord Vasudeva is about 2m (6 ft) tall. He stands with his associates Sri, Bhu, Nila, and Kama. This temple is about 30m from the Narasimhadeva Temple. To the left of the chief entrance is a deity of dancing Ganesh, which is said to be one of only two such deities in India. This temple is very ancient, and no one knows just how old it is.

Sankaracharya Math: The Shankaracharaya temple is located on the ridge above the upper part of the town. If you enter the temple and follow the signs to your left, you come to the cave where Sankaracharya is said to have meditated. If you go up the steps to the right of the temple entrance (before entering the temple complex), you come to the Kalpavriksa tree, where Sankaracharya is said to have attained self-realization. This 38m tall tree has a huge trunk and is said to be more than 2,400 years old. Sankaracharya wrote the Sankara Bhasya in Joshimath.

Kedarnath

In the mid of the dramatic mountain scopes of the majestic Kedarnath range stands one of the twelve 'Jyotirlingas' of Kedar or Lord Shiva. Lying at an altitude of 3584 mts. on the head of river Mandakini, the shrine of Kedarnath is amongst the holiest pilgrimages for the Hindus. The origin of the revered temple can be found in the great epic - Mahabharata. As per the legend, the Pandavas sought the blessings of Lord Shiva to atone their sins after the battle of Mahabharata. Lord Shiva eluded them repeatedly and while fleeing took refuge at Kedarnath in the form of a bull. On being followed, he dived into the ground, leaving behind his hump on the surface. This conical protrusion is worshipped as the idol in the shrine.The remaining portions of Lord Shiva are worshipped at four other places - the arms (bahu) at Tungnath, mouth (mukh) at Rudranath, navel (nabhi) at Madmaheshwar and hair (jata) at Kalpeshwar. Together with Kedarnath, these places are acknowledged as the Panch Kedar.

The Ling at Kedarnath is pyramidal, unlike its usual form. A status of Nandi – the celestial bull stands at the entrance of the temple and exquisitely carved images adorn the interiors of the temple. The present temple, built in 8th century AD. by Adi Guru Shankaracharya lies adjacent to the site of an ancient temple built by Pandavas. The walls of the exquisitely architectured temple are embellished with figures of deities and scenes from mythology. The temple has a conical Ling - the chief idol, a statue of Nandi - the celestial bull, a 'garbha grah' for assemblies of pilgrims and visitors. The temple is believed to be more than 1000 years old. Behind the Kedarnath Temple lies the samadhi or the final resting place of Adi Shankaracharya. It is believed, after establishing the four maths in India, he went for his samadhi at an early age of 32 years.

Kurukshetra

Kurukshetra is a place of great historical and religious significance, revered all over the country for its sacred associations. It was here that the battle of Mahabharta was fought and Lord Krishna preached his Philosophy of "Karma" as enshrined in the Holy Geeta to Arjuna at Jyotisar. In the very first verse of Bhagwat Gita, Kurukshetra is described as Dharamkshetra i.e. field of righteousness. Mythologically, the name Kurukshetra applied to a circuit of about 48 Kosh or about 80 miles (128

Kms) which comprises a large number of holy places, temples and tanks connected with the ancient Indian customs and the Mahabharata War and Kururu, the pious ancestor of Kaurvas and Pandavas.

Mathura

The city of Mathura lies in the state of Uttar Pradesh. Covering an area of about 3,800 sq. km., today, Brajbhoomi can be divided into two distinct units - the eastern part in the trans-Yamuna tract with places like Gokul, Mahavan, Baldeo, Mat and Bajna and the western side of the Yamuna covering the Mathura region that encompasses Vrindavan, Govardhan, Kusum Sarovar, Barsana and Nandgaon.

The land where Shri Krishna was born and spent his youth, has today little towns and hamlets that are still alive with the Krishna legend and still redolent with the music of his flute. Mathura, a little town on the River Yamuna was transformed into a place of faith after Lord Krishna was born here. Vrindavan, a village - once noted for its fragrant groves, is where he spent an eventful youth. There are numerous other little spots in the area that still reverberate with the enchantment of Shri Krishna.

The land of Braj starts from Kotban near Hodel about 95 km from Delhi and ends at Runakuta which is known specially for its association with the poet Surdas, an ardent Krishna devotee. A long line of picturesque ghats - with their steps leading to the water's edge, arched gateways and temple spires extending along the right bank of the River Yamuna, emphasise the sacred character of the town of Mathura. The birth place of Lord Krishna, "the best known, best loved and most complex of Lord Vishnu's expressions" - Mathura is today an significant place of pilgrimage.

An ancient city whose origins fade into the mists of history, Mathura's strategic location at the cross roads of various trade routes - that went westwards to West Asia and the Roman Empire; northwards, via Taxila, Pushkalavati and Purushapur to Central Asia and the Silk Route and eastwards to China - ensured its position as a centre of trade and a meeting point for varied cultures.

Pushkar

There is a belief among Hindus that no pilgrimage to the four principal pilgrim centres (Char Dham), namely, Badrinath, Jagannath, Rameshwaram & Dwarka would bear fruit unless one bathes in the holy waters of Pushkar Lake. Padma Purana, elaborately describes the origin and significance of this lake. It says that Brahma, the creator of the Universe, was once contemplating to locate a suitable spot on earth to perform a Yajna (sacrificial ritual), the lotus fell from his hand and rebounding, struck at the earth at three places within a circuit of 9 kms. Water issued forth, from all the three places and the creator called all the three as Pushkar (lotus) distinguishing them as Jyeshtha (Elder), Madhya (central) and Kanishtha (yonger). As per the mythology, he performed the Yajna at Jyeshtha Pushkar from Kartik Shukla Ekdashi to Purnima. Lakhs of devotees assemble and bathe in the holy waters during this period of the year; but bathing on the last day which is the full moon (Purnima) day, confers special blessing.

Though he may have no other temple sacred to his memory, Brahma seems to have take full advantage of the only one where prayers are offered to him. Not only did he perform a Yagya or ritual fire ceremony here, he also dropped a lotus form his hands to crated the lake where people bathe before offering him prayers. A silver turtle at the entrance of the marble temple is a symbol of his means of transport. Pushkar is best known for its Brahma Temple.

Pushkar Lake: The Pushkar Lake is bordered by 52 flights of steps, called ghats, a number of of them have special legendary significance. Lord Vishnu is said to have seem ed at the Varah Ghat in the form of a boar. Brahma took a bath here and performed Yajna at the Brahma Ghat, Accompanied by Vishnu and Mahadev. People regard the water of the Pushkar Lake to be very sacred and the ritual of taking dips in the holy water is believed to bestow salvation. The holy dip is most auspicious on Kartik Poornima. Even before sunrise, people descend the ghats, aided by the priests to take the sacred bath. Offerings of coconut, flowers and cash are made to the lake and the priests. After bathing at the lake, people proceed to pay homage to the creator of the Universe, Lord Brahma at the Brahma Temple.

It is accustomed to float lighted earthen lamps after placing them on pattals (plates made of leaves) on the waters of the lake. This creates a spectacular view in the evening when the sacred lake takes on a mystical tint sprinkled with twinkling spot of light. Aarti is bade at the Lake in the morning and evening.

Rameshvaram

In the Indian state of Tamil Nadu Rameshvaram is a town in Ramanathapuram district. It is located on an island separated from mainland India by the Pamban channel and is less than 40 kilometers from the Jaffna Peninsula, Sri Lanka. Together with Kashi, it is regarded to be one of the holiest places in India to Hindus. Hence, it is a bustling pilgrim centre. It is situated in the Gulf of Mannar at the very tip of the Indian peninsula. As per the legends, this is the place from where Lord Rama, built a bridge Ram Setu (also known as Adam's Bridge) across the sea to Lanka to rescue his consort Sita, from her abductor, Ravana. This is also the place where Rama worshipped Shiva to be absolved of the sin of killing Ravana, hence the name of Shiva, which became the name of the town - Rameswara ("lord of Rama"). Both the Vaishnavites and Shaivites visit this pilgrimage centre which is known as the Varanasi of the south.

People say that Rameshwaram is significant for the Hindus, as a pilgrimage to Benaras is not complete without a pilgrimage to Rameswaram. The presiding deity here is in the form of a Linga with the name Sri Ramanatha Swamy, it also happens to be one of the twelve Jyotirlingas. As per the Puranas, upon the advice of Rishis (sages), Rama along with Sita and Lakshmana, installed and worshipped the Sivalinga here to expiate the sin of Brahmahatya (killing of a Brahmin). Rama fixed an auspicious time for the installation and sent Anjaneya to Mount Kailas to bring a Ling. As Anjaneya could not return in time, Sita herself made a linga of sand. When Anjaneya returned with a linga from Mount Kailas the rituals had been over. To comfort the disappointed Anjaneya, Rama had Anjaneya's Ling (VisvaLing) also installed by the side of Ramalinga, and enacted that rituals be performed first to the VisvaLing.

Rishikesh

Rishikesh is not just recognized for its religious connection but also for its beautiful landscape. Surrounded by hills (the Lesser Himalayas) on three sides and holy Ganga river flowing through it, Rishikesh is an ethereal experience. Rishikesh is the gateway to famous Chardham which are Kedarnath, Badrinath, Gangotri and Yamunotri. In fact Rishikesh is a favourite of those coming to meditate and seek salvation. It is believed that meditation on the land of this holy place leads to salvation. Every year a number of people come here in the ashrams to meditate and gain peace of mind.

The place is also very famous with foreigners who come to India in search of spiritual quest. Rishikesh is famous for its ashrams on the banks of Ganga, at a number of such ashrams yoga is practiced and taught on a regular basis. Such is the feeling of Rishikesh that even Beatles could not escape from the magical experience. They had visited India in 1960 to pay visit to their Guru in Rishikesh. What else works in Rishikesh's favour is its altitude (1360 metres). It is higher than other holy cities of Haridwar and Varanasi, the water in Ganga here is cooler and cleaner.

The flow of the river is firmer here and the city is less populated than others. It is more calmer and peaceful here.

Somnath

Somnath at Somnath Patan, near Veraval in Gujarat is a pilgrimage center held in great reverence throughout India. Somnath is regarded to be the first of the 12 Jyotirlingas of Shiva. Somnath is situated on the south coast of Saurashtra. The Skanda Purana, in a chapter on Prabhasa Khanda, describes Somnath. Legend has it that Shiva in the previous aeons was looked up to as Mrityunjaya, Kaalagnirudra, Amritesa, Anamaya, Kritivasa and Bhairavanatha at Somnath.

Legend goes that the moon was married to the 27 daughters of Daksha Prajapati. He was partial to Rohini, his favourite and neglected the others. An angered Daksha cursed him to wane into nothingness. A disturbed Chandra, came down to Prabhasa with Rohini and worshipped the Sparsa Linga of Somnath after which he was blessed by Shiva to grow and shine in the bright half. As the moon regained his light here, this town came to be known as Prabhasa. Bhrama, one of the trinity, installed the Bhramasila, and paved way for the construction of the temple. Legend has it that the Kalabhairava Shivalinga (Bhairavanatha) at Prabhasa was worshipped by the moon, and hence Shiva here is referred to as Somnatha. The Skanda Purana describes the Sparsa Linga of Somnath as one bright as the sun, the size of an egg, lodged underground. The Mahabharata also refers to the Prabhasa Kshetra and the legend of the moon worshipping Shiva.

Tirupati

The town of Tirupati is one of the most ancient and spectacular places of pilgrimage in India. It is situated in the Chittoor district in southern Andhra Pradesh. The town owes its existence to the sacred temple of Lord Sri Venkateswara situated on the Tirumala Hill adjoining it. With a history that dates back to over twelve centuries, the temple is the jewel in the crown of ancient places of worship in southern India.

The Tirumala Hill is 3200 ft above sea level, and is about 10.33 sq miles in area. It comprises seven peaks, representing the seven hoods of Adisesha, thus earning the name, Seshachalam. The seven peaks are called Seshadri, Neeladri, Garudadri, Anjanadri, Vrishabhadri, Narayanadri and Venkatadri.

The sacred temple of Sri Venkateswara is located on the seventh peak, Venkatadri (Venkata Hill), and lies on the southern banks of Sri

Swami Pushkarini. There are several legends associated with the expression of the Lord in Tirumala.

The name Tirupati, meaning the 'the Lord of Lakshmi' should have been appropriately applied to the village on the Venkata Hill, the abode of the Lord. However, it has been popularly assigned to the Municipal town at the foot of the Hill, while the village around the Hill near His temple is called Tirumala (the Sacred Hill).

Vaishno Devi

The Vishno Devi temple is also a great religious place of Hindus. The Holy Shrine of Shri Mata Vaishno Devi Ji is regarded all over the world as where your wishes comes true. That is why the Holy Cave attracts lakhs of devotees of all faiths every year from all parts of India and abroad. It is one of the oldest shrines of India where the Mother Goddess is worshipped in the forms of Maha Kali, Maha Saraswati, and Maha Lakshmi. Shri Mata Vaishno Devi Shrine is one of the oldest shrine of India, located at a height of 5300 feet on the holy Trikuta Hills of the Shivalik Hill Range. The Holy cave is 13 Kms from the Base Camp Katra. The Town Katra is 50 Kms away from Jammu and 35 Kms from District HQ Udhampur and is linked by road. A rail link from Udhampur to Katra is being built to facilitate pilgrimage.

The Goddess Mata Vaishno Devi's abode is in 100 feet long cave with a narrow opening. The holy cold and crystal clear water washes the lotus feet of the Mata's "Pindian". There are three natural pindies representing Maha Sarswati, Maha Lakshmi, Maha Kali, which represent creative, preservative, and destructive aspects of the Super Power. It is an ancient shrine whose reference is found in the Vedas and ancient scriptures.

Yamunotri

The Yamunotri temple is located in Uttarkashi District of Uttarakhand, India, a full day's journey from Uttaranchal's chief towns — Rishikesh, Haridwar or Dehradun. Yamunotri, the source of the Yamuna River and the seat of the goddess Yamuna, is one of the four sites in India's Char Dham pilgrimage.

The actual temple is only accessible by a six kilometer walk from the town of Hanuman Chatti and a four kilometer walk from Janki Chatti (horses or palanquins are available for rent). The hike from Hanuman Chetty to Yamunotri is very picturesque with beautiful views of a number of water falls. The original temple was built by Maharani Gularia of Jaipur in the 19th century. The current temple is of recent origin, as past iterations have been destroyed by the weather and elements. Lodging at the temple itself is limited to a few small ashrams and guesthouses. Ritual duties such as the making and distribution of prasad (sanctified offerings) and the supervision of pujas (ritual venerations) are performed by the Uniyal family of pujaris (priests). Unique aspects of ritual practice at the site include hot springs where raw rice is cooked and made into prasad.

The queen Gularia of Jaipur built the temple in the 19th century. Destroyed by a major earthquake in 1923, it was subsequently rebuilt, then again damaged in 1982. It is located at a height of 3252 meters (10,700 feet), about 6 km below the glacier. The temple is dedicated to the river Yamuna, who is represented in the form of a silver idol, bedecked with garlands. Goddess Yamuna is the daughter of Surya, the sun God, and Sangya, the Goddess of consciousness. Yamuna is also the sister of Yama, the God of death, and so anyone bathing in the waters of the river is spared of a painful death.

Surya Kund is known for its thermal springs. The hot water pool here is used to prepare the prasad or holy offerings to the deity, which is normally rice and potatoes, cooked by tying the food in cloth bags and dipping it into the hot water which is as high as 190°F. Divya Shilla is a rock pillar that is worshipped by the pilgrims before they enter the Yamunotri temple.

RELIGIOUS PLACES OUTSIDE INDIA

Lake Manasarovar

The Manasarovar Lake lies at 4,556 14947 feet above mean sea level. It is one of the highest fresh-water lakes in the world. Lake Manasarovar is relatively round in shape. The circumference of Manasarovar is 88 km, depth is 90 m and it occupies a total area of 320 km². The lake freezes in winter and melts only in the spring. The Sutlej River, the Brahmaputra River, the Indus River, and the Karnali River (Ghaghara River) all trace their sources to its close vicinity. Like Mount Kailash, Lake Mansarovar is a place of pilgrimage, attracting religious people from India, Tibet and the neighbouring countries. Bathing in the Manasa Sarovar and drinking its water is believed to cleanse all sins. Pilgrimage tours are organized regularly, especially from India, the most famous of which is the Kailash Mansarovar Yatra which takes place every year. Pilgrims come to take ceremonial baths in the cleansing waters of the lake.

As per the Hindu religion, the lake was first created in the mind of the Lord Brahma. Hence, in Sanskrit it is called "Manas sarovara", which is a combination of the words manas (mind) and sarovara (lake). The lake, in Hindu mythology, is also supposed to be the summer abode of swans, who are regarded as very wise and sacred birds. It is also believed the Devas descend to bathe in the lake between 3 and 5 am the time of the day known as Brahma Muhurta. Buddhists also affiliate the lake to the legendary lake known as Anavatapta in Sanskrit and Anotatta in Pali, where Queen Maya is believed to have conceived Buddha. The lake has a few monasteries on its shores. The most notable of which is the ancient Chiu Gompa Monastery, which has been built right onto a steep hill. It looks as if it has been carved right out of the rock.

Mt. Kailash

The supremely sacred site of four religions and billions of people, Situated in Tibet, Kailash is one of the most sacred places in Hinduism. Origin myths speak of Kailash as the mythical Mt. Meru, the center and birth place of the entire world. The mountain was already legendary before the great Hindu epics, the Ramayana and the Mahabharata, were written. Indeed, Kailash is so deeply embedded in the myths of ancient Asia that it was perhaps a sacred place of another era, another civilization, now long gone and forgotten.

The Hindus believe Mt.Kailash to be the abode of Lord Shiva. As per the legend, immortal Shiva lives atop Kailash where he spends his time meditating. For a Hindu, to make the pilgrimage to Kailash and have the darshan (divine view) of Shiva's abode is to attain release from the clutches of ignorance and delusion. Pilgrims to Kailash, after the hard journey getting there, are then confronted with the equally arduous task of circumambulating the sacred peak. The walking around the mountain known as Parikrama normally takes three days. In hopes of gaining extra merit or psychic powers however, some pilgrims will vary the tempo of their movement.

Pashupati Nath Temple

The Lord Pashupatinath's magnificent temple is situated about 5 kms north-east of Kathmandu, amidst a number of other temples on the right bank of the river Bagmati. Pashupathinath is the guardian spirit and the holiest of all Shiva shrines in Nepal. Lord Shiva is known by a number of various names; and Pashupati is one. Pashu means leaving beings, and Pati means master. In other words Pashupati is the master of all living beings of the universe. This is how lord Pashupati is eulogized in the

Vedas, Upnisada and other religious books. Legends are numerous as to how the temple of Lord Pashupatinath came to existence here. As told in chronicles, the image of Lord Shiva in the form of Jyotirlinga was covered with earth over the years, and soft green grass sprouted over it.

Further, as the legend goes, a cow used to come here mysteriously every day and offer her milk to this holy but hidden Linga of Lord Shiva. When the Gwala (owner) saw that the cow had stopped giving milk since the last few days he started keeping eye on her; and ultimately came across the place where the cow used to offer her milk. With a natural curiosity to know the significance of the place, where his cow used to make offering of her milk, the gwala dug the place and found the Jyotirlinga of Lord Shiva.

After this number of gwalas gathered to worship this Linga as per the religious conformity, starting the custom of worshipping this Linga. As the time passed Lord Pashupatinath started gaining more and more popularity and reverence of the devotees as a guardian spirit and gradually the temple of Lord Pashupatinath became a great place of pilgrimage. In the sanctum of the temple, there is a very attractive, about three feet high Shivalinga with four faces. All these faces have various names and significance. The face facing east is known as Tatpurusha and the one facing south as Aghora. Similarly, the faces looking west and north are known by the name Sadhyojata and Vamadeva respectively. The upper portion of this linga is known as Ishan. These faces are also defined as the symbol of four dharmas (the most famous places of pilgrimage for Hindus) and four Vedas (sacred books of Hindus).

The images of Vishnu, Surya, Devi and Ganesh are also placed in the sanctum of the temple .Pashupati area is regarded as one of the most significant places of pilgrimages for the followeres of Hinduism. Thousands of devotees from within and outside the country come to pay homage to Pashupatinath every day. And on special occasions like Ekadasi, Sankranti, Mahashivratri, Teej Akshaya, Rakshabandhan, Grahana (eclipse), Poornima (Full moon day) people congregate here in great mass.

REFERENCES

E. J. Thompson and A. Marshman Spencer: *Bengali Religious Lyrics*, Calcutta, Association Press, 1923.

Evans-Pritchard, E.: *Nuer Religion*. London, Oxford University Press, 1956

F. E. Keay: *Kabir and His Followers*, Calcutta, Association Press, 1931.

F. E. Pargiter: *The Maarkandya Purana*, Calcutta, Asiatic Society, 1904.

F. Edgerton: *The Bhagavad-Gita*, Cambridge, Mass, Harvard University Press, 1944.

F. Kingsbury and G. E. Phillips: *Hymns of the Tamil Shaivite Saints*, Calcutta, Association Press, 1921.

Fairservis W. A.: *The Roots of Ancient India*: The archaeology of early Indian civilization, London, 1975.

Fuller, C. J.: *Gods, priests and purity: on the relation between Hinduism and the caste system*, 1979.

G. Buhler: *The Laws of Manu*, Oxford, Clarendon Press, 1886.

G. Buhler: *The Sacred Books of the East*, Oxford, Clarendon Press, 1897.

Gale, R.M.: *The language of time*, London, Routledge & Kegan Paul, 1968.

Gandhi: *An Autobiography*, Mahadev Desai, Ahmedabad, Navajivan, 1927.

Gell, A.: *The anthropology of time*, Berg, Oxford, 1992.

Gonda Jan: *Change and Continuity in Indian Religion*, Gravenhage, 1965.

Gonda Jan: *Vedic Literature,* Wiesbaden, 1975.

Good, A.: *Law, legitimacy, and the hereditary rights of Tamil temple priests*. Mod. Asian Stud., 1989.

Gopinatha Rao, T.A.: *Elements of Hindu,* Delhi, Motilal Banarsidass. 1997.

Gordon Matthews: *Shiva*, New York, Oxford University Press, 1948.

Gough, E.K.: *Brahman kinship in a Tamil village*, Am. Anthrop, 1956.

H. H. Wilson: *Select Specimens of the Theatre of the Hindus*, London, Trubner & Co., 1835.

18

Art and Iconography

In the Hindu religion much significance is given to the symbols than most other religions. The Hindu symbols range from the mark one puts on the forehead to the idols of the deities that get worshipped by the ardent Hindu devotees. Each one has its own significance. Hinduism at its core maintains that there is one God and many see it in different ways. This God is Formless and is beyond the limitations of the comprehension.

HISTORY

Simply speaking Iconography is the study and interpretation of images in art. This comprises both religious and secular images of all kinds. Images have been used by numerous different religions comprising Hinduism, Buddhism, and Christianity. Images of Hindu gods utilize a rich symbolism. Some figures are blue-skinned the colour of heaven or may have multiple arms holding various symbols showing aspects of the god the drums of change, the flower of new life, the fire of devastation, etc. The art of Hinduism represents one of the world's great customs, as active today as when the first images of Hindu gods were forged out of stone more than two thousand years ago. An invaluable survey looks at the entire period, covering shrines consecrated to Hindu cults as well as works of art that portray Hindu divinities, semi divine personalities, and mythological stories. The growth of Hinduism and the principal iconic forms of its pantheon, explains the system of royal patronage that led to the building of numerous temples and the commissioning of their attendant works of art. Then, in a liberal chronological span, he shows artistic persistences down to the present day in the various regions of the country, supporting the vibrancy of the ocular world of Hinduism.

After bringing in Hinduism, its gods, the symbolic basis for its architecture, and the system of royal patronage that led to the introduction of so many temples and their attendant works of art, the this religion adopts a chronological expanse that traces artistic persistences down to the present day in the various regions of India, through unfathomed and beautiful works of sculpture – such as Shiva dancing the eternal dance of creation and destruction – to exquisite pictures of the loves of Krishna.

ARCHITECTURE

Whilst a great deal of Indian secular art was developed, it was basically made of spoilable material and has not outlived. What has lasted in the medium of stone is religious art. In Hindu art, symbolism in gesture, posture, and attribute comprises numerous levels of meaning. In images of the Buddha, various hand positions (mudras) stand for religious states, such as the Enlightenment (Nirvana), Meditation, and Preaching. In Hindu sculpture, deities are frequently staged with numerous hands to show their power to execute multiple deeds at the same time, and the hands each carry their characteristic imputes. With the exclusion of Mughal art and architecture, which necessitates distinguish treatment, the major courses in Indian art-Hindu, Buddhist, and Jain-are talked about here.

Indus Valley Civilization: The earliest Indian art came out from the valley of the Indus River throughout the second half of the third millennium BC. The best-known sites are Harappa, destructed in the nineteenth century, and Mohenjo-Daro; these are amongst the earliest instances of civic planning. Houses, markets, storage facilities, offices, and public baths were ordered in a grid like scheme. There was also an extremely highly developed drainage system.

The Indus civilization gave rise to many statuettes constructed of steatite and limestone. Some statuettes match the hieratic style of contemporary Mesopotamia, while others are done in the smooth, wiggly style that is the prototype of later Indian sculpture, in which the plastic modelling brings out the animating breath of life (prana). Also discovered in this region are square steatite seals decorated with a range of animals, comprising naturalistically yielded bulls; ceramic storage jars with simple, stylized designs; toys with wheels; and figurines, which may be mother goddesses. Bronze arms, tools, and carvings show sophistication in craftsmanship rather than a major aesthetic ontogenesis.

Post-Indus Civilization through the Maurya Dynasty: Of the period from the destruction of the Indus civilization until Alexander the Great crossed the Indus, few traces persist. Notwithstanding, the principles of Indian architecture were formulated in wooden buildings, long since decomposed. From the great Maurya dynasty the most renowned remains are the edict pillars, erected throughout Northern India by the Emperor Ashoka to promulgate his devotion. The monolithic, smooth columns are over 50 ft (15 m) high and are surmounted by lotus capitals and animal figures. Some of the pillar capitals disclose forms that suggest Persepolitan determines. Also dating from the reign of Ashoka is the earliest stone ogival chaitya window, found on the portal of a small rock-cut sanctuary near Bodh Gaya. The chaitya halls were cloistral sanctuaries hewn out of rock. As they evolved, from the third century BC through the first millennium AD, they became elaborate colonnaded halls, or walls decorated with painting or sculpture.

Sunga and Andhra Dynasties: The earliest living stupas date from the Sunga dynasty second-first century BC and early Andhra dynasty first century BC. These relic agglomerates are encircled by railings and gateways covered with carved ornament. One of the chief stupas is at Bharhut, where the carving is archaic in character.

The significant stupa at Sanchi depicts a like style. Significant carvings on the gateways of another stupa at Sanchi date from the early Andhra period. The yakshis have assumed full, graceful forms, and high-relief writings are frequently gestated in a continuous method of story. In the far south, in the Deccan, the later Andhra dynasty extended to flourish into the first century AD. Its most outstanding monument is the carving at the Great Stupa at Amaravati, built in second century AD. The complex but tenacious composition, the chiaroscuro, and the liveliness of the crowded surfaces make out these bas-reliefs.

Gandhara and Mathura: During the period of Kushans rule, conquerors from central Asia, two of India's most significant styles were developed between the second and fifth century AD: Gandhara art and art of Mathura. Gandhara art, named after the region of Gandhara now in Pakistan, demonstrates some of the most former images of the Buddha. Earlier at Bharhut and Sanchi, the Buddha's comportment was symbolized by symbols, such as the pipal tree, the wheel of life, footprints, and an empty throne. The Gandhara style was deeply shaped by second-century Hellenistic art and was itself extremely important in central and eastern Asia. Ivories and imported glass and lacquer ware testify to the cosmopolitan tastes and across-the-board trade that characterized the period. Stupas and monasteries were decorated with relief friezes, often carved in dark schist, demonstrating figures in classical poses with flowing Hellenistic curtains. In farther east and south, present-day Mathura, also under Kushan rule, created a wholly Indian sculptural art. Reddish limestone was the common medium.

The Gupta Period: Hindu art prospered throughout this period, which has often been reported as a golden age. A notable rock-cut monastery at Ajanta consists of several chaitya halls and various residential viharas. Both facades and interiors comprise graceful relief sculpture, while interiors are covered up with painted murals that feature superb figures drawn with a graciously sinuous line. As in all periods, there is little divergence in the images of the major Indian religions, Buddhist, Hindu, and Jain. Large stone figures, stone and terra-cotta reliefs, and large and small bronzes are made in the refined Gupta style; the level of yield is uniformly high. After the seventh century although the rulers of the Pala and Sena dynasties in seventh and eleventh century AD were Hindu, significant art was created. Images in bronze and in hard black stone from Nalanda and elsewhere expose an ontogenesis of the Gupta manner, with broad care to ornamental details.

Architecture and Sculpture of the Hindu Dynasties: From the sixth century on, with the revitalisation of Hindu rulers throughout India, a characteristic temple plan was explicated. An entrance portico led to a pillared hall *mandapa* into the cella. The shrine was a great deal crowned by a large tower acknowledged as the shikhara. In South India the Dravida tower rose in a series of terraces, each representing a varied divinity; in the north, *nagara* spires came up in a monolithic conical shape. Countless temples were constructed that were so ebulliently decorated with sculpture that their style is called "sculptural architecture." The Khajuraho temples in central India symbolize one of the high points of the *nagara* buildings, and the damaged Temple of the Sun at Konarak brings out, in its famous erotic sculptures, cuttings that aggregate equilibrated mass with fine-spun execution.

In South India the seventh-century Pallava dynasty introduced the *dravida* style temple in numerous pyramidal *raths* (temples) at Mahabalipuram; a tremendous cliff-face at the site is cut up with a life-size representation of gods, men, and beasts, comprising the elephant family. The *dravida* style plan was used also in the eighth century in the quarried temple at Ellora. The Chola dynasty of South India further developed this form in the eleventh century, when they in all probability also cast most of multitudes of South Indian bronzes, of which the *Nataraja* images are possibly the best acknowledged.

The *dravida* style climaxed in a series of elaborated "temple townships," of which the most prominent is Srirangam, comprising of seven concentric enclosures. These finished in the relatively crude stucco sculptured architecture of seventeenth-century Mandura. Medieval bronze carving was highly developed in Southern India. The main subjects were the deities, figures of whom were utilized for processional and home ritual. Competent cire-perdue sculptures were developed until the late nineteenth century in numerous regions of India.

SCULPTURES

The most former prehistoric sculpture in India was brought forth in stone, clay, ivory, copper, and gold. Examples of the 3rd millennium BC from the Indus Valley, found among the remains of the burnt-brick buildings of Mohenjo-Daro, include alabaster and marble figures, terra-cotta figurines of nude goddesses, terra-cotta and faience representations of animals, a copper model of a cart, and a number of square seals of ivory and of faience depicting animals and pictographs. The similarities of these objects to Mesopotamian work in subject matter and stylized form shows an interrelatedness of the two cultures and a possible common ancestry. In Vedic and later times, from the second millennium to the third century BC, connections with Middle Eastern culture are not apparent. An example of the earlier phase of this period is a ninth-century BC gold figurine of a goddess, found at Lauriya Nandangarh. Later, from 600 BC to historical times, common instances comprise finely polished and ornamented stone disks and coins presenting many sorts of animals and religious symbols.

Hindu sculpture also grew throughout the Gupta period. Reliefs were carved in rock-cut sanctuaries in Udayagiri, Madhya Pradesh, and adorned temples at Garhwa, near Allahabad, and Deogarh. From the seventh to the ninth century numerous schools prospered. They comprise the highly architectural style of the Pallavas, exemplified by the work at Kanchipuram, Tamil Nadu; the Rashtrakuta style, of which the best-maintained instances are a colossal temple relief and the three-headed bust of Shiva at Elephanta, near Mumbai; and the Kashmir style, which shows some Greco-Buddhist impact in the remains at Vijrabror, and more autochthonal forms in figures of Hindu gods found at Vantipor.

From the ninth century to the consolidation of Muslim power at the commencing of the thirteenth century, Indian sculpture more and more inclined toward the linear, the forms coming out to be sharply outlined rather than voluminous. More so than antecedently, sculpture was applied as a decoration, subordinate to its architectural setting. It was complex and elaborate in detail and was characterized by perplexed, many-armed figures drawn from the pantheon of Hindu and Jain gods, which substituted the earlier simple figures of Buddhist gods. Stress on technical skill also added to the propagation of involved forms.

At this time the three distinguishable areas of production in sculpture were the north and east, Rajputana, and the south-central and western regions. In the north and east, one of the chief schools was centered in Bihar and Bengal under the Pala dynasty from 750 to 1200. A noteworthy source for sculpture was the monastery and university at Nalanda in Bihar. Black slate was a common medium, and the themes, at first still Buddhist, gradually became more and more Hindu. Another north-eastern school, in Orissa, developed typically Hindu work, comprising the monumental elephants and horses and erotic friezes at the Sun Temple in Konarak. In Rajputana the local style was represented in the hard sandstone temple of Khajuraho, which was literally enshrouded with Hindu sculptures. The south-central and western schools produced noteworthy works at Mysore, Halebid, and Belur. The temples were decorated with friezes, pillars, and brackets carved in fine-grained dark stone. After the Muslims turned prevailing, they adopted many of the native patterns as ornament. The customs have persisted until the present day, especially in the south, where art holds its indigenous purity.

CALLIGRAPHY

Ashoka's edicts established in 265–238 BC were committed to stone. These inscriptions are stiff and angular in shape. Following the Ashoka style of Indic writing, two new calligraphic types appear: Kharosti and Brahmi. Kharosti was used in the north-western regions of India from the third century BC to the fourth century of the Christian Era, and it was utilized in Central Asia till the eighth century.

Copper was a preferred material for Indic inscriptions. In the north of India, birch bark was used as a writing surface as early as the second century AD. Numerous Indic manuscripts were written on palm leaves, even after the Indian languages were put on paper in the thirteenth century. Both sides of the leaves were utilized for writing. Long rectangular strips were collected on top of one another, holes were drilled through all the leaves, and the book was tied together by string. Books of this type were vernacular to Southeast Asia. The palm leaf was a fantabulous surface for pen writing, making possible the delicate inscription utilized in numerous scripts of southern Asia. Along with it anyone can easily see calligraphic arts in symbols of Hinduism like the 'aum' and 'swastika' in many temples, and the verses from Ramayana, Gita and Mahabharta.

PRESENT DAY EXAMPLES

Many Hindu architectural designs are preserved up to this date in various places of the country. Some of most famous among them are as follows:

- Akshardham temple in Gujarat
- Famous Hindu Akshardham temple in East Delhi
- Virupaksha Temple, Pattadakal
- Swami Narayan Temple, Vadtal, Ahmedabad
- Thanjavur Temple, Tamil Nadu
- Dodda Basappa Temple, Dambal, Karnataka
- Rameshwaram Temple, Rameshwaram

REFERENCES

Alper, Harvey P.: *Understanding Mantras. SUNY Series in Religious Studies*, Albany, State University of New York Press, 1989.

Azad, A. K.: *India Wins Freedom*, London: Sangam Books, 1988.

Baartmans, Frans: *Aapaha, The Sacred Waters: an Analysis of a Primordial Symbol in Hindu Myths*, Delhi, B. R. Publishing Corporation, 1990.

Babb, Lawrence A.: *The Divine Hierarchy: Popular Hinduism in Central India*, New York, Columbia University Press, 1975.

Bacchetta, P.: '*Hindu Nationalist Women as Ideologues*' in Jayawardena and de Alwis eds, 1996.

Coward, Harold G. Bhart: *Twayne's World Autnors Series, no. 403. Boston*: Twayne Publishers, 1976.

Cunningham: *Alexander: "Report on a Tour in the Central Provinces and Lower Gangetic Doab in 1881-82"* Archaeological Survey of India, 1884.

Daniel, E.V.: *Fluid signs: being a person the Tamil way*, Berkeley, University of California Press, 1984.

Daniel, S.B.: *Marriage in Tamil culture: the problem of conflicting 'models*', Syracuse, N.Y: Maxwell School of Citizenship & Public Affairs, 1980.

Fairservis W. A.: *The Roots of Ancient India*: The archaeology of early Indian civilization, London, 1975.

Fuller, C. J.: *Gods, priests and purity: on the relation between Hinduism and the caste system*, 1979.

G. Buhler: *The Laws of Manu*, Oxford, Clarendon Press, 1886.

G. Buhler: *The Sacred Books of the East*, Oxford, Clarendon Press, 1897.

Homo Hierarchicus: *An Essay on the Caste System*, Mark Sainsbury. Chicago, University of Chicago Press, 1970

Hume, R. E.: *The Thirteen Principle Upanishads*, Delhi: Oxford University, 1931.

J. A. B. Van Buitenen: *Ramanuja on the Bhagvad-Gita*, The Hague, H. L. Smits, 1953.

J. Brough: *Selections from Classical Sanskrit Literature*, London, Luzac & Co., 1952.

J. Eggeling: *The Uatapatha-BrahmaGa*, Oxford, Clarendon Press, 1900.

M. Winternitz: *A History of Indian Literature*, Calcutta, University, 1927.

Macdonell A. A.: *Vedic Mythology*, Strassburg, 1897.

Nicol Macnicol: *Hindu Scriptures*, London, J. M. Dent, 1938.

Nicol Macnicol: *Psalms of Maraha Saints*, Calcutta, Association Press.

O'Flaherty W. D.: *Hindu Myths*, Harmondsworth, 1975.

O'Flaherty, W.D.: *Women, androgynes, and other mythical beasts*, Chicago, University Press, 1980.

O'Flaherty, Wendy D.: "*Asceticism and Sexuality in the Mythology of Siva, Part 1.*" History of Religions, 1969.

Thomas, F. W.: "*Sandanes, Nahapana, Cacmana and Kanicka : Tung-li P'an-ch'i and Chinese Turkestan.*" New Indian Antiquary, 1944.

Trautmann, T.R.: *Indian time, European time*, Ann Arbor: University of Michigan Press, 1995.

Vivekananda: *The Complete Works*, Almora, Advaita Ashrama, 1924.

W. G. Orr: *A Sixteenth-Century Indian Mystic*, London, Lutterworth Press, 1947.

Welbon, G.R. & G.E. Yocum: *Religious festivals in South India and Sri Lanka*, New Delhi, Manohar, 1982.

Zaehner R. C.: *Hinduism*, London, 1962.

19

Hinduism in Modern World

Hinduism as is already said is one of the ancient religions, in modern times it has undergone tremendous reformist changes and has tended to focus on peace rather than war. Though there has not been any scriptural development in Hinduism in relation to war, one stream of Hinduism espousing a theory similar to just war developed into the separate religion of Sikhism. Ancient doctrines of war and conflict continue to be significant, but hardly if that has motivated political conflicts. To put it in a bit of detail, Ancient doctrines like Digvijaya, and practices like Aswamedha Sacrifices were related to imperialism - such has not been a factor of modern history.

However a few times some zealous people would keep indicating that the political boundaries of Ancient India encompassed Afghanistan, Pakistan, Bangladesh, etc, and sometimes such maps would get displayed openly in political rallies of the right wingers. But then such depiction does not influence the politics, because the political leaders are well aware of launching such superfluous projects. Such issues are irrelevant even in the context of the international relations and diplomacy of India with its neighbours. Yet, such things do feed the popular imagination regarding the "Ancient Glory". Such ancient glory are relevant not merely in the context of history, but also in the context of religion - though the most popular false belief exploited by such leaders is the fact that throughout those ancient times there was no Islam, not even Christianity.

India was under British imperialism from 1757 to 1947. As part of this interaction, Hinduism was invoked on certain occasions of conflict. This has become part of political development of India and not gone into anything of scriptural significance. British Imperialism was a development that did not have any precedent in the scriptures- so scriptural motivation would not exist in the fight against the imperial power. Moreover scriptures written in Sanskrit were hardly understood by an illiterate population. Events as part of Imperial interlude led to use of Hindu motifs and idioms. This interaction happened in the realm of culture as well as politics. But this has not led to creation of "scriptures".

A number of texts have been written relating to Hindu religion, but unlike the medieval times, when texts like Hanuman Chalisa etc were written, nothing emerged in modern times as part of cultural or political development that has been accepted as part of Hindu scripture. The term scripture mean text that is regarded sacred. Though in modern times various sects and sub-sects have emerged and such sects and sub-sects have their own rules and texts written by the originator of such sects. The sect followers hold such text with reverence, but such texts cannot be regarded to be sacred for the Hinduism as a whole or even comparable with texts like Ramayana or Bhagwad Gita. The only significant development has been copious writings and commentaries on Hindu philosophy.

At last, in modern times there has not been anything like a "holy war" in the case of Hinduism. The struggle against imperialism was a secular one, mostly led by political leaders who had education in the west. There has although been the conflict between Islamists and the British imperialists based on "holy war"- for example the Wahabi movement, and the Khilafat movement, among others.

In that time the main focus of religious leaders was reform, and British imperialism rushed along that process. It would be incorrect to presume that if British were not present, reform would not happen or that reform happened under pressure of the British. Infect, on a number of instances British would support the orthodox sections and act in a reactionary manner. Hindu theologians and leaders were related with combating Christian missionary propaganda, that was an element of imperialism, on theological grounds. This was done by engaging in debates with the missionaries and at the same time by bringing in reforms to the various institutions of Hinduism. These reforms started in Bengal province, where Ram Mohan Roy (1772 -1833) started the Brahmo Samaj movement.

DIASPORA

The Indian diaspora today makes up a significant, and in some respects unique, force in world culture. The origins of the modern Indian diaspora lie mainly in the subjugation of India by the British and its incorporation into the British empire. Indians were taken over as indentured labour to far-flung parts of the empire in the nineteenth-century, a circumstance to which the modern Indian populations of Fiji, Mauritius, Guyana, Trinidad, Surinam, Malaysia, South Africa, Sri Lanka, and other places attest in their own peculiar ways. Over two million Indian men fought on behalf of the empire in numerous wars, including the Boer War and the two World Wars, and some remained behind to claim the land on which they had fought as their own.

As if in emulation of their ancestors, a number of Gujarati traders once again left for East Africa in large numbers in the early part of the twentieth century. Ultimately, in the post-World War II period, the dispersal of Indian labor and professionals has been a nearly world-wide phenomenon. Indians, and other South Asians, provided the labor that helped in the reconstruction of war-torn Europe, particularly the United Kingdom and the Netherlands, and in more recent years unskilled labor from South Asia has been the chief force in the transformation of the physical landscape of much of the Middle East. Meanwhile, in countries such as the United States, Canada, and Australia, Indians have made their presence visibly felt in the professions.

If we ever think that how we are to recognise the Indian diasporic community as 'Indian' given that it is constituted of such diverse elements as South Asian Hong Kong Muslims, Canadian Sikhs, Punjabi Californians, South African Hindus, and so forth. In the United States, at least, the Indian community has occupied a place of considerable privilege, and a number of Indians could deflect the moment of recognition that Indianness and being American do not always happily coincide. In recent past, with a declining economy on the one hand, and the congregation of Indians in clusters that visibly put them apart on the other hand, Indians have for the first time become the targets of racial attacks.

However different Indian communities across the world might be, they all maintain some sort of tenuous link with the motherland. Newspapers published by Indian communities flourish everywhere, and they invariably carry a section with matrimonial ads. Though these very ads help Indians to 'locate' one another, they pose hard questions about 'otherness', both the otherness' of Indians in relation to 'Americans', and the internal 'otherness' of certain Indians in relation to other Indians.

The religious practices of Hindus, Sikhs, and Muslims in the U.S. and other overseas communities might be assisting in transforming the nature of religious faiths in India itself. Hindus all over the world are showing alarming signs of susceptibility to a resurgent and militant Hinduism; indeed, it is even arguable that they seem to know the meaning of Hinduism better than do Hindus in the motherland. Why do overseas Hindus, particularly in the North American diaspora, seem always to out-Hindu the Hindu? In thinking of the Indian diaspora, other questions that come to the fore include: relations between parents and children; race relations between Indians, blacks, and whites; the place of Indian food and music in the preservation of Indian communities; the responsibility, if any, of the Indian Government to overseas Indians; and the future prospects of the Indian community in the U.S. However, after all the discussions it can be concluded that Indian diaspora is unique in whole world.

MODERN RELIGIOUS MOVEMENTS

Meanwhile, reform measures among Hindus addressed improving the status of women and bringing about equality in society by reforming the caste system. The two most influential reformers of the late nineteenth century were Dayananda Sarasvati (1824 -1883) and Vivekananda (1863 -1902). They were also influential as sources of inspiration to the freedom fighters opposing British colonialism. At the political level religion came to be used as a rallying point as exemplified by B. G. Tilak's (1856 - 1920) use of the Ganapati festival from 1893 onwards to propagate nationalist ideas. In such festivals, patriotic songs and speeches were incorporated that tended to radicalize the people.

Another panorama was the use of religion by some of the revolutionary organizations, that included swearing oaths by religion in pursuing revolutionary objectives against the imperial regime. By the 1920s, revolutionary organizations were influenced more by leftist ideology than by religion. But popular vernacular literature would use Hindu imagery to invoke patriotic sentiments against imperial rule; for example , India was depicted as a divine mother, Bharat Mata, that had been enslaved. As imperialism developed, the imperial masters created a division between Hindus and Muslims. This on various occasions led to sectarian violence on religious grounds. The response of Hinduism to such developments was that of Gandhian nonviolence.

Mohandas Karamchand Gandhi (1869 - 1948) was a political leader and social reformer with deep roots in the Hindu religious customs. He brought to the fore the concept of Ahimsa (nonviolence) as the theoretical and doctrinal dimension of his struggle against British imperialism and as a means of bringing about harmony between various sections of the population. The custom of Ahimsa has roots in the ancient scriptures of Hinduism. For Gandhi nonviolence was soul-force and was the positive kind of love. This meant that one should try to remove the evil, but not hate the evildoer. His concept of Ahimsa was concomitant with his other formulations like that of Satyagraha (meaning sticking to the truth or truth-force) even in situations of great adversity.

These concepts were useful in the struggle against imperialism as they helped to mobilize large numbers of unarmed people without any fear of the weapons of the state. Though Gandhi would draw inspiration from Hindu customs, his nonviolence was not sectarian. In the latter part of his life, he also extended his nonviolence to the extent of being a pacifist who opposed all war. This also meant that he was for disarmament and against the atom bomb. For him the atom bomb symbolized "the most diabolical use of science". Gandhi mentioned this in his journal - Harijan, 29-9-1946.: "I regard the employment of the atom bomb for the wholesale destruction of men, women and children as the most diabolical use of science." In an another article, he wrote: "The moral to be legitimately drawn from the supreme tragedy of the bomb is that it will not be destroyed by counter-bombs even as violence cannot be by counter-violence. Mankind has to get out of violence only through non-violence. Hatred can be overcome only by love. Counter-hatred only increases the surface as well as the depth of hatred."

A related aspect of his thought was tolerance and equality between various religions; for him various religions were equally sacred. This school of thought of equality of religions was very useful in a culturally diverse and plural society like India in welding people to nationhood. Thus Gandhian ideas have great philosophical relevance for modern Hinduism. Another aspect of Hinduism is politics of the right-wing which has existed since British times. Technically, religious leaders do not play politics! Politics is played by political parties - these political parties have their own left to the right spectrum of politics. These political leaders can at best claim that they have the blessings of the Gurus and Saints. Frankly, there is no "political Hinduism". There is nothing like the Christian Right or the Christian Left. At the doctrinal level, this movement derives its roots from the writings of the revolutionary V. D. Savarkar (1883 - 1966). The movement sees India as a Hindu nation and objectives to take it to glorious heights. In recent times, it has developed into the Hindutva movement. This strand on various occasions has taken violent positions vis-à-vis other religions on issues like temple construction, killing of cows, and religious conversions. It is a form of cultural nationalism and considers that Hinduism should be assigned its prime position in its own land.

The other aspects of modern Hinduism relate to social violence. These relate to the position of women in society and the ills of the caste system. Reformative Hinduism has led to considerable improvement in the position of women, and awareness and legal provisions have accomplished the eradication of the ills of the caste system, even though at social levels this only represents an unachievable utopia. The general tenor of modern Hinduism remains that of nonviolence combined with a pluralistic outlook and is determined by liberal customs of Vedanta and Upanishads. Outside India, the expression of Hinduism is in general not concerned with issues of war and violence, but is more concerned with Bhakti (devotion) and its philosophical dimensions.

It is not without consideration that Rammohan Roy (1772-1833) has been described as the father of modern India. His enthusiasm for reform may be attributed in part to the influence of Islamic thought and Western ideas, but, as his Vedanta grantha shows, he is also indebted to Vedantic teaching pertaining the unity and supremacy of Brahman as Eternal Being and One without a second. His defence of Hinduism against the attacks of Christian missionaries is an indication of the determine of his Brahminic upbringing and the part it played in moulding his desire to restore the religious purity of Hinduism. He strove to do this through his journalistic and literary activities and through the formation of the Brahmo Samaj, a society he founded in 1828 to promote the worship of the one eternal, immutable God and the rejection of image worship so characteristic of popular devotion. If the intellectual bent of the Brahmo Samaj deprived it of popular appeal, it however succeeded in producing an atmosphere of liberalism and rationality in which a reinterpretation of the Hindu custom could take place.

Roy's emphasis on logic and fact is looked upon to have characterised one of his earliest Persian works entitled Tuhfatul-ul-Muwahhiddin (Gift to Deists), in which belief in a Creator, the existence of the soul and life after death, are claimed to be the basic tenets of all religions (though such tenets could hardly be attributed either logically or factably, e.g. to Buddhism). The same work dismisses as irrational beliefs in miracles, anthropomorphic deities and the efficacy of rituals in man's salvation. It was his earnest endeavour to convince his fellow-countrymen and prove to his European friends that what he called irrational and idolatrous practices had nothing to do with the pure spirit of the Hindu religion. He was not confident of the symbolic nature of the images worshipped and maintained that Hindus of his day firmly believed in the existence of innumerable gods and goddesses.

His resistance to idolatry is matched by his state of affairs of some of the social customs of Hinduism, especially suttee, the practice of burning widows on the funeral pyres of their husbands. His advocacy of the provision of education for his fellow-countrymen, particularly in mathematics, natural philosophy, chemistry and other useful sciences, was objectiveed at the elimination of such customs, the cultural improvement of the native population and the harmonisation of Western science and Eastern spirituality for the gain of mankind. His pursuit of this goal justly earned him a place of eminence as one of the most creative attributes of nineteenth-century India.

A fellow member of the Brahmo Samaj, whose resistance to idolatry matched that of Roy, was Devendranath Tagore (1817-1905). It was his firm belief that the ultimate good of India would derive from the rejection of tantric and puranic myths and legends and the acceptance of Brahman. He showed great enthusiasm for the purification of the Hindu religion and joined the campaign to provide free education for Hindu children. A man of sensitive spirit, Tagore in his later years inclined to mysticism and his piety earned him the title Maharishi, 'great sage'. He attracted a number of able young men to the Samaj, including Keshab Chunder Sen (1838-84), who became equally committed to religious and social reform.

Sen's exuberance to propagate the message of the society led him to found the Indian Mirror and the Dharmatattva, journals of religion and philosophy, and to launch branches of the Samaj in a number of parts of India. Like Roy he rejected idolatry as erroneous and superstitious, but unlike his predecessor he recognised the popular need for visible and palpable expressions of the divine and the intense love, reverence and faith manifested in the worship of images. Hence his claim that Hindus ought to be grateful for the gods and goddesses of India and the legends of Hindu mythology. His boundless enthusiasm and vitality proved a mixed blessing to the society and schisms ensued which resulted in the founding of the Brahmo Samaj of India in 1865, and subsequently the setting up of the Sadharan Brahmo Samaj in 1878 by his disenchanted followers.

Sen's close conversance with Christian teaching provided him with the terminology he needed to express the principles of his New Dispensation. This he refers to as equivalent to the Jewish and Christian Dispensations; as the fulfilment of Christ's prophecy; as the harmonisation of all scriptures and all religions; and as exclaiming the message of love which prohibits all distinctions between Brahmins and Uuddras, Asiatics and Europeans. Its uniqueness for him lay in its insistence on the direct, unmediated worship of God. His acceptance of the divinity of Christ and the title of Jesudas, the servant of Jesus, suggests that he completely embraced the Christian faith. In fact he regarded Christ to be an Asiatic and his concept of the Incarnation is not 'once and for all' but the expression of God in history through great men and prophets. Christ, he claims, held the doctrine of divine humanity, which is essentially a Hindu doctrine and at one with the Vedantic notion of man's unity with the Absolute.

Sen's belief in the providential nature of British rule would not have been shared by Dayananda Sarasvati (1824-83), whose promotion of Hindi as a national language was not unrelated to the development of national self-consciousness. He was fully aware of the intimate relation that pertained between language, religion and nationalism, and was convinced that political independence was the natural corollary of the restoration of Vedic ideals. It was his firm belief that the Vedas contained true revelation and were the authoritative source of the Hindu religion. Through the generosity of his followers he founded schools to teach the Vedas but this proved an unsuccessful experiment. More productive was his insistence on the place of morality in true religion and his denunciation of idol worship as contrary to the teaching of the scriptures. In his view God, being formless and omnipresent, cannot be conceived of existing in any special object, and the evil practice of idol worship was responsible for widespread ignorance and mendacity in the country.

Dayananda in 1875 founded the Arya Samaj, provided him with the organisation necessary to propagate his religious and social ideals. Among the rules adopted by the society, belief in God, the authority of the Vedas and the rejection of idol worship and incarnational doctrines were paramount. The duty of all members of the Samaj was to promote spiritual monotheism, Vedic authority and social reform. The reforms he advocated related to child marriage, widow remarriage and niyoga. He was aware of the problems of early widowhood and child marriage and the relation between the dowry system and female infanticide.

The eradication of the practice of child marriage, he believed, would reduce the number of widows and he advocated niyoga, the temporary legal union of widows and widowers, as an interim solution to the problem of early widowhood. He approved of the education of both sexes, insisting that it was the basis of mutual respect between husband and wife. The best form of marriage, in his view, was marriage by choice after the education of the contracting parties had been completed. Education itself should involve Hindi and Sanskrit and a case should be made for making them the medium of instruction in schools. Dayananda's aggressive nationalism and deep desire to lead his fellow-countrymen back to the Vedas earned him the title of the 'Luther of India', a description which is not solely unfitting.

Of the religious mystic of modern India pride of place must go to Ramakrishna (1836-86), who from an early age is reputed to have experienced mystical trances. Though lacking formal education he possessed an abundance of native intelligence and for the greater part of his life served God at the KalI temple at Dakshineswar. Through his association with followers of the Tantric and Vedanta schools he acquired an understanding of yogic techniques and the ways of bhakti (devotion) and jñana (knowledge) as means of union with the divine. His personal experiences of other religious customs, especially Islam and Christianity, enabled him to make the claim that various religions are simply various paths to the same goal.

SPIRITUAL REVOLUTION

The Evolutionary scientists tell us that that birth and the growth of man, the Home Sapiens, marked the completion of evolutionary cycle of life on earth that took place in several stages over millions of years. Man is the only creature among millions of species on earth, who can imagine intelligently and synthesise thoughts. Due to the man's power of intelligent facting, the scientists have put him at the zenith of the evolutionary spiral. Man has made great strides in science and technology over the past one century. This is often mistaken as the evidence of man having reached the pinnacle of the evolutionary glory.

A closer look at this phenomenon tells that the growth of human mind has so far been limited to exploiting the potential of matter. This is reflected in the spectacular growth of physical science that has put man in space and begun unlocking the mysteries of human body through research in areas such as genome mapping, cellular biology and stem cells. However, human endeavor to look into the potential of spirit has not gone beyond the realm of psychophysical research. In fact, research into deeper aspects of human mind always invariably ends with scientists probing the brain. This is due to the fact that modern science cannot believe or perceive that human body and mind could be linked to another state of consciousness that exists beyond the limits of our physical world.

The result is that the potential possibilities of spirit, vis-à-vis matter, has been left to the interpreters of religious spirituality. This has caused a neat division between scientists and religious leaders, making them look at each with a degree of suspicion and even hostility. The developed West's excessive emphasis on exploiting the physical world has resulted in the near total neglect of the great potential of the spirit world with which human body and mind are closely linked, and are hence deeply impacted by it. The progress in science and technology has hence led to greater physical comforts but not to peace of mind. If anything, material progress stemming from new scientific discoveries has only led to competition, conflict, discord and internecine struggle in human society. What was really happening on the spiritual front in India and this world during the 19th century can only be speculated. If one starts reading the lifes and stories of well known spiritual leaders, one thing that stands out very blatantly is that all these events occurred in several parts of India.

One of the most outstanding Spiritual worker of India who carried the message to the world from Calcutta is Swami Vivekananda. Swami Vivekananda's address to the religions of parliament was in September 1893. Swami Vivekananda(1863-1902) was initiated by his Guru Sri Ramakrishna Parahmansa who incidentally lived from (1836-1886). Swami Vivekananda upon returning from his Chicago address met Shri BalaGangadhar Tilak a number of times, if one reads in the available literature. The same Tilak who went to seek Baba's blessings with Kharparde and later sent Geeta to be blessed by Baba.

Another great yogi who acted upon a number of lives and did lot of spiritual work in the west was Parmahansa Yogananda(1893-1952). Is it coincidental or what that in the same year when the west gets a taste of Indian spirituality, another great worker is born to continue the legacy by bringing the Indian Yoga system to the West in a very effective way. Yogananda was initiated into spirituality by his Guru Shri Yukteshwar Giri who was a disciple of Shri Lahiri Mahasya. The deathless Mahavtar(Babaji) gave Kriya Yoga initiation to Lahiri Mahasya in 1861. One finds very similar powers of travelling without a body, materializing somewhere else while seated in the front of others elsewhere, etc. attributed to the great teachers of Yogananda who did their work in silence. Speaking of successful yogis who worked outside India, another great spiritual seeker and philosopher who returned after studying in the west and took upon his spiritual practice in Pondicherry is Sri Aurobindo Ghosh(1871-1950).

Another Saint who created a strong spiritual presence and self-realized was the Saint of Arunachal, Sri Ramana Maharishi(1879-1950). It is said that in the early life of this great saint, when as a kid he quietly left his family to make Arunachal his home, he was met by a Maulvi on the train who helped him on his journey with some information that made his journey possible. Now there are a number of more great spiritual souls who acted their roles, some being Swami Rama Tirtha (1873-1906), Papa Ramdas (1884-1963), Swami Omkar (1895-1982), Sri Ananda Mayee Ma (1896-1982), Swami Sivananda (1887-1963) and probably scores of others.

Yogananda's and Vivekananda's centers to propagate their philosophies were put in place while they were still alive and continued to flourish. A number of such centers were started with direct disciples or with the participation of the family of the Saint.

We can only view these Saint's lives and events from their historical significance and by the value their lives, instances, sayings and preaching help us to make ourselves a better person. But considering what is going today, the growth of sprituality is at an exponential rate both in and outside India.

FUTURE

A number of people worry, what will happen to the future of the Hinduism, but in true sense, Hinduism will progress with enlightened people, and mere self centered people leaving and joining other religions do not weaken the Tree of Hinduism Today the Society is full of crime, Injustice, inequality created by few political, deviant persons at the cost of the living and suffering Humanity. A number of are enjoying the life at the cost criminalizing the society.

Hinduism stood the test time with multiple invasion from external sources and today faces the threat within our own nation with principles of pseudo secluralism,The facts of India's survival remain with the deep faith in Artha, Kama, Dharma, and if practiced to best of his ability attain Moksha Religion rarely imposed and controlled individuals against his wishes. Every one emphasized that you are creator of you destiny. All are for one reality that you are the Atman and your goal is to reach the Parmatman that is almighty. Even the enlightened westerns believe that Hinduism to be understood as Universal way of Living The sectarian identity with castes followed, for selfish ends has lost several masses leaving the Hindu faith embracing other religious identities . A number of who are knowledgeable used the understanding the Vedas and Upanishads for their survival rather than creating the love for Hinduism.

If a persons converts to other religion, he has not understood the philosophy of their own religion. Mere identity with religion don't turn sub human to human race. Every religion is a wonderful creation; people convert just for the advantage of the day or time. The beginning of the 20th century has great preachers of Hinduism and followed the Hinduism in real sense and practiced without hypocrisy. Mahatma Gandhi championed the cause of Ahimsa with slogan of "Ahimsa Parma Dharma" meaning non violence is the highest act of life. If understood in the true sense The Mahabharata great epic on human destiny teaches how Dharma win over Adharma, every character is hidden in us, only waiting for an opportunity to surface. If any Adharma committed with knowledge or ignorance will bear fruit how mighty you are. Every character, how noble in their attitudes has reaped the consequences. Today's problems in Hinduism are man made, but not God made, misinterpreted for selfish goals.

The strength of Hinduism lies in choice of way of life. The Doctrine of Karma, every living human guided by his acts of omission and commission, and also guides the destiny of the Nation or even the Universe. Few people in India take to crime and become immoral in spite of several hardships experienced in basic necessitatement s of life. The poor man is a great follower of the Hinduism as he still lives with faith in God. The recent Scientific and Economic advances brought in consumerism, greed, and selfishness more than any concern for Society, forgetting all the co humans which in turn contributing hungry helpless masses. Today people in power, mighty, and rich buy the Justice, trade with Human suffering. The unanswered question is, will be one happy with Injustice to others. Time is best teacher, great instrument in the hands of Almighty, yet no one escaped.

Every human being find hard to interpret the saying of the Bhagavat Gita, 'The life one speaks of it or hears of it as a Mystery but none know it" Those who left the Hinduism know very little, core of our religion. People create hatred on Hinduism, the Dharmic principles of life and living, and which may not be suitable to their needs. If one believes in the Doctrine of Karma, we are writing our own future, the Destiny, God is only a silent spectator, Our Vedas and Upanishad turned a number of Sub humans to Humans. Today we need more Humans to preach religion. A little practice of "whatever is not agreeable to him that he should not do unto others remains the best, Dharma" all else is only selfishness.

HINDUISM AS A GLOBAL RELIGION

The traditionalist definition of Hindu dictates that anybody consenting on the ancient Indian culture and customs is Hindu. The philosophical bankruptcy of the customalist definition is of the same order as that of the geographist definition. The traditionalist mind is inherently conservative and is opposed to all change and growth. Everything old is regarded good, while everything modern is looked down upon. The traditionalist treats the "puratan" (ancient) as "sanatan" (eternal or natural or essential) and sacred. The customalist invokes "bhakti" (devotion and faith) to close the mental doors to any fresh thought. This is contrary to the concept of Hindu.

A closed mind cannot be the discerning feature of a Hindu. If Hindu religion was a closed-minded religion, there would have been no Upanishads and Puranas after Vedas. Diversity of opinion and clash of opinions is a frequent phenomenon in ancient Hindu texts. Considering the ancient as sacred will block the growth of Hinduism. Moreover, when only a few remnants of the ancient are available and the circumstances in the present time and world (desh-kal) are completely various, it is necessary to begin the job of reconstruction and renaissance by starting from first principles and fundamental values. The old can be a guide, but it is necessary to give up the presumption that everything ancient is sacred. Hence, the customalist definition of Hinduism is not only not complete and shallow, it is a big obstacle in the growth of Hinduism.

It is significant to compare the commitment of a Hindu towards truth with that of the followers of other religions. For a Christian, every word in Bible is the ultimate truth. During the reign of the Church, any attempt to even collect evidence that might contradict something written in the Bible was regarded blasphemy and was punishable by death. Obviously, some holy book says that a man has more teeth and ribs than a woman has. During the medieval period, it was blasphemy and criminal offence to try to gather evidence against the sacred book by counting the teeth or ribs of men and women. For hundreds of years no one in Europe could hence count teeth or ribs. In any single-book-based religion such problems are likely to occur at some time or the other. Both Christianity and Islam have at some points in their history opposed science since it clashed with the truth as provided in their sacred books.

Hinduism has never and can never be opposed to Science due to the central belief in truth. It was this belief in truth that led to the development and growth of science and knowledge in ancient India. The glow of science and knowledge made the Hindu full of light and the region that was illuminated by this shower of light was called Bharatvarsh.

It may be further added that just as Lord Jesus Christ's sayings were misused and distorted by Church, there are attempts to narrow and restrict Hinduism. The churchification of Hinduism is a danger that needs to be guarded against. In recent years, people who know nothing of Hinduism have emerged as the self-proclaimed defenders of the faith. They are understanding Hinduism in their own way and are declaring their versions to be the official versions. For a religion which does not even prohibit the eating of human flesh, vegetarianism and non-violence are being declared as fundamental values. Hindus are being asked to be loyal to a geographic entity or a nation. There is even an attempt to show that Hindus are one race. The harm that such ignorant proclaimed defenders of the faith may inflict on Hinduism is enormous.

It must be thought of that the dark ages of Europe were not a result of anything that Lord Jesus said. European Renaissance was an attempt to break the vice-like grip of the church on all aspects of European life. It was a revolt against the Church and not against Lord Jesus Christ. As years have passed, the influence of church in European (and American) life has decreased considerably. Nowadays, a Christian takes almost all significant decisions of his life based on his own self assessment and intellect.

Concern with ecological considerations and serious attempts to live life as per nature's laws can also be seen as an attempt to attain the oneness with cosmos which is most fundamental to Hinduism. The move of the world to a more rational and humane existence is in fact a move towards Hinduism. It is time that Hindus realized this and took up the leadership in this ongoing historical movement which has transformed the world in the past four/five centuries.

As men and women across the world (from all races and communities) understand and adopt the "Global Religion of the Modern World" – Hindu Dharm based on Satyam, Shivam, Sundaram -- they will not only transform their own lives but will also make the world a better place to live in. Some modern Hindu teachers have stated that all religions are one, that they are all ultimately the same and all equally good. They look upon various religions as merely alternative ways to reach the same goal, as little more than various names for the same thing. This has caused them to mix various religions together, often with little discrimination, trying to be all things to all people. While their view may be motivated by a sincere effort to bring about religious harmony and world peace, it has led to a number of distortions. Above all it has gone against the pluralistic approach of the Hindu tradition.

Making all religions the same is a abnegation of pluralism and can breed another form of intolerance. Pluralism in any field does not mean that all alternatives are the same but that we do have various choices, which may not all be good or equal. Having pluralism in food, for example , means that we can choose from a number of various types of food. It does not mean that all food articles are of equal nutritional value or of the same taste. This corresponding of all religions as equal and good makes it seem wrong for religions to disagree with one another, even if their views are contrary. It destroys discrimination in religion and makes people blur over various views of God, immortality, the goal of life, and the ways to achieve these. Rather than honoring diversity in religion, it attempts to cut down this diversity to a vague identity that no one can challenge. Rather than giving people a number of various choices in religion it tries to make all these choices seem to be the same or inconsequential. In eliminating choice it destroys freedom and inhibits inquiry and growth.

The Hindu notion of an untouchable caste seems irreconcilable with universal rights. Gandhi famously rejected the idea of 'the untouchables' and discrimination on the basis of caste is illegal under Indian law. Despite a legal commitment to human rights HRW (Human Rights Watch) point out many areas where human rights abuse is a concern, for example the impunity of the police and security forces. The Hindu Human Rights Group explains their support for universal human rights as "it is in the spirit of Hindu Dharma, Hindu belief and action, that all are accorded with equity and respect, and that rights are not infringed". In the Vedas (Hindu scripture from between 7th and 5th centuries BC) twenty niyamas and yamas (ethical do's and don'ts) are prescribed. The seventh yama is compassion (daya) which enjoins Hindu to sympathise and assist all people, creatures and the earth itself. God is in everything, and a Hindu must have compassion on the world. For some Hindus, human rights are an expression of an ancient religious principle.

Religion has been assigned many roles in our modern global society. It is archaic and divisive in the discourse of the 'clash of civilisations' and terrorism. It is an expression of individuality against the idea of national homogeneousness and a cultural anchor against the forces of globalisation. But it is also an important moral and philosophical corroborating of the rights and obligations that come with global citizenship.

REFERENCES

Homo Hierarchicus: *An Essay on the Caste System*, Mark Sainsbury. Chicago, University of Chicago Press, 1970

J. A. B. Van Buitenen: *Ramanuja on the Bhagvad-Gita*, The Hague, H. L. Smits, 1953.

J. Brough: *Selections from Classical Sanskrit Literature*, London, Luzac & Co., 1952.

J. Eggeling: *The Uatapatha-BrahmaGa*, Oxford, Clarendon Press, 1900.

J. Jolly: *The Institutes of Vishnu*, Oxford, Clarendon Press, 1900.

J. Jolly: *The Minor Law-Books*, Oxford, Clarendon Press, 1889.

J. Mascaró: *The Bhagavad Gita*, New York, Penguin, 1962.

J. Muir: *Metrical Translations from Sanskrit Writers*, London, Trubner & Co., 1871.

J. Muir: *Original Sanskrit Texts*, London: Trubner & Co., 1872.

J. S. M. Hooper: *Hymns of the Alvars*, Calcutta, Association Press, 1929.

Jagadisvarananda: *The Devi-Mahatmyam or Sri Durga-Saptasati*, Mylapore, Sri Ramakrishna Math.

Jay, Edward J.: "*Bridging the Gap Between Castes: Ceremonial Friendship in Chhattisgarh*" Contributions to Indian Sociology, 1973.

K. H. Potter: *Presuppositions of India's Philosophies* (1963) and Guide to Indian Philosophy, 1988.

Kalynasuntaram, N.: *Tiruccentur Murukankoyil varalaru.: Tiruchendur: Tirukkumaran Patippakam*, 1980.

Kane, P.V.: *History of Dharmasastra* 5, Poona: Bhandarkar Oriental Research Institute, 1958.

Kapadia, K.: *Siva and her sisters: gender, caste, and class in rural South India*, Boulder, Col: Westview Press, 1995.

Kavyopadhyaya, Hira Lal: *A Grammar of the Chhattisgarhi Dialect of Eastern Hindi*, Calcutta, Baptist Mission Press, 1921.

Kersenboom, S.: *Word, sound, image: the life of the Tamil text*, Oxford: Berg, 1995.

Bibliography

A. Avalon: *The Great Liberation*, Madras, Ganesh & Co., 1927.

A. Embree: *The Hindu Tradition and, with S. Hay*, Sources of Indian Tradition, 1988.

A. L. Basham: *The Wonder That Was India*, London, Sidgwick and Jackson, 1954.

Agrawala, Vasudeva: *Sparks from the Vedic Fire: A New Approach to Vedic Symbolism*. Varanasi, Banaras Hindu University, 1962.

Ainley, Alison: "*The Ethics of Sexual Difference." In Abjection, Melancholia, and Love: The Works of Julia Kristeva*, London and New York: Routledge, 1990.

Allchin F. R.: *Neolithic Cattle-Keepers of South India*: A study of the Deccan ashmounds, Cambridge, 1963.

Alper, Harvey P.: *Understanding Mantras. SUNY Series in Religious Studies*, Albany, State University of New York Press, 1989.

Aurobindo Ghose: *Speeches*, Calcutta, Arya Publishing House, 1948.

Azad, A. K.: *India Wins Freedom*, London: Sangam Books, 1988.

Baartmans, Frans: *Aapaha, The Sacred Waters: an Analysis of a Primordial Symbol in Hindu Myths*, Delhi, B. R. Publishing Corporation, 1990.

Babb, Lawrence A.: *The Divine Hierarchy: Popular Hinduism in Central India*, New York, Columbia University Press, 1975.

Bacchetta, P.: '*Hindu Nationalist Women as Ideologues*' in Jayawardena and de Alwis eds, 1996.

Badrinath, C.: *Dharma, India and the World Order, Edinburgh*: Saint Andrew Press, 1993.

Bailey, Greg.: *The Mythology of Brahma*, Delhi, Oxford University Press, 1983.

Balslev, A.N.: *A study of time in Indian philosophy*, Wiesbaden, Otto Harrassowitz, 1983.

Banerjea, J. N.: *Pauragic and Tantric Religion (Early Phase)*, Calcutta, University of Calcutta, 1966.

Banerjee, S.: '*The woman Shiv Sainik and her sister Swayamsevika*' in Sarkar and Butalia eds, 1995.

Banerji, S. C.: *A Brief History of Tantra Literature*, Calcutta, Naya Prokash, 1988.

Barnett, S.A.: *Coconuts and gold: relational identity in a South Indian caste*, 1976.

Basham A. L.: *A Cultural History of India*, Oxford, 1975.

Basu, A.: '*Feminism inverted: the gendered imagery and real women of Hindu nationalism*' in Sarkar and Butalia eds., 1995.

Basu, K. and Subrahmanyam, S.: *Unravelling the Nation: sectarian conflict and India's secular identity*, New Delhi: Penguin Books, 1996.

Beck, B.E.F.: *The kin nucleus in Tamil folklore. In Kinship and history in South Asia*, Ann Arbor: University of Michigan, 1974.

Berreman, Gerald D.: "*Brahmans and Shamans in Pahari Religion*" Journal of Asian Studies, 1964

Biardeau, M.: *Hinduism: the anthropology of a civilisation*, Delhi, Oxford University Press, 1989.

Bowes Pratima: *The Hindu Religious Tradition*, A philosophical approach, London, 1978.

Bowker, J.: *Oxford dictionary of world religions*, Oxford, 'University Press, 1997.

Braaten, C.: "*The Problem of the Absoluteness of Christianity*" Interpretation 40/4, October 1986.

Brown W. N.: *Man in the Universe*, Some continuities in Indian thought, Berkeley, 1966.

Carman, J., and V. Narayanan: *The Tamil Veda: Pillan's Interpretation of the Tiruvaymoli*. Chicago, University of Chicago, 1989.

Carstairs, Morris G.: *The Twice-Born: A Study of High Caste Hindus*, Bloomington, Indiana University Press, 1961

Chapman, M.: '*Theology as Vocation'- Ernst Troeltsch as Philosophical Theologian*" Ph.D. diss., Oxford University, 1988.

Clayton, J. P.: *Ernst Troeltsch and the Future of Theology. Cambridge*, Cambridge University, 1976.

Clooney, F. X.: "*The Tiruvaymoli of Shatakopan*, 1998.

Clothey, F.W.: *Chronometry, cosmology and the festival calendar in the Murukan cult.*, New Delhi: Manohar, 1982.

Courtright, PB.: *Ganesa: Lord of obstacles, Lord of beginnings*, New York, Oxford University Press, 1985.

Coward, Harold G. Bhart: *Twayne's World Authors Series, no. 403. Boston*: Twayne Publishers, 1976.

Cunningham: *Alexander: "Report on a Tour in the Central Provinces and Lower Gangetic Doab in 1881-82"* Archaeological Survey of India, 1884.

Daniel, E.V.: *Fluid signs: being a person the Tamil way*, Berkeley, University of California Press, 1984.

Daniel, S.B.: *Marriage in Tamil culture: the problem of conflicting 'models'*, Syracuse, N.Y: Maxwell School of Citizenship & Public Affairs, 1980.

Daniélou Alain: *Hindu Polytheism*, London, 1964.

Danielou, Alain.: *The Gods of India: Hindu Polytheism*, New York, Inner Traditions, 1985.

Das, S. K: *Shakti or Divine Power*, Calcutta, University of Calcutta, 1934.

Das, Veena; *Structure and Cognition,* Delhi, Oxford University Press, 1982.

Davis, R.H.: *Ritual in an oscillating universe: worshiping Siva in medieval India*, Princeton, University Press, 1991.

De E. A. Brett: *Chhattisgarh Feudatory States*, Bombay, Times Press, 1909.

Devasenapathi, V.A.: *Saiva Siddhanta. Madras*, University of Madras, 1974.

DiNoia, J. A.: *The Diversity of Religions: A Christian Perspective*, Washington, D.C.: Catholic University of America, 1992.

Dubey, K. C. and M. G. Mohril: *Fairs and Festivals of Madhya Pradesh*, Delhi, Manager of Publications, 1965

Dumont, L.: *The Dravidian kinship terminology as an expression of marriage*, Man, 1953.

Dumont, Louis, and David Pocock: "*On the Different Aspects or Levels in Hinduism.*" Contributions to Indian Sociology, 1959

Dumont, Louis: *"World Renunciation in Indian Religions*" Contributions to Indian Sociology, 1960.

Durkheim, E.: *The elementary forms of the religions life*, London, George Allen & Unwin, 1915.

E. B. Cowelleau and A. E. Gough: *The Sarva-darœana-sacgraha*, London, Kegan Paul, Trench, Trubner & Co., 1904.

E. J. Thompson and A. Marshman Spencer: *Bengali Religious Lyrics*, Calcutta, Association Press, 1923.

Evans-Pritchard, E.: *Nuer Religion*. London, Oxford University Press, 1956

F. E. Keay: *Kabir and His Followers*, Calcutta, Association Press, 1931.

F. E. Pargiter: *The Maarkandya Purana*, Calcutta, Asiatic Society, 1904.

F. Edgerton: *The Bhagavad-Gita*, Cambridge, Mass, Harvard University Press, 1944.

F. Kingsbury and G. E. Phillips: *Hymns of the Tamil Shaivite Saints*, Calcutta, Association Press, 1921.

Fairservis W. A.: *The Roots of Ancient India*: The archaeology of early Indian civilization, London, 1975.

Fuller, C. J.: *Gods, priests and purity: on the relation between Hinduism and the caste system*, 1979.

G. Buhler: *The Laws of Manu*, Oxford, Clarendon Press, 1886.

G. Buhler: *The Sacred Books of the East*, Oxford, Clarendon Press, 1897.

Gale, R.M.: *The language of time*, London, Routledge & Kegan Paul, 1968.

Gandhi: *An Autobiography*, Mahadev Desai, Ahmedabad, Navajivan, 1927.

Gell, A.: *The anthropology of time*, Berg, Oxford, 1992.

Gonda Jan: *Change and Continuity in Indian Religion*, Gravenhage, 1965.

Gonda Jan: *Vedic Literature,* Wiesbaden, 1975.

Good, A.: *Law, legitimacy, and the hereditary rights of Tamil temple priests*. Mod. Asian Stud., 1989.

Gopinatha Rao, T.A.: *Elements of Hindu* , Delhi, Motilal Banarsidass. 1997.

Gordon Matthews: *Shiva*, New York, Oxford University Press, 1948.

Gough, E.K.: *Brahman kinship in a Tamil village*, Am. Anthrop, 1956.

H. H. Wilson: *Select Specimens of the Theatre of the Hindus*, London, Trubner & Co., 1835.

H. H. Wilson: *The Vishnu Puraana*, London, Trubner, 1864.

H. Jacobs: *Western Psychotherapy and Hindu-Sadhana*, London, G. Allen & Unwin, 1961.

H. Oldenberg: *The Grhya-Sutras*, Oxford, Clarendon Press, 1886.

Handelman, D. & D.D.: *Shulman Cod inside out: Siva's game of dice*, New York, Oxford University Press, 1997.

Harper, Edward B.: "*A Hindu Village Pantheon*" Southwestern Journal of Anthropology, 1959

Hauer J. W.: *Der Vratya*; Untersuchungen uber die nichtbrahmanische Religion altindiens, Stuttgart, 1927.

Heesterman, J. C.: "*Veda and Dharma*." New Delhi: Vikas Publishing House, 1978.

Heimann, Betty: *Facets of Indian Thought. London*: George Allen and Unwin, 1964.

Hill, John E.: *The Peoples of the West from the Weilue by Yu Huan: A Third Century Chinese Account Composed between 239 and 265 AD*, Draft annotated English translation, 2004.

Holdrege, Barbara A.: "*Hindu Ethics." In The Berkely-Harvard Annotated Bibliography on Comparative Religious Ethics,* Cambridge and New York: Cambridge University Press, 1991.

Homo Hierarchicus: *An Essay on the Caste System*, Mark Sainsbury. Chicago, University of Chicago Press, 1970

Hume, R. E.: *The Thirteen Principle Upanishads*, Delhi: Oxford University, 1931.

J. A. B. Van Buitenen: *Ramanuja on the Bhagvad-Gita*, The Hague, H. L. Smits, 1953.

J. Brough: *Selections from Classical Sanskrit Literature*, London, Luzac & Co., 1952.

J. Eggeling: *The Uatapatha-BrahmaGa*, Oxford, Clarendon Press, 1900.

J. Jolly: *The Institutes of Vishnu*, Oxford, Clarendon Press, 1900.

J. Jolly: *The Minor Law-Books*, Oxford, Clarendon Press, 1889.

J. Mascaró: *The Bhagavad Gita*, New York, Penguin, 1962.

J. Muir: *Metrical Translations from Sanskrit Writers*, London, Trubner & Co., 1871.

J. Muir: *Original Sanskrit Texts*, London: Trubner & Co., 1872.

J. S. M. Hooper: *Hymns of the Alvars*, Calcutta, Association Press, 1929.

Jagadisvarananda: *The Devi-Mahatmyam or Sri Durga-Saptasati*, Mylapore, Sri Ramakrishna Math.

Jay, Edward J.: "*Bridging the Gap Between Castes: Ceremonial Friendship in Chhattisgarh*" Contributions to Indian Sociology, 1973.

K. H. Potter: *Presuppositions of India's Philosophies* (1963) and Guide to Indian Philosophy, 1988.

Kalynasuntaram, N.: *Tiruccentur Murukankoyil varalaru.: Tiruchendur: Tirukkumaran Patippakam*, 1980.

Kane, P.V.: *History of Dharmasastra* 5, Poona: Bhandarkar Oriental Research Institute, 1958.

Kapadia, K.: *Siva and her sisters: gender, caste, and class in rural South India*, Boulder, Col: Westview Press, 1995.

Kavyopadhyaya, Hira Lal: *A Grammar of the Chhattisgarhi Dialect of Eastern Hindi*, Calcutta, Baptist Mission Press, 1921.

Kersenboom, S.: *Word, sound, image: the life of the Tamil text,* Oxford: Berg, 1995.

Kuenen, A.: *National Religions and Universal Religions*, New York: AMS Press, 1979.

Leach, E.R.: *Rethinking anthropology*, London, Athlone Press, 1961.

Leach, Edmund R.: *Political Systems of Highland Burma*; *A Study of Kachin Social Structure*. London, London School of Economics and Political Science, 1964.

Legge, James: *A Record of Buddhistic Kingdoms: Being an account by the (1886): Chinese Monk Fa-Hien of his travels in India and Ceylon (AD. 399-414) in search of the Buddhist Books of Discipline*. Oxford, Clarendon Press. Reprint: New York, Paragon Book Reprint Corp, 1965.

Long, J.B.: *Mahasivaratri: the Saiva festival of repentance*, New Delhi: Manohar, 1982.

M. Bloomfield: *Hymns of the Atharva-Veda*, Oxford, Clarendon Press, 1897.

M. Monier-Williams: *Indian Wisdom*, London, Allen, 1876.

M. Winternitz: *A History of Indian Literature*, Calcutta, University, 1927.

Macdonell A. A.: *Vedic Mythology*, Strassburg, 1897.

Mandelbaum, David: "*Transcendental and Pragmatic Aspects of Religion*" American Anthropologist, 1966.

Marriott, McKim: "*The Feast of Love." In Krishna: Myths, Rites and Attitudes*,M. Singer. Honolulu: East-West Center Press, 1966.

Mauss, Marcel: *The Gift, trans, Ian Cunnison*, New York, Norton and Co., 1967.

Mayer, Adrian C.: *Caste and Kinship in Central India*, Berkeley and Los Angeles, University of California Press, 1960.

McTaggart, J.M.E.: *The nature of existence 2*, Cambridge, University Press, 1927.

Mellor, D.H.: *Real time*, Cambridge, University Press, 1981.

Melville T. Kennedy: *The Chaitanya Movement*, Calcutta, Association Press, 1925.

Merrey, K.L.: *The Hindu festival calendar* , New Delhi: Manohar, 1982.

Moreno Arcas, M.: *Murukan: a god of healing poisons; the physics of worship in a South Indian center for pilgrimage*, University of Chicago, 1984.

Needham, Rodney: *Belief, Language, and Experience*, Chicago: University of Chicago Press, 1972.

Nelson, A. E.: *Central Provinces District Gazetteers: Raipur District*, Vol. A, Descriptive. Bombay: British India Press, 1909.

Nicol Macnicol: *Hindu Scriptures*, London, J. M. Dent, 1938.

Nicol Macnicol: *Psalms of Maraha Saints*, Calcutta, Association Press.

O'Flaherty W. D.: *Hindu Myths*, Harmondsworth, 1975.

O'Flaherty, W.D.: *Women, androgynes, and other mythical beasts*, Chicago, University Press, 1980.

O'Flaherty, Wendy D.: "*Asceticism and Sexuality in the Mythology of Siva, Part 1*." History of Religions, 1969.

Ortner, Sherry B.: "*Is Female to Male as Nature Is to Culture?" In Women, Culture, and Society*, Stanford, Calif. Stanford University Press, 1974.

Padoux, André. Vac: T*he Concept of the Word in Selected Hindu Tantras*, State University of New York Press, 1990.

Paktavatsalam, K.: *Kalukumalaittala varalaru: . Kovilpatti: Selvarajan*, 1972.

Panikkar Raimundo: *The Vedic Experience: Mantramanjari,* London,.1977.

Panikkar, R.: *The Intrareligious Dialogue*, New York: Paulist, 1999.

Patni, B: *Shiv Purana: A Poetic Analysis*, Delhi, Ajanta Publications, 1980.

Payne, Ernest A.: *The Saktas: An Introductory and Comparative Study*, 1933.

Pfleuger, Lloyd William: "*God, Consciousness, and Meditation: The Concept of Iúvara in the Yogasutra*." University of California, Santa Barbara, 1990.

Ph. J. Vogel: *Indian Serpent-Lore*, London, A. Probsthain, 1926.

Pintchman, Tracy: "*Deciphering the Goddess: The Rise of the Feminine Principle in Brahmanical Hindu Cosmogony and Cosmology.*" University of California, Santa Barbara, 1992.

Pocock, D.F.: *The anthropology of time-reckoning*, Contrib, Ind. Social, 1964.

R. C. Temple: *The Word of Lalla the Prophetess*, Cambridge, Mass, Cambridge University Press, 1924.

R. E. Hume: *The Thirteen Principal Upanishads*, London, Oxford University Press, 1931.

R. Tagore: *One Hundred Poems of Kabir*, Madras, G. A. Natesan.

Raja Rammohun Roy: *The English Works of Raja Rammohun Roy*, Allahabad, The Panini Office, 1906.

Ramakrishna: *The Gospel of Ramakrishna,* New York, The Vedanta Society, 1907.

Ramanama: *The Infallible Remedy*, Karachi, 1947.

Ramanujan, A. K. "*On Folk Mythologies and Folk PuraGas." In PuraGa Perennis: Reciprocity and Transformation in Hindu and Jaina Texts*, , State University of New York Press, 1993.

Redfield, Robert: *Peasant Society and Culture*, Chicago, University of Chicago Press, 1960.

Reynolds, H.B.: *The auspicious married woman,*. Syracuse, N.Y., Maxwell School of Citizenship & Public Affairs, 1980.

Rodhe Sten: *Deliver us from Evil: studies on the Vedic ideas of salvation*, Lund, 1946.

Russell, Robert Vane: *The Tribes and Castes of the Central Provinces of India, 4v*. London, Macmillan, 1916.

S. N. Das Gupta: *History of Indian Philosophy*, 4 vol., 1922–55.

S. Radhakrishnan and C. A. Moore: *Source Book in Indian Philosophy*, 1957.

S. Radhakrishnan: *The Principal Upanishads*, London, George Allen & Unwin, 1953.

S. Radhakrishnan: *The Bhagavad-gita*, London, George Allen & Unwin, 1948.

Sarvapalli Radhakrishnan: *An Idealist View of Life*, London, George Allen & Unwin, 1929.

Sastri, H.K.: *South Indian images of gods and goddesses*, New Delhi, Asian Educational Services, 1986

Sharma, Chandradhar: *A Critical Survey of Indian Philosophy*, Delhi, Motilal Banarsidass, 1987.

Shastri, P. D.: *The Doctrine of Maya in the Philosophy of the Vedanta,* London, Luzac and Co., 1911.

Sheridan, Daniel P.: *The Advaitic Theism of the Bhagavata Puraga*, Delhi: Motilal Banarsidass, 1986.

Shulman, D.D.: *Tamil temple myths: sacrifice and divine marriage in the South Indian Saiva tradition*, Princeton, University Press, 1980.

Siddhantashastree, Rabindra Kumar: *VaicGavism Through the Ages*. New Delhi, Munshiram Manoharlal, 1985.

Singer, Milton: *When a Great Tradition Modernizes*, New York: Praeger, 1972.

Singh, Renuka: *The Womb of Mind: A Sociological Exploration of the Status Experience of Women in Delhi*, New Delhi, Vikas Publishing House, 1990.

Sinha, Surajit: "*State Formation and Rajput Myth in Tribal Central India*" Man in India, 1962.

Sircar, D. C.: *Foreigners in Ancient India and Lakcmi and Sarasvati in Art and Literature*, Calcutta, University of Calcutta, 1970.

Stutley M. and J.: *Dictionary of Hinduism: its Mythology, Folklore and Development, 1500 BC. AD. 1500*, London, 1977.

Thapar, R.: *Time as a metaphor of history: early India*, Delhi, Oxford University Press, 1996. Census of India: *Data from the 2001 Census, including cities, villages and towns,* Census Commission of India, 2001.

Thomas, F. W.: "*Sandanes, Nahapana, Cacmana and Kanicka : Tung-li P'an-ch'i and Chinese Turkestan.*" New Indian Antiquary, 1944.

Trautmann, T.R.: *Indian time, European time*, Ann Arbor: University of Michigan Press, 1995.

Vivekananda: *The Complete Works*, Almora, Advaita Ashrama, 1924.

W. G. Orr: *A Sixteenth-Century Indian Mystic*, London, Lutterworth Press, 1947.

W. Norman Brown: *The Saundaryalahari*, Cambridge, Mass, Harvard University Press, 1958.

Wadley, S.B.: *The powers of Tamil women*. Syracuse, N.Y.: Maxwell School of Citizenship & Public Affairs, 1980.

Wasson R. G.: *Soma, Divine Mushroom of Immortality*, New York, 1968. Beck, Brenda E. F.: "*Colour and Heat in South Indian Ritual*", 1969.

Watters, Thomas: *On Yuan Chwang's Travels in India. Thomas Watters*. London. Royal Asiatic Society. Reprint: Delhi. Mushiram Manoharlal. 1973.

Welbon, G.R. & G.E. Yocum: *Religious festivals in South India and Sri Lanka*, New Delhi, Manohar, 1982.

Zaehner R. C.: *Hinduism*, London, 1962.

Index

S

T